BRITAIN'S PAINTINGS

The Daily Telegraph
BRITAIN'S PAINTINGS

THE STORY OF ART THROUGH MASTERPIECES IN BRITISH COLLECTIONS

NEIL MACGREGOR

IN ASSOCIATION WITH THE NATIONAL GALLERY

EDITOR: ALEXANDER STURGIS

LIST OF PAINTINGS IN THE CHRONOLOGY
COMPILED BY CHRISTOPHER WRIGHT

CASSELL
ILLUSTRATED

THE
NATIONAL
GALLERY

First published in Great Britain in 2003 by Cassell Illustrated,
a division of Octopus Publishing Group Limited
2-4 Heron Quays, London E14 4JP

A CIP catalogue record for this book is available from the British Library.

10 9 8 7 6 5 4 3 2 1

ISBN 1 84403 047 4

Colour reproduction by Graphic Facilities, London

Printed in Italy

BRITAIN'S PAINTINGS

FOR THE NATIONAL GALLERY

Contributors
Rachel Barnes
Linda Bolton
Mari Griffith
Lynda Stephens
Richard Stemp

Managing Editors
Kate Bell
Jane Ace

Copy Editor
Lise Connellan

Editorial Assistant
Sarah Perry

FOR THE DAILY TELEGRAPH

Editorial Projects Director
George Darby

Creative Director
Clive Crook

Designer
Mark Hickling

Picture Editor
Abi Patton

Production
Harry Coen,
Bill Owen

THOMAS MORAN
NEARING CAMP, EVENING,
UPPER COLORADO RIVER
1882

CONTENTS

INTRODUCTION 8

LOVE AND WAR

Introduction   24

LOVE

The joys of love   28

The pains of love   30

Dangerous love   32

The look of love   34

WAR

The spectacle of war   36

Heroes   38

Off the battlefield   40

The suffering of war   42

WORK AND PLAY

Introduction   46

WORK

The worker   52

Mass labour   54

Brain work   56

Domestic work   58

PLAY

Music and dance   60

Children's play   62

Leisure   64

Sport and games   66

GODS AND HUMANITY

Introduction   70

GODS

Power   76

God as man   78

Gods on earth   80

Transcendence   82

HUMANITY

Identity   84

Vice and folly   86

Body and soul   88

Death   90

NATURE AND TIME

Introduction   94

NATURE

Nature into art   100

Wild nature   102

Animals   104

Natural effects   106

TIME

The time of life   108

Passing time   110

The moment and movement   112

Timelessness   114

PAIN AND PLEASURE

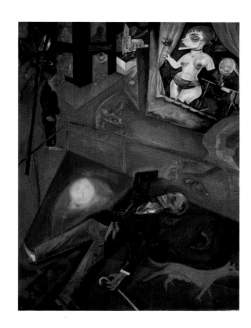

Introduction   118

PAIN

Violence   124

Sorrow   126

Desolation   128

Anguish   130

PLEASURE

Heaven on earth   132

Joy of the senses   134

Exuberance   136

Paint and pleasure   138

CHRONOLOGY

*Significant artists whose
work is on show in Britain*

1200–1600   142

1601–1700   152

1701–1800   160

1801–1900   170

1901–2002   178

GALLERIES

Where to see the paintings   186

INDEX

Page guide to the artists   194

INTRODUCTION

Wherever you are in the United Kingdom you are never very far from a great picture. They are housed in a dizzying variety of collections and buildings, their histories as varied and eccentric as anyone could wish. Together they form an extraordinary testimony to centuries of taste and erudition, wealth and acquisitiveness, generosity and philanthropy in Britain. Collecting pictures was something that the British came to rather late. At the beginning of the seventeenth century, when the palaces of Continental Europe were already bursting with the masterpieces of the Renaissance, you would have been hard-pressed to find any Italian picture of note in Britain. When the future Charles I visited the court of Philip IV of Spain in 1623, in a hopeless bid to marry his daughter, he was overwhelmed by the artistic riches on display. Six months later he left Spain, no closer to marriage but with a Titian or two in his trunk and, it seems, determined to emulate Philip as a collector.

He set about the task with impressive energy, his most spectacular coup being the purchase of the entire Ducal collection in Mantua from the sick, nasty and debt-ridden Vincenzo II, last of the Gonzaga dynasty. This great Renaissance collection included the series of canvases by Mantegna on *The Triumphs of Caesar (right)*, then some of the most famous works of art in the world and today still in the Royal Collection at Hampton

THE BRITISH CAME TO PICTURE-COLLECTING RATHER LATE, COMPARED WITH CONTINENTAL EUROPE. ONE OF THE FIRST INFLUENTIAL ENTHUSIASTS WAS CHARLES I. HE PURCHASED THE ENTIRE COLLECTION OF THE DUKES OF MANTUA, WHICH INCLUDED THE MAGNIFICENT SERIES OF PAINTINGS *THE TRIUMPHS OF CAESAR*, BY ANDREA MANTEGNA. RIGHT: *THE ELEPHANTS* FROM THAT SERIES

Court. Charles competed for the best picture collection with his closest courtiers, such as the Marquis of Hamilton and the Earl of Arundel – whose antique marbles are now in the Ashmolean Museum in Oxford. Within twenty years they had transformed the English court from one of the most artistically impoverished in Europe into one of the richest. When the great Rubens, painter to all the courts of Europe, surveyed his elevated clientele, he was unhesitating in describing Charles as 'the greatest amateur in painting of the princes of the world'.

This spectacular opening to the history of British collecting proved to be something of a false start. In 1649 Charles I lost his head and his paintings. At the end of January he stepped out from beneath Rubens' magnificent ceiling painting at the Banqueting House and onto the scaffold. Charles had commissioned the pictures – still to be seen there – which, with grim irony, celebrate the peaceful prosperity and the divine legitimacy of Stuart rule. Parliament seized on Charles's collection as a means of raising funds, and the great collectors of Europe – Philip IV, Cardinal Mazarin and the Archduke Leopold – circled like vultures and carried away the choicest pieces, which now hang in Paris, Madrid and Vienna. However, we should not regret these losses too much: the works that stayed in the country were returned to the monarchy (both voluntarily and by force) on the restoration of Charles II in 1660 and many were subsequently destroyed in a devastating fire at Whitehall Palace in 1698.

If the artistic poverty of Britain at the beginning of the seventeenth century was notable, it was even more evident sixty years later after civil war and a Puritan government had suppressed collectors' appetites. Even after the Restoration most people in Britain had very little chance of seeing a painting, let alone buying one. In stark contrast to Europe, where the art market was flourishing, it was illegal to import works of art for sale. Further, there were no public art exhibitions, no picture dealers and no auction houses. When the gossipy diarist John Evelyn travelled to Holland he was amazed by the number of paintings hanging in even modest Dutch houses. But even more remarkable than the bare walls of Britain's houses in the 1680s was the rapidity with which they became cluttered with pictures in the decades that followed.

Throughout the eighteenth century pictures flooded into the country and the British established themselves as Europe's most voracious and extravagant collectors. The figures are prodigious: between 1720 and 1770 about 50,000 paintings and ten times as many prints were imported from Italy, France and Holland. By the end of the century London had become the hub of the European art market, which was presided over by the charming

James Christie, founder of the famous auction house. English gentlemen travelled to Europe to finish their education, see the wonders of classical and Renaissance Europe and, if possible, bring them back in their suitcases. 'I never sent a gentleman to Italy,' complained an exasperated King George III, 'but he came back a picture dealer.' The taste of these travelling magpies for Italian masters of the sixteenth and seventeenth centuries is still reflected in the great strengths of many of Britain's collections today. Nowhere is this truer than in the number of paintings in Britain by Claude Lorrain. Claude was a seventeenth-century French artist who spent nearly all his working life in Italy. His golden-hued vision of the Roman countryside was the very essence of the Englishman's idea of Italy. It was to exert a huge influence on British cultural life; shaping both painting, through Richard Wilson and Turner, and the countryside through our gardens, as at Stowe or Stourhead, made in emulation of his landscapes. Among the Claude pictures amassed in Britain during the eighteenth and early nineteenth centuries were those gathered by Thomas Coke, which are still preserved at Holkham Hall in Norfolk, and the great collections of John Julius Angerstein and Sir George Beaumont, which form the heart of the National Gallery's outstanding holdings of the artist.

The grand tourists did not only collect the art of the past. Among their contemporaries they sought out portraits by the arch-flatterer Batoni (page 38) and the Venetian views of Canaletto. Collectors such as the Duke of Bedford and George III bought in bulk, virtually wallpapering rooms in

IN THE 18TH CENTURY HOGARTH COMPLAINED VOCIFEROUSLY ABOUT WHAT HE SAW AS THE SNOBBISH AND IGNORANT TASTE OF BRITISH COLLECTORS WHO INSISTED ON BUYING ANYTHING BEARING AN ITALIAN NAME. IN HIS PRINT, *THE BATTLE OF THE PICTURES,* BELOW, HE SHOWS HIS OWN WORK BEING ASSAULTED BY SWARMS OF 'POPISH' DAUBINGS

their London properties with the yards of Canalettos that are now housed at Woburn (*above*) and Windsor.

Not every eighteenth-century observer welcomed this craze for picture-buying. But, perhaps surprisingly, the most vociferous objector was himself a painter, the brilliant, if bigoted, William Hogarth. Hogarth railed against 'Picture Jobbers from abroad' importing 'Ship Loads of Dead Christs, Holy Families, Madona's (*sic*), and other dismal Dark Subjects, neither entertaining nor Ornamental.' As ever, Hogarth's worry was for the fate of the English artist – and more particularly himself. If ignorant collectors and slaves to fashion insisted on paintings with an Italian name tag, what hope for those artists closer to home? He stressed the point in a print, *The Battle of the Pictures (left)*, in which his own paintings are assaulted by swarms of foreign daubings of saints, holy families and similarly 'popish' subjects. But despite, or more probably because of, the taste for foreign painting, the appetite for the domestic product was also growing, even if – and this was the constant complaint of British artists – painters of the genius of Gainsborough, Reynolds, Raeburn, Romney and Lawrence were employed almost exclusively as mere portrait painters.

The foundations for Britain's collections were laid during the middle decades of the eighteenth century but they acquired much of their distinction in the years after the French Revolution and the wars that followed. This period saw the break-up of many Continental collections, more often than not to the benefit of the rapacious Brits. More paintings, of an ever-increasing quality, made their way on to the London market. In 1792, the pictures belonging to the Duke of Orléans, cousin of Louis XVI, the finest collection in private hands anywhere in the world, arrived for sale in the capital. 'I was staggered,' recalled William Hazlitt 'and looked at them with wondering and with longing eyes...' A large slice of the collection was bought by the Duke of Bridgewater, and many of these works, including paintings by Raphael, three superb Titians and Poussin's *Seven Sacraments* are still in the family and on loan from the Duke of Sutherland to the National Gallery of Scotland.

Where some took advantage of the saleroom the Duke of Wellington benefited rather more dramatically on the battlefield. On 21 June 1813, Wellington and his troops won the decisive battle of Vittoria that ended French rule in Spain and put to flight Joseph Bonaparte, who had been placed on the throne by his brother, Napoleon. Among the

THE 'VENETIAN ROOM' AT WOBURN ABBEY, IN BEDFORDSHIRE, IS LINED WITH A FINE COLLECTION OF WORKS BY CANALETTO. COMMISSIONED BY THE 4TH DUKE OF BEDFORD DURING HIS GRAND TOUR OF ITALY IN 1731, THEY ARRIVED AT HIS LONDON HOME OVER THE FOLLOWING FEW YEARS. THEY WERE TRANSFERRED TO WOBURN IN 1800

piles of captured baggage and equipment left behind by the French was Joseph's coach, which was found to contain (in addition to state papers and a silver chamberpot) about two hundred paintings – removed from their stretchers and rolled up. Wellington did not have time to give the pictures more than a cursory glance and sent them back to England where they were unrolled with ever-growing excitement by William Seguier, later to become the first Keeper of the National Gallery. The haul included masterpieces by Velázquez, Jan Brueghel, Correggio and Rubens. Seguier wrote back in breathless tones describing a 'most valuable collection of pictures, one which you could not have conceived.' This was no ordinary booty. In fact, the paintings had been looted by the French from the Spanish royal collection. On this discovery, Wellington, in some embarrassment offered to return them. Fortunately for him, the embarrassment was mutual and the Spanish king, conscious that he owed the Iron Duke both his throne and his kingdom, insisted he keep them as a fitting gift of gratitude. Over eighty of these pictures, including Velázquez's *Waterseller (facing page)*, and Correggio's *Agony in the Garden* – Wellington's favourite picture – still hang in Apsley House, the Duke's London residence at Hyde Park Corner.

The combined efforts of picture dealers, grand tourists and marauding soldiers were such that, within little more than a hundred years Britain's holding of paintings had been transformed from the derisory to the spectacular. When the German museum director Gustav Waagen went on a tour of the country to compile a catalogue of its paintings in the 1830s, he could report without any exaggeration that the private collections of Britain contained the richest assembly of works of art in the world.

Despite many losses – mostly to America and the power of the dollar – a large proportion of these paintings are still here. Perhaps more surprisingly, many of them are still in the nation's country houses and royal palaces where Waagen saw them. Britain's political history has left many pictures in the hands of those who bought them – with only the taxman, the need to mend the roof and the odd philanthropic urge depleting aristocratic collections with any consistency.

Today many important paintings enter public collections, both national and regional, in lieu of inheritance tax, but the most significant beneficiary of country house collections over the past half century has been the National Trust. Indeed, since 1942, when Mrs Ronnie Greville took the unprecedented step of bequeathing to the National Trust her house at Polesden Lacey, Surrey (*right*), along with her collection of Dutch paintings, it has become, in a large number of its

RIGHT: VELASQUEZ'S *WATERSELLER*, WHICH CAME TO THE COUNTRY VIA THE BATTLEFIELD. IT WAS ONE OF A VAST HAUL OF PAINTINGS SEIZED BY THE DUKE OF WELLINGTON AFTER HE HAD DEFEATED JOSEPH BONAPARTE, NAPOLEON'S BROTHER, IN SPAIN IN 1813

NATIONAL TRUST PROPERTIES HOUSE A SIGNIFICANT PORTION OF BRITAIN'S RICH STORE OF PAINTINGS. OVER THE PAST HALF CENTURY, SINCE MRS RONNIE GREVILLE BEQUEATHED TO THE TRUST HER HOUSE AT POLESDEN LACEY, SURREY, BELOW, THE TRUST HAS BEEN THE CHIEF RECIPIENT OF BRITAIN'S COUNTRY HOUSE COLLECTIONS

properties, an alternative national picture collection. But even the collections still in private hands are and have been public for some time. From almost the moment that the great country-house collections were being assembled they were, to some degree at least, accessible to the curious visitor. At Wilton House in Wiltshire, home to the unrivalled collection of the Earls of Pembroke, guidebooks were produced as early as the 1720s. By the 1760s books such as *The English Connoisseur: Containing an Account of Whatever is Curious in Painting and Sculpture in the Palace and Seats of the Nobility and the Principal Gentry of England* helped people find their way to paintings of particular distinction. It was not unusual for great houses to have set opening times; at the end of the century Chatsworth was open two days a week and Fonthill, the extravagant gothic fantasy built by William Beckford – father of Gothic horror and 'the richest man in Britain' - was open daily between noon and 4pm. Other houses could be visited when the family were not in residence, which in practice meant most of the time. When Jane Austen's *Pride and Prejudice* was published in 1813, nothing could have been more usual than for Elizabeth Bennett to be shown round the pictures at Pemberley by Mr Darcy's housekeeper.

However, access to the country's paintings was certainly not universal. Elizabeth was a respectable young lady after all, and most of the aristocracy were not ready to throw their doors open to just anybody. Even more significantly, the Royal Collection remained virtually inaccessible to all but those of the highest rank. In 1793 some envious eyes looked over the Channel when the French Revolutionary government threw open the doors of the Louvre, transforming it from royal palace to national museum. Indeed, by the early years of the

nineteenth century London was alone among the major capitals of Europe in not having a significant collection of paintings on public display. Outside London, the situation was slightly better. The previous centuries had seen the foundation of university museums in Oxford and Glasgow and in 1816 Lord Fitzwilliam bequeathed his collection to Cambridge University. Meanwhile, in a southern suburb of London, the newly built Dulwich Picture Gallery opened its doors to all in 1817. There they could visit the elegant top-lit gallery, designed by Sir John Soane, eccentrically built around a mausoleum of the Gallery's three founders (*below*). The gallery still houses its impressive collection of paintings, many originally intended for the King of Poland but rendered homeless on his abdication.

Though the call for a National Gallery became ever louder in the early years of the nineteenth century, it was not until 1824 that the British government – feeling unusually flush after unexpectedly receiving Austria's long-overdue war debts – somewhat reluctantly paid £60,000 for the acquisition of the collection of the banker John Julius Angerstein as the nucleus of a National Gallery. Even then they failed to provide it with anything like decent accommodation and the collection remained for some years cramped in Angerstein's London residence at 100 Pall Mall.

BY THE START OF THE 19TH CENTURY, LONDON WAS ALONE AMONG THE MAJOR CAPITALS OF EUROPE IN NOT HAVING A SIGNIFICANT COLLECTION OF PAINTINGS ON PUBLIC DISPLAY. HOWEVER, INDIVIDUAL INITIATIVES HELPED TO IMPROVE THE SITUATION, GIVING ORDINARY PEOPLE ACCESS TO AT LEAST SOME SIGNIFICANT WORKS. ONE EXAMPLE WAS THE DULWICH PICTURE GALLERY, IN SOUTH LONDON, BELOW, AN ELEGANT SPACE DESIGNED BY SIR JOHN SOANE THAT OPENED ITS DOORS IN 1817

This act of grudging government patronage was followed by two magnificent acts of individual generosity when Sir George Beaumont and the Rev Holwell Carr both donated their entire collections to the fledgling institution. These gifts set the pattern of private generosity towards our public collections that still continues. Today, two-thirds of the National Gallery's Collection has been bequeathed to it from private individuals and the legacy of philanthropic donations is perhaps even greater in the regions.

Perhaps the most spectacular private initiative to introduce paintings to a regional public took place in Manchester in 1857, when a group of local businessmen took it upon themselves to bring together the greatest collection of paintings that had ever been seen anywhere in the country. This was the 'Great Art Treasures Exhibition', an extravagant collection of thousands of works of art drawn from British private collections. There were prints, sculptures, ivories, metalwork and at least one thousand paintings by the 'Ancient Masters' and many more by members of the British School (*right*). This was a public-spirited commercial venture; eager to attract people of all classes the organisers halved the one shilling entrance fee on Saturday afternoons, when the labouring classes would be most likely to be able to visit. There was

and the Laing Art Gallery in Newcastle, both the gifts of brewers who may have felt the need to add a little cultural lustre to their names in the age of the temperance movement. Such collections grew through yet more gifts and also, in many cases, through extravagant campaigns of acquisition – principally of modern British works – with substantial local council support as city galleries were increasingly seen as an important expression of civic pride and identity. They were also phenomenally successful. In 1886, its first year, Birmingham City Art Gallery was visited by over a million people, more than twice the population of the city. In the 1880s and 1990s, Manchester, Liverpool and Birmingham competed with each other in buying the most glamorous pictures of the year, resulting in their unrivalled collections of Victorian and Pre-Raphaelite works. Manchester reportedly sent its buying committee to the Royal Academy Summer Exhibition under instruction to buy the most expensive picture in the show. In 1889 it was Manchester alone that could contemplate buying the huge *Captive Andromache* (*next page*) by the Academy's then President, Frederic Lord Leighton, for which he was asking the enormous sum of £8,000. Even Manchester couldn't meet this price and they eventually secured the painting for exactly half.

As well as the great municipal galleries, nineteenth-century industrial and commercial wealth has left us many less predictable monuments. A very passable imitation of a French Renaissance château (*below*), incongruously planted on the moors of County Durham, houses the prodigious collection of painting and furniture that John Bowes amassed on the strength of an enormous coal fortune. In a similar architectural fantasy in Egham, Surrey, you can see some of the most famous of all Victorian images, bought with the proceeds of the popular Victorian patent medicine, Holloway's Little Liver Pills, acquired in

also a new attention to public comfort and amenities (all too familiar to today's museum directors). The exhibition halls included cafés and bars, while concerts – conducted by Charles Hallé – were put on in an attempt to attract the general public to paintings. And the public came. By the end of the year, at least a million people had visited the huge glass and metal basilica – a crystal palace – that had been specially erected for the show. The undisputed star of the exhibition, in front of which crowds pressed and swooned, was the painting of the Holy Women mourning over the body of the dead Christ known as *The Three Maries* by Annibale Carracci. It now hangs quietly dreaming of past glories in the National Gallery.

But the greatest legacy of the Manchester exhibition was its unequivocal demonstration of the public's appetite for art and, perhaps as important, the fact that this public was not confined to the capital. 'The Great Art Treasures Exhibition' became the inspiration and model for the large number of regional municipal museums that were established over the next fifty years. Almost all were founded through some great act of private generosity from the newly wealthy citizens of the great industrial cities. This could be the donation of a collection in search of a building – such as the railway and paper magnate Thomas Wrigley's collection, given to Bury by his children to mark Queen Victoria's jubilee in 1887 – or the provision of a building in search of a collection, as was the case for the Walker Gallery in Liverpool

the space of two years and presented by Thomas Holloway to his educational foundation, Royal Holloway College. Holloway, it seems, was not the most sure-footed philanthropist and he settled on the idea of a ladies college only after taking out an advertisement asking for suggestions as to 'How best to spend a quarter of a million or more', for which he apparently received seven hundred proposals, most of which were 'utterly worthless'.

Far more sure of himself was William Hesketh Lever, who, having made a fortune packing soap, founded the model village of Port Sunlight (named after his most popular brand) for his workers and provided it with its own art gallery and collection of pictures. His collection had started inauspiciously – in a search for suitable images with which to advertise his products; but it soon developed into the lavish collection of nineteenth-century British painting and eighteenth-century furniture we can see today. Despite their differences of approach, both Lever and Holloway shared the belief that pictures were a force for good – a means towards enjoyment certainly, but, as important, an aid to moral improvement. To this end Lever added suits

of armour to his collection, explaining that they were there to bring in the crowds who might not come for pictures alone.

Tales of outstanding generosity continue through the twentieth century. After the First World War, Dame Nellie Barber decided that Birmingham University should have a collection of pictures that could compare with those of the National Gallery in London and provided the money to buy them. The Barber Institute is the result. In 1973 the University of East Anglia received the collection assembled by Sir Robert and Lady Sainsbury, including African, Indian, Polynesian and Native American sculptures as well as paintings by Bacon, Giacometti and Picasso. It is now displayed in Norman Foster's Sainsbury Centre for the Visual Arts in Norwich. In the same year, the sculptor Jacob Epstein's widow Kathleen gave her collection to the city of Walsall where it can now be seen in the recently built and wonderfully popular New Art Gallery (*page 19*). Most spectacular of all, 1983 saw the opening of the Burrell Collection in Glasgow, showing the extraordinary collection of over 8,000 objects, ranging from medieval

Claude Monet 1905

tapestries to Degas pastels, collected by the shipping magnate Sir William Burrell and given to the city in the 1940s and 50s.

Yet the picture is not entirely rosy. While the galleries of Victorian and Edwardian Britain were enthusiastic in their purchase of modern British art they were altogether more nervous, if not actively hostile, towards developments on the Continent. The Impressionists – those dangerous radicals – were simply beyond the pale. Even the National Gallery did its best to resist being *given*, let alone buying, any pictures by this controversial bunch until it was almost too late to do so. As late as 1964 when the Gallery bought Cézanne's *Bathers* – a mere sixty years after it was painted – there were squeals of outrage from press and public over the purchase of this alarmingly 'modern' picture. The masterpieces by Van Gogh and Seurat in the National Gallery Collection were forced on them in the 1920s by Samuel Courtauld, who left his still greater collection to the Courtauld Institute, now to be seen in Somerset House in London. The other exceptional collection of Impressionists in the country was similarly the result of private enthusiasm, this time on the part of the sisters Gwendoline and Margaret Davies, who built up their collection in the early years of the century and gave it to the National Museum of Wales in Cardiff in 1951 and 1963. As far as later twentieth-

THE GIFT OF TWO SISTERS, MONET'S *WATER LILIES*, IS IN THE NATIONAL MUSEUM OF WALES

WALSALL'S POPULAR NEW ART GALLERY HOUSES SCULPTURES GIVEN BY THE WIDOW OF JACOB EPSTEIN

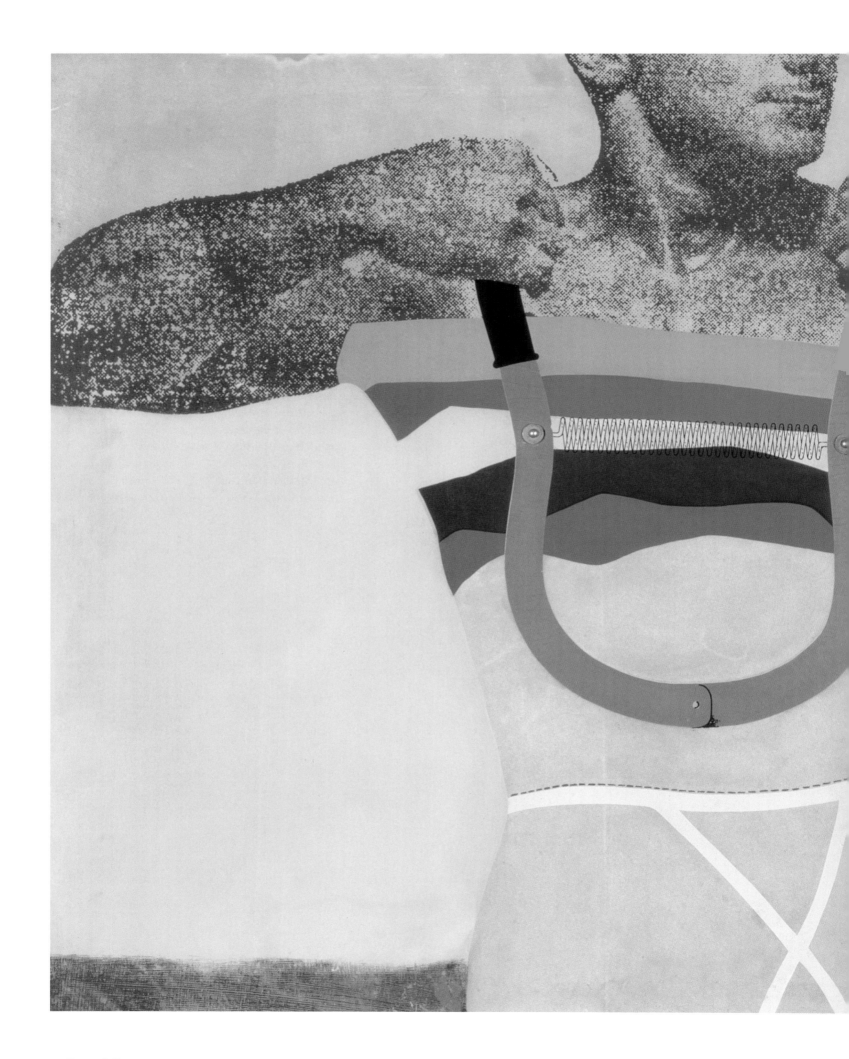

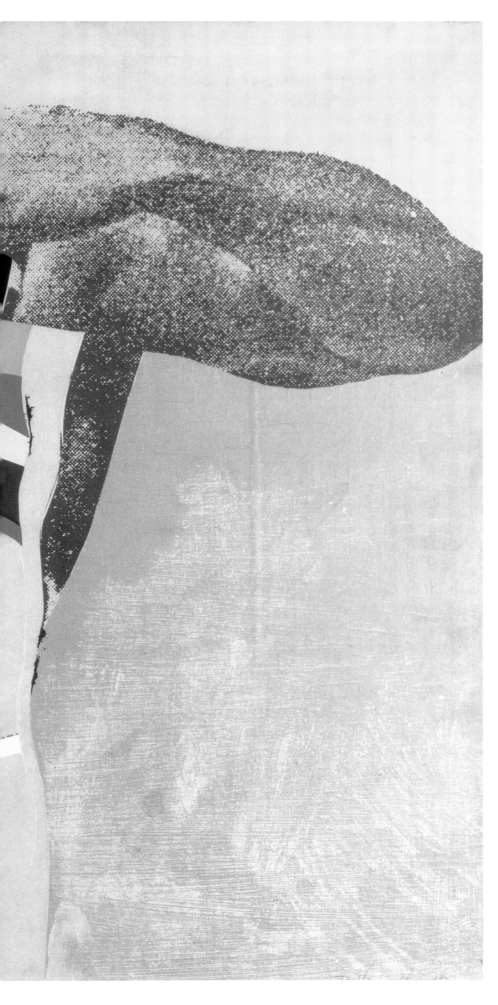

century painting goes we are even less well off. Beyond the walls of Tate Modern (and its satellites in Liverpool and St Ives), there are depressingly few works by even such giants as Picasso, Matisse or Jackson Pollock. But even here there are some bright spots. In the midst of the Second World War, Trevor Thomas, the Director of Leicester City Art Gallery, together with his curator Hans Hess, took the brave decision to collect German Expressionism and today the gallery still owns the country's only painting by Franz Marc on public display. A similar curatorial initiative in the 1960s in Wolverhampton resulted in the city's impressive collection of American and English Pop Art (*left*).

In this book, I want to look at all these collections – Britain's Paintings – as though they were one collection. All the pictures that we own or that we can go and see. Strangely, there is as yet no centralised inventory of the nation's paintings, an undertaking which the National Gallery strongly supports, working with colleagues in public collections everywhere. But that will take many years; and in the meantime this book aims to show you some of the best of what is there. In the chronology (*beginning on page 140*), we have organised the paintings by artist – so that you can easily find out where Britain's Rembrandts or Van Goghs are – and also by date. The works range from the beginning of the Renaissance to the present day and come from all over Europe.

Together, the pictures tell at the highest level the story of European art. But I think they also tell an even more extraordinary story: the story of us. Over the centuries artists have explored the way we look, the way we live and, above all, the way we think and feel. What it means to be alive. So I have decided to organise this guide, this very personal tour of Britain's pictures, not by date of painting, but by the areas of human experience that the painters addressed. We begin with the most important, Love, and the most destructive, War.

CURATORIAL INITIATIVE HAS BEEN RESPONSIBLE FOR THE EXISTENCE OF SOME NOTABLE COLLECTIONS AROUND THE COUNTRY. WOLVERHAMPTON ART GALLERY AND MUSEUM, FOR EXAMPLE, HOUSES AN IMPRESSIVE ARRAY OF AMERICAN AND BRITISH POP ART, INCLUDING *ADONIS IN Y-FRONTS* BY RICHARD HAMILTON, LEFT

PART I

LOVE AND WAR

'War and love are drawn together,
because they are at a deep level merely
different aspects of the same thing –
the moments of ultimate intensity
in every human life'

M ars and Venus here could be any
couple after a night of love. Like a
joke from a best man's speech, he
sprawls exhausted, everything about
him limp and drooping. She, on the
other hand, sits up, eager and alert, ready either to read
the Sunday papers, or – to judge by the cavorting satyrs
trying to rouse him – to tackle him again. Botticelli's
figures may indeed be a Florentine wedding joke,
perhaps part of an elaborate marriage gift of the 1480s,
but they are also the goddess of love and the god of war,
who, according to the myths of Greece and Rome, were
passionately, inextricably in love.

As always, the myths merely remind us of a great and
disturbing truth. Mars and Venus have to wind up in
bed together. It is unavoidable. War and love are
drawn together, because they are at a deep level merely
different aspects of the same thing – the moments of
ultimate intensity in every human life, where self
encounters other, is overwhelmed and perhaps
destroyed, where we behave like beasts or gods, where

life itself is or seems to be on the line, and we live each
moment, tragic or sublime, as though it alone existed.
Rich themes for artists in every age.

Where Botticelli milks the subject for its comic
potential, Rubens takes the sombre view. Europe's
central tale of destructive passion, in painting as in
literature, is Troy, the great city brought low by one
man's love. According to legend, the Greeks not only
destroyed the city, but killed or enslaved every
inhabitant, annihilating an entire civilisation. It was war
at its most brutal and it has haunted the European
imagination for thousands of years. Painting when the
Thirty Years' War was devastating his native Flanders
and much of Germany, Rubens shows us where the
Trojan War began: Paris, Prince of Troy, choosing
between the goddesses representing wisdom, power
and passion *(facing page)*. We know in the story, as we
know in our own lives, that there is no contest. Power
and wisdom haven't a chance once passion is in issue.
Paris chooses love and his boundless love for Helen
will lead to the dark chaos we see foreshadowed in the

▲ Sandro Botticelli
1445–1510
MARS AND VENUS
c.1485
*The shape of this panel suggests that
Botticelli conceived it not as an
independent painting, but as part of a
piece of furniture, perhaps a bedhead.
Panels like this were popular wedding
presents in Renaissance Florence. In
this grove of pleasurable fantasy,
Mars's surrender has been total.
Mischievous satyrs try to wake him;
if they fail, the wasps around his head
may succeed, another reminder of the
stings of love. Venus views her
conquest with a quizzical eye, her
gown concealing and revealing her in
equal measure. Indeed, Botticelli
seems to have been so concerned to rearrange Venus's body into a pleasing
pattern that she has lost her right leg.*

Tempera and oil on poplar,
69.2 x 173.4 cm
NATIONAL GALLERY, LONDON

George Frederic Watts
1817-1904
LOVE AND DEATH
EXHIBITED 1877

"Love," Watts explains, "stands upon the threshold of the House of Life, barring the entry against the fatal advance of Death. The bright wings of the god are already crushed and broken against the lintel of the door and the petals are falling from the roses that Love has set around the porch." In fiction, art and life, from Little Nell to the Duke of Wellington, the Victorians were fascinated by death and its details. They yielded delightedly to wither-wringing accounts of sick-room farewells and the elaborate grievings of the public funeral. Watts's picture was such a success at its first showing in 1877 that he made several replicas of it.

Oil on canvas, 64.5 x 33 cm
WHITWORTH ART GALLERY, MANCHESTER

Peter Paul Rubens
1577-1640
THE JUDGEMENT OF PARIS
PROBABLY 1632-1635

Three plump, pearly goddesses prepare to undress for the beauty contest between wisdom, power and love. The prize is a golden apple; the judge Paris, Prince of Troy. Behind Paris, Mercury, heavenly messenger, waits to announce the result. Minerva's owl watches over the goddess of wisdom's shield and helmet. Juno, Queen of Heaven, has brought her peacock, who has clearly taken against Paris's dog. In the middle, Venus looks confidently towards Paris, who offers her the apple. The winner.

Oil on oak, 144.8 x 193.7 cm
NATIONAL GALLERY, LONDON

heavens – the ruin of his family and the death of all his companions in arms. *Folie à deux* with a terrible price. Rubens, however, does no more than hint at the ultimate horror: when Mars, not Venus, is the victor, love and war coincide, compelling you to watch the killing of those you love.

Among the most harrowing images of Western painting are the mothers of Bethlehem struggling in vain to save their children from the murderous troops of Herod, sent to kill every baby boy. The subject is so powerful that Bruegel's picture of it in the Queen's collection *(above)* was clearly felt to be too distressing to live with and had to be toned down. Pain of this order could not be looked at. Watts gives a gentler view of love trying to ward off death, but it is hardly less tragic *(previous page)*. The scale of the figures leaves us in no doubt who will prevail. It is in the realm not of war but of faith that love survives and overcomes death. As we see later in this book, that theme too has inspired the greatest painters in every generation. But first, the violence and the tenderness of Love and War.

Pieter Bruegel the Elder
c.1525-1569
THE MASSACRE OF THE INNOCENTS
1565-1568

It is Bethlehem, but it could be any Flemish town. It is a biblical act of savagery, but the clothes, weapons and armour are all modern. The Massacre of the Innocents, Brueghel says, is a perpetual battle between the powerful and the helpless. It is happening now. We are in the middle of it. Matthew's gospel tells of King Herod's solution to the problem posed him by the birth of a so-called King of the Jews: he would kill every child in Bethlehem under two. His mounted troops mass in the town square. Foot-soldiers search house to house and slaughter as they find, overcoming the mothers' frenzied resistance. The action has no focus, for real tragedies do not turn into satisfyingly balanced compositions. Brueghel knew first-hand from the religious wars which ravaged his country that war produces ugly, individual horrors, griefs experienced singly, separate acts of butchery. His brilliant, disconcerting conception was too much for viewers: a later artist was instructed to paint out the murdered children, turning them into undisturbing bundles of washing, or animals. Nobody ever wants to confront the reality of massacre.

Oil on canvas , 109.2 x 158.1 cm
HAMPTON COURT PALACE, ROYAL COLLECTION

John Everett Millais
1829-1896
THE BLACK BRUNSWICKER
1860

In 1860, when Millais painted this picture, the British still clearly remembered the heroic role the German regiments had played at Waterloo, Blucher arriving at the critical moment to help defeat Napoleon (whose portrait hangs here on the back wall). The Black Brunswickers were the smartest, most dashing and most effective of the lot. And they died in large numbers. On the eve of battle, a young woman tries to persuade her sweetheart not to leave for the fight and almost certain death.

Oil on canvas, 104 x 68.5 cm
THE LADY LEVER ART GALLERY, PORT SUNLIGHT

Nicolas Poussin
1594-1665
TANCRED AND ERMENIA
1635-1640

Across the fierce battle-lines of the Crusades, Erminia, a Saracen princess, is in love with the Christian knight, Tancred. She rides out to look for him after battle, finds him dangerously wounded and, with his sword, cuts off her own hair to staunch his wounds. Her white horse looks nervously around in the moonlight, fearing a further attack. But over the lovers a pair of cupids provide extra light for this mission of mercy and romance, and reassure us that all will end well.

Oil on canvas, 75 x 100cm
BARBER INSTITUTE OF FINE ARTS, BIRMINGHAM

Edward Burne-Jones
1833-1898
LAUS VENERIS (THE PRAISING OF VENUS)
1873-1878

This, the latest of the pictures in this section, denies all the others. Through the window we see knights riding to combat, but we can be sure that the disagreeable aspects of battle will not trouble this private world of medievalising tapestries and languid self-regard. Venus, crown on her lap, listens to women of her court tell of the feats of love. But the true victor here surely is not love, but style.

Oil on canvas, 122 x 183 cm
LAING ART GALLERY, NEWCASTLE

THE JOYS OF LOVE

Painting love, with all its emotional and physical excitements, is always going to be a challenge for the artist. How do you suggest its intensity? How do you express its physical pleasures without drifting into the realm of pornography? In the paintings here each of the artists has resorted to metaphor – the visual pun. In Fragonard's playful, funny painting – which seems to provide incontrovertible proof of the helpless frivolity of pre-Revolutionary France – the swing itself provides the sexual metaphor, while also ferrying the smiling vision in pink between her lover and cheerfully ignorant husband. The painting is as light as meringue, the girl's slipper is caught mid-air, the trees and leaves take on her frilliness and her enraptured lover stares up her skirt.

Whereas Fragonard concentrates on physical excitement, the other paintings suggest the more profound way in which love can unite – and make two become one. Jan Gossaert, painting in sixteenth-century Netherlands, shows Hercules almost literally knotted to his wife Deianeira with his beautifully wrought depiction of intertwining legs. Picasso's painting is altogether more personal – a painting of his lover on to which he has grafted a blue profile – notionally his own. As they kiss, the two faces merge into one, yet maintain their individual forms. Hockney, on the other hand, links his embracing figures with strokes of red paint – reminding us of arteries, through which the essence of life and love can freely flow.

▲ Pablo Picasso
1881–1973
NUDE WOMAN IN A RED ARMCHAIR
1932
In rhythmic, yielding curves of plump flesh, Picasso shows us his lover, Marie-Thérèse Walter, who was 17 when she met the 45-year-old artist. Even the chair joins in this painted caress, its forward arm enfolding and embracing the rounded forms of buttock, hip and breast. But this is also a double portrait. Marie-Thérèse's pale face merges with Picasso's own blue profile, which kisses her on the lips. The noses meet, the lips combine, two individuals become one in this universal image of sensual love, as tranquil as it is erotic.

Oil on canvas, 130 x 97 cm
TATE, LONDON

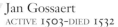
▼ Jan Gossaert
ACTIVE 1503–DIED 1532
HERCULES AND DEIANEIRA
1517
Hercules and Deianeira sit in a classical niche decorated with relief sculptures showing three of the Labours of Hercules. Clearly, Hercules is home after sorting out the problems of the world. They gaze cheerfully into each other's eyes as Hercules cradles his massive club – a playful phallic reference. They seem inseparable – one dreads to think what might happen should they try to stand up, but it seems more likely that they will soon be lying down. This is clearly a marriage of minds as well as bodies. Talk as well as sex. Harmony at every level.

Oil on panel, 36.8 x 26.6 cm
THE BARBER INSTITUTE OF FINE ARTS, BIRMINGHAM

◄ David Hockney
BORN 1937
WE TWO BOYS TOGETHER CLINGING
1961
The title comes from a poem by Walt Whitman: 'a marvellous, beautiful, poetic line', according to the artist. As is suggested, the painting deals with the inseparability of two people in love. The boys kiss and embrace, but they are also connected by red lines, which Hockney described as 'small tentacles that help keep the bodies together'. These lines suggest the mysterious dynamic that binds lovers together. Hockney drives home his point with graffiti on a shabby wall. Made in the early Sixties, when gay relationships were illegal in Britain, Hockney's painting suggests something of the danger that often attended homosexual love.

Oil on canvas, 121.9 x 152.4 cm
ARTS COUNCIL COLLECTION, LONDON

Jean-Honoré Fragonard
1732-1806
THE SWING
1767
*A statue of Cupid warns us to
be silent as Fragonard depicts*

*a love triangle in this lush
garden. A befrilled young
woman kicks off her slipper as
she swings merrily between
two men – her unknowing
husband who pulls the swing*

*in the shadows and, hiding in
the bushes, her young lover,
who had commissioned the
picture and given the artist
detailed instructions. The
husband smiles at his wife's*

*glee, but she has eyes for one
man only – the red-cheeked,
goggle-eyed lover, who is
captivated by the vision. Not
surprising, for the artist has
placed him so that he could see*

*his mistress's little feet, white
stockings and, indeed,
considerably more.*

Oil on canvas, 81 x 64.2 cm
WALLACE COLLECTION,
LONDON

THE PAINS OF LOVE

We don't need artists to tell us that love can hurt but nor should we be surprised that they often do. In the Bible, Adam and Eve, by tasting of the forbidden fruit of the Tree of Knowledge, forfeited the pleasures of paradise for a life of pain and labour. With this act of disobedience came death, but also regeneration – and consequently desire and sex. Unsurprisingly, artists have often suggested the sexual nature of Eve's temptation of Adam – even if, theologically speaking, this might be putting the cart before the horse. The sixteenth-century German court artist, Cranach, shows Eve as a golden-tressed *femme fatale* who has clearly got the measure of her feeble-minded partner.

The other paintings here suggest the multifarious forms of love's agonies. In Waterhouse's prettified vision of hopeless love we are shown the unrequited love of Echo, spurned by the handsome Narcissus; and the impossible love of Narcissus for his own intangible reflection. In Hilliard's famous portrait of an Elizabethan gentleman, we see a more complex inner conflict – torn between two women and two types of love. These forms of heart-rending affliction are presented as unthreatening, pleasing images but the same can not be said of Francis Bacon. Here style echoes subject – and both are viscerally painful.

▶ John William Waterhouse
1849-1917
ECHO AND NARCISSUS
1903
The nymph Echo looks longingly towards Narcissus but he is interested in nothing but his own reflection. Able to speak only the last words she hears spoken (a punishment from Juno for gossiping), Echo cannot express her own feelings, only those of others. Like the ivy to which she clings, she can have no independent existence. Narcissus spurns her, and is in turn punished with the opposite affliction – he falls in love with his own reflection, and can never know happiness in others. Enchanted by himself, he stays and stares until transformed into a flower – the yellow narcissus depicted here. Echo is dependent, even in death: broken-hearted at Narcissus's end, she wasted away until only her voice remained.

Oil on canvas, 109.2 x 189.2 cm
WALKER ART GALLERY,
LIVERPOOL

◀ Lucas Cranach the Elder
1472-1553
ADAM AND EVE
1526
Cranach gives us not a tragic view of the fall of mankind, but a humorous portrayal of the first seduction. A knowing Eve hands the forbidden apple to a hesitant Adam, who scratches his head, uncertain whether or not he should take it and, if he does, what to do next. They are surrounded by wild animals, arranged to provide visual interest and, in places, humour: right in front of Adam, an extremely horny deer almost winks at us. Behind them is the Tree of Knowledge, from which the serpent watches the plot develop. At the tree's base is a vine, which, besides hiding the couple's nudity, offers a theological lesson: the grapes symbolise the blood of Christ and, with it, the hope of redemption from the sinful state into which Adam and Eve are about to lead us. But Cranach's painting is no dry sermon – with its wry humour and delightful details, it amuses and enchants as it teaches.

Oil on canvas, 117.1 x 80.5 cm
COURTAULD INSTITUTE
GALLERIES, LONDON

Nicholas Hilliard
1547-1619
A YOUNG MAN LEANING AGAINST A TREE AMONG ROSES
1585-1595
Was anyone ever so unhappy with such style? Like a sonnet charting the delicious wretchedness of love, this painting encourages us to take delight in a young man's melancholy. He is thought to be Robert

Devereux, 2nd Earl of Essex, the dashing favourite of Elizabeth I, whose colours he wears. Essex met the disapproval of the queen when he married in secret, and this painting may be part of his effort to make amends. His languorous pose, hand on heart, suggests that he is thinking of his love – but which one? The wild roses surrounding him, emblems of Elizabeth I that

glow with special brilliance against the cape covering his heart, speak only of his devotion to the queen. The cryptic message at the top, 'praised faith causes pain', suggests there is no way out of his elegant impasse.

Body colour on vellum,
13.5 x 7.3 cm
VICTORIA AND ALBERT
MUSEUM, LONDON

Francis Bacon
1909-1992
TRIPTYCH – AUGUST 1972
1972
In these three images Bacon explores his tempestuous seven-year relationship with his companion and lover, George Dyer. In October 1971, Dyer committed suicide in a Paris hotel room, the day before the opening of a retrospective of

Bacon's work at the Grand Palais. What should have been a triumphant and joyous climax to the artist's career became perhaps the most devastating experience of his life. The traumatic losing of his lover inspired a series of works made in the following years. Many of these reflect the physical and violent nature of their love. In this one, we see George Dyer on the left, and Bacon

himself on the right. In the centre, the two are united in a contorted amalgamation of human flesh, both tender and savage, an image that echoes Bacon's view that '...one of the terrible things about so-called love... is the destruction'.

Oil on canvas, each canvas
198.1 x 147.3 cm
TATE, LONDON

DANGEROUS LOVE

All societies set limits to love, because all societies know that while love may end happily ever after, it can, and often does, go very nastily wrong. The pictures on these pages show how Renaissance Italy and Victorian England presented the consequences of love without control – violence, shame, misery, disease and disgust – and how the artists tackled the problem of how to delight the eye while disturbing the conscience.

These pictures offer us sex with a government health warning. Bronzino and Holman Hunt build stories out of endless small details, at the same time revealing the past and suggesting what happens next. Around Venus and Cupid are all the signs of the wretchedness that follows pleasure. The domestic minutiae of Woodbine Villa, St John's Wood, allow Holman Hunt to suggest that there is still hope that the worst can be avoided.

The winner, for my money, is without question Titian, who created at the age of 80 a picture which is one of the greatest feats of sheer painting on show in the whole of Britain. Even after 400 years, Titian's image of rape is terrifying. The victim, rigid with fear on her soft yielding pillows, gazes in silent panic at her attacker. The thrust of his knee is as brutal as the dagger he brandishes.

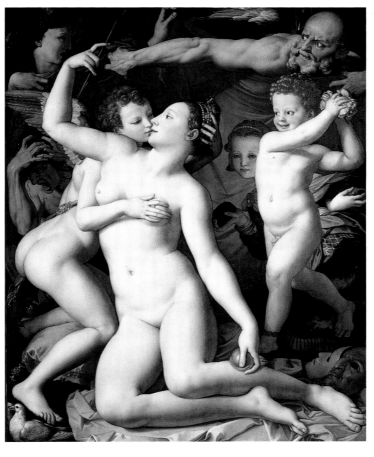

William Holman Hunt
1827-1910
THE AWAKENING CONSCIENCE
1853

She has many rings on her fingers, but – very visibly – no wedding ring. She is that widespread threat to Victorian domestic decency: the kept woman. But Holman Hunt clearly shows her to us as victim, not as seducer. And his view is optimistic. This woman may have been led astray, but she has come to her senses and is about to break free. On the floor lies sheet music for the song Tears, Idle Tears. Above it, a bird has just escaped from the claws of the cat and is about to take flight for the safety of the garden that we see reflected in the mirror behind. The woman looks out to us and to respectable life to which she is about to return – thus fulfilling the ambition of many Victorian social reformers.

Oil on canvas, 76.2 x 55.9 cm
TATE, LONDON

Titian
c.1487-1576
THE RAPE OF LUCRETIA
1570

Everything here is divided and in conflict – male and female, clothed and naked, power and helplessness, the white of her blameless sheets and the red of his breeches, already undone. Most important, he is split: his body is impossible, legs and groin apparently unrelated to head and heart, dislocated in a frenzy that will quickly destroy both man and woman as well as the political order of Rome. The virtuous Lucretia will commit suicide in anger and shame; and public outrage will banish Tarquin the prince and end for ever the monarchy in ancient Rome. This image of physical violence, of the ultimate abuse of power, was painted for – astonishingly – a king, Philip II of Spain. What on earth, one wonders, did he make of it?

Oil on canvas, 188.9 x 145.1 cm
FITZWILLIAM MUSEUM, CAMBRIDGE

Bronzino
1503-1572
AN ALLEGORY WITH VENUS AND CUPID
1540-1550

Cupid arches his buttocks as he caresses his mother. Their tongues touch. Father Time, his hour glass just visible at top right, pulls back the veil to show the inevitable consequences of illicit love. To the right of Venus, none of whose charms is concealed, lie the masks of deceit. Above, a child clasps the roses of pleasure with such intensity that he has not yet noticed that the spike of a thorn has pierced his left foot. Behind him, a sinister figure, half-smiling girl, half-serpent, offers us a honeycomb. As we look closer we see she has two right hands – this is the double-dealing of the sweet life. On the other side of the painting, a figure howls in lonely despair.

Oil on wood, 146.1 x 116.2 cm
NATIONAL GALLERY, LONDON

THE LOOK OF LOVE

It is hardly surprising that the transforming and enrapturing power of vision should be a popular subject for the visual artist. Titian, in his wondrous painting of the legend of Bacchus and Ariadne seems concerned above all else with the look of love. The riot and noise of Bacchus's drunken retinue and the leaping God himself seem to stop dead when we come to the vivid space between the gazes of the God and the abandoned Ariadne. The tension and potency of this look of desire is then echoed in a quieter key by other gazes in the picture – between the tambourine-wielding nymph and hairy-legged satyr, between the amorous cheetahs who pull Bacchus's chariot and even between the cheeky young satyr and us as we look at the painting.

The gaze out of the painting is a common device and we find it again in Burne-Jones's depiction of King Cophetua's enchantment by the beautiful beggar maid. Her look and charms are directed as much at us as at the king, even if we may resist falling under the spell of a particularly wan late-nineteenth-century idea of feminine beauty. In the paintings by Cranach and Rembrandt it is again we, the (male) viewers, who are invited – or, perhaps, forced – to take the position of the admiring lover or voyeur. Cranach's nude, a sixteenth-century pin-up and clearly 'on show', closes her eyes to invite our voyeuristic gaze. Rembrandt, as ever, creates a more ambiguous moment. Again we find ourselves in an astonishingly intimate situation, watching a woman in bed as she pulls back the curtains in apparent anticipation of someone joining her. But here her gaze is not directed towards us but towards someone offstage – we couldn't be closer but we shouldn't be there.

◄ Edward Burne-Jones
1833-1898
KING COPHETUA AND THE BEGGAR MAID
1884
King Cophetua, a handsome African king, sits on the lower ledge, looking up adoringly at the beautiful young beggar girl. He has removed his crown – a sign of humility, respect and much more. In Tennyson's poem, the king, renowned for his contempt of women, had spotted the girl from his palace window and, struck by her beauty, had fallen instantly in love. She on the other hand looks decidedly uneasy. She does not return his loving gaze, but stares blankly into space, allowing us to take in the endless contrasts between them – rich and poor, dark and fair, armour or thin, form-hugging cloth. As in all the best fairy tales, simplicity and goodness have conquered all.

Oil on canvas, 293 x 136 cm
TATE, LONDON

Lucas Cranach the Elder
1472-1553
THE NYMPH OF THE FOUNTAIN
1534

Cranach's nudes were extremely popular at the court of the Electors of Saxony, where he was court painter and where classical erudition was fashionable. This is the learned man's centrefold: a naked female figure presented in the respectable guise of a mythological character. An inscription in Latin tells us that this reclining woman is the nymph of the fountain. It also says: 'I am resting; do not wake me'. Being asleep, the nymph is powerless before us. We become voyeurs, allowed to scrutinise at leisure her naked body. But Cranach slips in a moral. She is laid out for the delectation of the (male) viewer, but if he is too beguiled he will fall victim to Cupid's love arrows (seen on the right) and then the power relationship will be suddenly and painfully reversed. He should heed the warning provided by the apples above: we should not be tempted by forbidden fruits.

Oil on panel, 51.3 x 76.8 cm
WALKER ART GALLERY,
LIVERPOOL

Titian
c.1487-1576
BACCHUS AND ARIADNE
1522-1523

The lonely Ariadne, abandoned by her lover, Theseus, on the island of Naxos, turns away from the ship in which he has just sailed away, and sees Bacchus, the god of wine, leaping to her rescue. Bacchus's movement is frozen: he hovers in mid-air, at the crest of a wave of merry-making and revelry, which is about to break over Ariadne. Titian also freezes the moment their gazes first meet: this look of love brings with it a moment of calm amid the frenzy and noise. Colour emphasises this contrast: vibrant and clashing tones on the right, and a clear, endlessly resonating blue on the left. This new love will endure, immortal like the crown of stars at the top – the constellation which Ariadne will become.

Oil on canvas, 175 x 190 cm
NATIONAL GALLERY, LONDON

Rembrandt van Rijn
1606-1669
YOUNG WOMAN IN BED
1640s

Hair beautifully groomed and stylishly held in place, she leans forward to push aside the curtain that closes off the bed, and peers into our space. There are no signs of recent waking. Although we do not know who she is, she must only just have gone to bed and is waiting expectantly (apprehensively?) for someone to join her. Breast, upper arm and pillow all show plump and yielding. Pleasure is surely hoped for.

Oil on canvas, 81.1 x 67.8 cm
NATIONAL GALLERIES OF
SCOTLAND, EDINBURGH

WAR: THE SPECTACLE OF WAR

W ar is of course nasty, muddy and bloody but it can also put on a hell of a show. Painters are not alone in glorifying war but, unsurprisingly, visual artists when expressing the glory of battle have concentrated on its role as spectacle. With the exception of a single prone soldier in Uccello's painting (rendered by inexpert if ambitious foreshortening as a barrel-chested midget) and the bugler in Lady Butler's cavalry charge, war in the four paintings on these pages is victimless. Uccello's knights, dressed in entirely impractical armour and headgear, prance on a smooth pink floor in front of rose bushes and orange trees – a glorious re-interpretation of what had been a fairly inglorious scuffle. In the sixteenth-century depiction of the naval Battle of Lepanto we float above the action – a splendid combination of flags and ships in which the billows of smoke are as decorative and benign as the clouds in the sky. Lady Butler's wonderfully muscular cavalry charge seems almost invincible and clearly unprepared for anything even suggesting resistance.

In contrast Charles Nevinson's paintings of the First World War, during which he was employed as an official war artist, were generally far from celebratory. But he, too, could be mesmerised by the purely visual spectacle of war. Here the great geometric beams of early searchlights marry perfectly with his characteristically simplified and angular artistic style.

▲ Christopher R.W. Nevinson
1889-1946
SEARCHLIGHTS
1916

Nevinson believed in an art which was 'strong, virile and anti-sentimental'. He painted powerful scenes of First World War conflict, but here he focuses not on the heroism of the individual soldier, but on the inhuman beauty of searchlights, long before the Nazis were to exploit their aesthetic potential to build cathedrals of light. With a group of artists who called themselves the Vorticists, Nevinson invented a new, self-consciously modern visual vocabulary of geometric lines and structures, wonderfully adapted to the new technology of killing.

Oil on canvas, 76.4 x 56 cm
MANCHESTER CITY ART GALLERY

▲ South German school (signed H Letter)
THE BATTLE OF LEPANTO, 7 AUGUST 1571
16TH CENTURY

A table-top representation of a battle that changed world history. In 1571 the Pope declared a Holy League of Christian Countries in an attempt to check the growing power of the Ottoman Turks. A fleet of more than 200 ships from Spain, Portugal, Venice and Genoa defeated the Turkish fleet at Lepanto, off the west coast of Greece. From then on, the balance of naval power in the Mediterranean was firmly in the West's favour. This bird's-eye view is typical of paintings of sea battles, intended to give an impression of scale and splendour, as well as showing particular incidents. Made soon after the event, it is at the same time a news report, a celebration and perhaps also an accompaniment to the tales of a participant.

Oil on canvas, 127 x 232.5 cm
NATIONAL MARITIME MUSEUM, GREENWICH

Paulo Uccello
1397-1475
THE BATTLE OF SAN ROMANO
1450s
The figure on the white charger, dressed in magnificent hat and brandishing his commander's baton, is Niccolò da Tolentino, one of the Florentine commanders at the Battle of San Romano. This skirmish between Florentine and Sienese mercenaries in 1432 – in which according to one account Niccolò was ambushed, burst into tears and tried to flee – was celebrated by Uccello in three huge paintings which are now in London, Paris and Florence. Uccello has transformed Niccolò into fearless hero and the squalid battle has become an elegant tournament. The armour of the soldiers is actually silver leaf, now tarnished, but which would once have shone brilliantly against the decorative landscape background and the perspectival puzzles of the foreground.

Tempera on wood, 182 x 320 cm
NATIONAL GALLERY, LONDON

Elizabeth Thompson
(Lady Butler)
1846-1933
SCOTLAND FOREVER
1881
The Victorians never tired of scenes of British heroism at Waterloo, and Lady Butler had huge popular success with works like this. The charge of the Scots Greys at the Battle of Waterloo was part of a counter-attack by the Heavy Cavalry, which defeated Napoleon's Cavalry attacks on June 18, 1815. They clearly would not have done so had the horses been in such chaotic formation in reality. But the light touches of paint, describing the wild galloping of the horses and cloudy skies, evoke a romanticised, fiery drama of noise and movement. According to her own account, the painting was brought on by Lady Butler's fury at limp-wristed, effete modern artists, such as Burne-Jones or Whistler, who lacked the kind of backbone that had helped win the war.

Oil on canvas, 101.6 x 194.3 cm
LEEDS CITY ART GALLERY

LOVE AND WAR
HEROES

War has always been a theatre for heroes, and countless portraits extol the military virtues of their sitters, few more exuberantly than Batoni's flamboyant Colonel William Gordon of Fyvie. He stands a hero, in his own eyes at least, a conqueror amid classical ruins, a worthy heir to the generals of ancient Rome. His Highland dress mimics a toga and the statue of Roma offers him an orb of command and a victor's wreath.

But painters also served the wider public's appetite for heroes. In Benjamin West's tableau of the death of Nelson, historical accuracy is hardly the point. West would have known that Nelson died below decks, but he shows us a carefully composed hero's death, depicted at the moment of victory, surrounded by his grief-stricken men. In contrast, Delaroche's painting of Napoleon ostensibly eschews such oratorical pretences. But the apparently painstaking realism is double-edged: the painting is actually bigger than West's and by stressing the unremarkable reality of the episode, the aim is to make the man in the middle more, not less, remarkable.

Today we are less comfortable with our military heroes – more aware of the cost of victory, and less deferential to our commanders. Renato Guttoso's Hero of the Proletariat, painted in the years after the Second World War, is no general but one of the nameless and faceless wounded.

▶ Pompeo Batoni
1708-1787
COLONEL WILLIAM GORDON OF FYVIE, 1736-1816
1766
Batoni was the portrait painter of choice for many eighteenth-century British travellers to Rome and we can see why. His powers of flattery and invention were seldom better deployed than in this fantasy of effortless domination. Nobody could mistake the Colonel's nationality. Painted full length in a pose of elegant power, he sports his kilt and full plaid of the Huntly tartan and carries a claymore in his outstretched right hand. If not quite the all-conquering hero, Gordon had seen distinguished active service in India. What, one wonders, did the Romans make of this Caledonian Caesar?

Oil on canvas, 101 x 73 cm
FYVIE CASTLE, ABERDEENSHIRE

▶ Paul Delaroche
1797-1856
NAPOLEON CROSSING THE ALPS
1850
Around 1800, when Napoleon was at the height of his fame, Jacques Louis David painted a flamboyant official portrait of Napoleon crossing the Alps, an isolated hero on a rearing white stallion (a print of it features on the back wall of Millais's The Black Brunswicker; see page 27). Delaroche's portrait is deliberately more low-key and based on what actually happened. In 1850, when Napoleon's nephew was attempting to become emperor in his turn, a new, more human image of the great man was needed. So Delaroche shows Napoleon humbly mounted on a mule he had borrowed, being led over the Great St Bernard Pass. He wears his trademark hat and strikes his typical pose: steadfast and unwavering among the icy peaks, he endures the same hardships as his men.

Oil on canvas, 279 x 214 cm
WALKER ART GALLERY, LIVERPOOL

▶ Renato Guttuso
1912-1987
A HERO OF THE PROLETARIAT
1953
The figure in the metal-framed bed, communist red flag at his side, is deliberately nameless and faceless. This is no general or leader of men but an anonymous worker killed in some unspecific conflict or accident. Guttuso was a Sicilian, a communist and the leader of the Italian socialist realist painters, who believed that the abstract art of many of their contemporaries was élitist and alienating. Most of Guttuso's work was politically motivated and here he paints a political martyr – the extremely foreshortened view recalls the famous picture of the dead Christ by the Renaissance master Mantegna – whose heroism actually depends upon his anonymity.

Oil on Canvas 88 x 103 cm
ESTORICK COLLECTION, LONDON

Benjamin West
1738-1820
THE DEATH OF NELSON
1806

West's painting of the much-loved admiral during his last seconds of life, centre stage on his ship, has positively operatic qualities. Many of the portraits were said to be taken from life, but the scene has been radically idealised and carefully staged. Crowds flocked to see the painting when it was exhibited in the artist's house, a few months after the Battle of Trafalgar. It was a huge success, a fitting epitaph for a national hero even if most who saw it would have understood that this was not how history was, but how it should have been. This is a myth in the making.

Oil on canvas, 182.5 x 247.5 cm
WALKER ART GALLERY,
LIVERPOOL

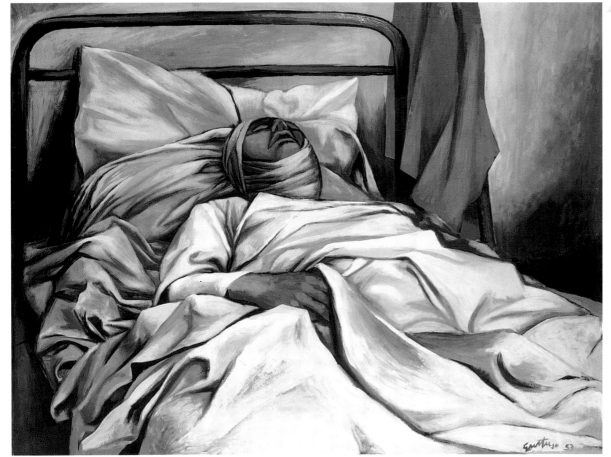

◀ David Wilkie
1785-1841
CHELSEA PENSIONERS READING THE GAZETTE OF THE BATTLE OF WATERLOO
1822
The Duke of Wellington had apparently asked Wilkie for a painting simply showing old soldiers outside a pub 'talking over their old stories'. It was Wilkie's own inspiration to include the reading of the victory despatch from Waterloo and that transformed the painting and accounted for its immediate popularity. The Duke himself was delighted with his picture, which had become an ingenious piece of flattery centred on his own deeds, and paid Wilkie, in cash and on the spot, the huge price of 1,200 guineas.

Oil on wood, 91 x 158 cm
APSLEY HOUSE, LONDON

OFF THE BATTLEFIELD

The drama of war – both in terms of triumph and disaster – is not confined to the field of battle. Wilkie's great scene of veterans reading news of the victory at Waterloo, painted for the Duke of Wellington himself and still hanging in his house at No. 1 London, is an ingenious depiction of the celebration of military victory at home, as well as being a tribute to the soldier's profession and heroism. The painting's anecdotal detail and clearly legible emotional responses made it immensely and immediately popular (when it was shown, the Royal Academy had to erect a barrier to protect it) and these qualities were to have a profound influence on later nineteenth-century British painting. The same elements can be found again in that other popular masterpiece And when did you last see your Father?, a Victorian vision of Cavalier and Roundhead that has coloured countless imaginings of the Civil War by memorably, if cloyingly, pitting blue-satinned innocence against unscrupulous grey-armoured severity.

Concentrating on the innocent sufferer has perhaps now become our characteristic response to war, especially since the waging of war on the whole civilian population has, since the 1930s, become the norm. During the Second World War the Blitz sent the population of London under ground where they were the subject of an astonishing series of works by Henry Moore. In contrast, Stanley Spencer's paintings for the memorial chapel at Burghclere took the soldiers of the Great War as their subject but showed them not as fighters but in scenes of quiet and homely calm – humanising and domesticating men in uniform.

▶ Stanley Spencer
1891-1959
MAP READING AND BED MAKING
1932
These two scenes are just part of Spencer's great scheme of decoration for the Sandham Memorial Chapel, built in memory of Lieutenant Henry Willoughby Sandham, who had died from war wounds in 1919. Behind the altar, the Resurrection of the Soldiers shows the men rising from their graves, but on the side walls Spencer painted scenes inspired by his own active service in Macedonia and the time he had spent in military hospital in Bristol. In all the scenes soldiers perform simple domestic tasks, often acts of charity – such as the bed-making and the berry-picking seen here. The map-reading scene is particularly idyllic, Spencer commenting that he loved it 'for the obvious reason of resting and contemplating'.

Oil on canvas, 213.5 x 185.5 cm and 105.5 x 185.5 cm
SANDHAM MEMORIAL CHAPEL, BURGHCLERE

William Frederick Yeames
1835-1918
AND WHEN DID YOU LAST SEE YOUR FATHER?
1878

The artist wrote: 'I had at the time I painted this picture living in my house a nephew of an innocent and truthful disposition and it occurred to me to represent him in a situation where the child's outspokenness and unconsciousness would lead to disastrous consequences. A scene in a country house occupied by the Puritans during the Rebellion in England suited my purpose.' The 'and' in the title indicates how subtly the interrogator introduced the treacherous question. Yeames carefully stages his drama. The boy's older sister weeps, aware of imminent catastrophe. But her upright little brother cannot understand the violent conflict. The Parliamentary soldiers appear gentle and considerate, comforting the weeping girl. Everyone – except the boy – knows what is at stake.

Oil on canvas, 131 x 251 cm
WALKER ART GALLERY,
LIVERPOOL

Henry Moore
1896-1986
SLEEPING SHELTERERS
(TWO WOMEN AND A CHILD)
1941

Down in the Underground stations, beneath the chaos of the Blitz, Moore, unnoticed in a corner, observed the shelterers. He produced rapid, intense sketches, recording what he saw in his sketchbook. Later, he would work these up into more finished works. The frenetic, almost frenzied lines describing the women and child seem strangely at odds with their sleeping, motionless figures, whose utter exhaustion is so tellingly conveyed. Moore's shelter drawings are among the most powerful images of the forlorn and battered, struggling through the horrors of the London Blitz. They were clearly very personal works.

After the war, when once again materials were available for making sculpture, Moore never translated these drawings into sculptural form.

Watercolour and pen on paper,
33.3 x 52.4 cm
SAINSBURY CENTRE, UEA,
NORWICH

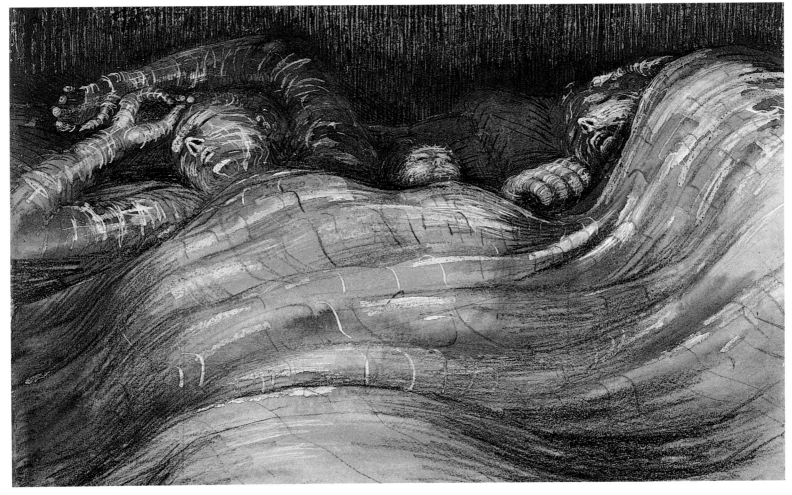

THE SUFFERING OF WAR

I f artists in the past were often called upon to glorify war, today such a response seems almost impossible. With the unprecedented suffering and slaughter of the two World Wars and the indiscriminate bombing of soldiers and civilians alike, war has become for us above all a subject of horror and pity. It is perhaps the poets who have left the most powerful memorial to the heroic sacrifice of a generation in the trenches of the First World War – eye-witness accounts of those who served. In contrast, painters were for the most part appointed as 'official' war artists (the first in Britain in 1916) and less free to record the raw horror of what they witnessed.

Sargent's huge Gassed was an official commission designed to capture 'the spirit, philosophy and sacrifice of war'. His subject is clearly horrific, but the painting subtly celebrates great courage: we see the soldiers from below, towering above us and silhouetted against the sunset. They are blinded (in a telling detail the third soldier lifts his foot far too high to clear a small step) but these strong-jawed epitomes of stoic and heroic suffering are not helpless. Bloodied, but not broken, they survive.

The two other responses to the wars of the last century shown here are less explicit, but perhaps in consequence all the more expressive. Paul Nash turns an aircraft dump into a barren metal sea, a chilling vision of the world transformed and buried by machines of destruction. Whereas Nash exploits the absence of a human presence, Picasso focuses on a single individual in one extraordinary weeping woman, part of a series of distorted, shattered, weeping figures mourning the dead of the Spanish Civil War.

Paul Nash
1889-1946
TOTES MERE (DEAD SEA)
1940-1941

Inspired by a set of photographs taken by the artist at a dump for wrecked German aircraft at Cowley, near Oxford, Nash's image of devastation has a visionary, nightmare quality. The year he painted it, Nash wrote to Kenneth Clark, then Chairman of the War Artists' Advisory Committee, describing the spectacle: 'The thing looked to me suddenly, like a great inundating sea. You might feel under certain influences – a moonlight night for instance – this is a vast tide moving across the fields, the breakers rearing up and crashing on the plain. And then no: nothing moves, it is not water or even ice, it is something static and dead. It is metal piled up, wreckage. It is hundreds and hundreds of flying creatures which invaded these shores... a sort of rigor mortis. No, they are quite dead and still.'

Oil on canvas, 101.6 x 152.4 cm
TATE, LONDON

Pablo Picasso
1881-1973
WEEPING WOMAN
1937

In 1937 Picasso responded to the German bombing of the Spanish Basque town of Guernica by producing his famous mural, which includes a figure of a weeping mother clutching her dead child. He continued to paint weeping women throughout the year, basing them on his mistress, Dora Maar. The contrast with his Nude in an Armchair (page 28) could not be starker. Here, hopeless, broken grief, a grief that can never be mended, is expressed in an astonishing assemblage of jagged edges, which replace the usual curves of the human face. These sharp points would hurt, as she has been hurt – quite literally broken up with grief. The putrid yellows, mauves and greens are sinister and unreal, and she clutches a handkerchief, which looks more like broken glass than anything soft or comforting.

Oil on canvas, 60.8 x 50 cm
TATE, LONDON

John Singer Sargent
1856-1925
GASSED
1919

The scene is one the artist witnessed at Le Bac-du-Sad on the Arras to Doullens road. The Germans put down a mustard gas barrage which failed to stem the advance but caught some of the units from the 99th Brigade. The effects of mustard gas varied from short-term damage to the eyes and lungs to permanent disablement or death, depending on the concentration of gas and the length of exposure. Photographs of mustard-gas victims show them walking in line, each one resting his hand on the shoulder of the man in front. Sargent gives his tragic procession a ritual, almost religious quality: his huge soldiers may be blinded, but through suffering they have grown in stature.

Oil on canvas, 231 x 611 cm
IMPERIAL WAR MUSEUM, LONDON

William Roberts

PART 2

WORK AND PLAY

'The nineteenth century was fascinated
by the new pleasures offered by
the great industrial cities and by
the new risks of all sorts that went
with them'

WILLIAM ROBERTS
LES ROUTIERS
C.1930-1932

▶ Édouard Manet
1832-1883
A Bar at the Folies-Bergère
1881-1882

The subject –what is the girl thinking, what is going to happen next? – and the teasing games of reflections – exactly who is standing where? – are the first things that fascinate us. But Manet's technique runs them a close second. He seems determined that we should understand how

much he has worked in order to give our eyes pleasure: the loose, bold strokes that distinguish a glass vase with water from a glass bowl with oranges, the bravura vagueness of the audience which captures attitude but not identity and the bottles waiting to be opened on a marble slab that you know is cold.

Oil on canvas, 96 x 130 cm
COURTAULD INSTITUTE
GALLERIES, LONDON

'What,' asked a French newspaper article of 1878, 'is the first thing the foreigner asks for when he reaches Paris?' The answer? 'The Folies-Bergère... Lightness, panache, charm, polish, dazzling brilliance...There are bars everywhere...tended by charming girls whose playful glances and delightful smiles attract a swarm of customers.'

Manet's impassive barmaid *(right)* works where the whole of Europe dreamed of playing. The audience in the mirror, glimpsed in a haze through the chandelier, is spellbound by the only other person in the picture who is actually at work – Little Bob, the trapeze artist, whose green bootees appear top left and who in the 1870s took the Folies-Bergère and most of Paris by storm.

But is the girl any safer than the acrobat? What does the customer, standing more or less where we the spectator must be as we look at the picture, want from her? This is a dangerous place for an unprotected single girl.

The nineteenth century was fascinated by the new pleasures offered by the great industrial cities – with London and Paris well in the vanguard – and by the new risks of all sorts that went with them. Politicians and journalists, churchmen and artists pondered the social dislocation caused by the railways, the anonymity that was possible in the huge population of the metropolis, and the tensions between the classes that were never far below the surface.

The pictures in this section suggest that, not surprisingly, the two capital cities produced very

different images of what was essentially the same phenomenon – the British eager to believe that the gulf between rich and poor could be bridged by high ideals, a moral political programme and shared good fun; the French taking a more distant view of the implications of rapid industrialisation for an increasing, and increasingly exploited, urban proletariat.

And where the English vision was communicated in the tight and laboured paint of the Pre-Raphaelites and their followers, the French brought the radicalism of their politics to the studio, the Impressionist brush-stroke every bit as revolutionary as the political upheavals of 1848 or 1870.

Different styles of painting, different responses to modern life, but in both countries a common belief that the artist had a key role to play in a crucially important and topical debate.

▲ Ford Madox Brown
1821-1893
WORK
1852-1863
This painstakingly executed picture (it took the artist over 10 years to complete) shows us not just Hampstead in 1852 but a moral vision of what British society was at the time and what it could become. In a crowded Heath Street, workmen take centre stage, toiling in heroic poses. This is manual labour in its rough dignity, with the workers' raggedly dressed children prominent in the incongruous foreground. Behind and to the side are those who benefit from the exertions of the poor, and who do not need to
work with their hands (or perhaps at all).
Ford Madox Brown leaves us in no doubt that this wider prosperity is built, almost literally, on the labour of others, and the two figures at the right urge us to a course of social and political action. Thomas Carlyle, whose 'Past and Present' (1843) sang the praises of the working man, looks out at us, beside F D Maurice, founder of the Working Men's College. Optimism with a hard edge.

Oil on canvas, 137 x 197.3 cm
MANCHESTER CITY ART
GALLERY

▶ François Boucher
1703-1770
**DAPHNIS AND CHLOË
(SHEPHERD WATCHING A
SLEEPING SHEPHERDESS)**
1743 OR 1745
From the days of classical Greece and Rome, European literature and music have conjured the fantasy of the lucky shepherds, young men who lived in a world with neither illness nor old age, where work was gentle and there was a great deal of time left for pleasure – especially with pliant shepherdesses. Boucher is perhaps the greatest painter of this enduring idyll, his young couples forever flirting in the sunlight. Do we need to disapprove?

Oil on canvas 109.5 x 154.8 cm
WALLACE COLLECTION, LONDON

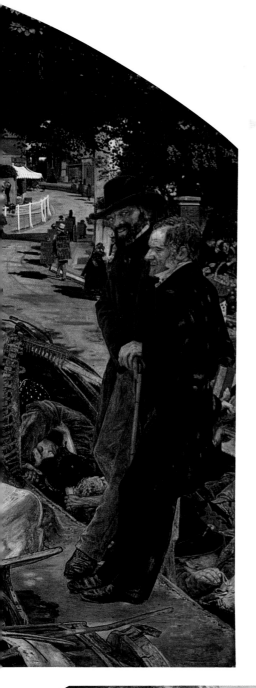

Gustave Courbet
1819-1877
YOUNG LADIES OF THE VILLAGE
1851

In eastern France, as in Hampstead, rich and poor cross in daily life, but to strikingly different effect. Three young ladies (in fact the artist's sisters), dressed rather too stylishly for outdoor activity and accompanied by a very urban dog, pause on a walk in the countryside around Ornans to give alms to a peasant-girl tending her cows. But Courbet is clearly more interested in a landscape in the sunshine than in this strangely desultory act of charity. The figures look inconsequential in the spacious valley and the cattle hover awkwardly, but grass and rock, water and sky glisten in the luminous, humid atmosphere.

Oil on canvas, 54 x 65.4 cm
LEEDS CITY ART GALLERY

Georges-Pierre Seurat
1859-1891
BATHERS AT ASNIÈRES
1884

This was the first great picture by the 25-year-old Seurat. The life-size figures bathing in the Seine presumably work in the factories we see in the background, on the industrial outskirts of Paris. Their clothes make it clear that these are prosperous working-class men, relaxing on their weekly day off. But these are clearly individual outings, with no hint of the community of pleasure of Frith's Derby Day (see next pages). This is the poor bank of the river: a small boat is ferrying a man in a top hat and a lady to the smarter side – the Grande

Jatte, which was to be the subject of Seurat's next large-scale picture. The different classes seek their pleasures separately. And even on this side, Seurat isolates each figure in space, imposing a pattern of ordered, silent calm. He focusses attention on how he has made the picture. The brush strokes are separate touches of colour – a technique he pioneered, known as 'pointillisme' – which, when orange sits next to blue for instance, can give effects of startling brilliance.

Oil on canvas, 201 x 300 cm
NATIONAL GALLERY, LONDON

▲ Augustus Egg
1816-1863
THE TRAVELLING COMPANIONS
1862

The railways opened new horizons of pleasure for the rich – on the horizon here you can see Menton on the French Riviera, to which the artist himself had travelled for his asthma. Two symmetrical sisters give a shimmering display of immaculate, well-bred and well-heeled elegance, with just enough difference between them to engage the eye and stimulate speculation. Is there a story? Or is the artist simply beguiled by the possibilities of a very pleasing pattern?

Oil on canvas, 64.5 x 76.5 cm
BIRMINGHAM MUSEUM AND ART GALLERY

▲ William Powell Frith
1819-1909
THE DERBY DAY
1856-1858

No painting better sums up the British belief (myth?) that whatever distinctions of class or income may exist, ultimately we can all of us – the rogues and the virtuous – get along together. And no sport more transcends social barriers than racing. In Derby Day Frith selected from the huge crowds that flocked to Epsom Downs representatives of different moral and social worlds, had a photographer record them and then, in his studio, worked up this enormously popular (and profitable) celebration of a national day at the races. The crowd

becomes more diverse the more you look, embracing the deserving and the undeserving poor; the demonstrably prosperous, the swindler and the kept woman. The picture is at once an inventory of different types of humanity and a Dickensian panorama of contemporary England.

Oil on canvas, 101.6 x 223.5 cm
TATE BRITAIN, LONDON

Jan Steen
1626-1679
A SCHOOL FOR BOYS AND GIRLS
ABOUT 1670

Even in seventeenth-century Holland, classroom discipline could be problematic and in a light-hearted bit of moralising, Steen shows the consequences of lazy, incompetent teachers and high-spirited children: chaos now, and a lack of self-control that can only lead to indigence. All is muddle – beautifully painted details of confusion, excess, indiscipline and sloth, the artist's precision reproaching his subjects' negligence.

Oil on canvas, 81.7 x 108.6 cm
NATIONAL GALLERY OF SCOTLAND, EDINBURGH

THE WORKER

W e know work can be hard – but does that make the worker an object of pity or of respect? The pictures on these pages present equivocal answers. All show workers performing menial tasks on a heroic scale – an approach that was quite revolutionary in the sixteenth century when Annibale Carracci painted his butcher's shop. But in all of them work is surely also a metaphor for our brief, hard and imperfect lives. In taking this perspective the artists have been influenced by the Genesis myth. After all, if Adam and Eve had not eaten the forbidden fruit they could have spent a carefree eternity in paradise. As it was, their eviction into our world carried the curse that they had to work for their 'daily bread'. These artists have picked up on the power of the biblical story to give resonance to our everyday lives. Daumier shows us a modern-day Eve or Hagar, cast out from society, with little hope of rest. For Carracci, some 400 years ago, the work of the butcher appears solid, honest and reliable, but evokes, nevertheless, the inevitability of death and the weakness of the flesh. For Bellany, with typical twentieth-century angst, the simplest of activities hides threatening intent. Meanwhile, in the setting of the Surrey hills, Brett shows a boy turning his back on the paradisical landscape as he prepares – quite literally – for the hard road ahead.

◀ John Bellany
BORN 1942
BETHEL
1967
Bethel – apparently the name of the boat on which this trio of fishermen work – means 'House of God' in Hebrew, and thus can imply any place where God is encountered. Christ told Peter, a simple fisherman, that he would make him a 'fisher of men' – and yet there is no sense of welcome here, no sense of the love of God. The grim, threatening stares of the men and their unforgiving stance appear condemnatory, while their stained clothing and sharp knives make their job look more like 'butchery'. In 1967, the year this work was painted, Bellany visited Buchenwald, the concentration camp, an all-too-clear reminder of man's ungodliness and another grim slaughter.

Oil on board, 248 x 320 cm
SOUTHAMPTON CITY ART GALLERY

John Brett
1831-1902
THE STONEBREAKER
1857-1858

The artist inscribed a sketch for this painting with the words 'The wilderness of this world' and 'outside Eden', making explicit the connection between work and original sin. It is probably not a coincidence that the setting, looking south towards Box Hill in Surrey, is on a route leading to the old Pilgrim's Way from London to Canterbury. With the attention to detail typical of the English Pre-Raphaelites, Brett depicts, in the foreground, brambles, thistles and gorse, all of which, like the stones the boy is breaking, are a contrast to the soft, grassy and flower-strewn meadows Adam and Eve would have trodden barefoot in Eden, represented perhaps by the beauty of the landscape in the background. The boy, however, absorbed in his menial task, appears oblivious of the 'heavenly' view behind him.

Oil on canvas, 51.3 x 68.5 cm
WALKER ART GALLERY,
LIVERPOOL

Honoré-Victorin Daumier
1808-1879
THE HEAVY BURDEN
1855-1856

In this monochrome version of a subject that Daumier painted at least seven times, a faceless woman carries an undefined bundle – and as she leans under the strain, the perspective of the buildings in the background makes this look like an uphill struggle despite the fact that the pavement is perfectly flat. The woman and her child are very much alone. The buildings form a forbidding barrier, closed to her except for the windows – almost like prying eyes – and she is cut off still more by the wall that runs along the path. Like Eve evicted from Eden, she moves away from the light – streaming from the top left of the painting – and casts her child in deep shadow as if they both face a sombre future of constant toil.

Oil on canvas, 39.3 x 31.3 cm
BURRELL COLLECTION, GLASGOW

Annibale Carracci
1506-1609
THE BUTCHER'S SHOP
1580s

The Carracci family, working in Bologna in the second half of the sixteenth century, took the direct observation of reality as their starting point, but this is reality heavy with meaning. Annibale's inspiration is a butcher's shop, and in his striking and original depiction of the life-size carcasses there is a suggestion that the difference between the living and the dead is not so great: the right-hand figure is stretched out like the carcass he is holding, while in the centre a man leans over the similarly slumped sheep. If we read this as a sacrificial 'lamb', the set of scales becomes an intimation of the Last Judgment, when all flesh will be weighed and assessed.

Oil on canvas, 190 x 271 cm
CHRISTCHURCH PICTURE
GALLERY, OXFORD

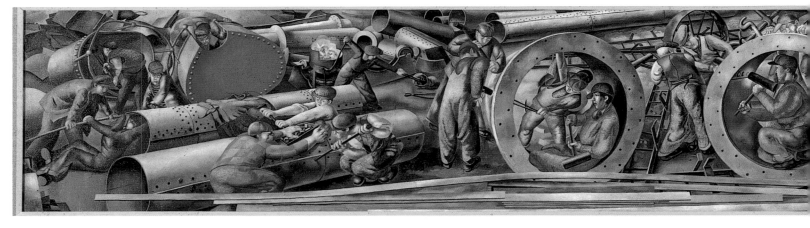

MASS LABOUR

The old adage has it that 'Many hands make light work', but this does not take into account the fact that certain kinds of work will never be easy: the most difficult of tasks will be readily achieved only with a very large number of toiling workers. So it is with the earliest of these paintings, Hawkins's astonishing depiction of the Penrhyn Slate Quarry. Whereas a single man could barely scratch the surface, the massed workers, like so many ants, are gradually eating into the majestic forms of nature. With Lowry we move from a natural to a man-made landscape, and we see how we have changed the appearance of the world, creating vast structures that need human labour to control, service and feed machines that do inhuman work. The scale is reflected by Lowry's tiny stick-like people – while the work inside one of these distant buildings must have been more like that depicted in Spencer's *Riveters*, which shows just one of the activities involved in shipbuilding. Much of this kind of labour no longer exists, giving these paintings an unexpected, and unintended, note of nostalgia.

▲ Stanley Spencer
1891-1959
SHIPBUILDING ON THE CLYDE: RIVETERS
1941
In the 1940s Spencer worked on a series of war paintings celebrating the workers at Lithgow's shipyards in Port Glasgow, which together form a modern, industrial 'altarpiece'. Riveters is one of the long, thin paintings which runs across the bottom, known as a predella. In a brilliant use of the unusual format, Spencer has depicted pipes running along the length of the painting, its elongation emphasised further by the strips of steel lying along the bottom and by the men pulling cables in from the right. In the centre this is counter-pointed by the large ring structures and the extraordinary vertiginous view of a man's legs, wonderfully foreshortened, disappearing into a cylinder.

Oil on canvas, 76.2 x 579.2 cm
IMPERIAL WAR MUSEUM, LONDON

▶ Henry Hawkins
ACTIVE 1822-1881
PENRHYN SLATE QUARRY
1832
Penrhyn was once among the world's largest slate quarries, and by the early nineteenth century tourists were attracted by its grandeur. The tiny scale of the figures working in the quarry reflects the contemporary taste for the 'sublime' (an eighteenth-century term whose modern equivalent is perhaps 'awesome'). It also, of course, reflects very cheap labour. The constant activity celebrates man's determination to master the world's resources. Hawkins shows a boy in the foreground pointing to the sky in the pose of Raphael's St John the Baptist, perhaps to suggest that this ceaseless labour is divinely ordained.

Oil on canvas, 132 x 188 cm
PENRHYN CASTLE GWYNMEDD,
NATIONAL TRUST

◀ Laurence Stephen Lowry
1887-1976
COMING FROM THE MILL
1930
For some the working day is over but as the stooped crowds leave the factory gates, the smoking chimneys and the pall of smoke over the scene suggest that the round of industrial labour is unbroken. The roads are full of people rather than vehicles, and it is this emphasis on the human – his 'matchstick men and matchstick cats and dogs' (the latter curiously absent) that makes Lowry's work so enduringly popular.

Oil on canvas, 42 x 52 cm
THE LOWRY, SALFORD

BRAIN WORK

The visual artist has no difficulty in depicting manual labour, the world of the human figure in action. More problematic is illustrating the workings of the mind. It is, of course, an easy matter to show a figure engrossed in a book, as the two fifteenth-century artists do here, but how do you suggest the depth or exceptional nature of what is being thought?

Foppa, in his beguiling painting of the young Cicero, does so through choosing to paint him as a child, oblivious, we might imagine, of the playful shouts drifting in at the open window. Antonello, in his painting of St Jerome, places the translator of the Bible within an ecclesiastical building, perhaps to suggest how fundamental his work is to the church itself. We look at the saint through a window through which light pours on to him, and artists often use light in this way to suggest intellectual and spiritual enlightenment.

Countless portraits of 'thinkers' show them with brightly-lit foreheads: Wright, in his great painting (still in his native Derby) of the orrery, uses light to suggest both understanding and wonder. Rego in *The Artist in her Studio* seems to give thoughts concrete form as the painter sits – in a pipe smoker's pose of contemplation – surrounded by her mental world.

◀ Antonello da Messina
ACTIVE 1456–DIED 1479
ST JEROME IN HIS STUDY
C.1475
St Jerome was responsible for translating the Bible into Latin, thus bringing it within reach of the monks and clergy, and so, indirectly, to the Church as a whole. He sits in quiet contemplation in his study, a curious, partitioned wooden structure within a vast stone hall, his shoes left at the bottom of the steps as if he has entered holy ground. The complexity of the depicted space perhaps echoes the complexity of Jerome's thought, while the light streaming into the painting from all sides – depicted thanks to Antonello's perfect understanding of the northern European technique of oil painting – is perhaps symbolic of the light Jerome is hoping to bring into the world.

Oil on wood, 45.7 x 36.2 cm
NATIONAL GALLERY, LONDON

◀ Joseph Wright of Derby
1734–1797
A PHILOSOPHER GIVING THAT LECTURE ON THE ORRERY IN WHICH A LAMP IS PUT IN PLACE OF THE SUN
1766
Wright's painting of The Orrery – a working model of the solar system – is a glorious study of the variety of human responses, from the fascination of the adults to the sheer delight illuminating the faces of the children. There is a single, hidden light source, a candle or lamp placed in the position of the sun, which acts as a fitting symbol of the enlightenment these people are experiencing. But while it is often assumed that Wright's paintings illustrate the popularisation of science displacing faith in God, at least one of the peripatetic scientists who performed such demonstrations, James Ferguson, did so precisely to show how perfectly God created the universe for us.

Oil on canvas, 147.3 x 203.2 cm
DERBY ART GALLERY

Paula Rego
BORN 1935
THE ARTIST IN HER STUDIO
1993
Paula Rego's artist pauses in contemplation of the many aspects of her life so far, illustrated by a fantastic array of people and things. Her two apprentices – in the bottom right and far left – are only two of seven representations of women in this painting. On a table to the right of the older apprentice is a small, crying doll, and further to the right a large and lolling sculpture like an over-grown baroque putto. A terracotta sculpture of a young and lithe woman reaches into the top left-hand corner while in the shadows on the right a cardboard cut-out swats a praying mantis. The artist, secure and serene, and taking centre stage, is the culmination of these seven ages.

Acrylic on paper on canvas,
180 x 130 cm
LEEDS CITY ART GALLERY

Vincenzo Foppa
ACTIVE 1456–DIED 1479
THE YOUNG CICERO READING
1460s
Frescos, painted on wet plaster, should by rights remain in situ but they can be detached like this one – unfortunately, this is all that remains of an entire cycle. The painting

is of the most charming informality: sitting with his foot up on a bench and a book resting on his knee, the child is absorbed in his reading.
To have grown up to be a great orator, Foppa is telling us, Cicero must have started young. More books lie on the desk, and in recesses above and below.

For Italians of the fifteenth century this would have constituted a library and only the richest – such as Cosimo de' Medici who commissioned this fresco – would have owned more.

Fresco on plaster,
99.1 x 133 cm
WALLACE COLLECTION,
LONDON

DOMESTIC WORK

Whatever the developments of technology, nothing will ever remove completely the need for domestic work. There will always be cooking and cleaning, and somebody has to do it.

It is essential work, something I suspect most of us would rather not do, but artists have always been fascinated by the quiet dignity of the humdrum.

Velázquez treats the act of cooking with the mystery and awe of alchemy as simple ingredients are magically transformed into food. For the Dutch, the Protestant work ethic moralises easily: in Netscher's painting, threads fashioned into lace show us that we must work if we want to make something of our lives. Hogarth, it seems, was lucky enough not to have to do menial work, but depicts six of his servants with a calm, respectful delicacy. Today, fortunately, we are helped by vacuum cleaners, washing machines and endless gadgetry, although Richard Hamilton appears to suggest that this move away from human to machine is one of the things that has helped to break up the fabric of our society.

◀ Caspar Netscher
1635/6-1684
THE LACE MAKER
1664
The Dutch traditionally associated lace-making with the idea of domestic virtue, further emphasised here by the broom leaning against the wall and the swept room – after all, 'Cleanliness is next to Godliness'. However, the carelessly discarded shoes and the mussel shells on the floor – which, like oysters, were accorded aphrodisiac properties – hint at sexual immorality. For this young girl, whose stark room is enlivened only by a print of The Flight into Egypt pinned to the wall, there are two possible paths to follow, perhaps even two ways in which she could make her living. Her studied application to honest, exhausting work suggests she has chosen morality.

Oil on canvas, 34.3 x 28.3 cm
WALLACE COLLECTION,
LONDON

◀ Diego Velázquez
1599-1660
OLD WOMAN COOKING EGGS
1618
This depiction of the nobility of a humble life is also the vehicle for a virtuoso display of painterly bravura. The 19-year-old Velázquez shows how well he can depict every possible surface, from the sparkle and transparency of a bottle to the roughness and solidity of a melon, and, in the fascinating procession along the front of the painting, from ceramic to metal via an onion and some garlic. The characters barely acknowledge one another: as the boy appears, presumably with more supplies for the kitchen, the old woman carries on her work. She holds an unbroken egg in one hand, while the other stirs a collection of increasingly opaque whites, and we witness the magic of cooking.

Oil on canvas, 99 x 117 cm
NATIONAL GALLERY OF
SCOTLAND, EDINBURGH

William Hogarth
1697-1764
HEADS OF SIX OF HOGARTH'S SERVANTS
1750-1755

In his satirical works Hogarth did not pull his punches. Master of the sly dig as much as the direct insult, he delighted in all that was ridiculous and futile in contemporary society. And yet here we have a hymn to the everyday, a poem of such directness, honesty and, above all, respect that we can be sure he was genuinely fond of his staff – it is a great pity we do not know their names. Symmetrically arranged in two arcs, the servants are turned out in their best to sit for the master, and are depicted with a tenderness and delicacy that makes this one of Hogarth's most touching works.

Oil on canvas, 63 x 75.5 cm
TATE BRITAIN, LONDON

Édouard Vuillard
1868-1940
THE MANICURE
1896-1897

Two people sit opposite each other, their heads bowed, almost immaterial amid the welter of brush strokes which concentrate more on the patterns of the furnishings than on the delineation of the people themselves. If we have intruded, the dark form in the foreground prevents our access, keeping us away from the more brightly lit figure on the other side of the table. Without the title it could be hard to work out what is happening in this atmospheric painting – Vuillard is as unconcerned with what these people are doing as he is with their identity. For him what is paramount is their total absorption and the intimacy of the activity within the homely setting.

Oil on card on wood,
33.5 x 30 cm
SOUTHAMPTON CITY ART GALLERY

Richard Hamilton
BORN 1922
INTERIOR STUDY (A)
1964

Hamilton's art has always attempted to reflect contemporary life, and celebrates and uses new developments, both as subject matter and technique. The individual elements of this work seem to show the attention to detail of a proud housewife: the room is clean and tidy, well-furnished and decorated with a number of floral arrangements. But there is no sense of calm and ease. The television, clearly a separate, collaged element, disruptively breaks into the room, blurring the boundary between private and public realms, between suburban reality and the glossy fantasies of advertisement.

Oil and collage on paper,
38.1 x 50.8 cm
SWINDON MUSEUM AND ART GALLERY

PLAY: MUSIC AND DANCE

Painting is essentially silent and still, but this has never stopped artists from trying to represent movement and noise. Indeed, it is a compelling challenge: to delight the eye by evoking the other senses and to show through visual imagery the precise timbre of the music or speed of the dance.

These paintings show completely different moods, from loud display to quiet introspection, from the brash and raucous to a calm and measured elegance. Seurat's painting is the wildest, the exuberance and energy of the dancers merely heightened by the measured application of individual dabs of paint, and the approving screams of an unseen audience adding to the music of the band.

A gentler noise for Vermeer, whose Guitar Player entertains herself. In this private setting, calm and still, the strumming of romantic tunes – bright and happy like the yellow of her coat – may herald the arrival of a lover. Similarly quiet – the only music the percussive tapping of a tabor – but with complete innocence, the children of the Gower family join in a measured round – neo-classical restraint holding off, if only for a while, the natural ebullience of youth.

▶ George Romney
1734-1802
THE GOWER FAMILY
1777
The challenge in making a group portrait is to create a realistic setting and activity for all the sitters while still being able to see them clearly – here Romney has succeeded through the use of dance in a composition often regarded as his most ambitious. To do this with children is no mean feat and, on top of this, he has captured not only their appearances but also a sense of their individual characters. The eldest and most serene beats time while among the elegant gestures and lightly flowing drapery of the four dancers there is the possibility that the most impetuous, on the far right, might just tear out of control.

Oil on canvas, 203 x 232 cm
ABBOT HALL ART GALLERY,
KENDAL

▲ Jan Vermeer
1632-1675
THE GUITAR PLAYER
c.1672
Vermeer is renowned for the sense of calm and solemn mystery with which he imbued his paintings, but here he is almost light-hearted. Typical, however, is his minute observation and delicate handling of the paint, and an interest in the way the atmosphere and space of a room is defined by the quality of light which pervades it. He focuses not on the surfaces themselves, but on the light which reflects off them. The girl's head – subtly picked out by the light and framed by the landscape painting behind her – is turned expectantly to the left. Someone has arrived:, perhaps we are about to witness an assignation.

Oil on canvas, 53 x 46.3 cm
KENWOOD HOUSE, THE IVEAGH
BEQUEST, LONDON

Georges Seurat
1859-1891
THE CHAHUT
c.1889
Seurat developed 'pointillism' – using dots of individually

coloured paint – in the hope that the pure colours would mix in the eye and make his paintings livelier and fresh. In this work he also wanted the lines to have a happy and

invigorating effect – the legs of the cancan dancers and the top of the double bass all rise up at exactly the same angle, in the same way that clocks are set at ten to two to make

them look more 'happy'. This is just a study – in the finished painting the dots are smaller, subtler and more delicate – but the freer and more energetic marks only

add to the depiction of a sparkling night's entertainment.

Oil on wood, 21.8 x 15.8 cm
COURTAULD INSTITUTE
GALLERIES, LONDON

CHILDREN'S PLAY

The games we play as children shape us for our roles and responsibilities in later life and the associations connected with children's games have long allowed artists to exploit apparent scenes of childhood innocence for deeper ends. The paintings on this page, through the antics of the young, make us see ourselves more clearly.

It would be a mistake to claim, as is sometimes done, that children are invisible in art from before the 1600s – there are countless images, after all, of playful Christ-childs before then – but certainly children in seventeenth-century Dutch paintings make themselves more

evident than ever before. Schalken's kite-flyers may be teaching us a lesson about the advantages of restraint and discipline but they are scarcely models of restraint themselves. Goya's children are similarly wild as they fight and play at soldiers, mimicking and parodying the struggles of their elders. It took the French still-life painter Chardin – one of the greatest painters of children – to catch a subtler truth in children's play; it is not all wild cavorting but, as often, quiet, absorbed and self-sufficient. In contrast, Symons, from a 1930s viewpoint, shows us the all-too-familiar face of post-Christmas excess and childish ennui.

▲ Jean-Siméon Chardin
1699-1779
THE HOUSE OF CARDS
c.1736-1737
There is nothing quite so beguiling as concentration on the face of a child, something which Chardin captures here with incomparable delicacy. The subject was the son of Chardin's friend, the cabinet-maker Le Noir, who perhaps made the gaming table on which the boy leans. His activity might seem little more than an innocent pastime, but a coin and ticket on the table remind us of the dangers of gambling. Engravings of this painting were published

with verses pointing out how our own endeavours could be as fragile as the boy's, again giving the painting a moralising context, and turning it from a private study into a public admonition, if a very gentle one.

Oil on canvas, 60.3 x 71.8 cm
NATIONAL GALLERY, LONDON

Mark Symons
1886-1935
THE DAY AFTER CHRISTMAS
1931

There is a slightly worrying tension in Symons's painting. A large family is crowded into a small room rendered festive with paper chains, Chinese lanterns and more, an altogether claustrophobic array of decorations. The children – eldest at the left, youngest, a baby, at bottom right – are increasingly supine with decreasing age. While the most mature are still engaged with the presents from the day before, the younger two seem to be ready to give up their struggle with excitement. One has collapsed, but the other ominously holds both a doll and a large stick. Children and toys are strewn across the floor with the alarming possibility of confusion as to which is which.

Oil on canvas, 91 x 68 cm
BURY ART GALLERY AND
MUSEUM

Francisco de Goya
1746-1828
BOYS PLAYING AT SEESAW AND BOYS PLAYING AT SOLDIERS
1777-1785

The title of one of these paintings is somewhat of an understatement – while there are boys 'playing at seesaw' there are also two couples locked in unrestrained combat as another pair stand by as if debating the odds. Goya, unlike his compatriot, Murillo, was not interested in the charming aspects of children: even the seesaw is essentially unfair, as the two on the left seem determined to keep their single playmate off the ground for good. Meanwhile, in the other painting, the boys 'play at soldiers', perhaps practising for international rather than interpersonal struggles. In both works Goya underlines how our childhood games contain the tensions of our future lives.

Oil on canvas, 29.8 x 41.9 cm
and 29.2 x 41.9 cm
POLLOK HOUSE, GLASGOW

Godfried Schalken (attrib)
1643-1706
BOYS FLYING KITES
c.1660

It is almost always possible to attribute an allegorical meaning to a painting. Here, for example, the kites blowing in the wind have been used as symbols of the benefits of restraint – a kite can soar in the air only if it is held firmly by someone on the ground. Or the painting could be seen as a representation of 'air': as such it would be one of a series of 'The Four Elements' – there is a painting in the Louvre, by Schalken, showing boys swimming from a boat, which could stand for 'water'. However, this should not blind us to the possibility that this painting, worked with the kind of freedom and energy that the boys themselves display, could simply be an illustration of fun, a celebration of the joys of childhood.

Oil on wood, 44.5 x 34.5 cm
UPTON HOUSE, WARWICKSHIRE,
NATIONAL TRUST

LEISURE

We take leisure for granted, but the idea of leisure for the masses was essentially a nineteenth-century invention. You would be hard-pressed to find two more different pictures than those by Burra and Forain on these pages but they both show the 'modern' city-dweller at play. Forain's top-hatted and waistcoated bourgeois sits suspended in a magical calm. But his is a suburban idyll, a moment captured at the end of the working day. In Burra's garish Boston bar, the chaos and noise of city-life is where the pleasure is sought, and the artist wrote enthusiastically about the 'human debris interspersed with dwarfs, gangsters, marines and hostesses' that he found there. The thrill or threat of the modern city has always been connected to these possibilities and mass transport made such encounters possible away from the city as well. Queen Victoria complained that the train had brought Brighton within the grasp of 'too many of the wrong kind of people'. The seaside holiday was another nineteenth-century innovation. In Spencer's wonderful painting of Southwold we have a recognisably British version of the seaside in which the the air is just that bit too cold and the sea that bit too grey.

Urban entertainment has always included the theatre. The poorest, found in the pit in Shakespeare's time, were restricted to the highest and most distant seats from the Restoration onwards. In his wonderful series of music-hall audiences, Sickert shows these crowds 'in the gods', their faces lit up by the unseen spectacle below them.

▶ Stanley Spencer
1891-1959
SOUTHWOLD
1937
Spencer's direct approach to the everyday, a view chosen to look spontaneous rather than a studied composition, provides a relaxed sense of informality. The patterns of the towels, the deck chairs and the textures of the pebbles and waves carefully emphasise the abstract qualities of the scene, but this is part of a human narrative. Only a few people now remain on the beach. Absent characters are implied by the chairs, some lined up as if an invisible audience watches the sea.

Oil on canvas, 57.9 x 89.9 cm
ABERDEEN ART GALLERY

▲ Edward Burra
1905-1976
SILVER DOLLAR BAR
1955
Burra's extraordinary graphic style was achieved by painting in watercolour over an initial drawing, and gives an almost cartoon-like feel to the bar he had first visited in 1937. The muscular barman turns to greet us with an almost threatening gaze – the effect gives us the sense of intruding into this louche world. The other side of the bar is depicted parallel to the picture plane, almost like a cinema screen.

Watercolour and bodycolour on paper, 104.8 x 73.3 cm
YORK CITY ART GALLERY

Jean-Louis Forain
1852-1931
THE FISHERMAN
1884

Forain achieves a wonderful sense of freedom in this painting, the delicate depiction of the reflected sky making it look as if the fisherman is suspended in mid-air rather than poised above the quiet river. It is a beautifully balanced painting, with the man, his belongings and patient dog in the middle, their silhouettes poetically echoed by the trees on the horizon. The luminous sky and sparse composition reinforce the lyrical tranquillity.

Oil on canvas, 94.7 x 100.1 cm
SOUTHAMPTON CITY ART GALLERY

Walter Richard Sickert
1860-1942
NOCTES AMBROSIANAE
1906

Sickert evokes the magic of theatre not by looking at the stage but by showing us the enchantment of the audience, in this case the working classes who have poured into the balcony, standing, leaning and craning their necks in order to get the best view of the night's entertainment. He evokes the sense of wonder in their faces as they loom out of the darkness, caught in the glare from the distant footlights, extra glitter added by the gilt decoration of the theatre's interior, which reflects the light more brightly. Ambrosia was the food of the gods and to this audience, up in 'the gods', the drama is intoxicating – hence the work's title.

Oil on canvas, 63.5 x 76.2 cm
NOTTINGHAM CASTLE MUSEUM

SPORT AND GAMES

Sport, like art, has existed since the earliest civilisations: the continuation of the play of children, a highly charged, ritually controlled expression of the rivalry between individuals and groups. As a subject for paintings, sport gives artists scope to use their skills to show the skills of others, and to play with us as the participants play with each other. Uccello shows us The Hunt, a darting, energetic painting with red figures bobbing through the green landscape and animals playing tag within a magical forest of ordered trees. He plays with colour and with perspective, challenging the rules and our expectations. De La Tour's soldiers think they know the rules of the game, but are unaware that they themselves are being played with, as a shifty onlooker prepares to steal their money, and Roberts plays games with shapes and lines to emphasise the energy, muscularity and potential speed of his cyclists.

But sport has not always been open to us all – through most of history women were generally excluded and during the nineteenth century were allowed to take part in only genteel pursuits reliant on concentration and precision rather than physical exertion. Of these, archery received the royal seal of approval and, as with so much else, where Queen Victoria went the nation followed. This is what Frith depicts, although not without a hint of male condescension.

▲ Georges De La Tour
1593-1652
THE DICE PLAYERS
c.1650
Caravaggio, the Italian master, had earlier made popular the depiction of low-life scenes, using strongly contrasting light to simplify and dramatise forms. Now De La Tour combines subject and form in a nocturnal game of dice. The light focuses attention on the absorbed expressions of the gamesters and on the apparent indifference of the onlooker on the left. But this indifference masks the fact that with his right hand he is about to pick the pocket of the soldier on the left.

Oil on canvas, 92.5 x 130.5 cm
PRESTON HALL MUSEUM,
STOCKTON ON TEES

▷ William Powell Frith
1819-1909
THE FAIR TOXOPHILITES
1872
Relatively few sports were open to women during the nineteenth century, but Queen Victoria herself was a keen archer or 'toxophilite'. Frith claimed that the subject matter was simply an excuse to depict contemporary female fashion. He positions his own daughters to show off their clothing. In the foreground is Alice, her back turned towards us, whereas on the right Louisa's stance allows us to see how the front is fashioned – the large tassel was used to clean the arrows. We see little of Fanny, although it is clear that she is dressed in an equally elaborate outfit.

Oil on canvas, 98.2 x 81.7 cm
ROYAL ALBERT MEMORIAL
MUSEUM, EXETER

Paolo Uccello
1397-1475
THE HUNT
C.1465-1470
*Dogs and deer seem to chase each
other along a lattice of
overlapping diagonals in the
centre of the painting, while the
huntsmen appear from left and
right. All is held together by
perspective, with the carefully
placed logs in the foreground and
the river on the right leading our
eye to a central vanishing point.
Uccello, however, was aware of
the deficiencies of one-point
perspective, particularly with a
wide panel like this (presumably
designed to decorate a chest), and
was happy to play games, both
visual and intellectual. He
created a variety of subsidiary
vanishing points so that the
systematically arranged trees
appear to recede into the distance
in whichever direction we look.*

Tempera on panel, 73.5 x 117 cm
ASHMOLEAN MUSEUM, OXFORD

William Roberts
1895-1980
LES ROUTIERS
C.1930-1932
*The broad and simplified forms of
these cyclists give them a strength
and monumentality that tells us
that here we have a winning
team, and the twists and turns
show that they are poised and
ready for action. Roberts simplifies
not only the human anatomy: it is
easy to miss the fact that the
bicycles do not have such
functional necessities as spokes,
chains or even pedals – their
omission adds to the sense of
streamlining and speed. The
potential for movement implied by
the use of the diagonal – the road
runs from top right to bottom left
– is wittily picked out by Roberts,
who signs his name parallel to the
kerb in the bottom right corner.*

Oil on canvas, 101.7 x 76.3 cm
ULSTER MUSEUM, BELFAST

PART 3

GODS AND HUMANITY

'The question at the centre of European
thought has been how the human form
relates to a divine creator and how
near or how far mankind is from being
itself divine'

ANDY WARHOL
MARILYN DIPTYCH (DETAIL)
1962

Blake's terrifying image of
God creating Adam is a
highly personal resolution of
centuries of argument and
picture-making across the
whole of Europe.

At the centre of the tradition of
European painting is the human body. Its
beauty and complexity have offered
limitless opportunities for artists of every
age. And for most of the period covered
in this book, the question at the centre of
European thought has been how that
human form relates to a divine creator –
and how near or how far mankind is from
being itself divine. It is a question that has
produced some of the greatest and most
disturbing works of Western art.

Inevitably, most of that art is Christian:
the only non-Christians in Renaissance
Europe were the Jews, who believed that
the second commandment forbade all
religious imagery. Yet because
Christianity saw itself as a universal faith,
the lives of Jesus and of the Old
Testament patriarchs were viewed as
reflecting every life, their different
episodes illuminating the experience of
every human being. The pictures,
accordingly, illustrate a particular faith,
but they explore a general truth. And in
almost every example in this section, the
episode from scripture is set not in the
ancient near-East but in a contemporary
landscape familiar to the spectator.
These mysteries happen in our world,
because they are about us.

Painters are not usually theologians.
On the whole they offer us not a
coherent system of belief but a series of
brilliant spot-lit insights into human
hope and fear. The exception is William
Blake. Almost alone among European
artists, Blake evolved a totally personal
reading of the Hebrew and Christian
scriptures and spent his life devising an
imagery that would convey that vision.
What we see on these pages is his view
of the creation of man. No hint in this
of the magnanimity of the Genesis story,
nor of the noble serenity of
Michelangelo's God calling Adam into
the fulness of life. For Blake the believer,
the creation was an act of punishment,
as man was banished from the realm of
the spirit, confined to the world of
matter, and made subject to the laws of
the material world: this cruel god of the

William Blake
1757–1827
ELOHIM CREATING ADAM
1795

This must be the bleakest of all visions of the creation of mankind. The huge wings of Elohim (Blake's name for the God of the Old Testament) combined with his rippling drapery and hair blowing free, emphasise his central attribute: his unfettered ability to move. Yet this God uses his power specifically to deny movement to his creation, pinning Adam to the curve of the earth, forcing his hand and his head down, preventing his spirit from soaring free. Blake shows us the act of creation as an act of oppression, flanked by ancient symbols of evil: the serpent of materialism entwines the newly created man in his coils, and a ghostly bat-wing parody of a rainbow shines against the dark sky. But there is hope. There will one day be a second, better creation. Adam's body, with its outstretched arms, is shown as though ready for crucifixion. Adam will be replaced by Jesus, and for Blake that means another view of God, this time not as oppressor but as pure love, and so another, blessed, vision of the relationship between God and man.

To achieve his rich visual effects, Blake evolved an original and highly elaborate system of colour printing, which required extensive reworking by hand – a new complex medium for an equally new and complex theology.

Colour print finished in pen and watercolour on paper, 43.1 x 53.6 cm
TATE BRITAIN, LONDON

GODS AND HUMANITY

Old Testament represents all the forces of repression – legal, moral and political – that constrain us every day. For Blake the ardent revolutionary, this image is as much a work of politics as of religion. And liberation – redemption – will come not so much through a change in us as through a change in God, by the birth of Christ and a new law of freedom and love. He sums up his unorthodox view of the relation between the Old and the New Testaments in characteristically quirky prose: '…thinking as I do that the Creator of this World is a very Cruel Being, and being a Worshipper of Christ, I cannot help saying: "The Son, O how unlike the Father! First God Almighty comes with a Thump on the Head, and then Jesus Christ comes with balm to heal it".'

It has of course always been central Christian orthodoxy to see Christ as making all things whole, righting even the greatest of earthly evils: death. Giovanni Bellini *(facing page)* tackles that subject – one every bit as momentous as Blake's – and imagines the ultimate confrontation, showing us one small figure taking on the dark.

Blake's political view of his religious imagery may seem startling to us today, but we find an unsettling echo of it in Ken Howard's Ulster Crucifixion *(next page)*, which uses the forms of traditional church art to make us reflect on the apparently no less traditional divisions of the faithful in Northern Ireland. Whether it carries the hope implicit in the work of Blake and Bellini I find it hard to say.

Most religious painting is not, however, about society but the individual. The Old Testament patriarch, Jacob, becomes for many artists *(next page)* the symbol of every believer who dreams of a closer relationship with God and struggles long to achieve it. Piero della Francesca's Baptism *(page 75)* shows us a man newly made aware of his nature and his destiny, and ready to accept the consequences of both. These are moments that we nearly all experience at some stage of our lives.

With the coming of Christianity the gods of Greece and Rome had died as objects of belief, but they lived on as a way of thinking about life, and perhaps

Edward Burne-Jones
1833-1898
THE WHEEL OF FORTUNE
ABOUT 1882

As the huge figure of Fortune slowly turns the wheel, the destinies of the three men – poet at the bottom, king and slave above – are irrevocably determined and transformed. The heroic musculature of the slave and the king makes it clear that these men, and the two roles they fill, are in all essentials the same. They are differentiated only by fate and, indeed, the figure with crown and sceptre looks considerably more anguished than the slave. The picture, with its subdued colouring, is a homage to Michelangelo, all four figures deriving from either the paintings of the Sistine Ceiling (which Burne-Jones had studied through opera glasses, lying on the floor, in 1871), or the marble sculptures of the Captives, which he sketched carefully in Florence in the same year. Burne-Jones painted at least five versions of this composition, an indication of how powerfully it spoke to the public. One of them was bought by the young A. J. Balfour, the future Conservative Prime Minister: there could hardly be a more apt subject for contemplation by a politician of any party.

Oil on canvas, 152 x 73.7 cm
NATIONAL MUSEUM OF WALES,
CARDIFF

Giovanni Bellini
ABOUT 1431-1516
DESCENT INTO LIMBO
ABOUT 1475-80

The scene Bellini has illustrated is not found in the gospels, but in four words of the Creed: 'He descended into hell'. Christ, a huddled figure wearing the shroud in which he was buried, but carrying the banner of his forthcoming resurrection, prepares to enter the mouth of hell, the gates of which he tramples underfoot. The light goes willingly into the dark and, so the faithful believe, vanquishes death for ever. The Cross is pitched triumphantly on the desolate rock. In the sky, furious devils howl with rage. Three figures – Adam and Eve and one other – emerge from the cavern, representatives of a humanity that now has a chance of redemption, the first beneficiaries of the sacrifice on the Cross.

Tempera or oil over a pen underdrawing on vellum stuck down on wood, 51.8 x 37.3 cm
BRISTOL MUSEUMS AND ART GALLERY

Nicolas Poussin
1594-1665
CEPHALUS AND AURORA
1627-1630

Aurora, goddess of the dawn, had a simple job: to open with her rosy fingers the doors of heaven for the chariot of the sun to pass through. But this took up only a small part of her time. She had a brief affair with Mars, which Venus punished by turning her into a nymphomaniac. Poussin's painting, made in Rome in the late 1620s, shows one of her many adventures with handsome young mortal men: Pegasus, the winged horse, looks coyly away, as Aurora cajoles Cephalus into yielding to her embraces. The young man is torn. He turns away to where a small cupid holds up a portrait of his true love, Procris. The myth has two endings – he breaks off now, or else makes love to Aurora and then goes home to a serious row. Poussin leaves the spectator to decide what happens next.

Oil on canvas, 96.5 x 130.8 cm
NATIONAL GALLERY, LONDON

above all as stories – a sort of heavenly soap opera, where familiar gods and goddesses tangled with mortals and with each other in a series of entertaining (and apparently endless) misdemeanours. One example, Poussin's Cephalus and Aurora *(previous page)*, shows how very intimately the gods of antiquity mingled with humanity and with what complex consequences.

There is of course another, more chilling possibility: that the gods have no interest in us at all and leave us to whatever fate they have determined. This uncomfortable thought finds full expression in Burne-Jones's monochrome, The Wheel of Fortune *(page 72)* in which he shows the sombre goddess, on whose ever-turning wheel our lives are changed, raised and broken.

▶ Ken Howard
BORN 1932
ULSTER CRUCIFIXION
1978
The miseries of Ulster's religious divisions are given a religious form, in the traditional altarpiece shape of a triptych. A stretch of graffiti-stained wall is filled with scrawled messages. Both sides inhabit this wall, as they do the province, and the Republican cry of 'Army Out' shares the space

with the loyalist summons to remember 1690. An altar-piece normally shows the suffering of Christ or a saint: here, in the centre, a child hangs from a cross-bar; presumably playing but disturbingly reminiscent of Christ crucified. On the right is a skeleton. Can redemption be found in this violence and suffering?

Oil on canvas,
centre panel 116.2 x 89.2 cm
ULSTER MUSEUM, BELFAST

◀ Aert de Gelder
1645-1727
JACOB'S DREAM
ABOUT 1700
Jacob is journeying in search of a wife when, overtaken by night, he sleeps, his pillow a pile of stones. Genesis (Chapter 28) tells us this took place between Beersheba and Haran, but there is nothing Middle-Eastern about

the scene: De Gelder, one of Rembrandt's most successful pupils, shows us a very Dutch traveller in a very north-European landscape. It is lit by a heavenly radiance as we share the exhausted traveller's dream of angels descending from heaven on a shimmering ladder. In the light above them God makes his promise to Jacob, the promise for

which every believer yearns: 'I am with thee and will keep thee in all places to which thou goest'.

Oil on canvas, 66.7 x 56.9 cm
DULWICH PICTURE GALLERY,
LONDON

Paul Gauguin
1848-1903
**THE VISION AFTER THE SERMON
(JACOB AND THE ANGEL)**
1888

In a letter to his friend Vincent van Gogh, Gauguin described this picture, painted in Brittany in the summer of 1888: 'To me…the landscape and the struggle exist only in the imagination of these praying people, as a result of the sermon'. Looking over the heads of the Breton women, dressed in their best for church, we see how they imagine the story told in Genesis, Chapter 32. Having sent his wives and household ahead to escape immediate danger, 'Jacob was left alone, and there wrestled a man with him until the breaking of the day'. The man turns out to be an angel, and Jacob eventually forces him to give him a blessing. It is the struggle of every soul to achieve a proper relationship with God. A good subject for prayer. Drawing heavily on the model of Japanese woodcuts, Gauguin sets the struggle on a ground of impossibly intense red, organises the headdresses into sharp abstract patterns, and then cuts the composition in half with a boldly flattened tree trunk. He saw this as a picture about belief, and offered it to the priest for the local church. It was refused.

Oil on canvas, 72.2 x 91 cm
NATIONAL GALLERIES OF
SCOTLAND, EDINBURGH

Piero della Francesca
1410/20-1492
THE BAPTISM OF CHRIST
1450s
In a stream in the central Italian hill country, John baptises Jesus. According to Mark, the Holy Spirit appeared above Jesus's head in the form of a dove, while a voice from heaven announced, 'Thou art my beloved son, in whom I am well pleased'. Piero places the head of Christ exactly in the centre of his composition and angels watch as this human body is proclaimed as divine. All is still: the dove hovers immobile and Christ himself seems to ponder the implication of what has been said. Only one man has missed this moment: the next candidate for baptism, still struggling to get his shirt off – a beautiful detail of human muddle.

Egg tempera on wood, 167 x 116 cm
NATIONAL GALLERY, LONDON

POWER

Divine power, in both paintings and literature, is often made manifest through representations of nature – usually through its most violent phenomena, such as storms, deluges, volcanoes and earthquakes. This should not surprise us. Since the beginning of time, nature has threatened and overwhelmed mankind, its terrifying effects interpreted as evidence of the wrath of God. The power of nature, like that of a God, is beyond our grasp – unpredictable and inexplicable.

The paintings on these pages demonstrate that the extremes, fire and ice, can be equally brutal: Martin's painting shows Sodom and Gomorrah engulfed by infernal fire and storm; Landseer's displays the inhospitable environment of an Arctic ice field. This is a place where divine benevolence is evidently absent. Wild animals, as well as nature, can evoke superhuman power: Landseer's rapacious polar bears, like Watts's unbridled horse, embody an elemental force that is greater than man's capabilities.

Titian, focusing on the power of a Classical goddess, shows it to be just as unforgiving. Diana, goddess of chastity and hunting, metes out her punishment on the hunter Actaeon with strength and determination. Having accidentally seen her bathing naked he is transformed into a stag.

▲ John Martin
1789-1854
THE DESTRUCTION OF SODOM AND GOMORRAH
1852

As raging fires sweep through the cities of Sodom and Gomorrah, Lot and his family escape to the mountains. His wife, ignoring God's instructions not to look back at the city, is turned into a pillar of salt. Such are the fearful consequences of disobeying God. Angered by the Sodomites' behaviour, God destroyed their city with fire. Martin translates this into a cataclysmic and infernal storm, and paints lightning striking with definite intention, as if it were the hand of God.

Oil on canvas, 135 x 213 cm
LAING ART GALLERY,
NEWCASTLE UPON TYNE

▶ George Frederick Watts
1817-1904
THE RIDER ON THE PALE HORSE
c.1882

The rearing horse carries the fourth horseman of the Apocalypse: Death. He sweeps his scythe through humanity, destroying everything in his path. Behind him is Hell, depicted as a gruesome, infernal beast. Taking these bare elements from the Book of Revelation, Watts gives his apocalyptic scene alarming visual impact. With vigorous brushstrokes, he conveys the rider's relentless movement and, with his palette of reds and oranges, the fearful fires of hell. Even the horse, with eyes wide open and nostrils flaring, seems terrified. Death's face is hidden, which makes him more sinister and frightening. The close-up view brings us into a direct confrontation, as if Death's scythe were heading directly towards us.

Oil on canvas, 66.5 x 53.4 cm
WALKER ART GALLERY,
LIVERPOOL

Edwin Landseer
1802-1873
MAN PROPOSES, GOD DISPOSES
1863-1864

*Two polar bears scavenge amid
the remains of a shipwreck. The
only evidence of human presence
is the discarded telescope in the
left-hand corner. Although
Landseer never visited the Arctic,
he succeeds in conjuring up its
fearsome environment – a wild
place where man has little hope of
survival. His theme is the
powerlessness of mankind in the
face of the will of God, a point
emphasised by the title. The artist
was inspired by the true story of
Sir John Franklin's 1845
expedition to discover the North-
West Passage, an arctic route
connecting the Pacific and
Atlantic oceans. Mysteriously, the
two ships, which were carrying
138 men, disappeared without
trace, and only years later were
some remains – a telescope and
human bones – discovered.*

Oil on canvas, 91.4 x 243.8 cm
ROYAL HOLLOWAY COLLEGE,
UNIVERSITY OF LONDON

Titian
ABOUT 1485-1490 -1576
THE DEATH OF ACTAEON
ABOUT 1565-1576

*Diana's dynamic figure
dominates the scene. Poised to
shoot, her bow is a symbol of
her overwhelming power.
Moonlit clouds echo the sweep
of her arm: as goddess of the
moon, she also has the force of
nature behind her. Diana
directs her fury at Actaeon,
transforming him into a stag.
The hunter becomes the
hunted. He is shown during
the process of change, still with
the body of a human, but with
the animal's head. As he falls
backwards, he is attacked and
ravaged by his own dogs.
Titian's painting technique
matches the subject. His broad,
expressive brushstrokes –
typical of his maturity – create
an impression of frenzied
movement and transmutation.
His deliberate lack of
definition demonstrates that,
in painting, suggestion is as
powerful as description.*

Oil on canvas, 178.8 x 197.8 cm
NATIONAL GALLERY, LONDON

GOD AS MAN

Jesus Christ combines the divine and the human: he has the miraculous powers and immortality of a God, and the vulnerability of a man. And if it is Christ's miracles that set him apart, it is his human aspects – from his childhood experiences to the later torture and suffering – that make him one of us, someone with whom we can identify and empathise. No surprise, then, that in paintings these fallible, human traits often take centre stage. It is these that elicit from us the most immediate and heartfelt responses.

Christ's humanity is most evident at the very beginning and very end of his earthly life. Images of his early childhood show him to be like any other baby – small and helpless, in need of love and care. Later, as Christ becomes victim, we again see his vulnerability. In El Greco's painting, he is a defenceless figure amid armed soldiers and torturers. His terrible suffering at the hands of other men – people like us – reminds us of the place we hold in the drama. Christ was born to die, and this for one reason – to absolve us of our sins. In paintings of the dead Christ, his sacrifice is shown as something real, painful, and inescapably human: as we see the anguish of a grieving mother who cradles her son's lifeless body, we are filled with both horror and compassion.

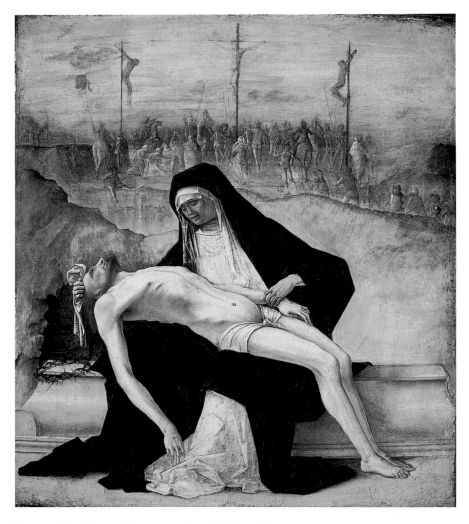

◄ Orazio Gentileschi
1563-1639

THE REST ON THE FLIGHT INTO EGYPT

LATE 1610S

The Holy Family fled to Egypt to escape Herod's massacre of infants. Here, we see them breaking their journey. Joseph, evidently exhausted, literally hits the sack, while Mary takes the opportunity to feed her baby. As Christ suckles at his mother's breast, we are reminded that despite his divine nature, he is as needy and dependent as any child. Gentileschi injects a strong element of realism into his scene (a defining feature of Roman art at this time) and, in doing so, gives the biblical story a striking immediacy. The figures are set against an old, dilapidated wall – so ordinary it seems familiar even to us today. And Joseph is shown with unrelenting honesty. It is difficult to think of a more convincing depiction of sleep: with this head thrown back, we almost feel we can hear him snoring.

Oil on canvas, 176.6 x 219 cm
BIRMINGHAM MUSEUM AND ART GALLERY

Ercole de' Roberti
ACTIVE 1479-1496
PIETÀ
c.1495

Mary grieves over Christ's dead body, which is drained of life. As she tenderly holds his head and wrist, her stooping face and pained expression convey the depth of her anguish. She sits on an altar-like block of stone – not dissimilar from the real altar the painting (as part of a larger altarpiece) originally stood behind. As a devotional image, the work was first and foremost an object of pious contemplation, reminding the congregation at Mass that the bread and wine represent the blood and flesh of Christ. Presented in such real terms, Christ's sacrifice becomes a universally recognised human experience, relevant and understandable to us all.

Egg tempera on panel,
34.4 x 31.3 cm
WALKER ART GALLERY, LIVERPOOL

Simone Martini
c.1284-1344
CHRIST DISCOVERED IN THE TEMPLE
1342

This unusual scene shows Mary, Joseph and Jesus caught up in a family feud. The artist shows the parents' annoyance with their son, who has returned after disappearing for three days during the Passover festival. Mary's question (seen on her open book) is 'Why have you done this to us?'. The 12-year-old Christ, who had been in the temple debating with the Elders, replies that he had needed to spend time in his Father's house. Through Martini's pronounced gestures and facial expressions we sense Mary and Joseph's bewilderment as they grapple with the fact that Christ, as well as being their son, is also the Son of God.

Egg tempera on panel,
49.6 x 35.1 cm
WALKER ART GALLERY, LIVERPOOL

El Greco
1541-1614
THE DISROBING OF CHRIST
ABOUT 1580

Christ is mocked, spat upon, and beaten. He is disrobed and his hands are tied. Engulfed in a sea of hostile faces, he is a lonely figure – vulnerable and defenceless. El Greco broke with convention by showing Christ's head at a lower level than his tormentors. This produces a strong feeling of claustrophobia. As Christ directs his gaze upwards, seeking solace from his Father, this seems his only way out. His evident faith and composure would have been an constant inspiration to the priests of Toledo Cathedral, for whom the original version of this painting was made. Hanging in the Sacristy, where priests dressed in and out of their robes, the subject was also entirely appropriate.

Oil on panel, 55.3 x 31.6 cm
UPTON HOUSE, WARWICKSHIRE,
NATIONAL TRUST

GODS ON EARTH

◀ Anthony van Dyck
1599-1641
CUPID AND PSYCHE
1639-1640

This is evidently no ordinary scene. With one figure winged and both naked, we are in the world of Classical mythology. The episode comes from the tortuous love affair of Cupid, god of love, with the mortal Psyche, a particular favourite of the court of King Charles I, for whom the painting was made. Psyche descended to the underworld to pick up some of Proserpine's beauty potion. Despite instructions not to touch it, she opened the box, releasing a mysterious, sleep-inducing substance. Here, it lies empty beside her. Cupid comes to the rescue of his mortal lover, reaching towards her to rouse her from her deep sleep.

Oil on canvas, 199.4 x 191.8 cm
ROYAL COLLECTION,
KENSINGTON PALACE, LONDON

I n the ancient world, gods were never very far away. There was always the danger that you might stumble on one in the woods, or be ravaged by another. But if Classical literature stresses the shared world of gods and humanity, in art we seldom mistake gods for mere mortals. For a start, each god can be identified by their individual attribute – here, for example, Cupid has his wings and bow – but, more importantly, they are always shown with perfect bodies, idealised according to the standards of Classical sculpture. This is an ideal whose potency still leads us to describe certain lucky, or strenuous, types as being built like Greek gods.

When painting Christ, artists were faced with a rather different challenge: Christ was both all God and all man, entirely divine and wholly mortal. The idea is difficult enough to grasp intellectually, so how on earth could artists suggest it visually? For Sebastiano, painting the raising of Lazarus in sixteenth-century Rome, the answer was to adopt Classical language. His dramatically-gesturing Christ is every inch the idealised Classical god, a perfect heroic body visible beneath clinging robes. Lievens, painting the same scene a century later in the Netherlands, shows Christ as a little man, but miraculously illuminated as he looks up to Heaven. Light again is all that marks out the stooped figure of Christ in Bruegel's haunting painting. In contrast to Sebastiano's giant, Jesus here is the figure placed lowest in the painting, the subject of amazement, ridicule and deep contemplation as he writes in the dust with his finger.

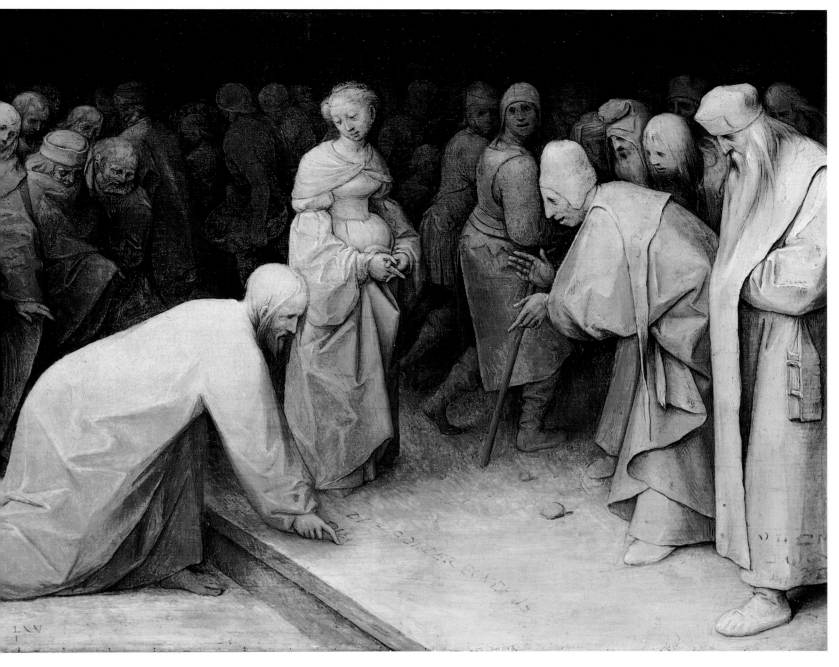

Jan Lievens
1607-1674

THE RAISING OF LAZARUS
1631

Lievens, a friend of Rembrandt, found a very different way from Del Piombo (right) of conveying the miracle of Lazarus. Here, two small hands emerge from the tomb, reaching upwards towards Christ's figure. His divinity is expressed through light: surrounded by a glowing halo, Christ illuminates the darkness around him. The white cloth removed from the tomb stands out prominently and, bathed in Christ's supernatural light, its ghostly appearance hints at the resurrection about to follow. Rather than illustrating the episode in detail, Lievens relies on suggestion and suspense. We eagerly await the body's emergence from the tomb.

Oil on canvas, 103 x 112 cm
BRIGHTON ART GALLERY AND
MUSEUM

Sebastiano del Piombo
c.1485-1547

THE RAISING OF LAZARUS
c.1517-1519

For Renaissance artists, the Classical ideal was one way of conveying Christ's divinity and power. The figures here, idealised and well-proportioned, are inspired by antique Roman sculpture. Christ is monumental in scale and stands on a plinth-like stone. He points his finger at Lazarus, who has lain dead for four days, bringing him back to life. Some people hold their noses, expecting the stink of a corpse. Instead, they see Lazarus emerging from his tomb, his body perfectly maintained. Thus, the miracle is emphasised.

Oil on wood, transferred to
canvas, remounted on synthetic
panel, 381 x 289 cm
NATIONAL GALLERY, LONDON

Pieter Bruegel the Elder
c.1525-1569

CHRIST AND THE WOMAN
TAKEN IN ADULTERY
1565

Christ, in his role as moral teacher, offers advice to the people of Jerusalem, clamouring to punish a woman found guilty of adultery. Christ turns their accusations back on them, writing his message in the dusty ground: let he who is without sin cast the first stone. Not one person responds. The story would have had added resonance in Bruegel's time, when Protestants and Catholics were at war .The artist never sold this painting (a monochrome work known as a 'grisaille'), perhaps an indication of its significance to him.

Oil on panel, 24.1 x 34.4 cm
COURTAULD INSTITUTE
GALLERIES, LONDON

TRANSCENDENCE

S ome paintings encourage us to stop in our tracks, and contemplate things that are above and beyond the material concerns of day-to-day life. Whether religious or secular in subject, figurative or abstract, such paintings are removed from the specifics of time and place. They do not tell a story, nor do they record a particular event, but are universal in nature. The paintings on these pages may strike us as being worlds apart – from a devotional image of Christ from fifteenth-century Europe to a twentieth-century abstract painting made in New York – but they share spiritual transcendence as a common theme.

The two paintings of Christ were painted over 500 years apart. Christus and Dalí worked in different countries, times and environments, but they shared a similar intention. Both focused on the body of Christ but, although displayed with his wounds in one and shown on the cross in the other, with no sense of physical suffering. Also, Christ is depicted above the clouds – they are just visible around his waist in Christus's little picture – removed from any particular time or place.

Blake does not show us Christ, but Albion. Although his specific meaning is unclear, the image itself – a naked man standing triumphantly against an explosive light – speaks volumes. In Rothko's case, the colours and size of the work become all-important, drawing us into an absorbing and silent meditation.

◄ Petrus Christus
ACTIVE 1444-1475/6
CHRIST AS THE MAN OF SORROWS
C.1450
Christ is shown after the Resurrection, in heaven, as indicated by the blue clouds at the bottom, and in majesty. In the fifteenth century, green curtains like these were usually used only for portraits of royalty. The painting, intended as a devotional image, was meant to inspire prayer and pious meditation. The magnificence of Christ is therefore combined with his sacrifice and sorrows. Still wearing the crown of thorns, he displays the wounds of his Passion, proffering them for our meditation. Christ is also shown as Judge: the sword held by the austere-looking angel represents judgment, while the lily stands for mercy, the symbols implying that at the Last Judgment, Christ will act with the appropriate degree of clemency.

Oil on panel, 11.2 x 8.5 cm
BIRMINGHAM MUSEUM AND
ART GALLERY

▲ Mark Rothko
1903-1970
BLACK ON MAROON
1958-1959
There is an intensity to Rothko's works: the enormous scale, which overwhelms us, and the subtle colours, which absorb us. In this painting, the black and maroon play against each other, and we constantly shift between surface and depth. While the dense colours seem flat, the rectangles seem like windows opening onto another space. We are drawn in, and taken beyond our immediate experiences into a seemingly infinite space. The painting, one of a series, was commissioned for a New York restaurant but Rothko withheld the works, deeming the location unsuitable for meditative pieces.

Oil on canvas, 266.5 x 366 cm
TATE MODERN, LONDON

► Salvador Dalí
1904-1989
CHRIST OF ST JOHN OF THE CROSS
1951
This must be one of the most original and unconventional depictions of the Crucifixion. Unusually, we look down at Christ, whose body is depicted with startling illusionism. At the same time, we find ourselves looking across at the landscape as if we were part of it. The painting combines heaven and earth, the divine and the real, the timeless and specific. A clever surrealist trick perhaps, but one that perfectly illustrates Christ's transcendence – he is shown existing continuously beyond time and place. His body is strong and fit, unmarred by wounds. Dalí said, 'My principal preoccupation was that my Christ would be beautiful as the God he is.'

Oil on canvas, 204.8 x 115.9 cm
THE ST MUNGO MUSEUM OF
RELIGIOUS LIFE AND ART, GLASGOW

William Blake
1757-1827
THE DANCE OF ALBION
c.1795
This pose strikes us as one of exultation and liberation.

Blake, however, was never explicit about Albion's meaning. Some see in him an idealised portrayal of the artist himself, while others suggest he stands for England, rising

again after the Industrial Revolution. Another version of the engraving suggests more. It is inscribed, 'Albion rose from where he labour'd at the Mill with Slaves:/ Giving

himself for the Nations he danc'd the dance of Eternal Death.' Albion displays close parallels with the Crucifixion, suggesting a life beyond death. And surrounded by a mystical

light, he seems to convey the ecstasy of true spiritual insight.

Colour-printed line engraving finished in pen and watercolour, 27.5 x 20.2 cm
BRITISH MUSEUM, LONDON

Anthony Van Dyck
1599-1641
PHILIP HERBERT 4TH EARL OF PEMBROKE AND HIS FAMILY
ABOUT 1635

In this huge portrait, which fills an entire wall of Wilton's famous Cube Room, the Earl, holding the staff and key of his office of Lord Chamberlain, sits beside his second wife, Anne Clifford. He is surrounded by his family, and sits beneath a huge shield emblazoned with his coat of arms. On the right is the Earl's daughter with her husband, the Earl of Caernarvon. Centre stage, in this most theatrical of compositions, is Lady Mary Villiers, glittering in her white satin. She was daughter of the King's late favourite, the Duke of Buckingham, now married to the Earl's eldest son, Lord Herbert, who stands above her.

Oil on canvas, 330 x 510 cm
WILTON HOUSE, WILTSHIRE

Rembrandt van Rijn
1606-1669
SELF PORTRAIT
ABOUT 1665-1669

One can't help feeling that Rembrandt's reputation has a lot to do with his face. The familiar potato features and bulbous nose seem to defy idealisation and carry with them the suggestion of no-nonsense honesty. But such prejudices should not blind us to the contrivance of this and his other self portraits. Here, x-rays have shown that Rembrandt originally intended to paint himself at work before altering his pose so that he faces us, holding brushes and palette as the regalia of his profession.

Oil on canvas, 114.3 x 94 cm
KENWOOD HOUSE, LONDON

HUMANITY: IDENTITY

Rembrandt in his monumental self-portrait at Kenwood House is an astonishing presence. His gaze demands our attention but it is also unflinchingly directed at his own sagging features and it is impossible not to respond emotionally. Rembrandt's self-portraits have forged his persona – when we think of him as uncompromising, honest and unconventional we are, perhaps naively, reacting to how he has presented himself to us.

Images have always been used to project desired personas and the portraits on these pages suggest the different ways in which identities can be forged through appearances and surroundings. Jan van Eyck's miraculous picture of the Italian banker Giovanni Arnolfini and his wife, painted in fifteenth century Bruges, may be all sorts of things but it is certainly a picture of a couple proud of their possessions. Clearly a banker might be expected to define himself in terms of what he owned. It is no less surprising to find a member of the English aristocracy presenting himself within his family, though few have done so as extravagantly as the Earl of Pembroke in Van Dyck's huge portrait at Wilton. And just as predictable, if no less gripping, is Degas's portrait of the intellectual Edmond Duranty surrounded by papers and books, in the traditional pose of the 'thinker'.

But the use of the image to construct and convey identity is double edged. Rembrandt's self-portraits have become Rembrandt in the popular imagination and today's celebrity culture is self-evidently image-driven, the countless pictures of celebrities creating an entirely fictional sense of intimacy with constructed personalities. Andy Warhol, the first great artist of celebrity, suggests in his Marilyn diptych how the image can subsume the individual – its endless multiplication making the subject less, not more real.

Andy Warhol
1928-1987
MARILYN DIPTYCH
1962
Working in the months after Monroe's suicide in 1962, Warhol took as his starting point a 1953 publicity shot for the film 'Niagara'. In the left panel, Marilyn is the glamorous blonde bombshell, but the fading and blurring of the image in the right panel suggest the loss of confidence and identity which led to her suicide. The contrast between black and white on the right and the brilliant colours on the left also suggests the divide between life and death. But Warhol leaves the interpretation open. Dispassionate as always, he will not direct our conclusions. The image is out there for us to make of what we will.

Acrylic on canvas, 205.4 x 114.8 cm
TATE MODERN, LONDON

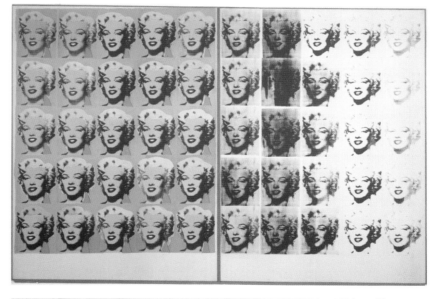

Jan van Eyck
ACTIVE 1422-1441
PORTRAIT OF GIOVANNI ARNOLFINI AND HIS WIFE
1434
Van Eyck's magical ability to paint the surface and textures of the material world seems to render the world more real than we actually find it. Perhaps this is why people have so often tried to read more into his paintings than is visible. This double portrait has been seen as a depiction of the couple's betrothal, each element – from the cheery dog to the single lit candle – pregnant with meaning. But perhaps it is simply a celebration of the Arnolfinis and their world, and Giovanni's gesture a greeting to the two figures who are just visible in the mirror on the back wall, entering the room in which we find him.

Oil on oak, 82 x 60 cm
NATIONAL GALLERY, LONDON

Edgar Degas
1834-1917
EDMOND DURANTY
1879
Degas depicts the art critic surrounded by his work, fingers pressed to his brow. Duranty was closely linked with Degas's circle and shortly before this portrait was made he had argued that the modern portrait should strike 'the special note of the modern person, wearing his usual clothes, amidst his social habits, at home or in the street...the observation of man's intimacy with the place he lives.' Degas's portrait is a clear response to his call.

Tempera, watercolour and pastel on linen, 100 x 100 cm
BURRELL COLLECTION, GLASGOW

VICE AND FOLLY

Artists of the past have often been called upon to glorify their subjects. But here we see painting as satire – the aim of which has always been to use the weapons of exaggeration, irony and ridicule to draw attention to hypocrisy and ridiculousness. Of course, it also hopes to make us laugh. The joke behind Massys's fantastically hideous old woman is not actually her ugliness, but that she believes herself so beautiful – dressed in low-cut and hopelessly old-fashioned finery and holding a rose-bud (a token of love): this is a cruel parody of a betrothal portrait. Her face is deliberately ape-like, and apes have a, possibly undeserved, reputation for unbridled lust. A grinning chained monkey also appears in El Greco's haunting and mysterious painting, adding to the uncertain sense that something devilish is afoot.

In Peter Howson's grotesque trio of baseball-capped thugs, the bestial is again emphasised, although here it is the snarling pit-bulls that characterise their owners.

Perhaps the greatest of all satirical artists was the Englishman William Hogarth, who came from the same bustling London as the arch-satirists Jonathon Swift and Henry Fielding. His ironically titled 'Progresses', made first as paintings before being published as prints, are morality tales in which – through a sequence of sharply observed, scabrous scenes – we follow the inexorable decline towards death or madness of contemporary urban types. In 'The Rake's Progress', whose third scene we see here, Tom Rakewell's appetites and his determination to live the fashionable life lead him in eight short steps from receiving his inheritance to lunacy.

▲ William Hogarth
1697–1764
THE RAKE'S PROGRESS III, THE ROSE TAVERN
1733–1734
We are in the Rose Tavern, a notorious haunt for prostitutes and criminals near London's Drury Lane. Two prostitutes are lifting a watch from Tom Rakewell's jacket which shows that it is three o'clock in the morning. The young drunk, clothes dishevelled and his sword hanging precariously from his belt, is slumped in his chair. In the foreground a girl is stripping for her routine as 'posture woman'. The metal

platter and candle being brought into the room by 'Leather Coat', a well-known porter at the tavern, form part of her act. She will dance naked on the table, striking various poses, as she spins around on the plate.

Oil on canvas, 62 x 74
SIR JOHN SOANE MUSEUM, LONDON

Peter Howson
BORN 1958
PATRIOTS
1991

Distortion and caricature have always been a tool of the artist in emphasising our grotesque and bestial qualities. Here Howson takes his lead from the snarling pit-bulls to characterise these contemporary bigots. According to the artist, he was walking through Gallowgate in Glasgow when 'across the road I saw three men running with two dogs. Both man and dog were aggressively posturing when they stopped, and then continued to run…I only saw them for a few seconds, but it left a strong impression on me. I wanted the painting to capture the atmosphere of the late '80s and early '90s, with its random violence, great bigotry (the patriots could come from any class) and moral confusion.'

Oil in canvas. 206 x 275 cm.
GLASGOW GALLERY OF
MODERN ART

Quinten Massys
1465-1530
A GROTESQUE OLD WOMAN
ABOUT 1525-1530

Perhaps most famous as the inspiration for Tenniel's depiction of the Ugly Duchess in 'Alice in Wonderland', this deeply curious painting was inspired by a grotesque caricature by Leonardo da Vinci. Massys has turned Leonardo's invention into a biting satire on misguided female vanity. It comes from the same world as the satirical poem 'In Praise of Folly' by Massys's contemporary, Erasmus, who wrote of foolish old women who 'can hardly pull themselves from the mirror…They show their withered flabby breasts and, with a quivering voice, they try to stir up a faint desire.'

Oil on wood. 64 x 46 cm
NATIONAL GALLERY, LONDON

El Greco
1541-1614
ALLEGORICAL NIGHT SCENE
1577-1578

Not all depictions of folly are grotesque, nor are they all straightforward. Indeed no-one is quite sure what this mysterious painting is trying to tell us. There is certainly a sense of conspiracy here, as the monkey on its chain and the foolishly grinning man on the right watch a young boy blowing on a lighted ember to light a candle. A number of sixteenth-century proverbs linked blowing on flames with arousing evil passions and it is probable that some warning of this kind is intended. Painted by El Greco, the Greek-born artist who spent most of his working life in the Spanish city of Toledo, the picture was probably meant to demonstrate his powers of invention, but perhaps even more powerfully to showcase his astonishing mastery of the depiction of light.

Oil on canvas. 71 x 92 cm
HAREWOOD HOUSE, YORKSHIRE

BODY AND SOUL

The human body has always been used by artists to express more than merely the facts of anatomy. Heroic nudes inspired by the art of the ancient world were often used to suggest the moral virtue of those who inhabited them. But here in four pictures painted over the last half century, we see the human body at its most vulnerable – twisted and distorted to painful ends. After the Second World War, possibly influenced by photographs of victims of the holocaust, Giacometti started to make the tall, elongated figures, both in sculptures and paintings, for which he is best known. His figures, even when they appear in otherwise conventional portraits, seem whittled away by the world around them – remote and isolated.

Where Giacometti creates his figures with scratchy lines of blacks and greys Francis Bacon and Lucian Freud – perhaps the two greatest flesh-painters of the late twentieth-century – revelled in the stuff of paint. In Bacon's figures paint – reds, whites and pinks – is smeared and dragged in ways that always remind you of the meat, blood and bones beneath the skin. Often faceless, usually contorted and isolated, his figures are pained and painful presences. Freud has talked of making oil paint 'work as flesh' and in front of his pictures you are often very aware of the work involved – paint worked up in thick worried layers – but in the beautiful small 'nude portrait' here, the effects seems almost effortless, body and limbs brushed in with simple confidence.

▼ Francis Bacon
1909-1992
TWO FIGURES IN A ROOM
1959
The experience of looking at a Bacon painting is unique; visceral, almost nauseating. Bacon himself saw beauty in unexpected ways. He spoke, for example, of very beautiful wounds. He also commented on how surprised he was when he walked into butcher's shops not to see his own body strung up. Here two figures crouch and lie in the corner of a featureless room. Isolated from us, their relationship to each other is unclear. They are close and naked but there is little sense of intimacy and certainly none of tenderness.

Oil on canvas, 198.1 x 141.8 cm
SAINSBURY CENTRE, NORWICH

▲ Alberto Giacometti
1901-1966
SEATED WOMAN
1949
This is probably a portrait of Giacometti's wife's cousin Elvezia. It was made during a trip back to Giacometti's home village Stampa, in Switzerland, when he took Annetta, his new wife, back to introduce her to his mother. As so often in his portraits Elvezia is framed or boxed in by the doorway behind – an effect he sometimes achieved in his sculptures by placing his figures in a cage structure. Confined and isolated by her surroundings, which are conjured up from the same worried network of hatched lines, Giacometti's figure emerges as an oppressed, and ghostly presence.

Oil on canvas, 74 x 38 cm
MANCHESTER CITY ART GALLERY

Jock McFadyen
BORN 1950
DEPRESSION
1990
The title of Scottish artist Jock McFadyen's disturbing painting is self-explanatory. Painfully twisted, distorted and caricatured, everything about this grimacing woman's physical appearance is contrived to emphasise the pain and isolation of her predicament. Her flesh is painted to appear scratched and scarred. Set – as are many of McFadyen's paintings – in an urban wasteland, she sits incongruously naked against the thorns beside her and the graffiti-covered wall behind. She has knotted her limbs into a helpless ball – and has no hands to defend or help herself.

Oil on canvas, 198 x 198 cm
GLASGOW GALLERY OF
MODERN ART

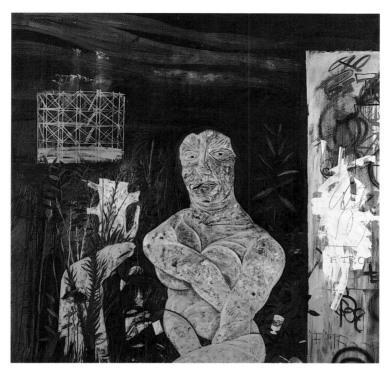

Lucian Freud
BORN 1922
SMALL NAKED PORTRAIT
1973-1974
Freud always describes his nudes as portraits and this is certainly a specific person, remarkably alive and vital despite her shut eyes and foetal hunch. Freud lingers on what is particular: the reddened hand against white breast, the dusty sole of her right foot and her hair across her forehead. Freud has said, 'I would wish my portraits to be of the people, not like them. Not having a look of the sitter, being them. I didn't want to get just a likeness like a mimic, but to portray them, like an actor…As far as I am concerned the paint is the person: I want it to work for me just as flesh'.

Oil on canvas, 22 x 27 cm
ASHMOLEAN MUSEUM, OXFORD

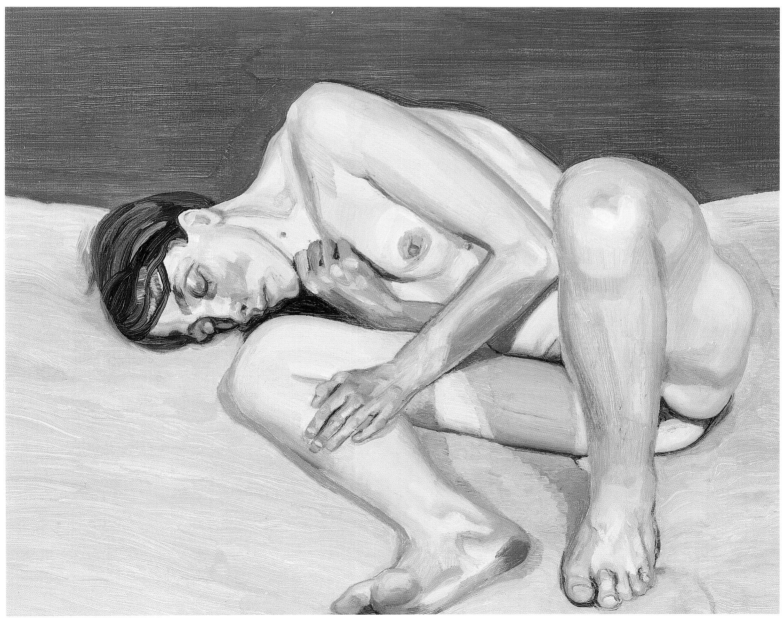

DEATH

eath will come to us all, but it is doubtful whether it will leave many of us as elegantly arranged as the purple-breeched Chatterton. Of course you can make death romantic, but you usually have to try quite hard and Henry Wallis has not stinted in his vision of the fantastically languorous passing of the boy poet. Chatterton – Wordsworth's 'marvellous boy' – killed himself in 1770 when only 17 and became at once the archetypal tragic genius for the Romantic age. Astonishingly, considering its stagy contrivance, when the final version of the picture was exhibited it attracted praise from the critic Ruskin for its accuracy and its success 'in placing before your eyes…an actual fact'. If Wallis's picture is a hymn to death, Van Dyck's similarly elegant cadaver is an attempt to defeat it. The beautiful Lady Venetia Digby 'dyed suddenly in bed', aged 33, and the following day her husband, the brilliant and dashing Sir Kenelm Digby, summoned his friend Van Dyck to draw her. The portrait was delivered seven weeks later as a permanent memorial to Venetia's beauty and a consolation to her grief-stricken husband.

It is the grief-stricken mourners who are the focus of Poussin's sober image of the moment of death from his series of pictures depicting the Christian sacraments. Here, a yellow-robed priest of the early Church anoints the dying man with holy oil while family and friends react with carefully distinguished degrees of grief. The painting was based on the funerary images to be found on Roman sarcophagi, and from them comes the figure of the man's wife, her face hidden in her hands to suggest the extremity of her grief – too great to be depicted.

▶ Henry Wallis
1830–1916
THE DEATH OF CHATTERTON
1855–1856
The doomed boy poet from Bristol killed himself at the age of 17, seeing his brief life as a hopeless failure. Wallis shows him heroically spread across the bed of his London garret, his torn-up poems and the exquisite clothes he loved a reminder of the life he rejected. The phial of arsenic has fallen from his lifeless hand. The burnt-out candle and the fading rose on the window ledge are familiar symbols of life's brevity. The dawn view of the City of London and St Paul's cathedral outside, suggests both the heartlessness of commerce and Christian certainties. Wallis clearly empathised with this tale of the neglected artistic genius although, ironically, his painting – for which this is a smaller study – made him famous virtually overnight.

Oil on wood, 17.4 x 25.4 cm
BIRMINGHAM CITY MUSEUM AND ART GALLERY

◀ Nicolas Poussin
1594–1665
THE SACRAMENT OF EXTREME UNCTION
ABOUT 1635
Poussin, noted for his knowledge of the classical past, paints a scene of the early Roman church in the style of a classical relief. The yellow-robed priest, dressed to resemble depictions of the apostles, anoints the head of the dying man. The figures are arranged in a narrow strip around the bed, their faces and gestures carefully modulated to express their grief. Such refinement seems beyond the servants, however, one of whom bustles out on the right with an entirely inappropriate swagger.

Oil on canvas, 117 x 178 cm
BELVOIR CASTLE, LEICESTERSHIRE

Anthony Van Dyck
1599-1642

VENETIA STANLEY, LADY DIGBY ON HER DEATHBED
1633

On the morning of Wednesday May 1, 1633, Sir Kenelm Digby found that his beautiful wife had died suddenly in the night. He immediately ordered the casting of her hands and a mould of her face to be set in metal. He summoned Van Dyck to draw her 'the second day after she was dead.' They 'brought a little seeming colour to her pale cheeks' by 'rubbing of her face.' The addition of the rose shedding its petals was an all-too-clear symbol of the swift passing of life and beauty. In the months after his wife's death

Digby wrote of the portrait's being 'the only constant companion I now have…All night when I goe to my chamber I sett it close by my beds side, and by the faint light of a candle, me thinkes I see her dead indeed.'

Oil on canvas, 74.3 x 81.8 cm.
DULWICH PICTURE GALLERY

PART 4

NATURE AND TIME

'The round of days, seasons and years, the cycle of decay and rebirth have for centuries been seen as metaphors for a moral order, within which individual human lives are simply aspects of a general truth'

JAN VAN OS
FLOWERS AND FRUIT (DETAIL)
c.1780

NATURE AND TIME

We have all walked on Renoir's hillside, watching the warm wind tousle trees and undergrowth, relishing the clouds on the move and the safe turbulence of European nature. In the landscapes of the Impressionists – and it is why we love them so much – this is how it always is. Everything is sun and light, with no dark side, no threats, nothing to unsettle us. It is the modern city-dweller's dream day-out in the country, and we come home restored and refreshed.

Yet in nature as it really is, the dark side is always present. Death is the precondition of any new life. Menace is everywhere. There is danger beneath the beauty.

The second painting on these pages, Piero di Cosimo's Forest Fire, is one of the earliest evocations of that other nature, incomprehensible and brutal, that destroys life and generates panic. This is a picture about ecological disaster. As their habitat burns, animals and birds scatter. It is also a picture about the uneasy boundary between man and beast: two of the animals have human faces. Are we watching a primal state of nature, part of a complex creation myth? Or is the artist (who had a reputation for highly quirky subjects) playing to our deep fears – cloning and BSE merely the latest examples – about what happens when the division between humans and animals is mysteriously or irresponsibly elided, and the natural order denied?

Piero's picture was painted in Florence 500 years ago. It is, I think, about uncertainties that exercise and alarm us today. Like poets, artists have always been fascinated by the balance in nature between the fleeting and the permanent. The round of days, seasons and years, the cycle of decay and rebirth have for centuries been seen as metaphors for a moral order, within which individual human lives are simply aspects of a general truth. On this view, change is merely part of a large pattern of constancy. The greatest of these painter-poets of the landscape is Nicolas Poussin, in whose works this country's museums are magnificently rich.

▷ Pierre Auguste Renoir
1841-1919
A GUST OF WIND
ABOUT 1878

How do you paint wind blowing across a hillside? Show trees bending? Leaves streaming in the gale? Renoir takes a subtler tack; he makes the paint itself quiver as though caught by the breeze, so that the whole surface of this little picture (only eighteen inches high) seems to move. The small scale means every stroke tells. They dance across the foreground, their different directions perfectly imitating the unsynchronised trembling of bush or grass. It is a moment made only of movement.

Oil on canvas, 52 x 82.5 cm
FITZWILLIAM MUSEUM,
CAMBRIDGE

Piero di Cosimo
1461/2-1522
THE FOREST FIRE
ABOUT 1505

The animal world is in turmoil. An ox bellows centre stage. On the right, a crane stands in the position of calling while, left of centre, the lion and the bear open their mouths as though growling. Noise on the ground is echoed by movement in the air. Birds open their wings to fly or are already in rapid movement. In the far distance on the left is the characteristic line of starlings in flight. Nearer to us are partridge and pheasant, woodcock and pigeon, all on the wing, all identifiable. The cause of the agitation is far from clear, but has presumably to do with the forest fire burning fiercely in the middle distance and smouldering on the left. All species are suddenly endangered. Conceived as part of a suite of luxury furniture, the picture was probably once the back of an elaborate storage chest, a popular wedding present in Renaissance Florence. It is an unsettling gift, entirely characteristic of its artist, a wild eccentric who lived largely on boiled eggs. On the left, a pig and a deer have a human face. Why, nobody knows for certain. Good subject for conversation in the newly-weds' house.

Oil on wood, 71.2 x 202 cm
ASHMOLEAN MUSEUM, OXFORD

Most famous and most loved among them is surely his Dance to the Music of Time *(facing page)*, which gave its title to Anthony Powell's magisterial cycle of novels plotting the transformation across decades of a whole section of English society. In both novel and painting fortunes rise and fall as characters – most memorably Widmerpool – come round again and again, more or less happy, more or less powerful or rich, until the long and ultimately futile dance is ended.

In his Landscape with the Ashes of Phocion *(above)*, Poussin I think gives a quite different reading of the same human story and, like no other artist in the European tradition, elevates landscape into a form of moral philosophy. The Athenian general, Phocion, had stood unflinchingly for an idea of political integrity and had been put to death by his fellow citizens as a consequence. This is the ignominious end of a noble career, a life which had apparently totally failed in its central purpose. Yet in nature, as in the world of ideals, an individual death is never the end of the story. Poussin shows a landscape fertile and ordered, governed by laws stronger than any man can make. Just as the laws of nature must always ultimately prevail, so will the moral law that governs human society, especially if proclaimed with courage and integrity. Phocion's reputation in due course will be restored. His ashes will return to Athens. More important, his ideas will triumph even though – indeed, perhaps because – he had to die for them. This landscape is about political hope, the need always to take the longer view, and it was painted at a moment – 1648 –

Nicolas Poussin
1594-1665
A DANCE TO THE MUSIC OF TIME
1638-1640

*As Time strums his lyre, four
women dance, and we know from
Poussin's biographer who they are.
At the back, Poverty, in green,
holds out a muscular arm to
Labour; who, like her, is barefoot.
Labour reaches out to Wealth,
dressed in gold and white, but
Wealth disdains to touch her hand.
Instead, she holds on to the blowsy
figure of Pleasure, in blue and red,
who leads us back to Poverty.
This is the dance of all mankind,
for individuals as for states,
either in one lifetime or across
generations. In the heavens, Apollo
drives the chariot of the days,
while two-headed Janus, symbol of
the turning years, looks sternly on;
for this rise and fall of fortunes,
like time, never ends. And what
does it all add up to? The bubble
blown by the sitting child.*

Oil on canvas, 82.5 x 104 cm
THE WALLACE COLLECTION,
LONDON

Ceri Richards
1903-1971
CYCLE OF NATURE
1944

*This swirling profusion of
dissolved forms, in which we can
(without total confidence)
decipher animal feet and sexual
organs among flowers and
leaves, all blown by the wind
against a brilliant blue sky, is
dominated by an unequivocal
bunch of grapes. It is, as the title
suggests, a vision of nature. It is
also a Bacchic fantasy of life as
intoxication. The picture owes a
great deal to Continental
surrealists such as Dalì, but
Ceri Richards was always very
conscious of his Welsh
inheritance, insisting that his
paintings were shaped by
a Celtic sense of 'proliferation
and metaphor'.*

Oil on canvas, 102.2 x 152.7 cm
NATIONAL MUSEUM OF WALES,
CARDIFF

Nicolas Poussin
1594-1665
LANDSCAPE WITH THE ASHES
OF PHOCION
1648

*I suspect that few people looking at
this picture for the first time would
guess that the hero is the heap of
ashes being gathered by the woman
in the centre foreground. The
dominant impression is surely the
controlled luxuriance of the trees
and a classical city that seems all
triangles and rectangles, in which
tiny figures go about the daily
business of ancient Greece. And this
is, I think, precisely what Poussin*

*intended. The hero, the Athenian
general Phocion, had been put to
death as a result of squalid political
intrigue. His dead body had to be
carried to nearby Megara to be
burnt there. His faithful widow
gathered his ashes and kept them
till his reputation was restored and
they could be returned to Athens
and honourably interred. A great
man is brought low; a faithful
widow remains true. Nature and
the rest of the world continue on
their pre-ordained way, unchanged
and unmoved.*

Oil on canvas, 116 x 178.5 cm
WALKER ART GALLERY, LIVERPOOL

when France seemed on the edge of civil war. Its owner must have been sustained and encouraged by a great example.

It is one of the most extraordinary things about paintings that artists can look at the things we all see every day around us and read in them such a bewildering range of meanings. Renoir's smiling countryside is uncanny and eerie to Piero di Cosimo. Where Poussin sees concealed in nature an ethical law, Ceri Richards finds demonic exuberance *(previous page)*.

Millais leaves us uncertain whether we are to enjoy the beauty of the world in stillness, or hurry to catch its pleasures while we can. The girls on the grass themselves seem undecided. But it is, I think, Van Os who sums everything up in what might at first seem the least ambitious of all these pictures – a vase of flowers with fruit. As you look more closely, it becomes clear that he has combined seasons with a god-like insouciance, telescoping time. The different flowers must have been drawn over many months, perhaps years, and then made into a satisfying, but imagined whole. Like all the other pictures here, it forces us to think about our place in time and in the world. Its virtuoso treatment of surface and tone sends us back in wonder to the beauties of the real world, and, I hope, also to the galleries where all these pictures hang and to the worlds that the artists have created.

▲ Sir John Everett Millais
1829-1898
SPRING (APPLE BLOSSOMS)
1859
At the edge of an orchard, eight well-dressed and good-looking young girls, jeunes filles en fleur if ever there were, are preparing to taste curds and cream in the spring sunshine. Flowers are everywhere – on the trees behind, in the baskets, bound in the hair of at least two of the girls. Millais

painted such pictures, he said, not to tell a specific story, but to induce 'the deepest religious reflection'. No less than Titian's Three Ages (page 109), this is a poem on the transience of life. On the right, the composition is balanced by a scythe, 'time's curbing sickle'. The time to gather rosebuds will not last. Think about it.

Oil on canvas, 110.5 x 45.7 cm
LADY LEVER ART GALLERY,
PORT SUNLIGHT

◄ Jan van Os
1744-1808
FLOWERS AND FRUIT
ABOUT 1780
Van Os has painted a bouquet of fruit and flowers that no amount of money could have bought in Holland of the 1780s. The spring tulip and narcissus would hardly be in bloom at the same time as the rose and the peony, and most certainly could not be surrounded by the fruits of high and late summer. The artist has combined the seasons and paint has triumphed over time in more senses than one. Morning glory and poppy will fade fast. Butterfly and bluebottle will live

and die almost as quickly. The picture, on the other hand, is still with us and the artist's skill in catching the bloom on the grapes is as astonishing now as it was over 200 years ago.

Oil on wood, 65 x 47 cm
WARRINGTON MUSEUM AND
ART GALLERY

Paul Nash
1889-1946
WINTER SEA
1925-1937
Paul Nash worked on this painting for 12 years, from 1925 to 1937, during which he slowly transformed the waves breaking low and long on the flat beach at Dymchurch (near Romney Marsh in Kent) into a potent image of desolate chill.
His experience as an official war artist on the Western Front had made him alert to the bleak poetry of a landscape with no salient features. This is one of his boldest designs. Like many of his contemporaries, Nash was influenced by Cézanne's capacity to reduce the confusions of nature to the order of geometry, but here the reduction of sea and sky to simple shapes betrays an emotional engagement of unusual intensity. Landscape has become a metaphor for feeling.

Oil on canvas, 71.2 x 96.6 cm
YORK CITY ART GALLERY

NATURE INTO ART

Even as late as the Renaissance landscape was not really established as a genre in its own right, but crept in through the background of narrative paintings, gradually pushing the story to the side until it completely took over. But even then, the depiction of realistic appearances was not always the artist's aim, and in some way all the works on these pages have gone through a transformation as the painters search for the 'artistic' in nature. Claude, although looking to nature for specific effects, portrayed vistas imagined from the Classical past. Even Constable, in his attempt to depict the world he knew, could not help but fall under Claude's charm, although if Claude evoked the age of Virgil, Constable was nostalgic only for his youth. Cézanne, too, went to the landscape of his childhood for inspiration, and found forms in nature that combined a palpable depth with two-dimensional patterning, the lines of foreground trees and distant hills on the surface of the painting breaking down the distance between them. It is this aspect of Cézanne's work that particularly appealed to twentieth-century artists such as Terry Frost.

◀ John Constable
1776-1837
THE HAYWAIN
1821
This painting appears in so many waiting rooms in bad prints that it is easy to forget its beauty and subtlety. The nostalgic calm, so effortlessly evoked, convinces us that Constable was showing 'truth', not 'art' – so it comes as a surprise to learn that this was painted in London, not the countryside. The carefully balanced composition and evidence of the odd change – there was a boy sitting on a barrel to the right of the dog – tell us that Constable had arranged nature, while details such as the mass of trees shielding the distant background signal his indebtedness to Claude.

Oil on canvas, 130.2 x 185.4 cm
NATIONAL GALLERY, LONDON

Claude
1604/5-1682
COAST VIEW WITH PERSEUS AND THE ORIGINS OF CORAL
1674

In his 'Metamorphoses', Ovid tells us how Perseus, having slain the gorgon Medusa, left her head on some seaweed, which was transformed by the dripping blood into coral. This miracle is observed with amazement by four nymphs, while Perseus washes his hands after his ordeal and the winged horse Pegasus stands nearby. As ever, Claude devotes little space to the narrative, but concentrates on the unifying effect of the light and the delicate balance of colour. The bright yellow sky shines through the trees and around the rock formation, while the more 'realistic' blue in the top right is picked up on the horizon and in the robe of one of the nymphs.

Oil on canvas, 100 x 127 cm
HOLKHAM HALL, NORFOLK,
VISCOUNT COKE

Terry Frost
BORN 1915
BROWN VERTICALS
1958-1959

Apparently abstract, this painting is in fact the result of Frost's profound involvement with the landscape. In 1954 he moved to Leeds to take up a teaching fellowship for three years, and his experience of the Yorkshire Dales was his inspiration. Their hypnotic expanse, bleak but beautiful in all weathers, is broken by a network of dry stone walls, patches of greens and browns defined by irregular outlines. It would, however, be a mistake to interpret this as an aerial view. It is not a depiction of a specific place, but an evocation of the mood of the landscape, which grows out of the relationship of colour, line and form as the work proceeds.

Oil on canvas, 213.4 x 172.7 cm
LEEDS CITY ART GALLERY

Paul Cézanne
1839-1906
MONT SAINT VICTOIRE
ABOUT 1887

Cézanne spent many hours in front of this mountain, trying to capture its splendour and majesty. He wanted to make 'something permanent' of the art of the Impressionists, to show timelessness and not the fleeting moment. He also wanted to combine this with expression of his visual experience: the equivalence he saw when looking at the sky and mountain, say, which share the same light blues and buffs, or the yellow-greens of the fields in the foothills and the leaves of the trees in the centre foreground. All this is held together by the lattice of black lines formed by the tracery of the branches and the outlines of the mountain and distant fields.

Oil on canvas, 66.8 x 92.3 cm
COURTAULD INSTITUTE
GALLERIES, LONDON

WILD NATURE

Manned space flight has shown us pictures of our planet, a mere fragment of the universe, and charter flights have put even the antipodes within our reach. But for the explorers and discoverers of the seventeenth and eighteenth centuries this was not a small world. The size and scale of the earth, of nature and all its splendours, were pitted against the small and insignificant figure of man, and became embodied in the concept of 'the sublime', the subject of thinkers, poets and painters alike. Martin's Bard inveighs against the tiny figures in the depths of the valley, his own minute form given strength by the massive rock on which he stands and the brilliance of the light above. There is no such support for Moran's four tiny horsemen, who are dwarfed, alone within an endless expanse. Turner, whose painting was once described as 'soapsuds and whitewash', takes us even further – away from the relative safety of the land to show nature's power at sea, the steamboat tossed by stormy waters almost a metaphor for our fragile existence. Stubbs, rather than setting man against nature, sets animals to fight against each other. There is no violence but the possibility of 'nature red in tooth and claw' tells us again that the landscape is not always the relaxed and hospitable place other artists would have us believe.

▷ Joseph Mallord William Turner
1775-1851
SNOW STORM, STEAMBOAT OFF A HARBOUR'S MOUTH
1842
At the black centre of the storm, the steamboat sits off-kilter, highlighted by a patch of light which silhouettes the frail mast bent by the strong winds. Around it the sea and sky are intent on destruction, a vortex of energy spinning in bands of overlapping sky, cloud and wave. Turner added to the title the enigmatic statement, 'The author was in this storm on the night the Ariel left Harwich' – but he does not tell us where he was, at sea or on land. Either way, his interest lies in the threatening power of nature, a threat which is beginning to be challenged by man's new weapon, steam.

Oil on canvas, 91.5 x 121.9 cm
TATE BRITAIN, LONDON

◁ John Martin
1789-1854
THE BARD
1817
Martin's fairy-tale painting is an illustration of Thomas Grey's poem of the same name, in which, after conquering Wales, Edward I orders the death of the country's Bards, focus of national culture and pride. We see the last Bard, 'loose his beard and hoary hair', defiantly standing on a massive and overhanging rock, cursing the departing armies. Brightly lit, as if partaking of the light of truth, he is almost part of nature, his hair, beard and drapery all flowing in the same direction as the rock strata. Hundreds of feet below, the gushing river echoes the departing army, whose procession curves in and out of the painting, dwarfed by the castle and icy mountains above.

Oil on canvas, 270 x 170 cm
LAING ART GALLERY,
NEWCASTLE UPON TYNE

△ Thomas Moran
1837-1926
NEARING CAMP, EVENING, UPPER COLORADO RIVER
1882
The backdrop to this painting is the brick-red rock formation towering

George Stubbs
1724-1806
WHITE HORSE FRIGHTENED BY A LION
1770

In the grand, forbidding landscape the horse stands out like the bright white clouds in the sky, its power and energy brought to a sudden halt by a lion. The horse's mane sweeps over his head and across his neck, his tail is blown forward between the hind legs, while the foreleg, on the same diagonal, braces the body. Stubbs, renowned for his animal portraits, here puts his skills to use to show, through the dramatic encounter of two animals, the savagery of nature.

above the Upper Colorado River, consisting of a single, monumental stack of rock, a gap, and then enormous cliffs receding like a giant exclamation mark that has fallen away from us. The scale is given by four tiny figures on horseback.

Moran, a Bolton man, has created a landscape of breathtaking enormity, a romanticised evocation of the West that is intended to remind us of the courage of the pioneers.

Oil on canvas, 206 x 111 cm
BOLTON MUSEUM AND ART GALLERY

Oil on canvas, 101.6 x 127.6 cm
WALKER ART GALLERY, LIVERPOOL

ANIMALS

The animals depicted on these pages are seen in different ways in terms of their relationship to man. In biblical terms, Noah was the greatest of conservationists, and his story is, for Griffier, an excuse for a display of painterly skill which also reflects a contemporary interest in natural history. There are two paintings by Stubbs (as we are looking at animal paintings, he should surely be represented twice), both of which are images of sport. Hunting may have originated in the need for food, but the cheetah depicted by Stubbs was presented as an exotic gift to provide spectacle and novelty. Although in reality it was tossed aside by one of George III's stags, it stands alert and ready for the chase, like Hambletonian, who, in one of Stubbs' most remarkable compositions, appears both racing and at rest. But animals are closest to us as our pets, and the two pictures of dogs here are paintings of unalloyed fun – in the first, Bonnard shows their natural energy, while in the other Landseer sees, through the dogs, our all-too-human foibles.

◀ Jan Griffier
1646-1718
NOAH'S ARK
c.1710
This huge canvas – over three metres square – gives Griffier, a Dutch artist working in England, ample space to portray the entire menagerie Noah was to save. In the distance, mild and obedient animals, elephants and bears among them, head towards the ark, while in the foreground, as if to stress man's discord and the difficulties Noah has to face, animals hiss and spit and bark at one another. Within this mass of possibilities, Griffier unifies the painting through a simple use of reds, blues and browns while varying his brushstroke to explore all the differences of fur and feather. Unexpectedly, a pair of unicorns is preparing to board – I had always thought they missed the boat.

Oil on canvas, 378 x 378 cm
BRISTOL CITY MUSEUM
AND ART GALLERY

▶ George Stubbs
1724-1806
HAMBLETONIAN
1800
Stubbs had the rare ability to portray elements of almost Classical idealism within a world of closely observed detail. In this painting he combines the balance and poise of a well-thought composition – notice the placing of the buildings and people around the champion's strong profile – with the dynamic energy of the horse. Painted as if simultaneously winning a race and being rubbed down, the well-groomed form is like an anatomical study, with bone and muscle structure showing clearly through the sleek and shiny coat. The intense and saturated colouring stands proud of the greys of the men and pastel tones of the background, leaving us in no doubt that Hambletonian himself should be the focus of our attention.

Oil on canvas, 209 x 367.3 cm
MOUNT STEWART HOUSE,
NORTHERN IRELAND,
NATIONAL TRUST

▲ George Stubbs
1724-1806
CHEETAH AND STAG WITH TWO INDIANS
c.1765
Stubbs would often accentuate the most important creature in his works by painting it in profile: the cheetah, tense and proud, the hairs bristling on the nape of his neck and his tail raised, adopts such a heraldic position here. Given to George III by Sir George Pigot, he is portrayed with his two Indian handlers as they pull back a red hood and gesture towards his prey – actually a cross-breed Stubbs seems to have invented, having the body of a red deer but the antlers of an Indian sambar. The hood and red sash – used to hold the cheetah back – chime in with the handlers' trousers and pull our attention to the foreground.

Oil on canvas, 250 x 305 cm
MANCHESTER CITY ART GALLERY

Edwin Landseer
1802-1873
LAYING DOWN THE LAW
BY 1840

A poodle, its fluffy head and chest appearing like a judge's wig, sits with one paw on a book next to a pair of glasses, presumably his. He is surrounded by dogs of stereotyped character – there's an eager terrier and bored spaniel on the right, and on the left a black Labrador who has 'retrieved' a brief. Landseer takes our tendency to find human traits in our pets to the limit. Although the work is believed to satirise individuals known by the artist, the in-joke doesn't need to be understood in order to amuse.

Oil on canvas, 120.7 x 130.8 cm
CHATSWORTH HOUSE, DERBYSHIRE

Pierre Bonnard
1867-1947
TWO DOGS
1891

This is a very bouncy painting – the dogs, their fur and the rich carpet of grass all depicted with the same energetic curves. Famous for his gorgeous and subtle colour harmonies, in this early work – painted when he was only 24– Bonnard is surprisingly bold. The vibrant green pushes the dark chocolate brown of the dogs into silhouette, while the delicate pink of the flowers is echoed on the left dog's nose. Bonnard signs the painting in a blue of intensity equal to the green, which can be seen breathing through the grass. The complex and bold outline, with its concentration on two-dimensional pattern, shows the influence of Japanese prints, an interest also made explicit in the depiction of the flowers.

Oil on canvas, 37 x 39.7 cm
SOUTHAMPTON CITY ART GALLERY

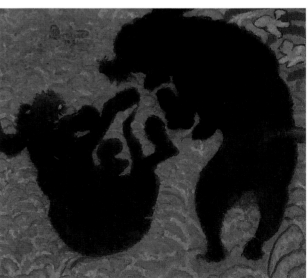

NATURAL EFFECTS

Artists have struggled for many years to catch the constant changes of weather. As soon as landscape painting emerged as an independent subject, it was essential to suggest reality, not only in the hills and trees but also in the sky. Rubens, an early master, would carry out studies to inform his finished works, and the painting here (top right), devoid of any narrative, might appear to be a study were it not for its size: this was to prove a fruitful innovation. For Constable, the clouds were all-important in showing the variation of light over time, and to furnish his paintings with pattern, contrast and mood. He executed studies of the changing skies *en plein air*, but would never have thought of finishing a painting outside. Neither would Seurat, for whom, unlike his Impressionist contemporaries, observed reality was only the starting point for his vision. Van Gogh plays with the same colours as Seurat, but with a different intensity and to achieve an expressive rather than a descriptive end. For Jones, years earlier, description was all: every surface of this sun-drenched scene is minutely plotted in a work which, in its play of shapes and planes, appears perhaps the most 'modern' here.

◀ Thomas Jones
1742-1803
BUILDINGS IN NAPLES
1782

Thomas Jones painted a number of these astonishingly detailed studies, which, given he was working in the eighteenth century, seem remarkably sparse and modern. Carefully planned – the tops of the door and window are half way up the painting, the left edge of the window half-way across – it could almost be an abstract composition. The sun must be high, given the angle of the shadow underneath the balcony, and lights the surface to reveal all the variation of tone and texture, the irregular whitewash and even the pockmarks left from scaffolding .

Oil on paper, 14 x 21.6 cm
NATIONAL MUSEUM OF WALES,
CARDIFF

John Constable
1776-1837
HAMPSTEAD, LOOKING TOWARDS HARROW
1821

For '5 o'clock afternoon' – written by Constable on the back of this painting – the sky is remarkably dark, particularly given that it was August. But it is a remarkably dramatic sky with overlapping bands of clouds like two opposing weather fronts. One band crosses from top right to middle left, the one behind is horizontal. Where they cross in the centre, we see both rain and sun. At the right, the striations of the deep blue clouds find a formal echo in the landscape below.

Oil on paper on canvas, 25 x 29.8 cm
MANCHESTER CITY ART GALLERY

Peter Paul Rubens
1577-1640
LANDSCAPE IN FLANDERS
c.1636

Late in life Rubens delighted in landscape painting, and here he enjoys not only the countryside but also the huge range of colours to be found in clouds. On the far right, the sun catches the side of the hills and trees, illuminating a back layer of clouds brilliant yellow. Further to the left, the same layer catches more direct light and appears white. The clouds in front of the sun, on the other hand, block the light with bluish greys.

Oil on panel, 89.8 x 133.8 cm
BARBER INSTITUTE OF FINE ARTS, BIRMINGHAM

Vincent van Gogh
1853-1890
RAIN, AUVERS
1890

Despite the violent appearance of the rain, the diagonals are painted with delicate overlaid strokes of black, white and violet. They form a screen in front of the landscape, an almost abstract construction of horizontal bands of violet and yellow, the colours softly modulating into one another as Van Gogh carefully places each individual mark. Paradoxically, it is this care that gives the landscape such tremulous power. As the rain slashes across the surface, trees corkscrew up from the centre and a nucleus of ravens bursts from the woods.

Oil on canvas, 48.3 x 99 cm
NATIONAL MUSEUM OF WALES, CARDIFF

Georges Seurat
1859-1891
SUNSET
c.1881

Three trees, whose bases lie on a diagonal, are painted in dots – or splodges, rather – of deep olive greens, black and purple, against a sky which varies from yellow around the trees to orange on the horizon. The handling of the paint conveys mood as strongly as colour. There is an intense energy in the brushstrokes around the central tree, with light burstsing through the leaves, while the ground is painted with calmer dashes of purple and tawny brown. This is a remarkable study of the relative value of colours, in which Seurat combines observation with his knowledge of scientific colour theory; the yellow light of the sunset causing the shadowed trees to be seen as dark purple – yellow's complementary colour.

Oil on wood, 15.2 x 24.8 cm
BRISTOL MUSEUMS AND ART GALLERY

TIME: THE TIME OF LIFE

Life need not always be nasty and brutish but it is undeniably short. The brevity and inconsequentiality of this life – especially when measured against the promise of an eternal after-life – is the subject of innumerable paintings, few as grim or dark as Rosa's Human Frailty. A child signs what is more or less his own death warrant, writing out a medieval poem whose sentiment is echoed much later in Samuel Beckett's Waiting for Godot: 'They give birth astride of a grave, the light gleams an instant, then it's night once more'.

Whereas Rosa is characteristically bleak, Titian, painting a century and a half earlier, is both more lyrical and less explicit. His Three Ages are experienced by a couple as two babies, a pair of lovers and two skulls (contemplated by an old man), and from sleep, through life to death. Mortality is also a central theme of Holbein's great double portrait, emphasised by the extraordinary stretched-out skull seen between the two men, which can only be understood correctly when the picture is viewed from an angle. But life's brevity is also challenged by the painting itself, which has 'immortalised' this odd couple. Indeed, one of the main aims of portraiture was to allow the sitter's appearance and achievements to live for posterity, although, as Gysbrechts suggests, even paintings do not live forever.

▷ Cornelius Gysbrechts
ACTIVE C.1659-C.1678
TROMPE L'OEIL STUDIO WALL WITH VANITAS STILL LIFE
1664
In a corner of the artist's studio a canvas is propped up behind a dripping palette and used brushes. The painting is a standard Vanitas still life, with a guttering candle, soap bubble and skull pointing to the brevity of our earthly span. The corn wrapped round the skull is perhaps more optimistic and may allude to future resurrection, as, once sown, the grains will grow new life. But where some claimed that immortality could be achieved through art, citing the epigram 'ars longa vita brevis' (art is long and life is short), Gysbrechts shows his canvas coming away from its stretcher. Even art is fragile – a further reminder of the illusory appeal of this world.

Oil on canvas, 87 x 70 cm
FERENS ART GALLERY,
KINGSTON UPON HULL

◁ Salvator Rosa
1615-1673
L'UMANA FRAGILITÀ
ABOUT 1656
A skeleton, winged to show the swiftness of death's approach, holds a piece of paper for a child who is transcribing the words of a twelfth-century poem: 'Conception is sinful; Birth a Punishment; Life, Hard Labour; Death, Inevitable.' This message is underlined by a plethora of symbols. One child blows bubbles, which, like the butterflies nearby, are short-lived. Another lights a fire, which will burn out as quickly as the spent rocket lying on the floor. At the top right is Terminus, god of death, and on the left an obelisk, like a funerary monument. This pessimism is understandable, as the painting probably dates from 1656, the year in which Rosa lost his brother and his son.

Oil on canvas, 197.4 x 131.5 cm
FITZWILLIAM MUSEUM, CAMBRIDGE

▷ Hans Holbein the Younger
1497/8-1543
JEAN DE DINTEVILLE AND GEORGES DE SELVE: 'THE AMBASSADORS'
1533
This painting records a specific time: the date is inscribed on the floor and the ages of the two men carefully recorded on the dagger held by Jean de Dinteville on the left and on the book under the arm of Georges de Selve on the right. But within the painting there are also many reminders of the passing of time – there are three different types of sundial on the top shelf, and the skull elongated across the bottom of the painting is a reminder of the vanity of human existence. That this life is lived in the knowledge of a future one is also suggested by the crucifix just visible behind the green curtain at the top left-hand corner of the painting.

Oil on wood, 207 x 209.5 cm
NATIONAL GALLERY, LONDON

Titian
ACTIVE BEFORE 1511, DIED 1576
THE THREE AGES OF MAN
ABOUT 1510-15

The meaning of Titian's apparently idyllic pastoral scene is hard to pin down, but the focus is clearly on the pair of lovers on the left. The pipes refer to their love – not just in the harmony they share together, but also physically – look at the position of the instruments. On the right are three babies in a pyramidal heap, but the wings of the uppermost tell us that only two are mortal:

they could grow up to be the couple on the left. This idea is taken further by the old man in the background contemplating not just one, but two human skulls. Whoever this couple are, the lesson is clear – we move from innocence, through experience, towards our inevitable death.

Oil on canvas, 90 x 150.7 cm
ON LOAN TO THE NATIONAL
GALLERY OF SCOTLAND, EDINBURGH
(DUKE OF SUTHERLAND)

PASSING TIME

Paintings may take time to contemplate but we tend to think of figurative paintings, at least, as representing single moments in time. In the first of Hogarth's witty pair Before and After, the falling apples are caught in mid-air to emphasise the split-second captured. Hogarth describes time's progress by showing two scenes, separated, we understand, by a short space of time and a large amount of frenzied activity. The Victorian painter Solomon achieved a similar – if less witty – effect with his two paintings set in the lawcourts. Intriguingly, the first of these paintings originally stood on its own, the original versions (these are copies by the artist himself) having been painted in 1857 and 1859. The narrative really did unfold over time, keeping the painter's audience in suspense for two years!

However, the idea that a painted image can show only one moment in time is confounded by the other paintings on this page. Both Giovanni di Paolo in the fifteenth century and Braque in the twentieth show the passing of time in a single image. In the earlier painting, the repeated figure of St John the Baptist implies his progress from city gate to mountain path. Braque, in his cubist still life, was responding to the fact that our knowledge of the world and its objects depends on time – and that we do not experience the world as a series of frozen moments.

◀ William Hogarth
1697-1764
BEFORE AND AFTER
1731
Despite the apparent innocence of Before, by the time we get to After the couple's dishevelment – not to mention their exhausted bewilderment – leaves us in no doubt as to what has passed. Hogarth jokes with colours – would you have guessed she had blue stockings, or that her garters matched the bows on her shoes? These colours show the couple to be 'well matched' as the stockings echo his suit, and we see more of the pink lining of his cuffs and collar, the same colour as her dress. But even 'before' we could have told what would ensue. The woman has been gathering apples – ever a symbol of temptation .

Oil on canvas, 37.2 x 44.7 cm
and 37.2 x 45.1 cm
FITZWILLIAM MUSEUM, CAMBRIDGE

Giovanni di Paolo
ACTIVE BY 1417, DIED 1482

**ST JOHN THE BAPTIST
RETIRING TO THE DESERT**
c.1453

*Within this tiny painting – just
one of the surviving fragments of
a far larger altarpiece –
Giovanni di Paolo comes up with
an ingenious solution to a
narrative problem. How do you
show the young St John the
Baptist leaving home and going
off into the wilderness? If you see
him in the wilderness you do not
know where he has come from,
and equally, if you show him
leaving home, how do you know
where he is going? But by
showing him twice you know
both, and can also 'fill in' the
intervening steps along the path.
Having clarified the point of the
narrative, ideas of scale and
'realism' become irrelevant.*

Tempera on wood, 31.1 x 38.8 cm
NATIONAL GALLERY, LONDON

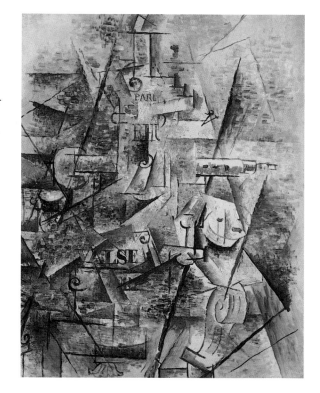

Georges Braque
1882-1963

**CLARINET AND BOTTLE OF
RUM ON A MANTELPIECE**
1911

*Linear perspective, as developed
in the Renaissance, only really
works if you shut one eye and
do not move. But we do move
and therefore see things from
different points of view. This is
what Braque tries to represent:
as time passes, he sees different
parts of an object and paints
them accordingly. The clarinet
seen from the side is a cylinder;*
*and looking from the end its
'bell' is a circle – both are
depicted simultaneously. What
he notices of the mantelpiece is
the curved bracket supporting
it – perhaps because it is like
an inverted treble clef.
Gradually, through time, you
piece the elements together in
the same way that the artist,
painting over time, interpreted
his subject.*

Oil on canvas, 81 x 60 cm
TATE MODERN

Abraham Solomon
1823-1862

WAITING FOR THE VERDICT
1857
THE ACQUITTAL
1859

*A family – a poor one judging by
the style of their dress – is
waiting to find out if the father
will be convicted of an unspecified
crime. If he is, the family will be
condemned to a life of penury.
The outcome is not clear – look at
the double door in the background:
one leaf is shut, the other could
go either way. When the sequel,
The Acquittal, was exhibited
two years later some people were
disappointed at the happy ending!
The painting is far lighter – and
both doors are flung wide open.*

Oil on wood, 31.8 x 39.3 cm
and 32.4 x 40.6 cm
TUNBRIDGE WELLS MUSEUM
AND ART GALLERY

THE MOMENT AND MOVEMENT

A 'moment' is frozen in time, whereas 'movement' implies time's continuity. The two would appear to be mutually exclusive, but in fact the former depends upon the latter: how can we tell it is 'frozen' if there is nothing to say it was moving? This is certainly the case with Caravaggio's Boy Bitten by a Lizard: whatever the interpretation of this painting (and there have been many), what is important is the depiction of the moment of shock.

With the title Rain, Steam and Speed, Turner is telling us that 'speed' is of the essence. Through the blurred atmosphere he shows the front of the on-rushing train with razor-sharp clarity – perhaps mimicking the way that we fasten on to moving objects, but also causing the locomotive to leap forward from the rest of the painting.

For Monet, like his fellow Impressionists, speed was important principally in terms of execution, as he wanted to catch the changing conditions of light and weather, its fleeting nature being one of his major preoccupations. On the other hand, for Balla, a member of the Futurist movement, speed itself was to be a defining feature of the twentieth century and something to be celebrated in its own right – and by this stage the influence of photography is clear.

Joseph Mallord William Turner
1775-1851
RAIN, STEAM AND SPEED: THE GREAT WESTERN RAILWAY
BEFORE 1844
As the train speeds towards us, the steam whips back across the roof of the carriages, smaller and smaller as they get further away. But whereas most artists use perspective to show us depth and space, Turner has turned it round. The bridge gets wider as it reaches us, exaggerating the perspective to show us how the train will look – almost like a cinematic 'zoom'. In the field on the right, a farmer steers a plough pulled by two horses plodding in the opposite direction, while on the track, about two-thirds of the way from the train to the corner of the painting, a hare runs at full speed to escape.

Oil on canvas, 90.8 x 121.9 cm
NATIONAL GALLERY, LONDON

Giacomo Balla
1871-1958
THE HAND OF THE VIOLINIST
1912
A century ago, photography began affecting painting. Balla was influenced by the work of, among others, Etienne Jules Marey, who took photographs that revealed the sequence of the movements of animals and people. There are five hands and, if you look carefully, five violins, all unified by the red and yellow brushstrokes that describe the movement of the hand, and by the cuff, which forms a continuous band. There are also five bows – slashes parallel to the left of the painting.

Oil on canvas, 56 x 78.3 cm
ESTORICK COLLECTION, LONDON

Michelangelo Merisi da Caravaggio
1571-1610
BOY BITTEN BY A LIZARD
1595-1600
Caravaggio gained his early reputation as a painter of still life, and his depiction of the crystal clear vase, delicate flowers and mouth-watering fruit make this easy to understand. Beyond the still life, however, everything is in motion – the boy's awkward position tells us as much. With the sensuous right shoulder thrust forward he looks towards us eyes half-shut and mouth open in shock. The left hand is flung up like the drapery. Dangling from his right hand is a wriggling lizard which must have been hiding among the fruit – Caravaggio has caught the very moment of his surprise.

Oil on canvas, 66 x 49.5 cm
NATIONAL GALLERY, LONDON

Claude Monet
1840-1926
THE CHURCH AT VARENGEVILLE
1882
This moment seems incredible – is the sky ever that yellow? – but once seen in a painting you will see it one day in nature. It is also a moment that was not seen independently. In the early 1880s Monet started to paint his 'series' paintings – to give a better idea of what something looked like he would paint it again and again at different times of day and in different weather conditions. This is one of three paintings of The Church at Varengeville, all of which have a more or less identical composition but extremely different colours. Here we see the church 'against the sunlight'.

Oil on canvas, 65 x 81.3 cm
BARBER INSTITUTE OF FINE ARTS, BIRMINGHAM

► Patrick Caulfield
BORN 1936
INSIDE A WEEKEND CABIN
1969
Caulfield plays games with both perception and representation. The clear black lines tell us the shape of the room, the position of the table and the pitch of the roof, but have the air of a designer's plan – there is no shadow, so no modelling, and no sense of texture whatsoever. The cabin, bench, stools and table are all wood – all brown to 'signify' wood without actually looking like it – with the cloth, just as featureless, as a bright contrast. With the supporting beam right in the middle of the painting, and with excess detail stripped down, Caulfield creates balance and removes all 'incident' to create a calm retreat.

Acrylic on canvas, 274.4 x 183 cm
MANCHESTER CITY ART GALLERY

◄ Raphael
1483–1520
THE CRUCIFIED CHRIST WITH THE VIRGIN MARY, SAINTS AND ANGELS (THE MOND CRUCIFIXION)
c.1503
The crucified Christ is flanked by his mother, Mary, and John the Evangelist, and on the right kneels the repentant Mary Magdalene. All three were present at the Crucifixion, unlike St Jerome, on the left, who would not be born for a few hundred years. He is present as another penitent (like the Magdalene) and is often represented kneeling before a crucifix: his presence here is symbolic rather than 'realistic'. It suggests that the Crucifixion, although a historical event, has a continuing reality. At the top are both sun and moon, which, according to Genesis, God created on the fourth day – to see both is a reminder that He endures throughout eternity. At the peak of the High Renaissance, Raphael looks back to medieval tradition to create an image outside of time.

Oil on wood, 280.7 x 165.1 cm
NATIONAL GALLERY, LONDON

► Piet Mondrian
1872–1944
COMPOSITION
1932
In his early work Mondrian painted realistic landscapes, but after the havoc of the 1914–18 war many artists wanted to bring order into the world. Hence the reduction of unnecessary distractions and any hint of instability. Mondrian concentrated on the absolutes – horizontal and vertical, black and white, and the three primary colours. In this painting the means are even more limited – the single yellow plane is balanced by the large white rectangle in the opposite corner.

Oil on canvas, 45.3 x 45.3 cm
EDINBURGH, SCOTTISH NATIONAL GALLERY OF MODERN ART

TIMELESSNESS

One of the aims of art is to tell us truths beyond the realm of visual reality. As such, paintings are vehicles for contemplation and for spiritual uplift, and in order to take us beyond the world in which we live they must show something that is outside the hubbub and activity of everyday life. The most direct route to stillness is through the balance of symmetry, and this is what Raphael employs. His calm description of the Crucifixion, unlike the horror of the actual event, is perhaps intended to show that God is everlasting, alpha and omega, the beginning and end of time.

Mondrian does not choose symmetry – he never did – but seeks a balance through the careful arrangement of limited means. For him, as for many artists at the beginning of the twentieth century, the fourth dimension was not time, as Einstein had shown it to be, but the spirit. If we want to reach an ideal or inner truth, he believed, the external, visible world is a distraction – so only abstract art can pierce through what we see and inspire us to a timeless 'reality'.

Although Caulfield is not interested in abstraction *per se*, he also strives to achieve balance, his reduction of detail leaving less for us to worry about or to find 'imperfect'. He gives us an almost platonic 'ideal' of a weekend cabin.

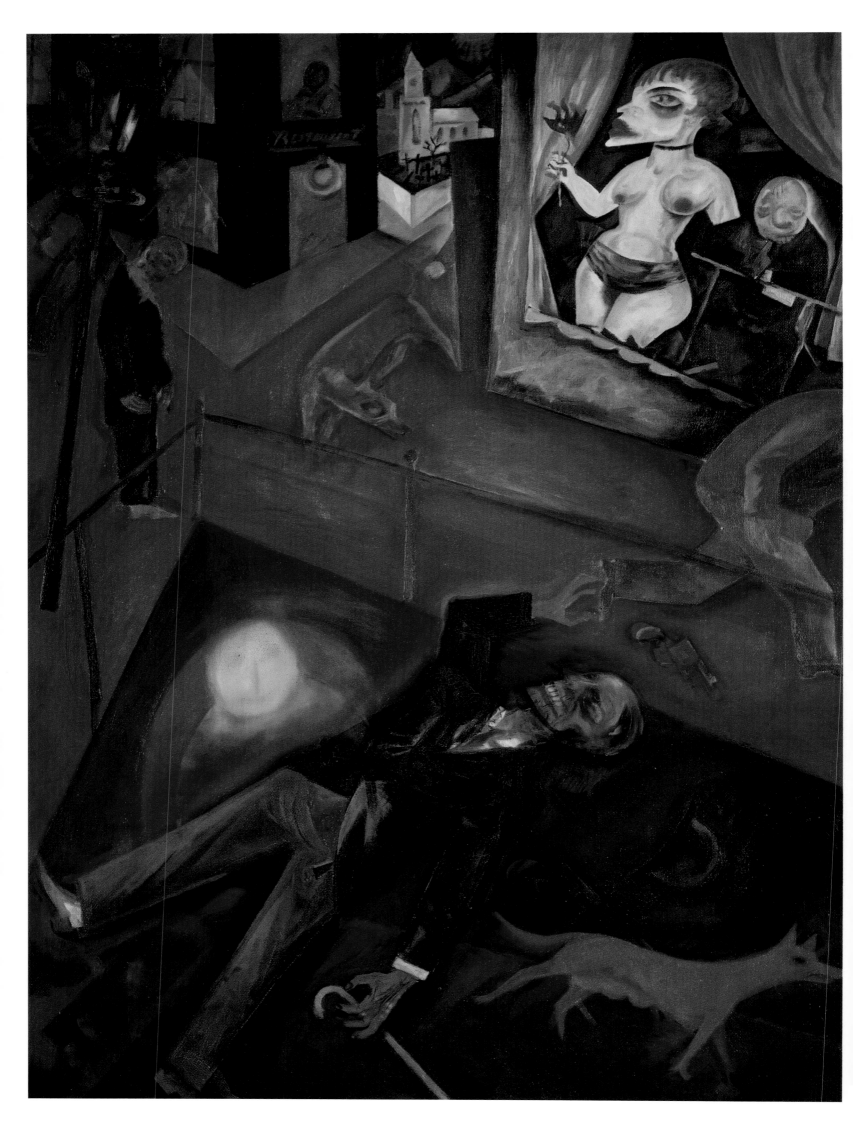

PART 5

PAIN AND PLEASURE

'Painting the passions has always been a
challenge for the artist: how to show, by face or
gesture, lighting or drapery what is going on in
the heart? The even bigger challenge is to show
two conflicting emotions at the same time'

GEORGE GROSZ
SUICIDE
1916

Rembrandt van Rijn
1606-1669
BELSHAZZAR'S FEAST
ABOUT 1636-1638
The king rises panic-stricken to his feet, his gold chain swinging forward as he turns to see the hand of God writing on the wall. The court (or are they courtesans?) stare and, to left and right, wine spills from the sacred vessels, looted from the Temple in Jerusalem and now sacrilegiously used only for partying. It is Belshazzar's moment of truth and the beginning of Babylon's fall. With the exception of the dramatic red on the right, Rembrandt paints the scene in a humble palette of greys, browns, and yellows, matching the turmoil of the figures with the violence of his heavily reworked paint. Earth colours for divine vengeance. Instantaneous alarm, very laboriously achieved.

Oil on canvas, 167.6 x 209.2 cm
NATIONAL GALLERY, LONDON

Nicolas Poussin
1594-1665
THE SHEPHERDS IN ARCADIA
ABOUT 1629
The sunlight catches the trees while a river god gently empties his urn. This is Arcadia, a Classical Shangri-la where shepherds and shepherdesses live and love in happy harmony. Three of them, legs carefully arranged to demonstrate just such harmony, have stumbled on an overgrown tomb on which sits a small skull. The shepherd nearest us leans forward to decipher the Latin inscription. The words 'Et in Arcadia ego' are clear, but their meaning is not. It could mean 'I, too, once lived in Arcadia' – words presumably of the dead shepherd whose tomb this is. Or it could be death itself announcing, 'I am present even in Arcadia.'

Oil on canvas, 101 x 82 cm
CHATSWORTH, DERBYSHIRE

Painting the passions has always been a challenge for the artist: how to show, by face or gesture, lighting or drapery what is going on in the heart? The even bigger challenge – and the one tackled here – is how to show two conflicting emotions at the same time. Easy in language; very, very hard in paint. Two giants, Rembrandt and Picasso, choose radically different approaches. Both, I think, succeed in convincing and disconcerting us.

Rembrandt *(right)* tackles a single moment of sudden change, when Belshazzar, King of Babylon, has decided to give a new twist of dissolute pleasure to his feasting. He has used the holy vessels seized from the Jewish Temple in Jerusalem, just for the extra kick of the sacrilege. The Book of Daniel tells what happened next. As the party was going full swing, a mysterious hand appeared, and wrote on the wall the fatal words, 'Mene, Mene Tekel Upharsin': you are weighed in the balance and found wanting, and your kingdom will be given over to the Medes and Persians. That very night Babylon was invaded and conquered, Belshazzar humiliated and killed. The writing is in Hebrew, in columns running from top to bottom, right to left. You can see that the two right-hand columns are the same – Mene, Mene – and we know that Rembrandt took top-level academic advice from a Jewish friend to ensure accuracy. Yet what intrigues him is the instant in which pleasure turns to panic. If some of the faces are blank with horror, the angle and posture of the bodies are

מנא
תקל
ופרסין

Pablo Picasso
1881-1973
THE THREE DANCERS
1925
In front of French windows, three figures join hands in a mysterious dance. The woman on the left is a frenzy of dislocated emotion, eyes wild and teeth bared as she throws her head back, tossing leg and breast in the air; her sexual availability unequivocal on the front of her skirt. But this is not a dance of pleasure shared. The figure on the right is all angles and awkwardness, while in the middle is an unmistakable echo of the Crucifixion. This is a Dance of Death. Picasso confirmed this by adding in the background the silhouette of a dead friend, and saying he thought it should be called not The Three Dancers, but The Death of Ramon Pichot.

Oil on canvas, 215 x 142 cm
TATE MODERN, LONDON

eloquent. Everything begins to totter. None of this pretentious profligacy will survive the night.

The same mix of religious imagery and party-time debauchery has shaped Picasso's Three Dancers *(left)*, one of his great achievements of the 1920s. It is an echo (a very resounding one) of great agitation in his personal life, of the suicide of one friend precipitated by sexual jealousy, and the early death of another. We do not need to know that, however, to see that the painting is about human misery in the middle of revelry. The shapes themselves have meaning. The woman on the left is, in both posture and gesture, the daughter of countless classical sculptures of the followers of Bacchus, God of Wine, who kill themselves in the destructive fury of drunkenness. Nobody used to western painting can look at these three figures

without seeing in them, or behind them, three others: the crucified Christ with the thieves writhing in pain on their crosses on either side. Only Picasso would dare to telescope the entire European tradition in this way – to bring the gods of the ancient Mediterranean, both pagan and Christian, into a 1920s jazz-turn and show us not one moment of dramatic change but a constant state of the human heart, the daily dialogue between the pursuit of pleasure and the panic fear of death. It is, I think, one of the most unsettling pictures on show in Britain.

Herbert Draper
1863-1920
ULYSSES AND THE SIRENS
1909
Ulysses, the cunning Greek, alone contrives to enjoy supreme pleasure and not pay the price. The song of the sirens, the sweetest music ever heard, lured men to follow the sexy sea-creatures and drown in the deep. Ulysses has blocked his crew's ears with wax so they cannot hear, and lashed himself to the mast so he cannot yield. Draper's crew may look more like Victorian lifeboatmen than Homeric wanderers, but the sirens' moist flesh, the swelling sea and Ulysses' eyes speak lust at any date.

Oil on canvas, 177 x 213.5 cm
FERENS ART GALLERY, HULL

▶ Anthony Van Dyck
1599-1641
THE STONING OF ST STEPHEN
1622-1624

*We are about to witness the first
Christian martyrdom. The newly
elected deacon, Stephen, as
Chapter 7 of Acts of the Apostles
tells us, had caused great offence by
his energetic preaching of the gospel
and was stoned to death for his
pains. His executioners' heads are
in shadow, but Stephen's bleeding
face receives the light of heaven as
he prays, 'Lord, lay not this sin to
their charge.' But Van Dyck goes
far beyond the text, imagining
two angels descending to the
suffering saint with the emblems
of victory – palm and laurel
wreath. The pains of death are
tempered by the certainty of
salvation. Van Dyck – a devout
Catholic – has dressed Stephen as
a seventeenth-century deacon,
underlining the fact that in the
Europe of the 1620s many were
called on to die for their faith.*

Oil on canvas, 99 x 121.9 cm
LEEDS CITY ART GALLERY

▶ Dante Gabriel Rossetti
1828-1882
BEATA BEATRIX
ABOUT 1864-1870

*The pictures on these two pages
are all visions of death opening
the way to spiritual renewal –
each one rooted in personal faith
or experience – Christian, Jewish
or, in this case, poetic. Rossetti has
turned, as he often did, to the
writings of his namesake, Dante,
who, around 1300, composed his
Divine Comedy in memory of
his dead love, Beatrice. The
painter wrote that this is not 'a
representation of the incident of
the death of Beatrice, but... an
ideal of the subject. Beatrice is
rapt visibly into Heaven, seeing,
as it were through her shut lids,
"Him who is Blessed throughout
all ages".' In the background on
the right Dante walks through
a desolate Florence while Love
holds Beatrice's flickering life.
This picture is at once poetic
fantasy and private memorial.
Rossetti's own love, his wife,
Elizabeth Siddal, had died a
few years earlier of an overdose
of laudanum, which surely
explains the white poppy on
Beatrice's arm.*

Oil on canvas, 86.4 x 66 cm
TATE BRITAIN

 Jacob Kramer
1892-1962
THE DAY OF ATONEMENT
1919

*Across the whole of Europe, the
years immediately after the First
World War saw artists address
the themes of communal
commemoration or mourning,
but Kramer's vision of painful
remembrance is like nobody
else's. This Ukrainian Jew,
whose family had fled the
pogroms to find refuge in Leeds
in 1900, when he was eight,
shows us not soldiers marching to
or from battle, but a frieze of
figures – their precise number is
strangely hard to tell – stock still
and dressed in white: a group of
Jewish men in their prayer
shawls. They are playing their
part in the most solemn moment
of the Jewish calendar, the Day
of Atonement, a time of fasting,
total abstinence and penitent
reflection on the year just past –
a year which, in 1919 when the
picture was made, would have
included the ending of the War.*

Oil on canvas, 99 x 121.9 cm
LEEDS CITY ART GALLERY

VIOLENCE

These four paintings of violent acts use very different means to extraordinarily varied ends. The most explicit is also, curiously, the least shocking. Rubens's muscular figures of the murderous Cain and cowering Abel are perhaps too artfully disposed and too physically idealised to engage us too directly with their plight. This is as it should be. Rubens was using the language of Classicism as a filter to render his scene less disturbing and more fitting, perhaps, for the wall of some wealthy patron.

Abel was the first biblical victim of violence, but it is the torture and murder of Christ that has most often been the subject of Western painting. The resulting focus on victimhood and suffering to evoke horror and pity is peculiar to Western art – a disturbing tradition evident on these and the following pages. In Rembrandt's Ecce Homo, the figure of Christ, stripped to the waist and facing outwards, is almost invisible, a little man lost amidst his torturers.

Anonymity also lies behind the unsettling power of the other paintings here. Cézanne's unpleasant picture of a nameless murder in a featureless setting is one of a number of violent and torrid images made by the young artist before he became the analytically measured painter with whom we are familiar. Where Cézanne opts for melodrama, the British artist Weight shows violence as something everyday and almost casual, but equally unexplained.

◀ Paul Cézanne
1839-1906
THE MURDER
1868

Cézanne uses the paint powerfully. Sweeping, gestural brushstrokes conjure up the power and force of two bodies combining to overwhelm another. It is a murder that could be happening anywhere at any time. Cézanne's great friend from school days, the writer Émile Zola, had recently written a grisly account of a murder in his novel, Thérèse Raquin. Cézanne might have been inspired by this or by reading an account of a recent murder in the popular press. It is an unusual work for him in that he concentrates completely on expressing raw emotion.

Oil on canvas, 65 x 80 cm
WALKER ART GALLERY, LIVERPOOL

▲ Rembrandt van Rijn
1606-1669
ECCE HOMO
1634

'Ecce Homo' (Behold the Man) were Pilate's words when he presented Christ to the people before the Crucifixion. Pilate considers Christ innocent of the charge of claiming to be king of the Jews: as he rises from his seat he impatiently rejects the rod of justice which the Jewish elders try to force upon him. The hand of the clock points to six in accordance with John's Gospel: 'At about the sixth hour... he saith unto the Jews, Behold your King!' The priests declared, 'We have no King but Caesar', and to reinforce this the bust on the right is a symbol of temporal Roman power.

Oil on paper mounted on canvas,
54.5 x 44.5 cm
THE NATIONAL GALLERY, LONDON

Peter Paul Rubens
1577-1640
CAIN SLAYING ABEL
c.1608-1609
The painting of heroic nudes in combat was popular from the Renaissance onwards. Rubens was perhaps more interested in displaying his mastery of anatomy and action, learned from his study of works by Michelangelo and others on his recent trip to Italy, than with engaging the spectator in the full horror of his subject. That said, the necessary elements are all in place. The burning offerings, the cause of Cain's jealousy, are visible behind them, and Abel's look of terror and cry of pain recalls Gods words to Cain: 'What hast thou done? The voice of thy brother's blood crieth unto me from the ground.'

Oil on panel, 131.2 x 94.2 cm
COURTAULD INSTITUTE GALLERIES,
LONDON

Carel Weight
1908-1997
ANGER
1955
The artist based his painting on a personal experience. One late afternoon he was wandering the streets around Bishops' Park in Fulham, enjoying the beauty of the sunset. Suddenly he heard the unmistakable sound of a woman screaming in pain. He never discovered the reason for the screams, but this picture shows his imaginings. The sunset and autumn trees dominate the picture and the act of violence, shocking in its intensity, is almost incidental, a small event in a seemingly peaceful suburban world.

Oil on canvas, 91.5 x 122 cm
MUSEUM OF LONDON

SORROW

A much-repeated story from the ancient world tells how the Greek artist Timantes, when painting the death of Iphigenia, painted each mourner more grief-stricken than the last, until he came to paint her father, Menelaos. Unable to raise the pitch higher still, Timantes 'threw a drape over his head and let his most bitter grief be imagined, even though it was not seen.' The grieving figure is an endlessly recurring theme in painting, the representation of the varieties of grief a constant challenge to the artist. The nymph in the background of Rubens's poignant oil sketch of the death of Adonis is just one of the innumerable heirs of Timantes's Menelaos, her face obscured by her hair, but here the hair itself takes on expressive qualities, falling like tears. In Bruegel's The Death of the Virgin, one of this country's great 'hidden' treasures, the mood is infinitely more restrained, grief mingling with prayer, sorrow accompanied by hope and expectation. But here again it is the figures sensed, but not wholly seen, that carry the emotional weight. Joseph Wright's solitary native American mourner – an example of the eighteenth-century concept of 'the noble savage' – follows a different tradition: stoic restraint in the face of not only her husband's death but of meteorological turmoil. Magritte, painting in a post-Freudian world and drawing on the imagery of dreams, offers a more mysterious and less concrete interpretation of sorrow.

René Magritte
1898-1967

THE TASTE OF SORROW
1948

Set against Magritte's characteristic cloudy blue sky, a plant sprouts from an otherwise barren ground. Fleshy, veined leaves grow upward, one of which turns into a dove. But all is not well with this leaf/bird, for a hungry caterpillar has been gnawing at its flesh. Magritte's image is, deliberately, an enigma. Why this strange creature should epitomise sorrow we do not know, but, remarkably, the fact that it does so does not seem absurd.

Oil on canvas, 59.4 x 49.5 cm
BARBER INSTITUTE OF ARTS,
BIRMINGHAM

Pieter Bruegel
c.1525-1569

THE DEATH OF THE VIRGIN
1564-1565

According to legend, on the eve of the Virgin's death the disciples were whisked up by a cloud from around the world and deposited at the door of her house. In Bruegel's haunting painting there are many more than the 12 disciples round the bed and in the shadows. Two candles shed a dim light on the back wall but they hardly register against the miraculous blaze coming from the bed itself. We see a sorrowful vigil over the bed of the dying woman, but also the miraculous moment at which her soul is transported to Heaven.

Oil on panel, 36 x 54 cm
UPTON HOUSE, WARWICKSHIRE,
NATIONAL TRUST

Joseph Wright of Derby
1734-1797

THE WIDOW OF AN INDIAN CHIEF WATCHING THE ARMS OF HER DECEASED HUSBAND
1785

The artist wrote of this subject: 'The picture is founded on a custom which prevails among the savage tribes of America, where the widow of an eminent warrior is used to sit the whole day, during the first moon after his death, under a... tree... on which the weapons and martial habiliments of the dead are suspended.' Wright dramatises the widow's ordeal by silhouetting her figure against nature gone wild, hinting at the emotions raging beneath her stoic façade.

Oil on canvas, 40 x 50 cm
DERBY ART GALLERY

Peter Paul Rubens
1577-1640

VENUS MOURNING ADONIS
ABOUT 1614

Weeping women surround a prostrate naked man. This is the characteristic format for paintings showing holy women mourning over the body of Christ but, here, Rubens has used this familiar arrangement to depict a secular scene. The subject is from Ovid's Metamorphoses. Venus, deeply in love with the mortal Adonis and 'enraptured by the beauty of a man', begs Adonis not to go hunting. He disregards her frantic pleading and is killed by a boar. Artists more usually depicted Venus imploring Adonis as he strides off for the hunt, but in this oil sketch Rubens shows the tragic denouement at the point when Venus 'saw him lifeless, writhing in his blood. She rent her garments, tore her lovely hair and bitterly beat her breasts and, springing down, reproached the Fates.'

Oil on panel, 19 x 26 cm
DULWICH PICTURE GALLERY

DESOLATION

Suffering need not be dramatic or histrionic and the paintings here all revel in their restraint. Understatement allows us, the viewers, to imbue the images with emotional depth. We cannot help reading emotion into even the most neutral of expressions given the right circumstances, a fact recognised by many great screen actors. Dyce and Goya both exploit the barrenness or inhumanity of their settings to suggest the desolation of their characters but they also use visual association: Dyce's Christ and Goya's central prisoner deliberately make us call to mind other images of the tortured and suffering Christ at the Crucifixion. Of course, such exploitation of a common visual language depends on the viewer's recognising the allusion.

The paintings by Gauguin and Van Gogh disturb us in rather different ways. In Gauguin's strange nude we are given no clear indication of the figure's state of mind beyond the suggestive hints of the ominous title, swivelled eyes, stunted bird and the secretive confiding couple. But it is precisely these ambiguous signs that create the undeniable mood of unease. In the case of Van Gogh's self portrait we perhaps know too much. Painted in the immediate aftermath of his infamous assault on his own ear, which marked the shattering of his hopes for a creative collaboration with Gauguin in their Provençal studio, we can not help but read emotional turmoil into what is, in fact, an almost expressionless face.

▼ William Dyce
1806-1864
THE MAN OF SORROWS
1860

The title 'Man of Sorrows' refers to a prophecy of Isaiah – 'He is despised and rejected of men, a man of sorrows' – and usually refers to depictions of Christ displaying his wounds, or else wearing the crown of thorns as he sits on a 'cold stone' awaiting the Crucifixion. Here he sits on a stone, but this is not an episode from the Passion. Dyce, a Scot, shows Christ praying alone on a barren Scottish moor. Presumably this represents Christ's 40 days in the wilderness, but Dyce is not concerned with narrative accuracy. As the title makes clear, this is a man rejected and alone, despised by the hard and rocky world he has come to save.

Oil on board, 34.9 x 48.4 cm
NATIONAL GALLERY OF
SCOTLAND, EDINBURGH

Vincent van Gogh
1853-1890
**SELF PORTRAIT
WITH BANDAGED EAR**
1889

*With bandaged ear deliberately
prominent, it is impossible for us
not to bring to this famous
portrait what we already know of
Van Gogh's circumstances and
future. Dressed in his hat and coat
– it is January and it is cold even
in the South of France – Van
Gogh's intense green eyes do not
meet ours (unusual in a self
portrait) but stare off into the
distance. The almost blank canvas
and Japanese print behind him
may have particular significance
but it is perhaps too easy to over-
interpret them. More telling is the
intense worked-over treatment of
the face – an astonishing array of
colours from greens to mauves
and pinks to yellows.*

Oil on canvas, 60 x 49 cm
COURTAULD INSTITUTE GALLERIES,
LONDON

Paul Gauguin
1848-1903
NEVERMORE
1897

*Both the title and the meaning of
this disturbing painting are
mysterious. Again, we are shown
a figure alone, this time, a nude
Tahitian laid out before us in the
manner of countless nudes. But
this woman, no alluring Venus,
appears under threat. A clothed
couple talk behind her – and her
eyes swivel towards them. On the
window edge, stands an ominous
bird. In the 1890s, the bird and
the painting's title would have
called to mind Edgar Allen Poe's
famous poem, The Raven, in
which the ill-omened bird sits
above the poet's door croaking,
'Nevermore'. Gauguin played
down this association as too literal
and preferred his paintings to be
read more allusively.*

Oil on canvas, 60.5 x 116 cm
COURTAULD INSTITUTE GALLERIES,
LONDON

Francisco Goya
1746-1828
THE INTERIOR OF A PRISON
1793-1794

*The inhumanity that man
inflicts on fellow man is a
recurring theme in the works of
Goya. This astonishing little
painting, made on tin, is one of a
number he made of the interior
of prisons, where his sympathies,
as ever, seem to be with the
victims. A dark cavernous
interior holds a number of
shackled men. Each seems
alone – none talk or look at each
other. One lies on his back, his
tied feet above him, while the
man in the centre, silhouetted
against the light, is deliberately
reminiscent of traditional images
of Christ, bound and awaiting
his Crucifixion.*

Oil on tin, 42.9 x 31.7 cm
THE BOWES MUSEUM,
BARNARD CASTLE

ANGUISH

These are disturbing pages of open mouths and contorted bodies. The artists here may have been attempting different things in these works but they have all used the same tool – the communicative power of the human figure and face. None of these paintings could be described as realistic: all resort to exaggeration, if not to caricature, to express the depths of mental despair.

The parallels are fortuitous but noteworthy: the crazed expression of Blake's Nebuchadnezzar exiled from humanity is almost identical to Ford Madox Brown's Manfred as he contemplates suicide on the peak of the Jungfrau. Nebuchadnezzar is a man reduced to the state of an animal, and the bestial nature of our strongest emotions is similarly suggested by Bacon, who uses the same stooped pose and open mouth. The Babylonian king's seemingly flayed body is similar in its effect to the skull-like face of Grosz's suicide figure.

Bacon's faceless creature, painted in the immediate aftermath of the Second World War, is apparently Mary Magdalene, one of the weeping mourners traditionally depicted at the base of the Cross. But here the figure and her emotion are exploited to more general ends. As Bacon himself admitted, 'Well, there have been so very many great pictures in European art of the Crucifixion that it's a magnificent armature on which you can hang all types of feeling and sensation.'

William Blake
1757-1827
NEBUCHADNEZZAR
1795
In the Old Testament book of Daniel, as punishment for his overreaching power, Nebuchadnezzar, the King of Babylonia, was 'driven out by men, and did eat grass as oxen, and his body was wet with dew from heaven, till his hair was grown like eagle's feathers, and his nails like birds' claws.' He was condemned to live the life of a beast, until he acknowledged God's universal dominion. The extraordinary body of Nebuchadnezzar, which gives the frightening impression that it has been flayed, may well derive from Blake's experience as an art student at the Royal Academy, where he made life drawings from the corpses of hanged criminals. But it is especially Nebuchadnezzar's crazed expression that grips us – a face contorted by a terror at what he has become.

Printed drawing finished in pen and watercolour, 44.6 x 62 cm
TATE BRITAIN, LONDON

George Grosz
1893-1959
SUICIDE
1916
'I lived in a world of my own at this time. My drawings expressed my despair, hate, disillusionment. I had utter contempt for mankind in general.' The Berlin-born artist Grosz came close to being shot in 1914, when he was court-martialled for insulting the German army. When he was invalided in 1915, he put his feelings of 'profound disgust for life' into his art. In Suicide, a grimacing figure, whose skull is already showing beneath the skin, lies dead, a gun near his outstretched hand. Behind him another man hangs from a lamp-post. Nearby, a prostitute entertains a bloated business man. In the background, the church presides over this sinister and cynical world. The garish reds add to the sense of a corrupt world.

Oil on canvas, 100 x 77.6 cm
TATE MODERN

Francis Bacon
1909-1992
FIGURE STUDY II
(STUDY FOR THE MAGDALEN)
1945-1946

The extraordinary sexless figure is bent low, an umbrella shielding her face. Only the screaming mouth is revealed. We do not know the reason for her pain, although the subtitle links her with the Crucifixion. The acuteness of the figure's torment is sharpened by the vivid orange background. This was painted at the end of the war as the horrors of the Holocaust were first being revealed. Bacon used an unusual combination of influences to create his grotesque figure: a book on mouth diseases and the screaming face from Sergei Eisenstein's film The Battleship Potemkin both played a part. 'I did hope one day to make the best painting of the human cry,' he said, and this was the first of many that focused on a screaming, tortured face.

Oil on canvas, 145 x 128.5 cm
HUDDERSFIELD ART GALLERY

Ford Madox Brown
1821-1893
MANFRED ON THE JUNGFRAU
1840

In the second scene of Lord Byron's poem, Manfred is brought close to suicide. Brown depicts him debating whether or not to jump off the mountain and end his life. As Manfred, like Hamlet, weighs up the pros and cons of continuing in so desolate a world, his cloak billows out behind him. In this vertiginous image of the despairing youth poised to plunge into the abyss and end it all, we are made intensely aware of Manfred's physical and mental isolation. Brown, a fan of Byron, has made a romantic image of suicide.

Oil on canvas, 140.2 x 115 cm
MANCHESTER CITY ART GALLERY

PLEASURE: HEAVEN ON EARTH

From the pleasurable groves of Arcadia to the lush richness of the Garden of Eden, our idea of an earthly paradise is firmly rooted in the world of nature. In both the classical and biblical worlds, nature – at its most temperate and nurturing – is shown to be a source of comfort and delight, of physical and spiritual sustenance. Claude conjured up an idyllic world where man and nature co-exist in perfect harmony. His landscapes, with their blue skies, green meadows and glowing light, evoke a lost Golden Age – a place of leisure and pleasure inhabited by shepherds and poets, a balm for the soul. The two other landscapes here focus on the plentiful abundance of nature: Palmer depicts a luxuriant wood with a tree weighed down with glowing fruit, Segantini creates a rural idyll in which workers are transformed into timeless piping rustics, resting on sheaves of corn, with little sense of the effort that would have been required to harvest them. Spencer identified heaven as a place familiar to him – his home village of Cookham. His painting shows the villagers kissing and embracing in a large-scale public celebration of love. For him, heaven on earth was a place of free and open love.

▲ Stanley Spencer
1891-1959
A VILLAGE IN HEAVEN
1937
Spencer's vision of heaven is located within his own personal experience. He sets the scene at Cookham war memorial, where the village girls traditionally met up with their loved ones. But, typically, he combines the familiar with the imaginary, and the secular with the religious. The war monument takes on a totally different role, becoming an altar to love.

Oil on canvas, 43.5 x 183.5 cm
MANCHESTER CITY ART
GALLERY

▶ Claude
1604/5-1682
**LANDSCAPE WITH ERMINIA
AND THE SHEPHERD**
1666
The painting depicts an episode from Tasso's epic poem, Gerusalemme Liberata, in which Erminia, a Saracen, falls in love with Tancred, a Christian knight. She sets off in search of her loved one, but instead finds a shepherd and his children in a shady grove. He convinces her of the rewards of a pastoral life and she decides to stay. Claude pushes to one side Erminia and the shepherd and directs our attention to the softly-lit landscape – the true subject of his painting. The balanced composition provides an aesthetic equivalent to the painting's peaceful subject.

Oil on canvas, 92.5 x 137 cm
NORFOLK, HOLKHAM HALL
(VISCOUNT COKE)

▲ Giovanni Segantini
1858-1899

AN IDYLL
1883

*This is a city-dweller's fantasy of
the countryside – as a place of
peace, innocence and simplicity.
With the day drawing to a close,
the labourers slump exhaustedly
on a haystack, enjoying a
well-deserved rest. One unwinds
by playing a pipe, which evokes
an atmosphere of calm. We see
nothing of the hard toil of
harvesting, only its peaceful
aftermath. Here, man is at
one with his environment: the
land provides him with work,
food and rest. Such idyllic scenes
of rural life were popular with
urban audiences during
the nineteenth century.
The inhabitants of large, modern
cities perhaps found in them an
attractive alternative to the
materialism and sophistication
of their own lives.*

Oil on canvas, 56 x 84.5 cm
ABERDEEN ART GALLERY

▷ Samuel Palmer
1805-1881

THE MAGIC APPLE TREE
c.1830

*Palmer spent a decade in the
Kent village of Shoreham,
hoping that the clean country
environment would improve
his poor health. While there,
he was inspired to paint idyllic
landscapes such as this one: a
pastoral scene where man and
nature are in a close and
harmonious relationship.
The shepherd and sheep are
surrounded by a glowing,
fertile paradise, which includes
a bountiful apple tree, wheat
fields and, at its heart,
a church spire. Nature
appears transformed.
As Palmer wrote, 'Sometimes,
when the spirits are in Heav'n,
earth itself, in emulation,
blooms again into Eden.'*

Pen, indian ink, watercolour
and gum arabic, 34.9 x 27.3 cm
FITZWILLIAM MUSEUM,
CAMBRIDGE

JOY OF THE SENSES

Paintings appeal first and foremost to our sense of sight, but they work only by awakening our other senses. Our response to painting is often almost physical, sight being the vehicle for a host of other sensations. Both Alma-Tadema and Hockney exploit sensual responses to depictions of bare skin with fur, feathers, water and heat in their very different tepidariums, one supposedly in ancient Rome, the other in 1960s Los Angeles. The ability of painting to evoke the tactile also lies behind Zoffany's splendid portrait of Charles Townley with his collection, the basis of the British Museum's holdings of antique sculpture. Here a selection of the most tactile of the arts is re-created on a single canvas, in which the seated Townley, shown in profile, is wittily juxtaposed with the bust of (the blind) Homer above him.

If all art appeals to our sense of touch, the evocation of the other senses in painting is more problematic. Taste can be appealed to through mouth-watering still lifes or, as here, in vibrant scenes of feasting. Far more restrained is Vermeer's painting of a well-dressed woman sitting at a virginal. We expect the evocation of sound but somehow sense stillness and silence – a song interrupted.

△ Honoré Daumier
1808-1879
LUNCH IN THE COUNTRY
c.1868
Without painting food or wine in any detail, Daumier succeeds in conveying the joys of eating, simply by focusing on body language. His skills and observation as a caricaturist are put to superb use: with fluent and cursory lines, he conveys the movement of the figures and, with that, their enjoyment of wining and dining in the open

air. The dog leaps up, his front legs on the table, eagerly awaiting the tasty morsel being offered him. No less reserved is the man in the middle, who clasps his cup and eagerly gulps down its contents. The other two men seem more interested in the dog's appetite than their own – the animal, unhindered by any sense of etiquette, reminds us of our own basic appetites.

Oil on panel, 25.4 x 33 cm
NATIONAL MUSEUM AND
GALLERIES OF WALES, CARDIFF

▷ Johan Zoffany
1733-1810
CHARLES TOWNLEY'S LIBRARY AT 7 PARK STREET, WESTMINSTER
1781-1783
Charles Townley, seated on the right, was a great collector of antiquities, and is shown surrounded by his beloved objects. They are mainly sculptures, works of art that appeal to the senses of both sight and touch. Zoffany, however, translated the tactile pleasures of sculpture into an entirely visual pleasure. Though each object is depicted with absolute accuracy, this is in fact an imagined scene, as the works of art were normally scattered around Townley's house. Some were even acquired after the painting was started: the discus thrower, for example, was added to the picture 15 years later. Such manipulations allowed the picture to show Townley his entire collection in a single glance.

Oil on canvas, 127 x 99 cm
TOWNELEY HALL ART GALLERY
AND MUSEUMS,
BURNLEY BOROUGH COUNCIL

Lawrence Alma-Tadema
1836–1912
IN THE TEPIDARIUM
1881

Alma-Tadema's painting sets out to tease and titillate. Set in a Roman tepidarium, a cool room between the hot and cold baths, the image itself is far from squeaky clean. A naked woman lies on a bearskin, an ostrich feather in one hand and a strigil in the other. For viewers in Victorian Britain, the remoteness of the Classical setting provided an acceptable context for a nude – even one as erotic as this. Everything here is suggestive. While the fur no doubt provided insulation against the cool marble, here it serves as a metaphor for soft female flesh. And although the feather fan conceals, its texture and form also suggest what lies beneath. Finally, the strigil, normally used to scrape oil off backs, is presented as overtly phallic.

Oil on panel, 24.1 x 33 cm
THE LADY LEVER ART GALLERY,
PORT SUNLIGHT

Johannes Vermeer
1632–1675
YOUNG WOMAN SEATED AT A VIRGINAL
c.1670

As the woman looks towards us, we wonder whether we are unwelcome intruders interrupting her play or are being invited to join her in a duet. The viola da gamba offers a clue. Turned outwards, perhaps it awaits a player – we are reminded of the traditional association of music and love. The atmosphere is still and refined, in contrast to the raffish scene in the picture hanging on the wall. A copy of a painting by the artist Dirck van Baburen, it shows a prostitute's madam taking money from a client in exchange for the young woman on the left. Quite what significance this scene of mercenary love was intended to have for the woman below is, perhaps deliberately, unclear.

Oil on canvas, 51.5 x 45.5 cm
NATIONAL GALLERY, LONDON

David Hockney
BORN 1937
PETER GETTING OUT OF NICK'S POOL
1966

In 1964, Hockney moved from rainy Britain to sunny Los Angeles. Inspired by the climate and relaxed lifestyle of California, he made a series paintings of sunlit swimming pools. In this one he focused on a single naked figure, half submerged in the cool water, and half exposed to the warm sunlight. The bright colours convey a sense of dry heat, while the deep blue water suggests its refreshing coolness. We are led to imagine the contrasting sensations of hot and cold, dry and wet – different, yet equally pleasurable. Hockney, like Alma-Tadema, was concerned with the pleasures of looking, but here the artist's focus is a man. In a painting that reflects his own homosexual viewpoint, he celebrates the beauty and desirability of the male body.

Acrylic on canvas, 213.4 x 213.4 cm
WALKER ART GALLERY, LIVERPOOL

Joseph Wright of Derby
1734-1797
THE ANNUAL GIRANDOLA AT THE CASTEL SANT'ANGELO, ROME
1775-1776
Glowing fireworks light up the night sky, illuminating the surrounding area – we see St Peter's Basilica in the background, and the Castel Sant'Angelo silhouetted in the foreground. From its roof, dazzling embers shoot up into the air, forming an exuberant fountain of light. This spectacular display took place twice a year, attracting large numbers of Grand Tourists who travelled to Rome at that time. Throughout his career, Wright was interested in depicting extreme effects of light, and this certainly would have attracted him to the firework display, but the scintillating effects and energy would also have appealed. He envisaged the painting hanging alongside another, of Vesuvius, the famous volcano above Pompeii: 'The one the greatest effect of Nature, the other of Art that I suppose can be.'

Oil on canvas, 138 x 173 cm
WALKER ART GALLERY, LIVERPOOL

EXUBERANCE

The means through which images can transmit emotions are essentially mysterious and no single explanation seems sufficient. Renaissance theorists urged artists to master the depiction of the emotions through facial expression and body language in order to elicit emotional response, arguing that a laughing figure could induce laughter in the viewer, a weeping figure, tears. There is some truth in the notion – it is hard not to raise a smile in front of Reynolds's depiction of maternal joy and childish playfulness – but it is clearly not the only way that paintings move us.

In the eighteenth century, Wright of Derby was one of many artists who attempted to exploit emotional responses to the spectacular and awesome in nature and art – what he would have termed 'the sublime'. Wright described the firework display he witnessed in Rome as the greatest 'effect of Art' he had ever witnessed, but it is the genius of its re-creation in paint that most excites us before his painting. The ability of paint itself to move us – transmitted through its colour, its substance and a magical sensation of the gestures with which it was applied – is where the true mystery lies. Both Van Gogh and Ayres give life and vitality to paint itself. We respond to these paintings physically, reacting to the energy of their making.

Joshua Reynolds
1723-1792
GEORGIANA, DUCHESS OF DEVONSHIRE, LADY GEORGIANA CAVENDISH
1786
Georgiana, Duchess of Devonshire, looks fondly at her daughter. With her hand playfully raised, she is either leading or copying the baby's enthusiastic motions. Reynolds, like other eighteenth-century artists, depicted children as children, celebrating their innocence and natural vivacity rather than painting them as miniature adults. The girl's actions are untouched by the self-consciousness of adulthood, and her entire body conveys her enjoyment. In a similar way, her mother's gesture, elegant yet sincere, captures something of her famously vivacious character.

Oil on canvas, 113 x 140 cm
CHATSWORTH HOUSE, DERBYSHIRE,
THE DUKE OF DEVONSHIRE

Vincent van Gogh
1853-1890
SUNFLOWERS
1888

In 1888, Van Gogh settled in Arles in the South of France. Soon after arriving, he painted a series of paintings of sunflowers, which grow profusely in the region. Using an explosive combination of bright yellows, he managed to capture the climate and bright sunlight of Provence. The painting was made to decorate a room in the artist's new home, which he was preparing for his first guest, Gauguin. Van Gogh hoped Gauguin would become a good friend and artistic partner, and expressed his aspirations in this painting. The colour is significant. Van Gogh believed that yellow had good connotations, conveying harmony and even friendship. His hopes were thwarted, however, when the two artists argued and Gauguin returned to Paris.

Oil on canvas, 92 x 73 cm
NATIONAL GALLERY, LONDON

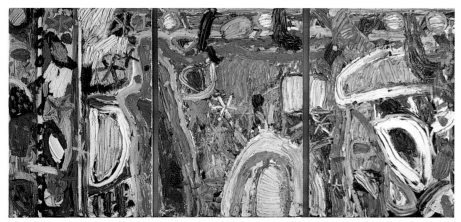

Gillian Ayres
BORN 1930
A MIDSUMMER NIGHT
1990

A riot of bold colours, dynamic patterns, and luscious textures – this painting has energy in its very making. Ayres has concentrated on the expressive power of the paint itself. She has applied it thickly and vigorously, in some places with brushes and elsewhere with her hands (a technique she encountered among the folk artists of Rajasthan during a trip to India). The richly textured surface gives the already vibrant colours and shapes an added dimension. Bright stars, crescents and circles evoke the life and energy associated with long summer nights. In this painting, Ayres combined her recent experience of India with her longstanding admiration for the great colourists of the past – Titian, Rubens and Matisse.

Oil on canvas, 183 x 369 cm
BIRMINGHAM MUSEUM AND ART GALLERY

PAINT AND PLEASURE

Artists and viewers alike derive pleasure from paint – artists from manipulating it and viewers from admiring it. No matter what the subject, the painted surface – the colours, textures and brushwork – always plays a part in drawing us in. The images on these pages can be divided by time, place and technique: they range from the fifteenth to the twentieth century, from the Netherlands and France to the United States. But, although the artists' intentions and techniques are worlds apart, in all of them we are struck and seduced by the quality of the paint itself, and the life that the artists bring to it.

We often marvel at an artist's ability to transform paint into an illusion of the real world. In the superbly refined work of Campin, because we struggle to find the individual brushstrokes with which he achieved his effects, the end result is both mysterious and magical. No such thing with Hals, who doubled the astonishment factor by drawing our attention to his fluent, virtuoso brushwork, while at the same time creating the illusion of sweeping fabric or weathered skin.

Our eye is constantly torn between the painted surface and the painted illusion. In the work of many modern artists, brushwork takes centre stage – nowhere more so than in the work of Seurat and Pollock, whose names we can scarcely separate from their signatory dots and drips.

▲ Robert Campin
1378/9-1444
THE VIRGIN AND CHILD IN AN INTERIOR
c.1435

In this minuscule painting, the artist paid close attention to the smallest detail – from the basket of nappies by the Virgin Mary's side to the burning logs in the fire. We marvel at his refined evocation of textures – the Virgin's silken hair, and the gleaming reflections on the brass bath. He even managed to capture three very different qualities of light: the light of day, which casts shadows around the room, the firelight, which fills the

hearth with a warm glow, and the single lit candle. The key to these effects lies in Campin's technique: he applied several thin layers of translucent oil paint one on top of the other. And did so with such skill and mastery that the results are seamless.

Oil on oak, 18.7 x 11.6 cm
NATIONAL GALLERY, LONDON

▷ Frans Hals
c.1580/3-1666
PORTRAIT OF AN UNKNOWN MAN
1660-1666

Hals is known for his seemingly effortless brushstrokes. We can safely say that he was an artist who knew when to put down his palette and brushes, and consider a painting finished. As a result, his works have a remarkable freshness. With the fluid, confident brushstrokes clearly visible, the luscious paint becomes as pleasing as the overall image to which it contributes. He used colour with similar economy, creating the illusion of skin, hair and fabric with just four colours – black, white, yellow and red. In this portrait, we find a perfect marriage of subject and technique: the man's pose, like Hals's brushstrokes, is jaunty and lively, yet at ease.

Oil on canvas, 79 x 65.4 cm
FITZWILLIAM MUSEUM, CAMBRIDGE

Jackson Pollock
1912-1956
SUMMERTIME: NUMBER 9A
1948

Placing his canvases on the ground, Pollock allowed the paint to drip freely across them. Abandoning traditional artistic instruments – the brush or palette knife – he let the paint create its own mark. This improvisatory technique was based on the idea that art could be determined by the unconscious mind – a view espoused by Surrealist artists. But the marks did not, of course, make themselves – they were influenced by the speed and proximity with which the artist released the paint. The artist's own physical action is therefore reflected in the flow and density of the drips. In a painting that is over five metres long – so long that Pollock would have had to move along it with his pots of paint – we feel we can trace the artist's energetic movement across the canvas.

Oil, enamel and house paint
on canvas, 84.8 x 555 cm
TATE MODERN

Georges Seurat
1859-1891
YOUNG WOMAN POWDERING HERSELF
c.1888-1890

In this painting of a young woman – possibly the artist's mistress – powdering herself, the separate dots create a scintillating effect, as if the powder itself had been released over the painting and magically transformed into specks of pure colour. In the 1880s, Seurat developed a technique of painting that entailed building up images with hundreds of dots of contrasting colours. Influenced by optical science, he believed these separate colours would combine in the eye of the viewer, while retaining their individual freshness and luminosity. The table and corset, for example, appear to be brown but are painted with separate strokes of red, blue and yellow.

Oil on canvas, 95.5 x 79.5 cm
COURTAULD INSTITUTE GALLERIES,
LONDON

CHRONOLOGY OF BRITAIN'S ART
1200-2002

1200-1600
Significant artists whose work may be seen in Britain

This is a comprehensive list of works by a selection of over 200 artists from the thirteenth century to the present day to be found in British collections accessible to the public. Britain's collection of paintings may be astonishingly rich, but, like any collection, it has its strengths and weaknesses, dictated by the history of taste and the enthusiasms of individuals. British collectors were among the first to collect so-called 'primitives' – masters of the early Renaissance – all but ignored from the sixteenth to the late eighteenth century. Among the trailblazers was the Liverpudlian reformer William Roscoe, who, at the turn of the nineteenth century, assembled a superb collection, part of which is now the city's Walker Art Gallery. The collection of fifteenth-century Italian paintings in the National Gallery, unrivalled outside Italy, was assembled in its essentials by the Gallery's first Director, Sir Charles Eastlake, in the mid-nineteenth century, at a time when artists such as Piero della Francesca were comparatively unrecognised in their own country.

Today, works by early Italian and Netherlandish masters are concentrated in the national galleries of London and Edinburgh, but there are also important Renaissance collections in university museums in Oxford (Ashmolean), Cambridge (Fitzwilliam), London (Courtauld Institute) and Birmingham (Barber Institute) and others in the city museums of Birmingham, Glasgow, Liverpool and Manchester. The Royal Collection is also rich in Renaissance masterpieces. Elsewhere, there are plenty of joys: a gripping painting by the Sienese master Sassetta in the Bowes Museum in County Durham; a Crucifixion by his compatriot Giovanni di Paolo in Rochdale; a haunting Bruegel in Upton House in Warwickshire and a great Tintoretto in Gateshead.

KEY CCPG: Christ Church Picture Gallery CMAG: City Museum and Art Gallery DPG: Dulwich Picture Gallery
NWMAG: New Walk Museum and Art Gallery NGS: National Gallery of Scotland NMM: National Maritime Museum
NT: National Trust NTS: National Trust for Scotland RC: Royal Collection RSCC: Royal Shakespeare Company Collection
SNGMA: Scottish National Gallery of Modern Art V&A: Victoria and Albert Museum • Painting illustrated

Many pictures are subject to conflicting views about who painted them. Unfortunately we are unable to detail the various opinions on each painting here. The blanket term 'attributed' indicates that there has been discussion at some time as to the status of the picture. New research is frequently presented and dismissed and the attributions within this book are subject to change and debate.

Similarly the inclusion of a particular picture does not mean that it will always be on view. Temporary exhibitions and necessary conservation mean that works are occasionally removed from their permanent homes. Items from the Royal Palaces may sometimes be included in exhibitions at the Queen's Gallery, Buckingham Palace and items from the Tate collections may be on display at St. Ives, Liverpool, Modern or Britain. Readers are therefore advised to telephone institutions before visiting to confirm that the items they wish to see are available.

Westminster Abbey: Westminster Retable

1200-1300

CIMABUE
?c.1240 – Pisa 1302
Often regarded as the founder of the Italian Renaissance and the master of Giotto (see col. 3) which he may or may not have been. Cimabue was a Florentine artist who worked in the Byzantine style, to which he gave a greater sense of three-dimensionality. He is best known for his Crucifixes and Madonna and Child altarpieces. He also painted frescos at San Francesco, Assisi. His name, meaning 'Bull-head', may refer to the pride he took in his work, a characteristic mentioned by Dante.
London National Gallery
•Virgin and Child Enthroned with Two Angels

DUCCIO DI BUONINSEGNA
Active 1278 – d.Siena 1319
The leading Sienese painter of his time. His most important work was the Maesta ('Majesty') for the high altar of Siena Cathedral. In this he illustrated scenes from the lives of Christ and his mother, three of which are in the National Gallery, depicting them in an original and readily understandable manner. His Madonna and Child images often show a touching tenderness as well as religious devotion.
Hampton Court Palace RC
Crucifixion and Other Subjects (triptych)
London National Gallery
•The Annunciation, Jesus opens the Eyes of a Man born Blind
The Transfiguration
The Virgin and Child with Saints Dominic and Aurea (triptych)
The Virgin and Child with Four Angels (follower)

Crucifixion (attributed)
Oxford CCPG
Virgin and Child with Saints (attributed)

GIOTTO DI BONDONE
Near Florence c.1267 – Florence 1337
The greatest painter of his time. Best known for his frescos. His realistic style is considered a forerunner of the Renaissance. In his famous poem The Decameron, written in about 1350, Boccaccio credited Giotto with restoring art after the dark ages, painting realistic figures from nature. Giotto worked in many places throughout Italy, but especially Florence, where he painted important and influential fresco cycles.
London National Gallery
•Pentecost (attributed)
Oxford Ashmolean Museum
Virgin and Child (attributed)

1300-1400

BERNARDO DADDI
1290 – 1348
Daddi was probably a pupil of Giotto. His most important paintings are small, made for private devotions or as portable altarpieces with hinged wings, which could be carried on journeys. Although his figures do not have the monumentality of Giotto's, he did acquire Giotto's ability to depict space and to relate a narrative.
Edinburgh NGS
•Crucifixion (triptych)
Hampton Court Palace RC
Marriage of the Virgin (predella panel)
London Courtauld Institute
Crucifixion with Saints (polyptych) (1348)
Saint Peter (attributed)
Virgin and Child with Angels and Saints (triptych) (1338)
London Wallace Collection
Nativity (attributed)

TADDEO GADDI
c.1300 – 1366
A pupil of Giotto, with whom he stayed for many years. He is credited with passing on Giotto's style to the next generation of painters. He worked principally for the Franciscan Order in Florence, for whom he painted the Life of the Virgin fresco in Santa Croce, which reveals his lively story-telling skills.
Bristol City Art Gallery
•Crucifixion and Lamentation over the Dead Christ
London Courtauld Institute
Virgin and Child enthroned with Two Angels (attributed)

PIETRO LORENZETTI
Active 1326 – d.1345
Sienese artist, influenced by Duccio. He was one of the earliest painters to depict a night sky: see the Last Supper and Betrayal scenes in the Lower Church of San Francesco, Assisi. He worked mainly in Siena as a painter of altarpieces, sometimes with narrative scenes which are set in a convincingly depicted three-dimensional space.
Cambridge Fitzwilliam Museum
Crucifixion (attributed)
London National Gallery
•Saint Sabinus before the Governor of Tuscany (?) (attributed)

SIMONE MARTINI
c.1284 – Avignon 1344
Best known for his elegant and courtly style. Probably a native of Siena, where he painted the fresco of Guidoriccio da Fogliano before Montemassi in the Palazzo Pubblico. He also worked in Naples and Assisi before moving to Avignon, where he sought papal patronage. While there he is supposed, according to Petrarch, to have painted the portrait of the poet's beloved Laura.

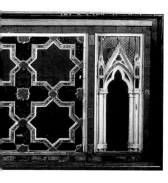

1400-1500

FRA ANGELICO
Near Vicchio c.1395 – Rome 1455

One of the leading Florentine Early Renaissance painters, he was also a Dominican friar. He painted at the convent of San Domenico di Fiesole, Florence, where he became Prior. He also worked for the Medici (the ruling family of Florence), for whom he painted altarpieces and devotional images, and the Pope in the Vatican palace, where his Nicholas V Chapel still survives. Known for his deep devotion, expressed in his painting through his use of light, luminous colours.

Hampton Court Palace RC
Saint Peter Martyr
London Courtauld Institute
Imago Pietatis surrounded by Saints,
Virgin and Child Enthroned between Two Saints (three predella panels; attributed)
London National Gallery
•Christ glorified in the Court of Heaven
A Martyr Bishop or Abbot (attributed)
Oxford Ashmolean Museum
Virgin and Child adored by Saint Dominic (triptych; attributed)
Oxford CCPG
Virgin and Child with Saints (triptych; attributed)

Birmingham Barber Institute
•Saint John the Evangelist (1320)
Birmingham CMAG
An Apostle
Cambridge Fitzwilliam Museum
Saint Geminianus, Saint Augustine, Saint Michael (triptych; attributed)
Liverpool Walker Art Gallery
Christ discovered by his Parents in the Temple (1342)

WESTMINSTER RETABLE
c.1270-90

A very rare, much damaged example of a surviving painting of the courts of King Henry III and Edward I. Of a very high standard and painted in a courtly style, it may have been the high altarpiece of Westminster Abbey. Copies of the figures, made in 1827 when its importance was finally recognised, indicate something of its original splendour.
London Westminster Abbey

WILTON DIPTYCH
c.1395

An outstanding painting (now in the National Gallery), yet no artist has been identified as the painter of this diptych (or two-panelled painting). It is named after Wilton House, where it used to be. It was almost certainly painted for the English king Richard II but the artist may have come from Continental Europe, perhaps France or Bohemia.
London National Gallery

Giovanni Bellini: Head of a Boy

ANTONELLO DA MESSINA
Messina c.1430 – Messina 1479

Probably trained in Naples, where he learned the oil painting technique. He was influenced by Netherlandish paintings and introduced the precise Netherlandish technique into Italian painting. He painted altarpieces but also small collectors' pieces such as his Saint Jerome in his Study (National Gallery) and portraits. His visit to Venice in the 1470s had a major impact on artists there.
London National Gallery

•Crucifixion (1475)
Salvator Mundi (1465)
Portrait of a Young Man
Saint Jerome in his Study

GIOVANNI BELLINI
Venice c.1431 – Venice 1516

The leading and long-lived painter of the Early Renaissance in Venice, who modernised Venetian painting following Florentine developments. He was one of the first Italian painters to begin painting with oil paint, instead of egg tempera. He and his busy workshop – perhaps including the young Titian – painted many images of the Madonna and Child as well as altarpieces and portraits.
Birmingham Barber Institute
•Head of a Boy
Saint Jerome in the Desert
Birmingham CMAG

Virgin and Child enthroned with Saint Peter, St Paul and a Donor (1505)
Bristol City Art Gallery
Descent into Limbo (after Mantegna)
Glasgow Art Gallery and Museum
Virgin and Child
Glasgow Burrell Collection
Virgin supporting the Child on a Parapet
Hampton Court Palace RC
The Concert (attributed)
A Young Man
Harewood House, Yorkshire
Madonna and Child with Donor
Liverpool Walker Art Gallery
A Young Man (much damaged)
London Courtauld Institute
Assassination of Peter Martyr (attributed)
London National Gallery
The Agony in the Garden
Assassination of Peter Martyr
The Blood of the Redeemer
Portrait of Doge Leonardo Loredan
The Madonna of the Meadow
Pietà
Saint Dominic
Virgin and Child
Virgin and Child
Oxford Ashmolean Museum
Saint Jerome in the Desert (attributed)
Southampton City Art Gallery
Virgin and Child (damaged)

BARTOLOMÉ BERMEJO
?Cordoba 1440 – ?Barcelona 1495

The greatest painter of fifteenth century Spain. Known as Bermejo ('red') perhaps because he had red hair. The influence of Netherlandish art on his paintings suggests that he trained in the Netherlands. His unreliability as a painter led one patron to threaten him with excommunication if he failed to complete an altarpiece on time. Even then he failed to meet the deadline, although he seems to have escaped excommunication.
London National Gallery
•Saint Michael triumphant over the Devil with the Donor Antonio Juan

SANDRO BOTTICELLI
Florence 1444-5 – Florence 1510

Although best known for his mythological paintings, such as The Birth of Venus, he also painted religious works and portraits. He was close to the circle of Lorenzo de' Medici, the head of the ruling family of Florence and was one of the artists to fresco the walls of the papal Sistine Chapel in Rome. He is reputed to have enjoyed jokes and puns but was also influenced by the puritanical religious teachings of the Florentine friar Savonarola.
Birmingham Barber Institute
Virgin and Child with the Young Saint John (attributed)
Birmingham City Art Gallery
Descent of the Holy Ghost (damaged)
Buscot Park, Berkshire NT
Nativity with the Young Saint John (attributed)
Cardiff National Museum of Wales
Virgin and Saint John adoring the Christ Child (attributed)

Fra Angelico: Christ glorified in the Court of Heaven

Edinburgh NGS
Virgin and Saint John adoring the Christ
Child (attributed)
• The Virgin adoring the Sleeping Christ
Child
Glasgow Art Gallery and Museum
Annunciation
London Courtauld Institute
Trinity with Saint John the Baptist, the
Magdalen, Tobias and the Angel
(attributed)
London National Gallery
Adoration of the Kings
Adoration of the Kings
Scenes from the Life of Saint Zenobius
(two panels)
Mystic Nativity (1500)
Venus and Mars
A Young Man
London V&A
A Woman (Esmerelda Bandinelli?)
Oxford CCPG
Five Sibyls seated in Niches (attributed)

DIERIC BOUTS
Haarlem c.1415 – Louvain 1475
His paintings are characterised by rather
thin, elongated figures with delicate heads
and limbs set in or before an atmospheric
landscape. One of his most important
commissions was a series of Justice
paintings for Louvain Town Hall. His two
sons inherited his workshop and
continued his style.
London National Gallery
• The Entombment
The Virgin and Child
The Virgin and Child
Portrait of a Man
Penrhyn Castle, Gwynned NT
• Saint Luke painting the Virgin (studio)

ROBERT CAMPIN
?Tournai 1406 – Tournai 1444
Surviving documents show Campin was
frequently employed on official
commissions for the city of Tournai as
well as by private patrons, but no signed
pictures survive. The works associated
with him are sometimes described as
being by 'the Master of Flemalle'. A painter
of extraordinary skill and refinement, he
probably taught Rogier van der Weyden.
London Courtauld Institute
• The Entombment (triptych)
London National Gallery
A Man and a Woman
The Virgin and Child in an Interior (workshop)
Portrait of a Man (follower)
The Virgin and Child Before a Firescreen
(follower)

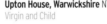

Gerard David: The Legend of Saint Nicholas

GERARD DAVID
Oudewater c.1460 – Bruges 1523
His paintings are almost exclusively
religious, painted for religious
organisations and clerics. Following his
move to Bruges in 1484, much of his work,
with its precise detail, shows the influence
of Jan van Eyck and Memlinc. The
participants in his paintings tend to look
impassive and detached. In 1507 he joined
the Brotherhood of Our Lady of the Dry
Tree, a religious society whose members
were of high social status.
Edinburgh NGS
• The Legend of Saint Nicholas (three
panels)
London National Gallery
Christ nailed on the Cross
An Ecclesiastic Praying
Canon Bernardinus de Salviatis and Three
Saints
The Virgin and Child with Saints and Donor
The Deposition
The Adoration of the Kings
Upton House, Warwickshire NT
Virgin and Child

PETRUS CHRISTUS
Active 1444 – d.Bruges 1475/6
Influenced by Jan van Eyck and Rogier
van der Weyden, Petrus Christus had a
successful career in the Netherlandish city
of Bruges. He bought citizenship there in
1444 so that he could join the local
painters' guild, thus giving him the right to
work there. Both his portraits and
religious paintings are frequently set in
domestic interiors.
Birmingham CMAG
Christ as the Man of Sorrows
London National Gallery
Edward Grimston (on loan)
• Portrait of a Young Man

Jan van Eyck: A Man in a Turban

DOMENICO VENEZIANO
Active 1438 – d.Florence 1461
Little is known about him, although he was
presumably from Venice and moved to
Florence by 1438. One of the leading
contributors to the Florentine Renaissance
style, he combined perspective with
convincing naturalistic depiction of light.
His colours tend to be bright and light, as
typified by his best-known surviving work,
The St Lucy Altarpiece.
Cambridge Fitzwilliam Museum
• Annunciation; Miracle of Saint Zenobius
(predella panels from the Saint Lucy
Altarpiece, Florence, Uffizi)
Glasgow Burrell Collection
The Judgement of Paris (attributed)
London National Gallery
Virgin and Child Enthroned and Two Heads
of Saints (much damaged fresco
fragments)

ERCOLE DE'ROBERTI
Ferrara c.1450 – Ferrara 1496
Court painter to Duke Ercole I d'Este of
Ferrara in North East Italy and his
Duchess, Eleonora of Aragon, for whom he
painted religious and allegorical works. He
also contributed to the Salone dei Mesi
frescos in Ferrara's Palazzo Schifanoia, for
the previous ruler. He made many of the
splendid objects, including the nuptial bed
produced for the marriage of the Duke
and Duchess's daughter, Isabella d'Este, to
the Marquis of Mantua.
Liverpool Walker Art Gallery
• Pietà
London Courtauld Institute
Christ carrying the Cross (attributed)
London National Gallery
The Israelites gathering Manna
Last Supper
Nativity; The dead Christ upheld by Angels
(diptych)

JAN VAN EYCK
?Maaseyck c.1390 – Bruges 1440
Probably the best-known Early
Netherlandish painter. He was court
painter to Philip the Good, Duke of
Burgundy, and had the title varlet de
chambre. He travelled to Portugal for the
duke to record in paint the portrait of the
princess the Duke was to marry. Van Eyck
used oils to great effect, creating lustre
and luminosity, which has earned him the
highest praise during and since his lifetime.
London National Gallery
Portrait of a Young Man
• A Man in a Turban
The Arnolfini Portrait

GENTILE DA FABRIANO
Fabriano c.1370 – Rome 1427
Painted a fresco in the Doges' Palace,
Venice, before moving to Brescia, where
he attracted the attention of Pope Martin V,
who invited Gentile to work for him. The
artist joined the Pope in Florence where
he executed his most famous work, the
Strozzi Altarpiece. He arrived in Rome in
1427, receiving a major commission to
paint in the Lateran church of St John, but
died before it was barely begun.
London National Gallery on loan from HMQ
• Virgin and Child with Angels

DOMENICO GHIRLANDAIO
Florence 1449 – Florence 1494
Leading painter of fresco cycles during the
late fifteenth century in Florence, he was
also one of the team which worked in the
Sistine Chapel in the Vatican. The subjects
of his religious paintings are often placed in
a familiar contemporary world, frequently
with a mountainous landscape, showing
the influence of Netherlandish painting. He
was assisted by his brother and nephews,
and was Michelangelo's master.
Cambridge Fitzwilliam Museum
Virgin and Child enthroned between St
Ursula and Saint Catherine (attributed)
London National Gallery
• The Virgin and Child
A Legend of Saints Justus and Clement of
Volterra
Portrait of a Young Man in Red
Oxford Ashmolean Museum
A Young Man (attributed)

Giovanni di Paolo: Crucifixion (predella)

GIOVANNI DI PAOLO
Siena 1403 – Siena 1482

Worked as a manuscript illuminator illustrating Dante's Divine Comedy, and was also a panel painter. His early paintings show little awareness of the developments in nearby Florence but later, influenced by Sassetta, he introduced a greater sense of three-dimensional space and volume. He was chosen by Pope Pius II to paint an altarpiece for the new cathedral at Pienza.
Cambridge Fitzwilliam Museum
Entombment of the Virgin; St Bartholomew; A female saint (predella)
Saint Bartholomew
London National Gallery
The Birth of Saint John the Baptist (predella)
Saint John the Baptist retiring to the Desert (predella)
The Baptism of Christ (predella)
The Feast of Herod (predella)
Saints Fabian and Sebastian
Oxford Ashmolean Museum
Baptism of Christ (predella)
Virgin and Child
Oxford CCPG
Crucifixion
Rochdale Art Gallery
•Crucifixion (predella)
Upton House, Warwickshire NT
Presentation of the Virgin in the Temple (predella)

be damned. Although he recovered, he died shortly afterwards. His Portinari Altarpiece, transported to Florence in 1483, greatly influenced Florentine artists.
Bath Victoria Art Gallery
Adoration of the Kings (attributed)
Edinburgh NGS
•The Trinity Altarpiece (shutters on loan from the Royal Collection)
Oxford CCPG
The Deposition (very damaged fragment)
Wilton House, Wiltshire
Nativity

LEONARDO DA VINCI
Vinci 1452 – Amboise 1519

The 'Renaissance man'. A polymath who studied nature and science, designed buildings, military equipment and machinery. He made numerous anatomical studies. As a painter he completed few works, preferring to experiment, sometimes disastrously, as with his Last Supper in Milan, which was falling off its wall almost

as soon as it was finished. He was court painter to the Duke of Milan, but after the French invasions he returned to Florence before spending his last years in France.
Bowhill, Selkirkshire
The Madonna of the Yarnwinder (attributed)
London National Gallery
•The Virgin of the Rocks

FILIPPINO LIPPI
Prato 1457 – Florence 1504

The son of Fra Filippo Lippi (see below), and a contemporary of Botticelli, Filippino ('Little Filippo') worked mainly in Florence for leading citizens including Lorenzo de'Medici. His paintings are characterised by a highly energetic and linear style.
Edinburgh NGS
Nativity with Two Angels
Saint John the Baptist in the Wilderness
Glasgow Art Gallery and Museum
Virgin and Child with Saint John and Two Angels
Liverpool Walker Art Gallery
Virgin and Child (attributed)
London National Gallery
Adoration of the Kings
The Virgin and Child with Saint John
The Virgin and Child with Saints Jerome and Dominic

HUGO VAN DER GOES
Active Ghent 1440 – d.Brussels 1482

Probably born in Ghent in the Netherlands, where he became a member of the painters' guild in 1467. He entered the monastery of Rode Klooster near Brussels in about 1475 and continued to live and work there until his death. Returning from a visit to Cologne, he went mad, believing himself to

Leonardo da Vinci: The Virgin of the Rocks

Filippo Lippi: Virgin and Child with Angels and Saints

An Angel Adoring (fresco fragment)
London (Blackheath) Ranger's House EH
Rest on the Flight into Egypt
(on loan from the Wernher Collection)
Oxford CCPG
Five Sibyls in Niches (attributed)
•The Wounded Centaur

FILIPPO LIPPI
Florence c.1406 – Spoleto 1469

Left an orphan, he grew up in the convent of Santa Maria del Carmine, Florence, later taking orders as a priest. He may have assisted Masaccio in frescoing the Brancacci Chapel in that church and his early paintings certainly owe a debt to Masaccio's works. While painting the choir of Prato cathedral (then the parish church), he set up house with a nun, Lucrezia Buti, who bore him a son, Filippino (see above).
Cambridge Fitzwilliam Museum
•Virgin and Child with Angels and Saints (triptych)
Corsham Court, Wiltshire
Annunciation
London Courtauld Institute
Female Saint with a Flail (attributed)
Saint Dominic (attributed)
Saint James the Less (attributed)
Saint Peter (attributed)
London National Gallery
Saint Bernard's Vision of the Virgin
The Annunciation
Seven Saints
Oxford Ashmolean Museum
Meeting of Saint Joachim and Saint Anne at the Golden Gate (predella)

ANDREA MANTEGNA
Isola da Carturo 1431 – Mantua 1506

Trained as a painter in Padua, near Venice, he became court artist to Ludovico Gonzaga, Marquis of Mantua, where he was able to indulge his passionate interest in antiquity. He produced many paintings, frescos, altarpieces, devotional works and portraits for successive Gonzaga rulers, the best known being the Camera Picta (or

Carmera degli Sposi), in which members of the Gonzaga family are depicted gathered together in family groups.
Hampton Court Palace RC
•The Triumphs of Caesar (nine panels)
(This panel: Trumpeters, Bearers of Standards and Banners)
London National Gallery
The Agony in the Garden
The Virgin and Child with the Magdalen and Saint John the Baptist
Tuccia
A Woman Drinking
Samson and Delilah
The Holy Family with Saint John
The Introduction of the Cult of Cybele at Rome

MASACCIO
San Giovanni Val d'Arno 1401 – Rome 1428

Despite a short career, probably the most influential Early Renaissance artist. He developed a highly realistic style, setting his monumental, three-dimensional figures in a naturalistic setting and using the newly developed system of perspective. Abandoning his most famous work, the Brancacci Chapel frescos, he went to Rome probably in search of more important patrons, but died shortly after his arrival.
London National Gallery
•The Virgin and Child
Saints Jerome and John the Baptist
Saints Liberius and Matthias (with Massolino)

Piero di Cosimo: A Satyr mourning over a Nymph

MASTER OF THE ST BARTHOLOMEW ALTARPIECE

Active Cologne after 1450 –
d.Cologne c.1510
The most accomplished painter and manuscript illuminator working in Cologne in the later fifteenth century. Like most German artists of the period he never signed his works and so he is named after the Altarpiece made for the Carthusian church of St Columba in Cologne and is now in Munich. His idiosyncratic and instantly recognisable paintings show the influence of Netherlandish artists.
London Courtauld Institute
Head of a Saint
London National Gallery
The Virgin and Child with Musical Angels
•The Deposition
Saints Peter and Dorothy
Polesden Lacey, Surrey NT
Head of a Youth (attributed)
Waddesdon Manor, Buckinghamshire NT
Virgin and Child with Saints

HANS MEMLINC

Seligenstadt 1430–40 – d.Bruges 1494
German artist who settled in Bruges in 1465, becoming its leading painter. He painted altarpieces, devotional images and portraits, which with a vivid immediacy make the sitters seem alive. His most important works were the triptych of St John the Baptist and

St John the Evangelist, and a reliquary of St Ursula for the Hospital of St John, Bruges, now the Memlinc Museum.
Birmingham CMAG
Nativity (companion to Glasgow; attributed)
Glasgow Burrell Collection
Rest on the Flight into Egypt (companion to Birmingham)
•The Virgin of the Annunciation (attributed)
London National Gallery
The Virgin and Child with an Angel, Saint George and a Donor
Saints John the Baptist and Lawrence
A Young Man at Prayer
The Donne Triptych
The Virgin and Child
London Wallace Collection
The Archangel Michael
London (Blackheath) Ranger's House EH
Virgin and Child (on loan from the Wernher Collection)
Upton House, Warwickshire NT
A Man
Windsor Castle RC
A Man

PERUGINO

Citta della Pieve c.1450 – Fontignano, Perugia 1523
Trained in Florence, Perugino worked for many important patrons, including Pope Sixtus IV, for whom he led the team of artists who frescoed the walls of the Sistine Chapel in the Vatican. Many of his paintings include lyrical landscapes, based on that of his native Umbria. He fell out of fashion in the early sixteenth century and worked mainly for small, provincial centres during his last years.
Cambridge Fitzwilliam Museum
Virgin and Child in a Landscape (attributed)
Edinburgh NGS
Apollo with Three Male Nudes standing
Liverpool Walker Art Gallery
Birth of the Virgin (predella; attributed)
London National Gallery
The Virgin and Child with an Angel.
St Michael
•The Archangel Raphael with Tobias ; The Virgin and Child with Saint John; The Virgin and Child with Saints Jerome and Francis (three panels of an altarpiece)
London V&A
Nativity (fresco)
Polesden Lacey, Surrey NT
Miracle of the Founding of S. Maria Maggiore (predella; attributed)

PIERO DI COSIMO

?Florence 1461/2 – Florence 1521
A Florentine contemporary of Botticelli and Filippino Lippi, he developed a highly idiosyncratic style and often painted unusual subject matter. He made many furniture paintings with mythological subjects, which were fashionable at the time, often displaying deep sensitivity. His first biographer, Vasari, described him as an eccentric recluse living on hard-boiled eggs that he boiled in batches of fifty.

Edinburgh NGS
Two censing Angels holding a Crown (attributed)
London National Gallery
•A Satyr mourning over a Nymph
The Fight between the Lapiths and the Centaurs
London (Dulwich) DPG
A Young Man
Oxford Ashmolean Museum
A Forest Fire

PIERO DELLA FRANCESCA

Borgo San Sepulcro 1410-20 – Borgo San Sepulcro 1492
Now regarded as one of the greatest of all artists of the Italian Renaissance, Piero was all but forgotten in the years after his death. He was rediscovered in the nineteenth century and championed by many twentieth-century critics who responded to the geometrical rigour and calm monumentality of his works, which make his characters seem remote and introverted. He was also a theorist of perspective and mathematics.
London National Gallery
The Baptism of Christ
Saint Michael
•The Nativity

SASSETTA

Siena 1395 – Siena 1450
The first Sienese painter to take account of Florentine developments in the depiction of perspective, while still retaining the Sienese style. His most important work was the altarpiece for San Francesco, Borgo San Sepulcro, made up of a number of panels of great charm and tenderness illustrating the life of St Francis. Seven of these are now in the National Gallery.
Barnard Castle Bowes Museum
•Miracle of the Holy Sacrament
London National Gallery
Seven Scenes for the Life of Saint Francis

PAOLO UCCELLO

Florence 1397 – Florence 1475
Painter of the early Florentine Renaissance, who was famously obsessed by the perspective construction. According to one story, he refused his wife's calls to bed in order to devote himself to his perspective studies. His best-known works are the three panels illustrating The Rout of San Romano, one of which is in the National Gallery, in which the foreground perspective is established by broken lances on the ground, while the background landscape appears to rise abruptly in a decorative pattern.
London National Gallery
The Battle of San Romano
•Saint George and the Dragon
Oxford Ashmolean Museum
The Hunt in the Forest

Piero della Francesca: The Nativity

ANDREA DEL VERROCCHIO
Florence 1435 – Venice 1488
Primarily a sculptor and much employed by the Medici in his native Florence. A number of paintings are attributed to him and his thriving workshop, in which many young artists studied. One of them, Leonardo da Vinci, is thought to have contributed to a number of Verrocchio's paintings.
Edinburgh NGS
• Virgin adoring the Child ('The Ruskin Madonna')
London National Gallery
Tobias and the Angel (attributed)
The Virgin and Child with Two Angels (attributed)

ROGIER VAN DER WEYDEN
Tournai c1399 – Brussels 1464
One of the greatest and most influential of all early Netherlandish painters, Rogier trained in Tournai under Robert Campin before working for both the city of Brussels and the Burgundian court. He painted portraits, altarpieces and religious works famous for their ability to convey depth of emotion.
London Courtauld Institute
Portrait of Guillaume de Filastre (attributed)
London National Gallery
• The Magdalen Reading
The Exhumation of Saint Hubert
Lamentation over the Dead Christ (workshop)
Saint Ivo (?) (workshop)
Portrait of a Lady (workshop)
Upton House, Warwickshire NT
A Man

Sassetta: Miracle of the Holy Sacrament

ALBRECHT ALTDORFER
c.1480 – Regensburg 1538
German painter of extraordinary and intense religious scenes, he may also be the first artist to have painted landscapes without figures. He also made some of the first recognisable topographical drawings and prints. As city architect of Regensburg, he built a municipal slaughterhouse and a wine-storage warehouse. Also, as a member of the city council, he represented the city on official business.
London National Gallery
Landscape with a Footbridge
• Christ Taking Leave of his Mother

ANDREA DEL SARTO
Florence 1486 – Florence 1530
Leading Florentine painter in the early sixteenth century, painting principally religious works and portraits. When King Francis I of France acquired some of his paintings, Andrea del Sarto was invited to Paris as court painter, staying only briefly before returning to his new wife. He trained many of the leading artists of the next generation.
Alnwick Castle, Northumberland
Self Portrait
Ascott, Buckinghamshire NT
Virgin and Child with Saint John
Edinburgh NGS
• Domenico di Jacopo di Matteo Becuccio

1500-1600

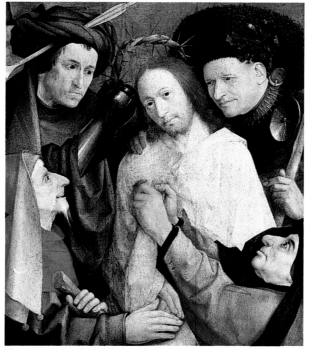

Hieronymous Bosch: Christ Mocked

Hampton Court Palace RC
Virgin and Child with Saint John
London National Gallery
The Madonna and Child with Saint Elizabeth and Saint John
Portrait of a Young Man
London Wallace Collection
Virgin and Child with Saint John and Two Angels
Petworth House, Sussex NT
Virgin and Child with Saint John and Angels
Windsor Castle RC
Woman in Yellow

JACOPO BASSANO
Bassano del Grappa c.1510 – Bassano del Grappa 1592
The leading artist from a family of painters. Assisted by his brother and sons, he created a virtual industry producing religious scenes, often set at night. Although most of his life was spent in his native town, he visited nearby Venice, where he came into contact with Tintoretto and Veronese. He studied contemporary artistic developments elsewhere by examining prints by German and Italian artists. He was a very keen musician.
Birmingham Barber Institute
Adoration of the Kings
Cambridge Fitzwilliam Museum
Christ on the Road to Calvary
The Penitent Saint Jerome
Corsham Court, Wiltshire
The Agony in the Garden
Edinburgh NGS
Adoration of the Kings
Adoration of the Shepherds (attributed)
Christ and the Money-Changers in the Temple (attributed)
A Gentleman
Hampton Court Palace RC
• Adoration of the Shepherds
Christ in the House of Mary and Martha

(attributed)
Consecration of the Host by Saint Denis (attributed)
The Flood (attributed)
The Good Samaritan
Jacob's Journey
A Man holding Gloves
Martyrdom of Saint Mark
Nativity (attributed)
The Supper at Emmaus (attributed)
Liverpool Walker Art Gallery
Noah's Sacrifice
London National Gallery
The Way to Calvary
The Good Samaritan
The Purification of the Temple
Oxford Ashmolean Museum
Christ disputing with the Doctors
An Unknown Man and his Secretary
Oxford CCPG
Christ Crowned with Thorns (attributed)

PARIS BORDONE
Treviso 1500 – Venice 1571
Although trained by Titian in Venice, they argued and Bordone did most of his work outside the city. He worked principally for northern Italian patrons and for rulers and aristocrats throughout Europe, who enjoyed his mythological paintings and his paintings of beautiful women. He visited the imperial court at Augsburg in Bavaria and Fontainebleau to work for the French king.
Birmingham Barber Institute
Mythological Scene
Chatsworth, Derbyshire
Family Group
Edinburgh NGS
Venetian Woman at her Toilette
The Rest on the Return from Egypt
Glasgow Art Gallery and Museum
Virgin and Child with Saints

Virgin and Child with Saints and a Donor
Hampton Court Palace RC
Man with a Laurel Wreath
Harewood House, Yorkshire
Knight and Two Pages
London Courtauld Institute
• Rest on the Flight into Egypt
London National Gallery
Pair of Lovers
Christ as the Light of the World
Christ baptising Saint John Martyr,
Duke of Alexandria
Portrait of a Young Woman

HIERONYMOUS BOSCH
s'Hertogenbosch c.1450 – s'Hertogenbosch 1516
Best known for his fantastic, grotesque beings which inhabit strange, nightmarish worlds. While some of his paintings have clear moralising symbolism, others elude explanation. Many were painted for the Burgundian aristocracy and later in the sixteenth century were collected by Philip II of Spain. Bosch married a wealthy widow, becoming one of the richest citizens in his home town, where he enjoyed high social status.
London National Gallery
• Christ Mocked
Petworth House, Sussex NT
Adoration of the Kings (attributed)
Upton House, Warwickshire NT
Adoration of the Kings (attributed)

AGNOLO BRONZINO
Monticelli 1503 – Florence 1572
Florentine painter who became court painter to Cosimo I de'Medici, Duke of Tuscany, painting many portraits of the ducal family. He also painted religious paintings and frescos, contributing to the decoration of the Palazzo Vecchio in Florence as a ducal residence. His refined, polished style created the image of the grand-ducal court. He was very learned and wrote poetry.
Corsham Court, Wiltshire
Saint Catherine
Hampton Court Palace RC
Lady in Green
London National Gallery
An Allegory with Venus and Cupid
The Madonna and Child with Saint John and Saint Anne
Portrait of a Young Man (on long term loan)
Portrait of Piero de' Medici
Oxford Ashmolean Museum
• Don Grazia de' Medici

Pieter Bruegel the Elder: Landscape with the Flight into Egypt

PIETER BRUEGEL THE ELDER
?Breda c.1525 – Brussels 1569
The leading artist of sixteenth-century Netherlandish painting and founder of a painting dynasty. He painted all kinds of subjects but, even in religious works, often focused on the activities of ordinary people: hence his nickname 'Peasant Bruegel'. His figures are often set in huge panoramic landscapes, while his allegories, such as the Children's Games, although appearing to show a carefree world, on closer inspection reveal a brutal side.
Hampton Court Palace RC
Massacre of the Innocents
London Courtauld Institute
Christ and the Woman Taken in Adultery (1565)
•Landscape with the Flight into Egypt (1563)
London National Gallery
Adoration of the Kings (1564)
Upton House, Warwickshire, NT
Dormition of the Virgin

ANNIBALE CARRACCI
Bologna 1560 – Rome 1609
A founding member, with his brother and cousin, of the Bolognese school of painters. As well as painting conventional religious and mythological subjects, he was among the earliest artists to paint large-scale scenes of everyday life and

created a new genre based on scenes of people hunting, fishing and boating in lyrical landscapes. After his move to Rome in 1595 he executed his masterpiece, the Loves of the Gods frescos in the Palazzo Farnese. In his last years he suffered from severe depressions.
Boughton House, Northamptonshire
Virgin and Child
A Young Man
Cambridge Fitzwilliam Museum
Head of an Old Woman
Saint Roch and an Angel
Corsham Court, Wiltshire
Self Portrait
Hampton Court Palace RC
The Agony in the Garden
Allegory with Truth and Time
Man in Profile
Virgin and Sleeping Child with Saint John
Harewood House, Yorkshire
A Man
Leicester NWMAG
The Youthful Bacchus (fragment)
London Kensington Palace RC
Virgin and Child (fresco: attributed)
London National Gallery
Silenus Gathering Grapes
Marsyas and Olympus
Christ Appearing to Saint Anthony
Christ Appearing to Saint Peter on the Appian Way
The Dead Christ Mourned
Oxford Ashmolean Museum
The Infant Christ Blessing the Virgin (1602)
Oxford CCPG
The Butcher's Shop
Portrait of Giacomo Filippo Turrini
•Man Drinking
Saint Francis in a Swoon supported by Angels (attributed)
Virgin and Child in Glory above Bologna
Woburn Abbey, Bedfordshire
Noli me Tangere
York City Art Gallery
Monsignor Agucchi (sometimes attributed to Domenichino)

CORREGGIO (ANTONIO ALLEGRI)
Reggio Emilia 1489 – Reggio Emilia 1534
His best-known works are in the north Italian city of Parma, where he frescoed the domes of the cathedral and Santa Giovanni Evangelista with stunning illusionistic visions of heaven, seen from a sharply foreshortened angle. He was influenced by Leonardo da Vinci's sfumato method, which gives a soft, atmospheric quality to his religious paintings, while his mythological works are sometimes sensual, sometimes playful.
Edinburgh NGS
Allegory of Virtue
Glasgow Art Gallery and Museum
An Angel (fresco fragment; attributed)
Hampton Court Palace RC
Holy Family with Saint Jerome
Saint Catherine Reading
London National Gallery
Christ Taking Leave of his Mother
Heads of Angels (fresco fragments)
The Madonna of the Basket
•The School of Love
Christ presented to the People (Ecce Homo)
The Magdalen (attributed)
London Wellington Museum
The Agony in the Garden

LUCAS CRANACH THE ELDER
Kronach 1472 – Weimar 1553
Founder of a leading family of German painters and also a printmaker. He was court painter to the Electors of Saxony, where he met Martin Luther, who became a close friend and whose portrait he painted several times. In addition to religious paintings and portraits, he also painted mythological subjects, often as an excuse to include his popular, lithe-limbed nudes.
Bristol City Art Gallery
Portrait of Martin Luther
Burghley House, Stamford
Portrait of Martin Luther
Edinburgh NGS
Venus and Cupid
Glasgow Burrell Collection
Judith with the Head of Holofernes
•The Stag Hunt
Venus and Cupid
Knightshayes Court, Devon NT
Nativity
Liverpool Walker Art Gallery
The Nymph at the Fountain (1534)
London Courtauld Institute
Adam and Eve (1526)
London National Gallery
Saints Genevieve, Apollonia, Christina and Ottilia (two wings of an altarpiece)
Johann the Steadfast and Johann Friedrich the Magnanimous (diptych) (1509)
Portrait of a Man (1524)

Portrait of a Woman
The Close of the Silver Age (?)
Cupid complaining to Venus
Charity

ALBRECHT DÜRER
Augsburg 1497/8 – Nuremberg 1528
Regarded as the greatest German Renaissance master, Dürer developed printmaking and introduced greater realism to German painting. He travelled twice to Italy and made a journey to the Netherlands, always recording sights and scenes that he saw, often in watercolours. He worked for several German rulers, painting both religious works and portraits.
Windsor Castle RC
A Young Man
London National Gallery
•Saint Jerome
The Painter's Father (attributed)

GIORGIONE
Castelfranco c.1477 – Venice 1510
Credited with the creation of a new style in Venetian painting, softening contours and shadows. He also created a new type of painting, the poesia, landscapes without a specific subject, peopled by goddesses, nymphs and shepherds, evoking a lost pastoral world. He painted the first female nude in a landscape, the Sleeping Venus (in Dresden).
Glasgow Art Gallery and Museum
See under Titian
London National Gallery
•The Adoration of the Kings
The Sunset
Oxford Ashmolean Museum
Virgin and Child 'The Tallard Madonna' (attributed)

JAN GOSSAERT (MABUSE)
Mauberge 1478-88 – Middelburg 1532
Netherlandish painter often considered the first to adopt the classicising style of the Italian Renaissance. He travelled to Rome in 1508, where he made copies of antiquities and painted a number of large-scale, classically inspired nudes (such as those in the National Gallery and Birmingham). His work is most remarkable, however, for his exceptionally refined oil-painting technique in the Netherlandish tradition.
Birmingham Barber Institute
•Hercules and Deianeira
Brighton Preston Manor
A Gentleman
Glasgow Burrell Collection
Virgin and Child
Hampton Court Palace RC
The Three Children of Christian II of Denmark
London Courtauld Institute
Portrait of Anne de Bergues and her Son
Virgin and Child
London National Gallery
The Adoration of the Kings
An Elderly Couple
A Little Girl
Adam and Eve (on loan from HMQ)
Virgin and Child (on loan)
Man with a Rosary
The Virgin and Child (1527)
Damião de Goes (?)
Oxford Ashmolean Museum
Saint Catherine of Alexandria
Wilton House, Wiltshire
The Children of Christian II of Denmark (attributed)

EL GRECO (DOMENIKOS THEOTOKOPOULOS)
Candia, Crete 1541 – Toledo 1614
One of the most original of sixteenth century painters, best known for his elongated figure style and intensity of emotion. He worked in Venice and Rome before arriving in Spain and settling in Toledo. He received one commission from King Philip II, which the king did not like. He painted mainly

Lucas Cranach the Elder: The Stag Hunt

Giorgione: The Adoration of the Kings

El Greco: The Tears of Saint Peter

for the religious institutions of Toledo, which were attracted to his work by the deeply religious expressiveness of his paintings.

Barnard Castle Bowes Museum
●The Tears of Saint Peter

Boughton House, Northamptonshire
The Adoration of the Shepherds

Cardiff National Museum of Wales
The Disrobing of Christ
Saint John the Baptist (attributed)

Edinburgh NGS
Christ as the Redeemer
The Penitent Saint Jerome
An Allegory (Fábula)

Glasgow Pollok House
A Man
A Woman in a Fur Wrap

Harewood House, Yorkshire
Fábula

London National Gallery
The Adoration of the Name of Jesus
Christ Driving the Traders from the Temple

Oxford New College Chapel
Saint James

Upton House, Warwickshire NT
Christ Mocked

MAERTEN VAN HEEMSKERCK
Heemskerck 1498 – Haarlem 1574
Painter of the Northern Netherlands who travelled to Rome in the 1530s where he produced a vast collection of drawings of antiquities and contemporary buildings

such as St Peter's, which he depicted frequently during the course of its construction. Strongly influenced by his Italian trip, he returned to Haarlem, where he enjoyed a highly successful career, receiving commissions for religious paintings and portraits from the leading citizens of Haarlem and elsewhere.

Barnard Castle Bowes Museum
Allegory of Innocence and Guile
Christ appearing to the Apostles on Lake Tiberias (1567)

Cambridge Fitzwilliam Museum
●Self Portrait

Hampton Court Palace RC
The Four Last Things (1565)

London National Gallery
The Virgin, Saint John the Evangelist, Mary Magdalen and a Donor (two wings of an altarpiece)

Manchester City Art Gallery
Portrait of Margaretha Banken

NICHOLAS HILLIARD
Exeter c.1547 – London 1619
Most famous English miniaturist, who also painted some larger portraits, he was granted the monopoly to paint the portraits of Queen Elizabeth I. However, the queen's slowness in paying led to him complaining that he had to find other patrons, many of whom were leading members of her court. He wrote 'The Arte of Limning' on the art of portraiture, the first book by an English artist.

Hatfield House, Hertfordshire
Queen Elizabeth I (The Ermine Portrait) (1585)

Liverpool Walker Art Gallery
●Queen Elizabeth I (The Pelican Portrait)

London Tate
Queen Elizabeth I (attributed)

HANS HOLBEIN THE YOUNGER
Augsburg 1497/8 – London 1543
German artist whose paintings of Henry VIII and his wives and children have formed our image of the Tudor dynasty. He arrived in England from Basle, where he had painted religious works as well as portraits. In England he painted a series of penetrating portraits of the merchant and political classes including Sir Thomas More, Chancellor of England, before becoming court painter to Henry VIII. An exceptional collection of his portrait drawings is preserved at Windsor.

Audley End, Essex EH
Portrait of an Unknown Gentleman

Cambridge St John's College
Bishop Fisher (attributed)

Castle Howard, Yorkshire
Howard Collection
Henry VIII (attributed)

Corsham Court, Wiltshire
The Wife of Sir Thomas More (attributed)

Edinburgh NGS
An Allegory of the Old and New Testaments

Hampton Court Palace RC
Johannes Froben
'Noli me Tangere'

London Surgeon's Hall
Henry VIII and the Barber Surgeon's Company (attributed)

London Lambeth Palace
●Archbishop Warham (1527)

London National Gallery
Erasmus of Rotterdam (on loan)
Lady with a Squirrel and a Starling
The Ambassadors (1533)
Christina of Denmark

London National Portrait Gallery
Henry VII and Henry VIII (cartoon)

London V&A

Maerten van Heemskerck: Self Portrait

A Man (miniature)
Miniature Portrait of Anne of Cleves

Upton House, Warwickshire NT
A Young Man with a Carnation (miniature) (1533)

Weston Park, Shropshire
Sir George Carew

Windsor Castle RC
Derich Born (1533)
A Merchant of the German Steelyard (1532)
Sir Henry Guildford (1527)
Thomas Howard, 3rd Duke of Norfolk
William Reskimer

LUCAS VAN LEYDEN
Leiden c.1494 – Leiden 1533
From Leiden in the Northern Netherlands Lucas was a printmaker as well as a painter, his prints bringing him international fame during his lifetime. He married a magistrate's daughter, which brought him social status. Many of his paintings were religious, but he also painted unusual subjects such as The Chess-players. He met Dürer, who made a portrait drawing of him.

London Courtauld Institute
The Scorning of Job

London National Gallery
A Man Aged 38

Wilton House, Wiltshire
●The Card-Players

LORENZO LOTTO
Venice c.1480 – Loreto 1556
Painter of religious works and strikingly curious portraits, Lotto spent much of his life outside his native Venice. He spent over twelve years in Bergamo, then in Venetian territory, returning to Venice for some years before moving down the East coast of Italy to the Marches, where he remained until his death, frequently

changing accommodation. His idiosyncratic style enjoyed a considerable reputation with his provincial patrons.

Alnwick Castle, Northumberland
Cupid crowning a Skull

Ascott, Buckinghamshire NT
A Prelate

Edinburgh NGS
Virgin and Child with Saints

Hampton Court Palace RC
Portrait of Andrea Odoni (1527)
A Bearded Man
A Man holding a Glove (attributed)

Harewood House, Yorkshire
Portrait of Sebastian Cabot(?)

London Courtauld Institute
Entombment
Holy Family with Saint Anne

London National Gallery
The Physician Giovanni Agostino della Torre and his son Niccolò (1515)
The Virgin and Child with Saint Jerome and Saint Nicholas of Tolentino
●A Lady with a Drawing of Lucretia
Portrait of Giovanni della Volta and his Family

Oxford CCPG
Supper at Emmaus

Upton House, Warwickshire NT
A Dominican Monk

QUINTEN MASSYS (METSYS)
Louvain c.1466 – Antwerp 1530
The son of a blacksmith, he supposedly began painting in order to woo his beloved away from another painter. He moved to Antwerp, a thriving centre of artistic patronage, where his success enabled him to buy two houses. He painted religious works and portraits. His most famous 'portrait' is The Ugly Duchess, based on a drawing of a grotesque woman by Leonardo, which Sir John Tenniel in turn used for his illustration of the Duchess in Alice in Wonderland.

Birmingham Barber Institute
An Ecclesiastic (attributed)

Cambridge Fitzwilliam Museum
Virgin and Child

Edinburgh NGS
A Man

Hampton Court Palace RC
Erasmus of Rotterdam
A Man (1527)

London Courtauld Institute
Christ and the Cross between the Virgin and Saint John and Two Donors
Virgin and Child

London National Gallery
The Virgin and Child Enthroned with Angels
The Virgin and Child with Saints Barbara and Catherine
●A Grotesque Old Woman

MICHELANGELO BUONARROTI
Caprese 1475 – Rome 1564
Painter, sculptor, architect and poet, one of the greatest of all artists, best known for his frescos on the ceiling of the Sistine Chapel. He regarded himself primarily as a sculptor and grieved that his ambitious plans for the tomb of Pope Julius II were not carried out, regarding this as the tragedy of his life. He was active throughout his long life, his last years devoted to the rebuilding of St Peter's in Rome.
Liverpool Walker Art Gallery
Christ and the Woman of Sumaria (grisaille; attributed)
London National Gallery
'The Manchester Madonna'
•The Entombment
Oxford Ashmolean Museum
Return of the Holy Family from Egypt (unfinished, grisaille, attributed)

PALMA VECCHIO
Bergamo c.1480 – Venice 1528
Venetian painter known as 'il Vecchio' (the old) because his nephew was also called Palma ('il Giovane' - the young). He painted many classical subjects, often featuring nude goddesses and nymphs within a landscape. He also painted half-length, partially clothed, anonymous women, possibly courtesans, which were fashionable as images of ideal female beauty.
Alnwick Castle, Northumberland
A Man
A Young Woman
Buscot Park, Berkshire NT
Mystic Marriage of Saint Catherine
Cambridge Fitzwilliam Museum
•Venus and Cupid in a Landscape
Glasgow Art Gallery and Museum
Virgin and Child with Saints (attributed)
Hampton Court Palace RC
Virgin and Child with Saints
A Sibyl
London Courtauld Institute
Venus in a Landscape

Michelangelo Buonarroti: The Entombment

London National Gallery
Portrait of a Poet
A Blonde Woman
Oxford Ashmolean Museum
Virgin and Child with Saints

PARMIGIANINO (FRANCESCO MAZZOLA)
Parma 1504 – Casalmaggiore 1540
Named after his native town, where he mostly worked, Parmigianino went to Rome in 1524 to work with his uncle, where he was regarded as the new Raphael and where he was caught in the sack of the city by the German Imperial troops in 1527. The figures in his paintings tend to be elongated, elegant and refined. As well as religious and mythological subjects, he painted some exquisite portraits, especially of women.
Hampton Court Palace RC
Pallas Athene
A Young Nobleman
London Courtauld Institute
Holy Family
Virgin and Child
London National Gallery
Portrait of a Man
The Madonna and Child with Saints John and Jerome
The Mystic Marriage of Saint Catherine
York City Art Gallery
•A scholar

JOACHIM PATENIER
?Dinant c.1480 – Antwerp 1524
A specialist in small paintings of huge panoramic landscapes in which the religious subject matter is subordinated and often very small. He sometimes collaborated with Quinten Massys, the latter painting the figures. His surviving oeuvre is small - fewer than 20 paintings - but his contribution to the development of landscape painting was major.
Brighton Art Gallery
Building the Tower of Babel (attributed, damaged)
London National Gallery
Saint Jerome in a Landscape (attributed)
Oxford Ashmolean Museum
•The Destruction of Sodom and Gomorrah
Upton House, Warwickshire NT
The Temptation of Christ

JACOPO DA PONTORMO
Pontormo 1494 – Florence 1556
A highly successful painter in mid-sixteenth-century Florence despite his neurotic personality, which to some extent is reflected in his style. He painted portraits, mythological and religious works for the ruling Medici family. In his last years he isolated himself, allowing only a former pupil, Bronzino, to visit him and take care of him.
Hampton Court Palace RC
Virgin and Child (attributed)

Jacopo da Pontormo: The Story of Joseph (four panels)

London National Gallery
•The Story of Joseph (four panels)
A Discussion
Oxford CCPG
A Scholar holding Two Gilt Statues

RAPHAEL
Urbino 1483 – Rome 1520
Leading painter of the early sixteenth century, especially in Rome, where he frescoed the papal apartments of Pope Julius II, which became known as the Raphael Stanze. His genius and his evidently charming personality ensured him continual patronage. His portrait of Julius II (National Gallery) provided the model for subsequent papal portraits. According to his own account, he was financially successful and was building a palace for himself at the time of his early death.
Edinburgh NGS
The Bridgewater Madonna (Sutherland loan)
•Holy Family with the Palm Tree (Sutherland loan)
The Madonna del Paesaggio (Sutherland loan)
Hampton Court Palace RC
Self Portrait (?)
London National Gallery
The Procession to Calvary (predella)
'The Mond Crucifixion'
An Allegory ('Vision of a Knight')
'The Ansidei Madonna' (1505)

Saint John the Baptist Preaching (predella) (1505)
The Madonna of the Pinks (on loan)
Saint Catherine of Alexandria
'The Garvagh Madonna'
'The Mackintosh Madonna'
Pope Julius II
London V&A
Nine Tapestry Cartoons
London (Dulwich) DPS
Saint Francis and Saint Anthony of Padua (two predella panels)

SEBASTIANO DEL PIOMBO
Venice c.1485 – Rome 1547
Trained in Venice, probably with Giorgione, Sebastiano moved to Rome to work for the Sienese banker Agostino Chigi. He became a close friend of Michelangelo, who helped him by providing drawings for some of his paintings. He was appointed Keeper of the Papal Seals, from which his nickname 'Piombo' derives. This necessitated his becoming a friar, despite having a wife and two children.
Alnwick Castle, Northumberland
The Visitation; Mary and Elisabeth; Joseph and Four Maidens carrying Gifts (fresco fragments)
Buscot Park, Berkshire NT
Head of a Girl (attributed)
Cambridge Fitzwilliam Museum
Adoration of the Shepherds (damaged)
Madonna and Child
Glasgow Pollok House
Pope Clement VII (attributed)
Harewood House, Yorkshire
Sophonisba
Kingston Lacy, Dorset NT

•The Judgement of Solomon (unfinished)
London National Gallery
The Daughter of Herodias
The Raising of Lazarus
The Madonna and Child with Saints and Donor
A Lady as Saint Agatha

BARTHOLOMEUS SPRANGER
Antwerp 1546 – Prague 1611
An international artist who worked in Bohemia, Italy and Austria before becoming court painter to the Habsburg Emperor Rudolf II in Prague. His paintings combined Netherlandish realism with Italian intellectualism, producing an elegant style which greatly pleased the Emperor. His mythological works often have a strained sensuality.
London National Gallery
•The Adoration of the Kings
Oxford CCPG
Faith, Hope and Charity (attributed)

TINTORETTO (JACOPO ROBUSTI)
Venice 1519 – Venice 1594
One of the most prolific painters of his day, he worked almost exclusively in Venice, undertaking large-scale works for the Venetian state as well as religious paintings and portraits. His famous works for the Scuola di San Rocco in the city show his very rapid, sketchy brushwork and the dark hues he generally used, as well as dramatic composition. He employed many assistants, including his children.
Alnwick Castle, Northumberland
Ecce Homo

Birmingham Barber Institute
A Youth Aged 22 (1554)
Cambridge Fitzwilliam Museum
Adoration of the Shepherds
Castle Howard, Yorkshire
Howard Collection
The Sacrifice of Isaac
Chatsworth, Derbyshire
Samson and Delilah
Seated Man
Seated Young Man
Edinburgh NGS
Christ Carried to the Tomb
A Man
A Venetian (Sutherland loan)
Venetian Family Presented to the Virgin
Firle Place, Sussex Gage Collection
Bearded Man
Gateshead Shipley Art Gallery
•Christ Washing his Disciples' Feet
Glasgow Art Gallery and Museum
The Ordeal of Tuccia
Hampton Court Palace RC
A Dominican Friar (attributed)
Girolamo Pozzo
A Knight of Malta (attributed)
Portrait of Mario Grimani (attributed)
A Maze (attributed)
Virgin and Child
A Young Man
Harewood House, Yorkshire
Seated Man with a Praying Nun
Kingston Lacy, Dorset NT
Apollo and the Muses (ceiling)
London Courtauld Institute
Apollo and Diana killing the Children of Niobe
Esther before Ahasuerus
Latona turning the Lycian Peasants into Frogs
London Kensington Palace RC
Esther before Ahasuerus
The Nine Muses (ceiling)
London National Gallery
Christ washing his Disciples' Feet
Saint George and the Dragon
The Origin of the Milky Way
Portrait of Vincenzo Morosini
London V&A
Self Portrait as a Young Man
Longleat, Wiltshire
Allegorical Couple in a Garden
Oxford Ashmolean Museum
Head of a Bearded Man
Resurrection

Oxford CCPG
A Gentleman
Martyrdom of Saint Lawrence
Upton House, Warwickshire NT
The Wise and Foolish Virgins
Wilton House, Wiltshire
Christ washing the Feet of the Apostles

TITIAN (TIZIANO VECELLIO)
Pieve di Cadore c. 1485/1490 – Venice 1576
The first artist to have a truly international career, working for rulers throughout Europe although he rarely left Venice. His early paintings are notable for their brilliant colour and fine technique, but in his later works he developed a more sombre palette and looser brushstrokes. He worked in all subject areas of the time, being a popular portraitist, painter of altarpieces and small devotional works and also brilliantly bringing classical myths to life.
Alnwick Castle, Northumberland
Bishop Armagnac and his Secretary
Cambridge Fitzwilliam Museum
Tarquin and Lucretia
Venus and Cupid with a Lute Player
Edinburgh NGS
Allegory of the Three Ages of Man (Sutherland loan)
•Diana and Actaeon (Sutherland loan)
Diana and Callisto (Sutherland loan)
Venus Anadyomene (Sutherland loan)
Virgin and Child with Saint John and a Donor (Sutherland loan)
Glasgow Art Gallery and Museum
Christ and the Woman Taken in Adultery (formerly attributed to Giorgione)
Hampton Court Palace RC
Boy with a Pipe (attributed)
Jacopo Sannazaro
Virgin and Child with Tobias and the Angel (attributed)

Ickworth, Suffolk NT
A Man (attributed)
Kingston Lacy, Dorset NT
Francesco Savorgnan della Torre?
London National Gallery
The Holy Family and a Shepherd
Noli me Tangere
Portrait of a Lady
Portrait of a Man
Portrait of a Young Man (Halifax loan)
Bacchus and Ariadne
The Virgin and Child with Saints
The Vendramin Family
The Tribute Money
The Death of Actaeon
The Allegory of Prudence
The Madonna and Child
London Wallace Collection
Perseus and Andromeda
Longleat, Wiltshire
Rest on the Flight into Egypt (stolen, not recovered)
Oxford Ashmolean Museum
Portrait of Giacomo Doria
Oxford CCPG
Adoration of the Shepherds (attributed)
Petworth House, Sussex NT
Young Man in a Plumed Hat

VERONESE (PAOLO CALIARI)
Verona 1528 – Venice 1588
Worked in his native Verona before settling in Venice in the 1550s, where he painted many of the decorative schemes in Venetian churches and palaces, including the Doges' Palace. He is most renowned for his ability to render texture and for his brilliant colour. He was brought before the Inquisition for suspected

heresy in a Last Supper, but on being ordered to make essential changes, he merely changed the title to The Feast in the House of Levi.
Birmingham Barber Institute
The Visitation
Burghley House, Stamford
The Calling of the Sons of Zebedee
Saint Augustine
Saint James
Saint Paul
Saint Peter
Cambridge Fitzwilliam Museum
•Hermes, Herse and Aglauros
Castle Howard, Yorkshire
Howard Collection
Sappho (fragment)
Chatsworth, Derbyshire
Adoration of the Kings
Edinburgh NGS
Saint Anthony Abbot and a Donor
Venus and Mars
Edinburgh Holyrood House
David and Goliath
Judith with the Head of Holofernes
Edinburgh Talbot Rice Gallery
Venus and Adonis
Hampton Court Palace RC
Mystic Marriage of Saint Catherine (attributed)
Harewood House, Yorkshire
Seated Man in Furs
Liverpool Walker Art Gallery
The Finding of Moses (attributed)
London Courtauld Institute
Baptism of Christ
London National Gallery
Christ addressing a Kneeling Woman
The Vision of Saint Helena
The Consecration of Saint Nicholas
The Family of Darius before Alexander
Four Allegories of Love
The Adoration of the Kings
The Rape of Europa
London (Dulwich) DPG
Saint Jerome and a Donor (fragment)
Oxford Ashmolean Museum
The Story of Judith and Holofernes (five paintings)
Holy Family with the Infant Saint John and Saint George

Tintoretto: Christ washing his Disciples' Feet

1601-1700

Britain has always been a good place to see seventeenth-century paintings. Charles I (1625-1649), the greatest of all royal collectors, enticed numerous artists to his court, such as Rubens, Honthorst, Gentileschi and, of course, Van Dyck, many of whose suave portraits still adorn the walls of our country houses. During the eighteenth century, when the British aristocracy began collecting art in earnest, seventeenth-century works predominated. Particularly popular were the landscapes of Claude, which are better seen in this country than anywhere else. There was a similar vogue later in the century for the golden landscapes of the Dordrecht painter, Cuyp.

Although some artists, such as Rembrandt, have always been collected in Britain, others have been the victims or beneficiaries of fashion. The nineteenth-century rage for Murillo and the late nineteenth-century 'rediscoveries' of Frans Hals and Vermeer have all left their positive mark on our collections. At the same time, the dazzling polemics of the critic John Ruskin managed to turn the whole country against seventeenth-century Italian art : for a century after the 1860s no significant Italian seventeenth-century painting was bought by the National Gallery, a shortcoming recently magnificently rectified by Sir Denis Mahon's promised gift to the nation's galleries of his unrivalled collection of Baroque masterpieces.

Claude Lorrain: Landscape with Ascanius shooting the Stag of Silvia

HENDRICK AVERCAMP
Amsterdam 1585 – Kampen 1634
One of the most popular painters of winter landscapes and one of the earliest painters of the subject. He was born a deaf-mute and spent most of his life in Kampen where his father was a pharmacist. His paintings, with their anecdotal detail of ordinary people in an everyday world, were sought-after from the start, enabling him to charge high prices.
Edinburgh NGS
Winter Landscape with Figures
London Mansion House
Pleasures on the Ice
Winter Pleasures on the River Ijssel near Kampen
London National Gallery
Winter Scene on the Ice near a Town
•Winter Scene with Skaters near a Castle

Hendrick Avercamp: Winter Scene with Skaters near a Castle

Vase of Flowers
Vase of Flowers
Corsham Court, Wiltshire
Flower Piece
Glasgow Art Gallery and Museum
Nature adorned by the Graces (with Peter Paul Rubens)
Hampton Court Palace RC
Flemish Fair
London Mansion House
Scene outside a Village
Village on the Banks of a River (1612)
London National Gallery
Adoration of the Kings (1598)
London V&A
The Garden of Eden
London Apsley House
The Wellington Museum
Country Road with Figures
Entering the Ark (1615)
River Scene with Boats and Figures (1606?)
Road Scene with Travellers and Cattle
Travellers on a Country Road with Cattle and Pigs (1616)
Oxford Ashmolean Museum
Ferry Boats by a Wooded Riverbank
•Vase of Flowers
Wilton House, Wiltshire
Winter Scene

JAN BRUEGHEL I
Brussels 1568 – Antwerp 1625
Son of Pieter Bruegel the Elder and sometimes known as 'Velvet' or 'Flower' Brueghel because of his smooth painting style and numerous flower paintings. He was court painter to the Archdukes Albert and Isabella, the Hapsburg regents of the Netherlands, and he actually painted a wide range of subjects, including religious and mythological. These were usually painted on a small scale and often executed on copper.
Burghley House, Stamford
Air, Earth, Fire and Water
Cambridge Fitzwilliam Museum
Basket of Flowers
Landscape with a Mill and Carts

HENDRICK TER BRUGGHEN
The Hague 1588 – Utrecht 1629
One of the leading painters of Utrecht in the Netherlands, ter Brugghen worked in Italy for ten years, where he was one of a number of Northern artists to fall under the spell of Caravaggio. His scenes of musicians and others, often shown with strong contrasts of light and shade, as in the National Gallery's Concert, show Caravaggio's influence, but his later works are lighter and more colourful.
Gateshead Shipley Art Gallery
Pilate washing his Hands (attributed)

Hampton Court Palace RC
Laughing Bravo with a Glass
London National Gallery
Concert
Jacob, Laban and Leah
Singing Lute Player
Oxford Ashmolean Museum
•Bagpipe Player

JAN VAN DE CAPPELLE
Amsterdam 1626 – Amsterdam 1679
Perhaps the greatest and most original of all Dutch seascape painters, Van de Cappelle specialised in expansive scenes of calm, glassy seas. He did not rely on painting for his income, being a wealthy owner of his family's dyeing works. He was an enthusiastic collector of paintings and drawings, many by his Dutch contemporaries, and he had his portrait painted by both Rembrandt and Frans Hals.
Barnsley Cannon Hall
Seascape with Ships Becalmed
Birmingham Barber Institute
Ruffled Water with Boats
Cardiff National Museum Wales
•A Calm (1654)
London Mansion House
Shipping in a Calm
Winter Landscape
London National Gallery
Coast Scene with Passengers Disembarking
River Scene with a Dutch Yacht firing a Salute
River Scene with a Large Ferry
River Scene with Dutch Vessels Becalmed
Shipping Scene with a Dutch Yacht firing a Salute
Small Dutch Vessel before a Light Breeze
Small Vessel in Light Airs
Vessels in Light Airs
Vessels moored off a Jetty
London (Greenwich) NMM
Estuary Scene at Dawn with the Incoming Tide
London (Hampstead)
Kenwood (Iveagh Bequest)
Boats in Shallow Water
Manchester City Art Gallery
Ships at Anchor in a Calm Sea (attributed)
Winter Scene
Upton House, Warwickshire NT

River Estuary
Woburn Abbey, Bedfordshire
Harbour Scene

CARAVAGGIO
Caravaggio 1571 – Porto Ercole 1610
One of the most famous and influential painters of the seventeenth century, known for his dramatic scenes, dramatically lit and for the sometimes violent activities of his life. In Rome he attracted important patrons for whom he executed innovatory works which sometimes invited controversy because of their realistic approach to religious subject matter. He fled from Rome after killing a man and, after travelling in the south, was returning to Rome when he died.
London National Gallery
•Supper at Emmaus
Boy bitten by a Lizard
Salome with the Head of Saint John the Baptist

CLAUDE LORRAIN
Chamagne, Lorraine 1604 – Rome 1682
The most important painter of idealised, classically inspired landscapes of the seventeenth century, Claude trained as a pastry cook in his native country before travelling to Rome at the age of 12 to train as a painter. His idyllic, sun-drenched landscapes - usually the settings for mythological and religious subjects - were immensely popular in his lifetime. They were much sought-after by British collectors in the eighteenth and nineteenth centuries, which explains their number in this country.
Anglesea Abbey, Cambridgeshire NT
Landscape with Psyche sacrificing at the Temple of Apollo (1663)
Landscape with Shepherds
Landscape with the Arrival of Aeneas at Pallanteum (1675)
Birmingham Barber Institute
Landscape with Shepherds
Birmingham CMAG
Landscape with Shepherds, the Ponte Molle (1645)
Marine with the Embarkation of Saint Paula
Bowhill, Selkirkshire
Harbour Scene (1633)
The Judgement of Paris (1633)
Cambridge Fitzwilliam Museum
Landscape with Lake Albano and Castel Gandolfo
Cardiff National Museum of Wales
Landscape with Saint Philip baptising the Ethiopian Eunuch

Aelbert Cuyp: View of Dordrecht

Corsham Court, Wiltshire
Landscape with the Baptist
and Angels (1647)
Edinburgh NGS
Landscape with Apollo and the Muses (1652)
Holkham Hall, Norfolk
Landscape with Apollo guarding the Herds
of Admetus
Landscape with Argus looking after Io
Landscape with Erminia and the Shepherds
Landscape with Esther and the palace of
Ahasuerus (fragment)
Landscape with Shepherds
Landscape with Shepherds
Landscape with the Flaying of Marsyas
Landscape with the Rest on the Flight
into Egypt (1676)
Marine with Perseus and the Origin of Coral
London Buckingham Palace
The Rape of Europa
London Courtauld Institute
Imaginary View of Tivoli (1642)
London National Gallery
12 works including:
Landscape with Hagar and the Angel (1646)
Landscape with Psyche at the Castle of
Amor ('The Enchanted Castle') (1664)
Port Scene with the Embarkation of
the Queen of Sheba
London Wallace Collection
Landscape with Mercury stealing the
Herds of Admetus from Apollo (1660)
London (Dulwich) DPG
Gathering Grapes near an Arch
Landscape with Jacob and Laban (1676)
Manchester City Art Gallery
Landscape with the Adoration of the
Golden Calf (1660)
Nostell Priory, Yorkshire NT
Landscape with the Flight into Egypt
Oxford Ashmolean Museum
•Landscape with Ascanius shooting the
Stag of Silvia (1682)
Landscape with Shepherds

Petworth House, Sussex NT
Landscape with Jacob and Laban (1654)
Stratfield Saye, Hampshire
Landscape with Shepherds
The Port of Ostia with the Embarkation
of Saint Paula
Sudeley Castle, Gloucestershire
Ashcombe Collection
The Rape of Europa
Woburn Abbey, Bedfordshire
Landscape with Dancing Figures (1640)

AELBERT CUYP
Dordrecht 1620 – Dordrecht 1691
A member of a family of landscape
painters, Cuyp was little known outside
Dordrecht until the eighteenth century,
when his paintings became all the rage
with English collectors. There are now
many more of his works in England than
Holland. His landscapes often incorporate
recognisable features of his native
Dordrecht but they are always idealised,
often showing fat and contented cattle
beneath golden skies.
Anglesey Abbey, Cambridgeshire NT
Saint Philip baptising the Ethiopian Eunuch
Ascott, Buckinghamshire NT
Landscape with a Horseman on a Road
•View of Dordrecht
Birmingham Barber Institute
Equestrian Piece: Setting Out for the Chase
Burghley House, Stamford
Old Man with an Owl
Old Woman with a Turkey
Cambridge Fitzwilliam Museum
Sunset after Rain
Cardiff National Museum of Wales
Landscape with a Horseman and Ubbergen
Castle
Drumlanrig Castle, Dumfriesshire
Group of Horsemen
Edinburgh NGS
View of Het Valckhof, Nijmegen

Glasgow Art Gallery and Museum
The Entry of Christ into Jerusalem
Hill of Tarvit, Fife NTS
Sea Piece
Kedleston Hall, Derbyshire NT
Landscape in the Rhine Valley (attributed)
London Buckingham Palace
Landscape with a Negro Page
London Mansion House
Cows watering at a River
Extensive Landscape with Shepherds
and Sheep
London National Gallery
11 works including:
The Maas at Dordrecht in a Storm
River Landscape with Horsemen
and Peasants
London Wallace Collection
The Avenue at Meerdervoort, Dordrecht
The Ferry Boat on the Maas
River Scene with a View of Dordrecht
Shipping on the Maas, Dordrecht
London (Dulwich) DPG
Cattle near the Maas, Dordrecht in the
Distance
Evening Ride near a River
Herdsmen and Cattle, Rhenen
Herdsmen with Cows
Landscape with Cattle and Figures
Road near a River
London (Hampstead)
Kenwood (Iveagh Bequest)
View of Dordrecht
Manchester City Art Gallery
Poultry with a Distant View of Dordrecht
(attributed)
River Scene with the Rietdijkspoort,
Dordrecht
Oxford Ashmolean Museum
Still Life of Fruit
Petworth House, Sussex NT
Landscape near Nijmegen
Polesden Lacey, Surrey NT
Landscape with a Herdsman and a Bull
Waddesdon Manor, Bucks NT
Landing-party on the Maas at Dordrecht
Landscape with Herdsmen driving Cattle
over a Bridge
Landscape with Horsemen, Figures
and Cattle
Shipping on the Maas
Woburn Abbey, Bedfordshire
Flat Landscape, View at Elten
Skating Scene on the Maas at Dordrecht
View of Het Valckhof at Nijmegen

Anthony van Dyck: Johann, Count of Nassau, with his Wife and Family

GERRIT DOU
Leiden 1613 – Leiden 1675
Although he was a pupil of the young
Rembrandt, Dou's art developed in very
different ways from his master's. He
specialised in small portraits and scenes
of every day life, painted in meticulous
and minute detail. Perhaps unsurprisingly,
he worked slowly but his highly finished
paintings commanded high prices and his
patrons included Charles II.
Brodick Castle, Isle of Arran NTS
An Old Lady
Brodie Castle, Morayshire NTS
The Alchemist
The Dentist
Cambridge Fitzwilliam Museum
The Schoolmaster
Woman at a Window
A Young Man
Cheltenham Art Gallery
Self Portrait
Edinburgh NGS
Interior with a Young Violinist
London Mansion House
A Boy (Self Portrait)
Seated Woman making Lace
with Two Children
London National Gallery
Anna and the Blind Tobit
Man with a Pipe (Self Portrait?)
A Poulterer's Shop
Woman in a Dark Green Jacket
London Wallace Collection
A Hermit
Hermit at Prayer
London (Dulwich) DPG
•Interior with a Woman playing
a Clavichord

Manchester City Art Gallery
A Girl
Waddesdon Manor, Buckinghamshire NT
Girl with a Basket of Fruit at a Window

ANTHONY VAN DYCK
Antwerp 1599 – London 1641
Van Dyck was born in Antwerp, worked in
Rubens's studio and spent six years in
Italy. For the British, however, his fame
rests on his elegant, glamorous portraits
of Charles I and his courtiers, which
have forever coloured our view of the
Stuart court in the period before the
Civil War. The demand for portraits
by him, many painted with the
aid of assistants, is testified to by the
astonishing number that remain
throughout the country.
Alnwick Castle, Northumberland
Algernon Percy
The 10th Earl of Northumberland
Althorp, Northamptonshire
Spencer Collection
Anne Lady Dalkeith
Dorothy Sidney, Countess of Sutherland
George Digby and William Russell (War and
Peace)
Margaret Lemon
Saint Jerome
Arundel Castle, Sussex
Thomas Howard, Earl of Arundel and his
Grandson Lord Maltravers
Charles I
Henry Frederick, Earl of Arundel
Thomas Howard, Earl of Arundel and his Wife
Thomas Howard, Earl of Arundel
Birmingham Barber Institute
Ecce Homo
François Langlois (shared with NG)
Boughton House, Northamptonshire
Virgin and Child
Broadlands, Hampshire
Knatchbull Collection
Charles I
Henrietta Maria
A Woman (pair of painting in Antwerp,
Koninklijk Museum voor Schone Kunsten)
Burghley House, Stamford
Anne Carr, Countess of Bedford
Crucifixion
Death of Tullius
Henrietta Maria
Lady Ann Cecil

Caravaggio: Supper at Emmaus

Cambridge Fitzwilliam Museum
A Man
Mystic Marriage of Saint Catherine
Virgin and Child
Rachel de Ruvigny, Countess of
Southampton, as Fortuna
An Old Woman
Cardiff National Museum of Wales
A Man
Castle Howard, Yorkshire
Howard Collection
Henrietta Maria
Henry Percy, 9th Earl of Northumberland
Chatsworth, Derbyshire
Arthur Goodwin
Dorothy Sidney, Countess of Sunderland
Elizabeth Cecil, Countess of Devonshire
Joanne de Blois
Philip Herbert, 5th Earl of Pembroke, with
his Sister Sophia
William Cavendish, 3rd Earl of Devonshire
Claydon House, Buckinghamshire NT
Sir Edmund Verney
King Charles I
Corsham Court, Wiltshire
The Betrayal of Christ
Gentleman in a Ruff
Edinburgh NGS
An Italian Nobleman
The Lomellini Family
Saint Sebastian
A Young Man (on loan from the Duke of
Sutherland)
Edinburgh
Scottish National Portrait Gallery
Princess Elizabeth and Princess Anne (1637)
Firle Place, Sussex Gage Collection
•Johann, Count of Nassau, with his Wife
and Family
Goodwood, Sussex Trustees
Charles II in Civilian Dress
Hampton Court Palace RC
Margaret Lemon
Hatchlands, Surrey NT
A Man in a Ruff
Holkham Hall, Norfolk
The Duc d'Arenberg
Kingston Lacy, Dorset NT
Alice Bankes, Lady Borlase
Sir John Borlase
Knole, Kent NT
The Countess of Dorset
London Apsley House,
The Wellington Museum
Saint Rosalie of Palermo crowned with
Roses by Two Angels
London Buckingham Palace
Charles I and Henrietta Maria with their
Two Eldest Children ('The Greate Peece')
Christ Healing the Paralytic
The Mystic Marriage of Saint Catherine
Virgin and Child
London Courtauld Institute
Adoration of the Shepherds
Christ on the Cross (attributed)
Crucifixion with Saint Francis (sketch)
A Man in an Armchair
Man of Sorrows
Virgin and Child with a Bishop, Donor and
Saint Anthony Abbot (sketch)
London Kensington Palace, RC
Cupid and Psyche
London National Gallery
16 works including:
Cornelis van der Geest
King Charles I on Horseback
London National Portrait Gallery
Lady Venetia Digby
London Tate Gallery (Tate Britain)
A Lady of the Spencer Family
London Wallace Collection
Isabella Waerbeke
Marie de Raet, Wife of Philippe Le Roy
Philippe Le Roy

Self Portrait as the Shepherd Paris
London (Dulwich) DPG
Emmanuel Philibert of Savoy
George, Lord Digby, later Earl of Bristol(?)
Lady Venetia Digby on her Deathbed
Samson and Delilah
Sunset Landscape with a Shepherd and
his Flock
Virgin and Child
London (Hampstead)
Kenwood (Iveagh Bequest)
Henrietta of Lorraine
James Stuart, Duke of Richmond
and Lennox
Oxford Ashmolean Museum
Bearded Man with a Wheel Ruff
Deposition
Head of a Negro
The Grand Procession of the Order of the
Garter
Oxford CCPG
The Continence of Scipio
Mars going to War (sketch)
Martyrdom of Saint George (sketch)
Soldier on Horseback (sketch)
Petworth House, Sussex NT
11 works including:
Lady Shirley
Sir Robert Shirley
Thomas Wentworth, Earl of Strafford
(two versions)
Southampton City Art Gallery
A Man; His wife (two paintings)
Tatton Park, Cheshire NT
Martyrdom of Saint Sebastian
Wilton House, Wiltshire
14 paintings including:
The Countess of Morton and Mrs Killigrew
Mary Villiers, Duchess of Richmond and
Lennox, and Mrs Gibson the dwarf
The Three Eldest Children of Charles I
Windsor Castle RC
16 paintings including:
Charles I in Three Positions
The Five Eldest children of Charles I
Thomas Killigrew and William Lord Crofts
Woburn Abbey, Bedfordshire
12 paintings including:
Francis Russell, 4th Earl of Bedford
The painter Daniel Mytens and his Wife
York City Art Gallery
Albert de Ligne, Prince of Arenberg

ADAM ELSHEIMER
Frankfurt am Main 1578 – Rome 1610
A German painter of small paintings with a
huge influence. He spent most of his career
in Italy, painting small-scale landscapes on
copper, a large number of which have
made their way into British collections.
The lighting in his paintings is wholly
naturalistic, with brilliant, evocative effects
of dawn or night skies, and was to exert a
strong influence on artists as diverse as
Claude, Rembrandt and Rubens..
Cambridge Fitzwilliam Museum
Interior with Minerva as Patroness of the
Arts and Sciences
Venus and Cupid in a Landscape

Edinburgh NGS
'Il contento'
The Stoning of Stephen
Liverpool Walker Art Gallery
Landscape with Apollo and Coronis
London Apsley House,
The Wellington Museum
•Judith and Holofernes
London National Gallery
Baptism of Christ
The Shipwreck of Saint Paul on Malta
Saint Lawrence prepared for Martyrdom
Tobias and the Angel (attributed)
London Wellcome Gallery
Saint Elizabeth visiting a Hospital
Petworth House, Sussex NT
Eight small panels of saints (one more in
series at Montpellier)

CAREL FABRITIUS
Midden-Beemster 1622 – Delft 1654
Only 12 paintings survive by this innovative
pupil of Rembrandt. He has always captured
the imagination, both for the originality of
his works and his short life, which was
brought to a dramatic end, at the age of 32,
when a gunpowder warehouse in his native
Delft exploded. His works were to influence
Vermeer and it has even been suggested
that he was his master.
Liverpool Walker Art Gallery
Head of an Old Man (attributed)
London National Gallery
Perspective View in Delft
•Self Portrait (?)

ARTEMESIA GENTILESCHI
Rome 1593 – Naples 1652/3
One of the very few women artists to
achieve international stature in a period
when most women were denied the
opportunity of an artistic training or
career. Artemesia was trained by her
father, Orazio , with whom she worked for
Charles I in England. She refused to be
confined to painting 'women's subjects'
and worked in all fields, producing
especially dynamic images of such
dramatic subjects as Judith and
Holofernes.
Hampton Court Palace RC
•Self Portrait as Pittura

ORAZIO GENTILESCHI
Pisa 1563 - London 1639
May have become a painter only in his
twenties and was much influenced by
Caravaggio. He was employed on the
mosaics of the dome of St Peter's, Rome,
where he enjoyed much success. After
working for the Duke of Savoy in Genoa
and the Queen of France, he moved to
England, becoming court painter to
Charles I, for whom he painted the ceiling
of the Queen's House, Greenwich.
Birmingham CMAG
Rest on the Flight into Egypt
Hampton Court Palace RC
•Joseph and Potiphar's Wife
A Sibyl

**GUERCINO
(GIOVANNI FRANCESCO BARBIERI)**
Cento 1591 – Bologna 1666
His nickname 'Guercino' means 'squint-
eyed', a condition said to be due to his
nurse dropping him as a baby. He was
a leading painter of the Bolognese school
and attracted the patronage of Bologna's
Archbishop who, on becoming Pope,
summoned him to Rome. Unfashionable
since the later nineteenth century,
Guercino has recently been championed
by the collector and art historian,
Sir Denis Mahon, who promised five of his
paintings to the National Gallery and
one to the Ashmolean, where they can
now be seen.
Audley End, Essex English Heritage
Saint Catherine of Siena (attributed)
Birmingham CMAG
Erminia and the Shepherd
Burghley House, Stamford
Head of David
Jacob receiving the Bloody Coat of Joseph
Joseph reading a Scroll
Cambridge Fitzwilliam Museum

•The Betrayal of Christ
Saint Sebastian succoured by Angels (1617)
Cardiff National Museum of Wales
The Agony in the Garden
Castle Howard, Yorkshire
Howard Collection
Tancred and Erminia
Corsham Court, Wiltshire
Christ and the Woman of Samaria
Christ visited by Nicodemus at night
The Infant Christ as Salvator Mundi
Saint James the Greater
Edinburgh NGS
Erminia finding the Wounded Tancred
The Penitent Saint Peter
Virgin and Child with Saint John
London Apsley House,
The Wellington Museum
Mars as a Warrior
Venus and Cupid
London Buckingham Palace RC
The Libyan Sibyl
London National Gallery
The Angel appears to Hagar and Ishmael
(on loan)
Angels weeping over the Dead Christ
The Cumaen Sibyl with a Putto (on loan)
Elijah fed by Ravens (on loan)
Saint Gregory the Great with Saints
Ignatius Loyola and Francis Xavier (on loan)
The Incredulity of Saint Thomas
The Presentation of Jesus in the Temple
(on loan)
London (Dulwich) DPG
Christ and the Woman taken in Adultery
Oxford CCPG
Head of an Old Man (on loan)
Saint John the Baptist (attributed)
Tatton Park, Cheshire NT
Absalom and Tamar
Mars

FRANS HALS
Antwerp 1581-5 – Haarlem 1666
Today one of the most famous of all Dutch
artists, but until his rediscovery in the
late nineteenth century only really known
in his local Haarlem. He was principally a
portrait painter, painting an elaborate
and vivacious series of group portraits of

Meindert Hobbema: The Avenue, Middelharnis

Pieter de Hooch: Courtyard of a House in Delft (1658)

the Haarlem militia companies. The
extraordinary freedom of his brushwork
was not to be matched until the
nineteenth century and can be seen
to excellent effect in his most famous
work, The Laughing Cavalier, in London's
Wallace Collection.
Birmingham Barber Institute
Man holding a Skull
Cambridge Fitzwilliam Museum
A Man
Chatsworth, Derbyshire
A Man with Folded Arms
A Woman (wife of Man holding a Skull)
Edinburgh NGS
A Standing Man
A Standing Woman
'Verdonck'
Glasgow Burrell Collection
A Man (attributed)
Hull Ferens Art Gallery
A Smiling Woman
London Mansion House
The Mandolin Player
The Merry Lute Player
London National Gallery
Family Group in a Landscape
Jean de la Chambre (1638)
A Man
A Man (1633)
A Middle-aged Woman
A Woman
A Woman holding a Fan
A Young Man holding a Skull
London Wallace Collection
•A Man (The Laughing Cavalier) (1624)
London (Hampstead)
Kenwood (Iveagh Bequest)
Pieter van den Broecke (1633)
Oxford CC Senior Common Room
A Seated Woman

MEINDERT HOBBEMA
Amsterdam 1638 – Amsterdam 1709
Today one of the most popular of all
Dutch landscape painters, thanks to his
most famous work, The Avenue
at Middelharnis (National Gallery).
He was apprenticed to Jacob van Ruisdael
and initially became a painter of river
scenes before turning to wooded
landscapes. He painted little after
his marriage in 1668 and his
appointment as wine-gauger to the
Amsterdam customs.
Ascott, Buckinghamshire NT
Cottages in a Wooded Landscape
Cambridge Fitzwilliam Museum
Cottages under Trees and a Hunting Party
(1667)
Wooded Landscape and Cottages (1665)
Edinburgh NGS
Landscape with a View of the Bergkerk,
Deventer (loan from the Duke
of Sutherland)
Landscape with a Waterfall
Wooded Landscape with Cottages
amid Trees
Edinburgh Talbot Rice Gallery
Wooded Landscape (1659) (attributed)
Elton Hall, Peterborough
Proby Collection
Landscape with a Mill
Glasgow Art Gallery and Museum
River Landscape with a Fisherman
London Mansion House
View in Westphalia
London National Gallery
•The Avenue, Middelharnis
Cottages in a Wood
The Haarlem Lock, Amsterdam
Road winding past Cottages
The Ruins of Brederode Castle
Stream by a Wood
The Watermills at Singraven,
near Denekamp
Woody Landscape
Woody Landscape with a Cottage
London Wallace Collection
The Outskirts of a Wood
Ruin on the Bank of a River
Stormy Landscape
The Watermill

Wooded Landscape
London (Dulwich) DPG
Woody Landscape with a Large Watermill
Norwich Castle Museum
Landscape with Anglers
Petworth House, Sussex NT
Landscape with a Coppice

GERRIT VAN HONTHORST
Utrecht 1592 – Utrecht 1656
One of a group of artists from Utrecht who
travelled to Rome and fell under the
influence of Caravaggio. His speciality of
painting nocturnal scenes with
dramatically cast shadows gave him the
Italian nickname of 'Gherardo delle Notti'
or 'Gerard of the Night'. He spent the
1620s in Utrecht before being summoned
to London by Charles I. In England, he
started painting portraits and these make
up most of his works in this country.
Ashdown House, Oxfordshire NT
12 portraits
Boughton House, Northamptonshire
Charles II
Elizabeth, Queen of Bohemia
Frederick V, King of Bohemia
Cambridge Fitzwilliam Museum
Portrait of William Earl of Craven (1642)
Hampton Court Palace RC
Apollo and Diana (1628)
Elizabeth, Queen of Bohemia
The Four Eldest Children of the King
and Queen of Bohemia
George Villiers, 1st Duke of Buckingham,
and his Family
London National Gallery
Christ before Caiaphas
Elizabeth, Queen of Bohemia (1642)
Saint Sebastian
London National Portrait Gallery
•Charles I
Elizabeth, Queen of Bohemia (attributed)
Frederick V of Bohemia
London (Brentford) Syon House
Elizabeth, Queen of Bohemia (The Winter
Queen)
London (Dulwich) DPG
A Lady (1639)
Jacob de Witt
Upton House, Warwickshire NT
A Man
Wilton House, Wiltshire
Prince Rupert
Princess Sophia of Bohemia
Windsor Castle RC
Frederick Hendrik, Prince of Orange (1631)
Willem II, Prince of Orange

PIETER DE HOOCH
Rotterdam 1629 – Amsterdam 1684
He spent most of his career in Delft, where
he painted some of the most intimate
Dutch genre interiors of great appeal.
These often provide an idealised, model
view of family life, paying particular
attention to children's upbringing.
London Apsley House,
The Wellington Museum
Cavalier talking to a Lady
A Musical Party
London Buckingham Palace
A Courtyard in Delft at Evening: a Woman
Spinning
London Mansion House
Interior with a Woman Knitting, a Serving
Woman and a Child
London National Gallery
•Courtyard of a House in Delft (1658)
Interior, Woman drinking with Two Men
Man with Dead Birds and Other Figures
in a Stable
Musical Party in a Courtyard (1677)
A Woman and her Maid in a Courtyard
(166?)
London Wallace Collection
Boy bringing Pomegranates
Woman peeling Apples
London (Blackheath) Ranger's House EH
(on loan from the Wernher Collection)
Interior with a Mother and baby
Luton Hoo, Bedfordshire
Wernher Collection
Dutch Interior
Manchester City Art Gallery
Interior with a Gentleman and two Ladies
conversing (attributed)
Lady seated with a Dog in her Lap
(attributed)
Polesden Lacey, Surrey NT
The Golf-players
Saltram Park, Devon NT
Interior with Card-players
Waddesdon Manor, Buckinghamshire NT
The Game of Skittles

WILLEM KALF
Rotterdam 1619 – Amsterdam 1693
Perhaps the greatest of all Dutch
seventeenth-century still-life painters. He
would often rearrange and paint the same
objects. Kalf first painted humble farm
interiors before specialising in still lifes of
expensive and refined objects: silver,
Persian carpets, exotic fruit. He was a
master of depicting the effects of light on
reflective surfaces.
Glasgow Art Gallery and Museum
Still Life
Still Life
London Mansion House
Still Life with a Chinese Bottle
London National Gallery
•Still Life with a Drinking Horn
Manchester City Art Gallery
Still Life with Fruit, Goblet and Salver
Oxford Ashmolean Museum
Still Life with an Oriental Rug

GEORGES DE LA TOUR
Vic-sur-Seille 1593 – Lunéville 1653
Famous today as the painter of
astonishing night-time scenes which
have an extraordinary meditative quality,
with very still, simplified figures lit by
the warm glow of candle or flame.
De la Tour's paintings were bought by
the French king, Louis XIII, but he fell into
obscurity after his death.
Hampton Court Palace RC
Saint Jerome
Leicester NWMAG
•The Choirboy
Stockton-on-Tees Preston Hall Museum
The Dice-Players

Georges de la Tour: The Choirboy

Murrillo: The Marriage at Cana

FRANS VAN MIERIS
Leiden 1635 – Leiden 1681
The founder of a dynasty of artists, he painted genre scenes with a meticulous and refined technique learned from his master, Gerrit Dou. His small-scale works have always commanded high prices and in his lifetime were collected by rulers across Europe. Despite the astonishing control of his painting, he apparently drank heavily and was unable to handle his wealth.

Ascott, Buckinghamshire NT
Portrait of Greffier Fagel (?)
A Man
Barnsley Cannon Hall
Boy blowing Bubbles (1663) (attributed)
Bowood, Wiltshire
A Lady with a Cavalier
Glasgow Art Gallery and Museum
•A Sick Woman and her Doctor (1657)
London Mansion House
Lady with Pearls and a Maidservant
London National Gallery
The Artist's Wife (?)
Self Portrait (1674)
Woman feeding a Parrot
London Wallace Collection
Venus and Cupid with Two Amorini
Polesden Lacey, Surrey NT
Self Portrait (1667)
Wilton House, Wiltshire
Self Portrait

MURILLO
Seville 1618 – Seville 1682
Murillo was the leading painter in Seville in the seventeenth century and painted most of his works for the religious houses of the city. Known for his deeply religious paintings but, in this country, perhaps more admired for his scenes of everyday life, such as the two paintings of peasant children in the Dulwich Picture Gallery. The sentimental nature of many of his paintings made them particularly popular in the nineteenth century.

Belvoir Castle, Leicestershire
Holy Family

Birmingham Barber Institute
•The Marriage at Cana
Birmingham CMAG
Vision of Saint Anthony of Padua
Boughton House, Northamptonshire
Saint John the Baptist
Buscot Park, Berkshire NT
Faith presenting the Eucharist
Cambridge Fitzwilliam Museum
Saint John the Baptist with the Scribes and Pharisees
The Vision of Fray Lauterio
Chatsworth, Derbyshire
Holy Family
Dyrham Park, Avon NT
Peasants
Edinburgh NGS
A Young Man with a Basket of Fruit
Glasgow Art Gallery and Museum
Rest on the Flight into Egypt (attributed)
Glasgow Pollok House
Virgin and Child
Virgin and Child with Saint John
Glasgow University
A Boy's Head
Christ as the Good Shepherd
Kingston Lacy, Dorset NT
Saint Rosa of Lima (attributed)
Liverpool Walker Art Gallery
Virgin and Child in Glory

London Apsley House, The Wellington Museum
A Gentleman (attributed)
Isaac blessing Jacob
Saint Francis receiving the Stigmata
London National Gallery
Adoration of the Shepherds (attributed)
Boy leaning on a Parapet
Christ healing a Paralytic at the Pool of Bethesda
Portrait of Don Justino de Neve (1665)
The Immaculate Conception (attributed)
The Infant Saint John the Baptist with the Lamb
Self Portrait
Saint John the Baptist in the Wilderness (attributed)
The Two Trinities (The Pedroso Murillo)
London Wallace Collection
Adoration of the Shepherds
Annunciation
Assumption of the Virgin
The Charity of Saint Thomas of Villanueva
Holy Family with Saint John
Joseph and his Brothers
Marriage of the Virgin
Virgin and Child
Virgin and Child (attributed)
Virgin and Child in Glory with Saints
London (Dulwich) DPG
The Flower Girl
Two Peasant Boys
Two Peasant Boys and a Negro Boy
The Virgin of the Rosary
Sheffield Sheffield Galleries (Graves)
Christ sleeping on the Cross
Tatton Park, Cheshire NT
Virgin and Child with Saint Anne
Woburn Abbey, Bedfordshire
Cherubs scattering Flowers
York City Art Gallery
Saint Thomas of Villanueva healing a Lame Man (attributed)

NICOLAS POUSSIN
Les Andelys, Normandy 1594 – Rome 1665
French artist who settled in Rome in 1624 and developed a highly classical style, derived from his study of antique sculpture. His only papal commission was rejected but he enjoyed the patronage of

Rembrandt: Young Girl leaning on a Windowsill (1645)

leading aristocrats in Italy and France, including Cardinal Richelieu, the Chief Minister of France. To aid his composition he posed wax models in a box so that he could observe light and shadow falling across the figures.

Belvoir Castle, Leicestershire
The Sacraments: Confirmation, The Eucharist, Marriage, Ordination, Extreme Unction
Birmingham Barber Institute
Tancred and Erminia
Brighton Preston Manor
Virgin and Child

Cambridge Fitzwilliam Museum
Rebecca and Eleazar at the Well
Cardiff National Museum of Wales
The Exposition of Moses (owned jointly with London, National Gallery)
Landscape with the funeral of Phocion (loan)
Edinburgh NGS
Moses striking Water from the Rock (Sutherland loan)
Mystic Marriage of Saint Catherine (Sutherland loan)
The Sacraments (second series): Extreme Unction, Confirmation, Baptism, Confession, Ordination, Eucharist, Marriage (Sutherland loan)
Leicester NWMAG
Holy Family with Saint John
Liverpool Walker Art Gallery
Landscape with Shepherds
Landscape with the Gathering of the Ashes of Phocion
London National Gallery
11 works including:
The Adoration of the Golden Calf
The Annunciation
A Bacchanalian Revel before a Term of Pan
The Triumph of Pan
London Wallace Collection
Dance to the Music of Time
London (Dulwich) DPG
The Nurture of Jupiter
The Return from Egypt
Rinaldo and Armida
Saint Rita of Cascia
•The Triumph of David
Venus and Mercury (fragment in Paris, Louvre)
Oxford Ashmolean Museum
The Exposition of Moses
Stourhead, Wiltshire NT
The Choice of Hercules
Tatton Park, Cheshire NT
Noah's Sacrifice (attributed)
Woburn Abbey, Bedfordshire
Moses trampling on Pharaoh's Crown

Nicolas Poussin: The Triumph of David

REMBRANDT

Leiden 1606 – Amsterdam 1669
Perhaps the best-known artist of the seventeenth century. As well as a painter of portraits, Biblical and mythological scenes and occasional landscapes, he was a prolific draughtsman and an extraordinarily innovatory printmaker. Hugely successful as a young man, he was famous for his ability to capture and convey character and the emotions. Extravagance led to bankruptcy in 1656 and his later works tend to be more introspective in mood, if more adventurous in technique.

Buscot Park, Berkshire NT
Portrait of Clement de Jonghe (?)
Cambridge Fitzwilliam Museum
Man in Fanciful Costume holding a Sword (attributed; companion in Sarasota) (1650)
Chatsworth, Derbyshire
King Uzziah stricken with Leprosy (1635)
Drumlanrig Castle, Dumfriesshire
Old Woman reading (1655)
Edinburgh NGS
Hannah and Samuel in the Temple (1648) (Sutherland loan) (attributed)
Hendrickje Stoffels in Bed
Self Portrait (1657) (Sutherland loan)
Glasgow Art Gallery and Museum
Alexander (?) (1655 (?))
Glasgow Burrell Collection
Self Portrait (1632)
Glasgow University
Entombment (sketch)
Liverpool Walker Art Gallery
Self Portrait
London Buckingham Palace
Christ and Mary Magdalen at the Tomb
London National Gallery
21 paintings including:
Belshazzar's Feast (163[?])
Saskia as Flora (1635)
Self Portrait at the Age of 34 (1640)
Self Portrait at the Age of 63 (1669)
London V&A
The Departure of the Shunammite Woman (attributed) (1640)
London Wallace Collection
The Centurion Cornelius (attributed)
Child in Fanciful Costume (attributed) (1633)
The Good Samaritan (attributed) (1630)
Portrait of Jan Pellicorne and his Son Caspar (attributed)
Landscape with a Coach (attributed) (1638)
Portrait of Susanna van Collen, Wife of Jan Pellicorne, with her Daughter Eva Susanna (attributed) (163[?])
Titus
London (Dulwich) DPG
Portrait of Jacob de Gheyn III (1632)
Titus (1663)
 •Young Girl leaning on a Windowsill (1645)
London (Hampstead)
Kenwood (Iveagh Bequest)
Self Portrait
Penrhyn Castle, Gwynned NT
Catrina Hooghsaet
Wilton House, Wiltshire

'Rembrandt's Mother' reading (attributed)
Windsor Castle RC
'Rembrandt's Mother' (?)
Self Portrait (attributed)
Young Man in a Turban (1631)

RIBERA

Jàtiva, near Valencia 1591 – Naples 1652
Spanish painter who spent his whole career in Italy and was much influenced by Caravaggio. He settled in Naples, at the time under Spanish rule, where he achieved much success, both professionally and socially, being knighted by the Pope in 1625. Ribera's dark and sombre works exerted a considerable influence on the next generation.

Attingham Park, Shropshire NT
Death of Archimedes
Buscot Park, Berkshire NT
Jacob with Laban's Flock (attributed)
Cardiff National Museum of Wales
Saint Jerome in the Desert
Corsham Court, Wiltshire
A Mathematician
Glasgow Art Gallery and Museum
The Penitent Saint Peter
Glasgow Burrell Collection
Christ disputing with the Doctors
Hampton Court Palace RC
A Philosopher
Harewood House, Yorkshire
Saint John the Baptist
Hull Ferens Art Gallery
A Philosopher
Leith Hall, Aberdeenshire NTS
The Flight into Egypt
London Apsley House,
The Wellington Museum
 •Hecate
Saint James
Saint John the Baptist
London National Gallery
An Apostle
Jacob and the Sheep
Lamentation over the Dead Christ
Perth Museum and Art Gallery
Saint Andrew
West Wycombe Park, Buckinghamshire NT
Pythagoras
Wilton House, Wiltshire
Democritus

SALVATOR ROSA

Naples 1615 – Rome 1673
An unconventional artist and poet who refused to work for patrons, choosing to paint his own subjects. These were often fantastical landscapes peopled by weird and frightening beings, which were much admired, particularly in the eighteenth and nineteenth centuries. He worked for Giovanni Carlo de'Medici in Florence but left because of the court's restrictions. He also found buyers by exhibiting in the annual Pantheon exhibition in Rome.

Althorp, Northamptonshire
Cincinnatus called from the Farm

Salvator Rosa: Rocky Landscape with a Hermit

Diogenes receiving a Visit from Alexander
Attingham Park, Shropshire NT
Christ and the Money Changers
Birmingham CMAG
Head of a Man with a Turban
Burghley House, Stamford
Landscape
Buscot Park, Berkshire NT
A Man
Cambridge Fitzwilliam Museum
'L'Umana Fragilità'
Cardiff National Museum of Wales
Rocky Landscape with Cattle
Castle Howard, Yorkshire
Howard Collection
Saint John the Evangelist
Chatsworth, Derbyshire
Jacob wrestling with the Angel
Joseph's Dream
Corsham Court, Wiltshire
Landscape
Landscape with a Mill
Landscape with Tobias and the Angel
Seascape
Edinburgh NGS
Desolate Landscape with Two Figures
Landscape with Saint Anthony Abbot and Saint Paul the Hermit
Edinburgh Talbot Rice Gallery
Rocky Landscape with Figures
Glasgow Art Gallery and Museum
Landscape with Saint John the Baptist
Landscape with the Baptism of Christ
Glasgow University
Laomedon detected
Kedleston Hall, Derbyshire NT
A Philosopher
Kingston Lacy, Dorset NT
Sir James Altham as a Hermit
Knole, Kent NT
Bandits robbing Travellers
Liverpool Walker Art Gallery
 •Rocky Landscape with a Hermit
London Apsley House,
The Wellington Museum
Battle Scene
London National Gallery
Landscape with Mercury and the Dishonest Woodman
Landscape with Tobias and the Angel
Landscape with Travellers asking the Way
Scene of Witchcraft
Self Portrait
London Wallace Collection
Landscape with Apollo and the Cumaean Sibyl

London (Dulwich) DPG
Soldiers Gambling
Newcastle upon Tyne Hatton Gallery
Soldiers and Peasants in a Rocky Landscape
Oxford CCPG
Erichthonius delivered to the Daughters of Cecrops
Hermit contemplating a Skull
Rocky Landscape with Figures
Rocky Landscape with Soldiers
Saul and the Witch of Endor
Tobias and the Angel
Southampton City Art Gallery
Landscape with Soldiers
Tatton Park, Cheshire NT
Landscape with Mercury and Argus
West Wycombe Park, Bucks NT
View of an Estuary with Shipping
Wilton House, Wiltshire
Landscape

Ribera: Hecate

PETER PAUL RUBENS

Siegen, Westphalia 1577 – Antwerp 1640
An international superstar, Rubens was a highly educated and erudite man of seemingly boundless energy and enterprise. He received commissions from rulers throughout Europe, receiving many honours. He was also employed on diplomatic missions to England, one result of which was the painted ceiling of the Banqueting House, Whitehall.

Ascott, Buckinghamshire NT
Virgin and Child
Birmingham Barber Institute
Landscape near Malines (Mechelen)
Portrait of a Carmelite Prior
Birmingham CMAG
Sketch for the Whitehall Ceiling
Buscot Park, Berkshire NT
Portrait of the Marchesa Brigida Spinola Doria
Cambridge Fitzwilliam Museum
12 works including seven sketches for the Eucharist series of designs and Teresa of Avila's Vision of a Dove
Cambridge King's College Chapel
Adoration of the Kings (altarpiece)
Cardiff National Museum of Wales
Four Tapestry Cartoons depicting the Story of Aeneas (attribution disputed)
Castle Howard, Yorkshire
Howard Collection
Herodias and Salome
Edinburgh NGS
Adoration of the Shepherds
The Feast of Herod
Saint Ambrose
Glasgow Art Gallery and Museum
Nature adorned by the Graces (with Jan Brueghel)
Glasgow University
Head of an Old Man
Hampton Court Palace RC
Jupiter and Antiope (with Snyders, qv)
Holkham Hall, Norfolk
Return of the Holy Family

Peter Paul Rubens: Portrait of Susanna Lunden, née Fourment ('Le Chapeau de Paille')

Jacob van Ruisdael: The Banks of a River

Kingston Lacy, Dorset NT
Portrait of the Marchesa Caterina Grimaldi
Portrait of the Marchesa Maria Grimaldi
Levens Hall, Cumbria Bagot Collection
Portrait of Anne of Hungary
Liverpool Walker Art Gallery
Virgin and Child with Saint Elisabeth
and Saint John
London Apsley House,
The Wellington Museum
Portrait of Anna Dorothea, Daughter
of Rudolf II
Head of an Old Man
London Banqueting House, Whitehall
Ceiling paintings celebrating King James I
London Buckingham Palace
Landscape with Saint George and the
Dragon
The Assumption of the Virgin
The Family of Balthasar Gerbier
London Courtauld Institute
31 works including oil sketches and
Cain slaying Abel
Death of Achilles
Landscape by Moonlight
London National Gallery
24 works including:
Autumn Landscape with a View of the
Château de Steen in the Early Morning
Minerva protects Pax from
Mars (Peace and War)
Paris awards the Golden Apple to Venus
(The Judgement of Paris)
Samson and Delilah
•Portrait of Susanna Lunden, née
Fourment ('Le Chapeau de Paille')
London V&A
War and Victory (sketch)
London Wallace Collection
Adoration of the Kings
Adoration of the Kings (sketch for
Altarpiece in King's College Chapel,
Cambridge)
Christ on the Cross
Christ's Charge to Saint Peter
The Defeat and Death of Maxentius
Holy Family with Saint Elisabeth
and Saint John
Portrait of Isabella Brandt
Rainbow Landscape
The Triumphal Entry of Henri IV into Paris
London (Brentford), Syon House
Diana returning from the Hunt
London (Dulwich) DPG
12 works including:
Venus weeping over Adonis
Venus, Mars and Cupid
Normanby Hall, Lincolnshire
Scunthorpe Corporation
Head of a Roman Emperor
Oxford Ashmolean Museum
13 oil sketches including:
The Conversion of Paul (sketch)
Landscape with Farm Buildings
at Sunset (sketch)

Saltram Park, Devon NT
Portrait of Francesco IV Gonzaga, Duke of
Mantua
Waddesdon Manor, Buckinghamshire NT
The Garden of Love
Wilton House, Wiltshire
Christ with Saint John the Baptist
and Two Angels
Landscape with Shepherds

JACOB VAN RUISDAEL
Haarlem 1628/9 – Amsterdam 1682
The greatest Dutch landscape painter,
Ruisdael painted all types of scenery, unlike
most of his contemporaries, who tended to
specialise. He often invested his landscapes
with a moody atmosphere, conveyed by
dramatic contrasts of light. Popular in
Britain in the eighteenth and nineteenth
centuries, his naturalistic landscapes
influenced English landscape painters such
as Gainsborough and Constable.
Birmingham Barber Institute
Wooded Landscape
Bristol City Art Gallery
A River in Spate
Burghley House, Stamford
Landscape
Cambridge Fitzwilliam Museum
Landscape with a Blasted Tree near
a House
Landscape with a River and Pines
Landscape with a Waterfall
View on the Amstel looking towards
Amsterdam
Drumlanrig Castle, Dumfriesshire
Landscape
Edinburgh NGS
•The Banks of a River (on loan from the
University)
Edinburgh Talbot Rice Gallery
Woodland Scene
Floors Castle, Roxburghshire
Rocky River Scene
Glasgow Art Gallery and Museum

Landscape with a Cottage, Bridge
and Sheep
Landscape with a Ruined Tower
View of Egmond aan Zee
Wooded Landscape with Fishermen by
a Pond
Hull Ferens Art Gallery
Woodland Scene with a Cornfield
Leeds Temple Newsam House
Storm off Egmond aan Zee
London Mansion House
The Castle of Bentheim
Landscape with Cornfield
View of Haarlem from the Dunes
London National Gallery
18 paintings including:
A Pool surrounded by Trees
A Landscape with a Ruined Castle and
a Church
London Wallace Collection
Landscape with a Farm (attributed)
Landscape with a Village
Landscape with a Waterfall
Rocky Landscape
London (Dulwich) DPG
Landscape with Windmills near Haarlem
A Waterfall
London (Greenwich) NMM
Rough Seas breaking over a Jetty
Manchester City Art Gallery
Storm off the Dutch Coast
A Wooded Country Lane (1649)
Nostell Priory, Yorkshire NT
Landscape with Cattle
Oxford Ashmolean Museum
Landscape near Muiderburg
Landscape with a Waterfall
Oxford Worcester College
Wooded Landscape (The Pond)
Petworth House, Sussex NT
Waterfall
Polesden Lacey, Surrey NT
The Coast of the Zuider Zee near Muiden
Southampton City Art Gallery
The Dunes near Haarlem
Sudeley Castle, Gloucestershire
Ashcombe Collection
The Watermill
Upton House, Warwickshire NT
'Le Coup de Soleil'
Waddesdon Manor, Buckinghamshire NT
Wooded Landscape with a Waterfall
Woburn Abbey, Bedfordshire
Landscape
Landscape

Diego Velázquez: The Infante Balthasar Carlos as a Sportsman with Three Dogs

PIETER SAENREDAM
Assendelft 1597 – Haarlem 1665
By far the greatest of the many Dutch
artists who specialised in painting the
bare whitewashed interiors of the
Protestant churches of Holland. His
mastery and manipulation of perspective,
together with the clarity and subtlety of
his depiction of light, give his paintings an
almost abstract quality.
Edinburgh NGS
•Interior of Saint Bavo, Haarlem
Glasgow Art Gallery and Museum
Interior of Saint Bavo, Haarlem (1633)
London National Gallery
Interior of Saint Bavo, Haarlem
Interior of the Buurkerk, Utrecht (1644)
Upton House, Warwickshire NT
Interior of the Catherijnekerk, Utrecht

JAN STEEN
Leiden 1626 – Leiden 1679
Prolific and popular painter of genre
scenes frequently depicting disorderly
behaviour and giving rise to the Dutch
saying, 'a Jan Steen household'. These

paintings are intended as warnings that
over-indulgence can only ever have
catastrophic outcomes and they
sometimes illustrate well-known
moralising sayings.
Ascott, Buckinghamshire NT
Children playing with a Cat
Itinerant Musicians (1659)
Belvoir Castle, Leicestershire
Grace before Meat
Birmingham Barber Institute
The Wrath of Ahasuerus
Cambridge Fitzwilliam Museum
Interior with Figures
A Painter and his Family
A Village Festival
Cheltenham Art Gallery
•The Fat Kitchen
The Lean Kitchen
Edinburgh NGS
The School for Boys and Girls
Edinburgh Talbot Rice Gallery
The Doctor's Visit
Glasgow Pollok House
Christ in the House of Martha and Mary
Glasgow University
A Boy showing his Drawings
London Apsley House,
The Wellington Museum
The Dissolute Household
The Egg Dance
The Physician's Visit
A Wedding Party (1667)
London Buckingham Palace
A Village Revel
Interior of a Tavern with Cardplayers and a
Violin Player
London Mansion House
Sleeping Couple
The Young Suitor
London National Gallery

Jan Steen: The Fat Kitchen

10 works including:
The Effects of Intemperance
A Peasant Family at Meal-time
London Wallace Collection
The Christening-Feast (1664)
The Harpsichord Lesson
The Lute Player
The Village Alchemist
Manchester City Art Gallery
The Rommelpot: Interior with Three
Figures
Penrhyn Castle, Gwynned NT
The Burgomaster of Delft
Upton House, Warwickshire NT
The Sense of Hearing
The Sense of Sight
The Sense of Smell
The Sense of Taste
The Tired Traveller
Woburn Abbey, Bedfordshire
The Twelfth Night Feast

GERARD TERBORCH
Zwolle 1617 – Deventer 1681
A leading Dutch genre painter, mainly of
refined middle-class scenes. His depictions
of wealthy, elegant people, are often
contemplative in tone and are marked by
his exquisite rendering of surface texture,
particularly the sheen of silks and satins.
Bowood, Wiltshire
Head of a Woman
Edinburgh NGS
Singing-practice
London Mansion House
A Gentleman seated beside a Table,
holding a Paper
London National Gallery
Hermana van der Cruis
Officer dictating a Letter
The Signing of the Peace of Münster, 1648
A Young Man
Young Woman playing a Theorbo, and
Two Men
London V&A
Cavaliers (1638)
London Wallace Collection
Lady at her Toilette
Lady reading a Letter
Manchester City Art Gallery
Cornelis de Vos, Burgomaster of Deventer
Hendrick Casimir II, Prince of Nassau-Dietz
(1670)
Polesden Lacey, Surrey NT
•Interior with a Dancing Couple
A Man
Waddesdon Manor, Buckinghamshire NT
The Duet (1675)
Wilton House, Wiltshire
Battle Scene

DIEGO VELÁZQUEZ
Seville 1599 – Madrid 1660
One of the best-known seventeenth-
century Spanish painters, he became
court artist to King Philip IV at the age of
24, painting numerous portraits of all the
royal family, as well as religious paintings.
He visited Italy twice, painting a famous
portrait of Pope Innocent X, a small

version of which can be found in Apsley
House in London. He also painted a
number of scenes of everyday life.
Edinburgh NGS
Old Woman cooking Eggs
Ickworth, Suffolk NT
•The Infante Balthasar Carlos as a
Sportsman with Three Dogs
Kingston Lacy, Dorset NT
Cardinal Massimi
London Apsley House,
The Wellington Museum
A Man
The Poet Francisco de Quevedo y Villegas
(attributed)
Pope Innocent X (attributed)
Two boys at a Table
The Water-Seller of Seville
London National Gallery
Archbishop Fernando Valdés (fragment)
Bust Portrait of Philip IV
Christ after the Flagellation contemplated
by the Christian Soul
The Hunt
The Immaculate Conception
Kitchen Scene with Christ in the House of
Martha and Mary (1618)
Philip IV in Brown and Silver
Saint John on Patmos
Venus and Cupid before a Mirror (The
Rokeby Venus)
London Wallace Collection
The Infante Balthasar Carlos
A Lady with a Fan

WILLEM VAN DE VELDE
THE YOUNGER
Leiden 1633 – London 1707
From a Dutch family of painters, he
specialised in marine paintings. His many
early works depict shipping on calm seas
or fishing boats along the coast. From
1672, after he moved to England, he began
painting marine battle scenes, principally
for King Charles II and the Duke of York,
and often from sketches by his father.
Barnsley Cannon Hall
A Calm (attributed)
Belvoir Castle, Leicestershire
Ships of the Dutch Fleet
Boughton House, Northamptonshire
Seascape
Bristol City Art Gallery
A Calm Sea
Culzean Castle NTS
Seascape
Edinburgh NGS
Fishing-bots in a Calm
Felbrigg Hall, Norfolk NT
Six seascapes
Floors Castle, Roxburghshire
Seascape
Hampton Court Palace RC
A Calm
London Buckingham Palace
A Calm: a States Yacht under Sail
'The Golden Leeuw' at Sea in Heavy
Weather
London Mansion House
Fishing boats at a Jetty in a Calm Sea
Shipping in a Calm
Shipping in a Calm Sea
London National Gallery

17 seascapes
London V&A
Shipping in a Calm
London Wallace Collection
Eight seascapes
London (Dulwich) DPG
A Brisk Breeze
A Calm (1663)
London (Greenwich) NMM
58 seascapes including:
• Calm: A Dutch Flagship Coming
to Anchor before a Light Air
London (Hampstead)
Kenwood (Iveagh Bequest)
Sea piece
London (Richmond) Ham House NT
Four seascapes
Polesden Lacey, Surrey NT
Shipping in a Calm
Tatton Park, Cheshire NT
Shipping in a Rough Sea
Waddesdon Manor, Buckinghamshire NT
The Cannon Shot
Shipping in a Calm
Wilton House, Wiltshire
Three pictures called Shipping in a Calm
Woburn Abbey, Bedfordshire
Seascape

JOHANNES VERMEER
Delft 1632 – Delft 1675
Vermeer is now a figure of near mythic
status but he was forgotten almost
immediately on his death and
rediscovered only in the later nineteenth
century. Only 35 authenticated paintings
by him survive, mostly of interior
scenes. They are characterised by a still,
remote quality and a near-miraculous

Johannes Vermeer: Interior with a Young Woman standing at the Virginals

depiction of light. His characteristic
subject matter is a single female, unaware
of the viewer's presence and absorbed by
careful activity, set in the corner of a room.
Edinburgh NGS
Christ in the House of Martha and Mary
London National Gallery
Interior with a Woman seated at the
Virginals
•Interior with a Young Woman standing at
the Virginals
London (Hampstead)
Kenwood (Iveagh Bequest)
Interior with a Woman playing a Guitar

FRANCISCO DE ZURBARAN

Fuente de Cantos, Badajoz 1598 –
Madrid 1664
Leading painter of religious works in Seville
and in Madrid, who worked principally for
religious houses. He was also employed by
Olivares, King Philip IV's chief minister, to
decorate the Buen Retiro Palace in Madrid.
Owing to Spain's economic decline in the
1640s, he sought and found a market in the
newly-discovered Americas. His few still
lifes are particularly striking for their spare
beauty.
Birmingham Barber Institute
Saint Marina (attributed)
Bishop Auckland, Co Durham, Palace
•Asher, Dan, Gad, Isaachar, Jacob, Joseph,
Judah, Levi, Naphthali, Reuben, Simeon,
Zebulun (all paintings attributed: for the
final painting in this series see
Grimsthorpe Castle)
Cambridge Fitzwilliam Museum
Saint Ruffina (attributed)
Edinburgh NGS
The Immaculate Conception with Saint
Joachim and Saint Anne
Grimsthorpe Castle, Lincolnshire
Benjamin (attributed)
Kingston Lacy, Dorset NT
Saint Augustine (attributed)
Saint Dorothy (attributed)
Saint Justa (attributed)
London National Gallery
Cup of Water and a Rose on a Silver Plate
Saint Francis in Meditation
Saint Francis in Meditation (1639)
Saint Margaret

1701-1800

The eighteenth century was the first in which the British began collecting art in earnest, but for the most part they preferred their art to be by dead Italians, Frenchmen and possibly Dutchmen than by their European contemporaries. There were, of course, exceptions. The young nobles who travelled to Italy on the Grand Tour might have been buying works by Renaissance masters and Claude Lorrain where they could find them, but they also stuffed their trunks with Canaletto's Venetian views and celebratory portraits painted in Rome by the arch-flatterer Pompeo Batoni. Today there are more Canalettos in Woburn Abbey alone than can be seen in the whole of Italy.

Even more importantly for British collections, the eighteenth century saw the birth of a truly British school of painting. Unsurprisingly, the list of pictures here is dominated by the British, most obviously by the portraits produced in huge quantities by the rival studios of Reynolds and Gainsborough in England and Raeburn and Ramsay in Scotland. The rococo extravagances of French artists such as Boucher and Fragonard were deplored by the British, a prejudice that continued into later centuries, making their work difficult to see here. The only really significant collection in the country was amassed in Paris during the nineteenth century by the 4th Marquess of Hertford and bequeathed to the British nation in 1897 by his son and daughter-in-law, Sir Richard and Lady Wallace.

Antonio Canaletto: Venice: The Grand Canal with the Palazzo Balbi

WILLIAM BLAKE
London 1757 - London 1827
Visionary, mystic, poet-painter of the Romantic Age, communicator with angels and the other world, Blake created, wrote and depicted an entire personal mythology. Known for his Songs of Innocence and Experience that he produced in limited handmade editions, these works integrate word and image.
Arlington Court, Devon NT
Vision of the Cycle of Life in Man (1821)
Brighton Art Gallery
Adoration of the Kings
Cambridge Fitzwilliam Museum
Allegory of the Spiritual Condition of Man
The Judgement of Solomon
Glasgow Pollok House
Adam naming the Beasts (1810)
Christ's Entry into Jerusalem (1800)
Entombment
Eve naming the Birds
•Sir Geoffrey Chaucer and the Nine and Twenty Pilgrims on Their Journey to Canterbury (1808)

Vision of the Last Judgement (1806)
London British Museum
The Dance of Albion
London Tate Britain
The Agony in the Garden
The Bard from Gray
Bathsheba at the Bath
The Body of Abel found by Adam and Eve
The Body of Christ borne to the Tomb
Christ blessing the Little Children (1799)
The Ghost of a Flea
Satan smiting Job with Sore Boils
The Spiritual Form of Nelson guiding Leviathan
The Spiritual Form of Pitt guiding Behemoth
Winter
London V&A
The Virgin and Child in Egypt (1810)
Manchester City Art Gallery
16 portraits of poets
Petworth House, Sussex NT
Characters from Spenser's Faerie Queene
Last Judgement (1808)
Satan calling up his Legions
Swimming Horses at Brighton

FRANÇOIS BOUCHER
Paris 1703 - Paris 1770
Rococo decorator, great admirer of Tiepolo's work, and patronised by Madame de Pompadour, Boucher designed tapestries and painted scenes of classical mythology, often in questionable taste, for which the philosopher Diderot censured him on moral grounds. He is best represented in London's Wallace

Collection.
Ascott, Buckinghamshire NT
Cupids representing the Arts (four pictures)
Barnard Castle Bowes Museum
Landscape with a Watermill (1743)
Edinburgh NGS
Portrait of Mme de Pompadour (attributed)
London National Gallery
Landscape with a Watermill (1755)
Pan and Syrinx (1759)
London V&A
Portrait of Mme de Pompadour (1758)
London Wallace Collection
23 paintings including:
Mme de Pompadour (1759)
•The Rising of the Sun (1753)
London (Hampstead)
Kenwood (Iveagh Bequest)
The Flower-Gatherers
Landscape with Figures gathering Cherries (1768)
Man offering Grapes to a Girl (1768)
Manchester City Art Gallery
Landscape with a Young Fisherman (1768)
Upton House, Warwickshire NT
Venus and Vulcan (sketch)
Waddesdon Manor, Buckinghamshire NT
Five Naked Children playing by a Rocky Pool
Four Naked Cupids and Flowers
Philippe Egalité as a Child (1749)
Shepherd teaching a Shepherdess to play the Flute
Three Cupids (1754)
Three Naked Cupids and a He-goat amid Vines

ANTONIO CANALETTO
Venice 1697 - Venice 1768
Referred to as 'The Merchant of Venice' on account of his astute business sense, Canaletto's views of Venice were highly sought after by Grand Tourists as souvenirs of their travels. Canaletto's success with the wealthy English aristocrats led him to visit London to test the home market and paint a number of scenes along the Thames. He subsequently returned to Venice and the more lucrative tourist market.
Alnwick Castle, Northumberland
London: Northumberland House
Venice: St Mark's Square
Venice: The Doge's Palace, the Scala dei Giganti
Angelsey Abbey, Cambridgeshire NT
Self Portrait (attributed)
Badminton House, Gloucestershire
Badminton from the Park
The Park from Badminton House
Barnard Castle Bowes Museum
Venice: Regatta on the Grand Canal
Venice: The Bucintoro
Barnsley Cannon Hall
Capriccio with a Colonnade and Courtyard
Birmingham Barber Institute
Venice: The Logetta of Sansovino
Birmingham CMAG
Warwick Castle, the East Front
Warwick Castle, the East Front from the Courtyard
Blickling Hall, Norfolk NT
London: Chelsea Hospital and Ranelagh House and Rotunda (fragment)
Bowhill, Selkirkshire
London: Whitehall and the Privy Garden towards the North
Cambridge Fitzwilliam Museum
Venice: Courtyard of the Doge's Palace
Venice: The Grand Canal, the Salute and Dogana
Venice: St Mark's Square
Cardiff National Museum of Wales
Venice: The Bacino di San Marco
Goodwood, Sussex
London and the Thames

London: Whitehall and the Privy Garden
Venice: The Grand Canal looking towards the Rialto Bridge
Venice: The Grand Canal with the Rialto Bridge
Holkham Hall, Norfolk
Venice: The Bucintoro and the Molo on Ascension Day
Venice: The Grand Canal
Venice: The Rialto Bridge
Hull Ferens Art Gallery
•Venice: The Grand Canal with the Palazzo Balbi
Leeds Temple Newsam House
Venice: Regatta on the Grand Canal (attributed)
London Museum of London
London: Westminster Abbey, Interior of Henry VII's Chapel
London National Gallery
11 works including:
Venice: The Campo San Vidal and S. Maria della Carità (The Stonemason's Yard)
Venice: The Feast Day of St Roch
London Sir John Soane's Museum
Venice: St Mark's Square
Venice: The Rialto Bridge
Venice: The Riva degli Schiavoni
London V&A
Capriccio: Ruined Bridge with Figures
London Wallace Collection
13 views of Venice
London Westminster Abbey
Westminster Abbey with the Procession of the Knights of the Bath (1749)
London (Dulwich) DPG
Venice: The Return of the Bucintoro to the Molo on Ascension Day
London (Greenwich) NMM
Greenwich Hospital from the Thames
Oxford Ashmolean Museum
Dolo on the Brenta
Penrhyn Castle, Gwynned NT
The Thames at Westminster
Campo Santo Stefanin
St Mark's Square
Tatton Park, Cheshire NT
Venice: The Molo and S. Maria della Salute
Venice: The Riva degli Schiavoni and the Doge's Palace
Upton House, Warwickshire NT
Venice: The Bacino di San Marco
Windsor Castle RC
44 paintings including 34 views of Venice and
London: The Thames from Somerset House looking towards Westminster
Woburn Abbey, Bedfordshire
22 views of Venice

JEAN-BAPTISTE-SIMÉON CHARDIN
Paris 1699 - Paris 1779
The finest eighteenth-century painter of still-life and genre scenes. Inspired by Netherlandish pictures so popular in eighteenth-century France, his range of subjects is modest and restricted: kitchen utensils, vegetables, baskets of fruit, fish and game furnish the still lifes, while his

William Blake: Sir Geoffrey Chaucer and the Nine and Twenty Pilgrims on Their Journey to Canterbury

scenes of everyday life tend to be of quiet domesticity in simple interiors.

Edinburgh NGS
Still Life, the Kitchen Table
Vase of Flowers
Glasgow Burrell Collection
'Pierrot Thief' (attributed)
Still Life with a Ray
Still Life with Pâté (attributed) (1760)
Still Life with Pâté and Bottles (attributed)
Still Life, the Kitchen Table
Glasgow Hunterian Art Gallery
The Cellar Boy
The Scullery Maid
Woman taking Tea (1735)
London National Gallery
The House of Cards
Woman drawing Water from a Cistern
The Young Schoolmistress
Oxford Ashmolean Museum
Still Life with Kitchen Utensils
Tatton Park, Cheshire NT
•The Governess

JEAN HONORÉ FRAGONARD
Grasse 1732 - Paris 1806
Pupil of first Chardin and then Boucher, and an admirer of Tiepolo. His early serious subjects of biblical and mythological scenes were replaced by light-hearted, often erotic, scenes. Typical of these is The Swing, painted for a patron desiring 'a good view of the legs of this pretty little thing'. The Revolution put an end to this style of painting.
Brodick Castle, Isle of Arran NTS
A Girl
London National Gallery
Psyche showing her Sisters her Gifts from Cupid (1753)
London Wallace Collection
10 paintings including:
•The Fountain of Love
The Swing
Manchester City Art Gallery
An Actor after Domenico Fetti

JOHANN HEINRICH FUSELI
Zurich 1741 - Putney Hill, near London 1825
Fuseli left his native Switzerland for England, where he worked as a translator of French and German until Reynolds suggested he become a painter. Creator of some of the greatest works of Romantic horror, he painted a series of works from Shakespeare and Milton before becoming Professor of Painting at the Royal Academy.
Birmingham CMAG
The Dispute between Hotspur, Glendower, Mortimer and Worcester about the division of England
Cardiff National Museum of Wales
Teiresias foretells the Future to Odysseus in the Underworld
Hinton Ampner House, Hampshire NT
Two Scenes from The Winter's Tale
Leeds University Gallery
Mistress Page in The Merry Wives of Windsor
Liverpool Walker Art Gallery
The Child Milton instructed by his Mother
Mary Powell, Milton's Wife, imploring his Forgiveness for having abandoned him
Oedipus receiving in the Presence of his Daughter the Prediction of his own Death
London Sir John Soane's Museum
Bracciaferro meditating over the Body of his Wife (1779)
London Tate Britain
The Dream of the Shepherd (1793)
Lady Macbeth and the Assassins
Percival liberating Belisane from the Spell of Urma
Titania and Bottom
London V&A
The Dream of Queen Catherine (three fragments)
The Fire King
Lytham St Anne's Town Hall
The Dream of Queen Catherine
Petworth House, Sussex NT
Five Courtiers
The Knight finding the Old Woman transformed into a Young and Beautiful One
Salome receiving the Head of Saint John the Baptist
The Witches appearing to Macbeth and Banquo
Stratfield Saye, Hampshire

Satan calling Beelzebub on the Sea of Fire
Satan calling up his Legions
Stratford-upon-Avon RSCC
Henry V condemning Cambridge, Scrope and Grey to Death
•The Three Witches from Macbeth
Tabley House, Cheshire
University of Manchester
Friar Puck
Wolverhampton Art Gallery and Museum
The Apotheosis of Penelope Boothby
York City Art Gallery
Prospero (fragment)

THOMAS GAINSBOROUGH
Sudbury, Suffolk 1722 - London 1788
One of the very greatest of the eighteenth-century portraitists, Gainsborough maintained that he wished to be a landscape painter but was obliged to make his living painting portraits. His charming early portraits, painted in his native Suffolk (his house in Sudbury is now a museum), may be somewhat stiff, but the virtuoso, loose painting technique of his later paintings often mesmerises in its seemingly effortless evocation of lace, silk and pearl.
Anglesey Abbey, Cambridgeshire NT
Coast Scene
Arundel Castle, Sussex
Bernard, 12th Duke of Norfolk as a Boy
Charles, 11th Duke of Norfolk
Ascott, Buckinghamshire NT
The Duchess of Richmond
The Hon. Thomas Needham
Barnard Castle Bowes Museum
Landscape with Elmsett Church, Suffolk
Bath Assembly Rooms
Captain Wade (1771)
Bath Holburne Museum of Art
Dr Rice Charleton
A Lady
Lady Clarges playing the Harp
•Mr and Mrs George Byam and their Eldest Daughter
Belfast Ulster Museum
Arthur, 5th Earl and 1st Marquess of Donegal
Theodosia Magill
Belvoir Castle, Leicestershire
Landscape
The Woodcutter's Return
Beningbrough Hall, Yorkshire NT
Edward Vernon
John Russell, 4th Duke of Bedford (lent by National Portrait Gallery)
Joseph Gibbs
Birmingham Barber Institute
Giusto Ferdinando Tenducci
The Harvest Waggon
The Hon. Harriott Marsham

Birmingham CMAG
Landscape with a Cottage and a Cart
Matthew Hale
Sir Charles Holte
Thomas Coward
Blickling Hall, Norfolk NT
The 2nd Earl of Buckinghamshire
Caroline Conolly, Countess of Buckinghamshire
Bowhill, Selkirkshire
George, Duke of Montagu
Henry, 3rd Duke of Buccleuch (1770)
Mary, Duchess of Montagu
Bowood, Wiltshire
Landscape with Cattle returning Home
Bradford Cartwright Hall
Sir Francis Bassett, Bt
A Young Man
Bristol City Art Gallery
A Gentleman of the Leybourne Popham Family
A Lady of the Leybourne Popham Family
Brodick Castle, Isle of Arran NTS
The 5th Earl of Rochford
Landscape with a Cottage and Cows drinking
Landscape with a Peasant and Two Cows
Burghley House, Stamford
Jane Lady Whichcote
Sir Thomas Whichcote, Bt

Burton Agnes, Yorkshire
Boynton Collection
Wick Rocks, Bath
Buscot Park, Berkshire NT
Cattle returning along a Wooded Lane
Cambridge Fitzwilliam Museum
A Forest Road
Heneage Lloyd and his Sister
The Hon. William Fitzwilliam (1775)
John Joshua Kirby
John Kirby
Mrs John Kirby
Landscape with a Pool
Philip Dupont
Canterbury Royal Museum
A Naval Officer
Cardiff National Museum of Wales
Sir Richard Lloyd
Thomas Pennant
Wooded Landscape with Hagar and Ishmael
Castle Howard, Yorkshire
Howard Collection
Girl with Pigs
Isobella Byron
Charlecote Park, Warwickshire NT
George Lucy (1760)
Corsham Court, Wiltshire
Paul Cobb Methuen
Paul Methuen
Croft Castle, Herefordshire NT
Elizabeth Cowper, Lady Croft
Dorchester, Dorset County Museum

Thomas Gainsborough: Mr and Mrs George Byam and their Eldest Daughter

Francisco de Goya: Scene at a Bullfight: Spanish Entertainment

FRANCISCO DE GOYA
Fuendetodos 1746 - Bordeaux 1828
Principal Painter to the King of Spain and official court painter, whose unofficial work depicted some of the most biting attacks on the church and on the savagery of the occupying French troops. His extraordinary imaginative depictions mark him out as curiously modern. He had an immense influence on nineteenth-century French art.
Barnard Castle Bowes Museum
Don Juan Antonio Meléndez Valdes (1797)
Interior of a Prison
Edinburgh NGS
The Doctor
Glasgow Pollok House
Children playing at Soldiers
Children playing on a See-saw
London Apsley House,
The Wellington Museum
The Duke of Wellington on Horseback (1812)
London Courtauld Institute
Don Francisco de Saavedra (1798)
London National Gallery
Andrés del Peral (1798)
The Duke of Wellington
Isabel de Porcel (1805)
Scene from The Forcibly Bewitched
Oxford Ashmolean Museum
•Scene at a Bullfight: Spanish Entertainment
Scene at a Bullfight: The Divided Ring
Upton House, Warwickshire NT
Don Francisco Bayeu y Subias (attributed)

WILLIAM HOGARTH
London 1697 - London 1764
One of the most inventive of artists, Hogarth as well as painting portraits, developed what he called his 'modern moral subjects'. These were series of narrative tableaux that satirised contemporary morals in society and politics, and shape our vision of eighteenth-century London. He sold his works as engravings, which ensured that they reached a wide audience.
Aberdeen Art Gallery
David Lewis
Mrs Mary Lewis
Ascott, Buckinghamshire NT
Miss Woodley (?)
Barnard Castle Bowes Museum
A Courtesan
Barnsley Cannon Hall
Lady Byron
Birmingham CMAG
The Distressed Poet
Brighton Art Gallery
A Girl
Bristol City Art Gallery
Ascension; The Sealing of the Sepulchre;
The Three Marys at the Tomb (The St Mary Radcliffe Altarpiece)
Edwin Sandys (1741)
Cambridge Fitzwilliam Museum
'Before' and 'After'

John Bragge
Drumlanrig Castle, Dumfriesshire
Mary, Duchess of Montagu
Dyrham Park, Avon NT
Peasant Girl (after Murillo)
Edinburgh NGS
The Hon. Mrs Graham
Landscape with a Distant View of Cornard Village, Suffolk
Mrs Hamilton Nisbet
Rocky Landscape
Edinburgh
Scottish National Portrait Gallery
John Campbell, 4th Duke of Argyll
Elton Hall, Peterborough Proby Collection
Landscape
Egham, Surrey Royal Holloway College
Peasants going to Market, Early Morning
Erddig, Denbighshire NT
Philip Yorke I
Exeter Royal Albert Memorial Museum
William Jackson playing the Harp
Firle Place, Sussex Cage Collection
The 2nd Viscount Gage
Floors Castle, Roxburghshire
Captain Henry Roberts, Cartographer
Fyvie Castle, Aberdeenshire NTS
Major William Tennant
Glasgow Art Gallery and Museum
Woody Landscape near Bath
Glasgow Burrell Collection
William Pitt
Gloucester CMAG
Landscape
Harewood House, West Yorkshire
George Canning as a Boy
Holkham Hall, Norfolk
Thomas William Coke, 1st Earl of Leicester
Hove Museum and Art Gallery
Landscape
Ickworth, Suffolk NT
Augustus Hervey
Augustus John Hervey, later 3rd Earl of

Bristol
John Augustus, Lord Hervey
Ipswich Christchurch Mansion
15 paintings (portraits and landscapes) including:
Holywells Park, Ipswich
William Wollaston playing the Flute (1760)
Knole, Kent NT
Lord George Sackville
Lacock Abbey, Wiltshire NT
John Talbot
Liverpool Sudley House
Elizabeth, Viscountess Folkestone
Liverpool Walker Art Gallery
Isabella, Viscountess Molyneux, later Countess of Sefton
Sir Robert Clayton
London Buckingham Palace RC
Diana and Actaeon
London Courtauld Institute
The Artist's Wife
Charles Tudway
Landscape
London Foundling Hospital
The Charterhouse
London National Gallery
11 works including:
The Morning Walk (1785)
Mr and Mrs Andrews
The Painter's Daughters chasing a Butterfly
London National Portrait Gallery
15 paintings including:
Self Portrait
David Garrick
London Tate Britain
30 paintings including:
Giovanna Baccelli
Gypsy Encampment, Sunset
London V&A
16 paintings including:
The Painter's Daughters
Queen Charlotte
London Wallace Collection

Miss Haverfield
Mrs Robinson (Perdita)
London (Brentford) Syon House
The 1st Duke of Northumberland
London (Dulwich) DPG
Mrs Moodey and Two of her Children
Mrs Sheridan and Mrs Tickell (The Linley Sisters)
Philippe de Loutherbourg
Thomas Linley the Elder
Thomas Linley the Younger
Samuel Linley
Unknown Couple in a Landscape
London (Greenwich) NMM
John Montagu, 4th Earl of Sandwich
London (Hampstead) Kenwood (Iveagh Bequest)
Going to Market
Lady Brisco
Mary, Countess of Howe
Miss Brummell
Two Shepherd Boys with Dogs Fighting
John Joseph Merlin
Wooded Landscape with Hounds coursing a Fox
Manchester City Art Gallery
The Faggot-Gatherer (1782)
Landscape with Figures
Landscape with Sheep
Mrs Prudence Rix
A Young Gentleman
Norwich Castle Museum
Sir Harbord Harbord, Bt
Oxford Ashmolean Museum
George Drummond
Landscape with Cattle and a Pond (unfinished)
Miss Gainsborough gleaning
Oxford CCPG
Sir John Skinner (1785)
Welbore Ellis, Baron Mendip (1769)
Parham Park, Sussex
Major Norton Knatchbull

Penrhyn Castle, Gwynned NT
Wooded Landscape
Petworth House, Sussex NT
A Pool with Shepherd and Cattle
A Setter
Port Sunlight Lady Lever Art Gallery
Anne, Duchess of Cumberland (?)
Mrs Charlotte Freer
Powis Castle, Montgomeryshire NT
The 1st Earl of Powis as a Boy
Southampton City Art Gallery
George Venables Vernon, 2nd Lord Vernon
Stourhead, Wiltshire NT
The Woodcutters
Sudbury, Suffolk Gainsborough's House
24 paintings including:
Peter Darnell Muilman, Charles Crokatt and William Keable in a Landscape
Wooded Landscape with Herdsmen
Upton House, Warwickshire NT
Crossing the Ford
Waddesdon Manor, Buckinghamshire NT
Alexander, 10th Duke of Hamilton (1786)
George IV, when Prince of Wales, with a Horse (1782)
Lord Archibald Hamilton (1786)
Master Nicholls (The Pink Boy) (1782)
Mrs John Douglas (1784)
Mrs Robinson (Perdita) (1781-2)
Sophia Charlotte, Lady Sheffield (1785)
Wallington, Northumberland NT
Susanna Trevelyan
Weston-super-Mare Woodspring Museum
John Pigott
Whitby Captain Cook Memorial Museum
John Montagu, 4th Earl of Sandwich
Windsor Castle RC
26 paintings including:
Johann Christian Fischer
Woburn Abbey, Bedfordshire
The 4th Duke of Bedford
Wolverhampton Art Gallery and Museum
Sir Edward Turner, Bt

The Bench
Dr Arnold of Ashby Lodge
Dr Benjamin Hoadley
Frances Arnold
A Man
A Musical Party: The Mathias Family
Richard James of the Middle Temple
Cardiff National Museum of Wales
A Children's Tea Party
A House of Cards
The Jones Family Conversation Piece
Clandon Park, Surrey NT
Arthur Onslow, Speaker of the House of
Commons with Sir Robert Walpole (with
James Thornhill) (1730)
Edinburgh NGS
Sarah Malcolm
Glasgow Burrell Collection
Mrs Anne Lloyd
Glasgow Pollok House
James Thomson
St Peter's Chapel
Ickworth, Suffolk NT
Conversation Piece with Lord Hervey
Leicester NWMAG
The Wollaston Family (loan) (1730)
Liverpool Walker Art Gallery
Garrick as Richard III
A Lady
London Foundling Hospital
Captain Coram (1740)
The March to Finchley (1746)
Moses brought before Pharoah's Daughter
London National Gallery
The Graham Children
'Marriage à la Mode': 6 paintings
The Shrimp Girl
London National Portrait Gallery
The Gaols Committee of the House
of Commons
Self Portrait painting the Comic Muse
London Sir John Soane's Museum
The Election Series: 4 paintings
The Rake's Progress: 8 paintings (1732-3)
London Tate Britain
19 paintings including:
'Oh, the Roast Beef of Old England' (The
Calais Gate) (1748)
Heads of Six of Hogarth's Servants
• Self Portrait with his Pug (1745)
London (Dulwich) DPG
A Fishing Party (The Fair Angler)
A Gentleman (1741)
London (Greenwich) NMM
Inigo Jones
Lord George Graham in his Cabin
Sir Alexander Schomberg (1763)
Woodes Rogers and his Family (1729)
London (Twickenham)
Marble Hill House EH
Sir Robert Pye Bt (1731)
Manchester City Art Gallery
A Gentleman (1739)
The Pool of Bethesda
Nostell Priory, Yorkshire NT
A Scene from Shakespeare's Tempest
Oxford Ashmolean Museum
The Enraged Musician
The Marriage Contract
The Suicide of the Countess or The Ill
Effects of Masquerades
Truro Royal Cornwall Museum
Scene at a Ball
Upton House, Warwickshire NT
Gerard Anne Edwards in his Cradle
Morning and Night
Windsor Castle RC
David Garrick with his Wife, Eva Maria Veigl
York City Art Gallery
Elisabeth Betts, Mrs Benjamin Hoadley (1741)

THOMAS JONES
Trevonen, Powys 1742 - Pencerrig,
Powys 1803

Welsh landscape painter and pupil of
Richard Wilson. He travelled to Naples and
Rome where he painted modest scenes
observed from his room - rooftops and
walls in the sun – and small landscapes
rendered on the spot, very like those later
painted by Corot in the nineteenth century.
Birmingham CMAG
A Hilltop near Naples (1782)
Penkerrig (1772)
Brecon Brecknock Museum
Llangorse Lake, Breconshire
Cambridge Fitzwilliam Museum
Scene near Naples (1783)
Cardiff National Museum of Wales
The Bard (1774)
The Bay of Naples (1777)
Buildings in Naples (1782)
Buildings in Naples (1782)
Classical Landscape (1772)
• Radnorshire
London National Gallery
A Wall in Naples
London Tate Britain
Capella Nuova, Naples (1782)
An Excavation
In the Colosseum, Rome
Mount Vesuvius from Torre
dell'Annunziata near Naples (1783)
The Outskirts of London (1785-6)
Rousham House, Oxfordshire
Cottrell-Dormer Collection
View of Rousham
Swansea Glynn Vivian Art Gallery
On the Road from Albano to Rome
Ruins in Naples

SIR THOMAS LAWRENCE
Bristol 1769 – London 1830
A prodigiously talented draughtsman and
painter, Lawrence was the finest portrait
painter of his generation in Europe and
regarded as the last English inheritor of
van Dyck's legacy. His public success was
swift and enduring. His pre-eminence as
the leading portrait painter was
established by his early 20s when he
painted George III and Queen Charlotte.
Aberdeen Town Hall
George Gordon, 5th Duke of Gordon
Arundel Castle, Sussex
Charles Howard, 11th Duke of Norfolk
Charlotte Sofia, Countess of Surrey
Attingham Park Shropshire NT
Henrietta Maria, Marchioness of Ailesbury
(1809)
Audley End, Essex EH
Louisa, Marchioness Cornwallis
Badminton House, Gloucestershire
Georgiana, Marchioness of Worcester
Bath Victoria Art Gallery
Prince Hoare
Sarah Kemble
Self-portrait
Belfast Ulster Museum
Harriet Anne, Countess of Belfast
Beningbrough Hall Yorkshire NT
Elizabeth Carter
Horace Walpole

Thomas Jones: Radnorshire

Biggleswade, Bedfordshire
Shuttleworth Agricultural College
Abel Rous Dottin with his Wife and Sister
Birmingham Barber Institute
A Lady
Birmingham CMAG
Elizabeth Marchioness Conyngham
Matthew Robinson Boulton
Bishop Auckland, County Durham Palace
The Hon. Shute Barrington
William van Mildert
Blair Castle, Perthshire
Viscount Beresford
Bodelwyddan Castle, Denbighshire
Sir Francis Burdett, 5th Bt (on loan from NPG)
Sophia, Lady Burdett (on loan from NPG)
Bowhill, Selkirkshire
Archibald Stewart, Baron Douglas of Douglas
The Duke of Wellington (unfinished)
Elizabeth Montague, Duchess of Buccleuch
Bowood, Wiltshire
Henry Petty-Fitzmaurice, 3rd Marquess of
Lansdowne
The Hon. Margaret Mercer Elphinstone
Louisa Emma, Marchioness of Lansdowne
Brighton Art Gallery
Emily and Harriet Lamb as Children
Bristol City Art Gallery
Head of a Young Girl
Lady Caroline Lamb (1809)
Bristol Corporation
William Henry Cavendish Bentinck, 3rd
Duke of Portland
Broadlands, Hampshire
Emma, Lady Hamilton (centre of a garland
of flowers by Monnoyer)
Henry John Temple, 3rd Viscount Palmerston
Lady Palmerston
Brodsworth Hall, Yorkshire EH
Mrs Charles Thellusson with her son Charles
Burghley House, Stamford
Henry Cecil, 10th Earl and 1st Marquess of
Exeter with his Wife and Daughter
Calke Abbey, Derbyshire NT
Sir Henry Harpur 6th Bt
Sir Henry Harpur 7th Bt
Cambridge Fitzwilliam Museum
Samuel Wooburn
Cambridge Trinity College
George Henry Fitzroy, 4th Duke of Grafton
John Jeffreys Pratt, 2nd Earl and 1st
Marquess Camden
Capesthorne Hall, Cheshire
Harriet Katherine, Lady Williams
Mrs Davies Davenport
Cardiff National Museum of Wales
Study of a Girl
Thomas Williams
Castle Howard, Yorkshire
George Howard, 6th Earl of Carlisle
William Spencer Cavendish, 6th Duke of
Devonshire
Cawdor Castle, Nairn
The 1st Earl Cawdor

Elizabeth, Countess of Cawdor
Chatsworth, Derbyshire
The Hon. William Lamb
Lady Charlotte Bentinck
Coventry Herbert Art Gallery
King Geoge III
Croft Castle, Herefordshire, NT
George IV (attributed)
Mrs Jens Wolff
Edinburgh National Gallery
Lady Robert Manners
Edinburgh Scottish National Portrait Gallery
Dr John Moore
George IV
Exeter Royal Albert Memorial Museum
A Gentleman in Academic Dress
Firle Place, Sussex
William Spencer Cavendish, 6th Duke of
Devonshire
Fyvie Castle, Aberdeenshire NTS
Susanna Archer, Countess of Oxford
Glasgow Art Gallery
A lady (sketch)
Mrs John Trower
Glasgow University
Lady Maria Hamilton
Gloucester Art Gallery
The Revd Daniel Lysons
Goodwood, Sussex
Caroline, 5th Duches of Richmond
Carolin, Duchess of Argyll
The Duke of Richmond
Haddo House, Aberdeenshire NTS
George Gordon, 4th Earl of Aberdeen
Lady Charlotte Bentinck
Philip Kemble
Harewood House, Yorkshire
Henry Lascelles, 2nd Earl of Harewood
The Rt Hon. George Canning (1825)
William Huskisson
Harrogate Mercer Gallery
'Prosperity Robinson'
Hatfield House, Hertfordshire
Frances Mary, Marchioness of Salisbury
Ickworth, Suffolk NT
The 2nd Earl of Liverpool
Charles Rose Ellis, 1st Lord seaford
Frederick William Hervey, 1st Marquess of
Bristol
Kendal Abbot Hall Art Gallery
Lord George Granvill Leveson-Gower, 1st
Duke of Sutherland
Killerton, Devon NT
Lydia Fortesque, Lady Acton and her Two
Sons
Henrietta Hoare
Matthew Fortesque
Kingston Lacy, Dorset NT
Anne Frances Bankes, Viscountess Falmouth
Charlotte Dee, Lady Nugent (1789)
Maria Woodley, Mrs Riddell
Lamport Hall
Northamptonshire Preservation Trust
Sir John Vaughan

Leeds, Temple Newsam House
Sir John Beckett
Leicester Museum and Art Gallery
William Brabazon Ponsonby, 1st Baron
Ponsonby
Liverpool Sudley Art Gallery
Mrs Charles Lock
Liverpool Walker Art Gallery
John Bradburne
The Rt Hon. George Canning (attributed)
Thomas William Coke, 1st Earl of Leicester
George III
London Apsley House,
The Wellington Museum
The 1st Duke of Wellington
Henry William Paget, 1st Marquess of
Anglesey
Lieutenant-Colonel Thomas Graham, Baron
Lynedoch
William Carr, 5th Earl Viscount Beresford
London British Museum
Sir Joseph Banks, 1st Bt.
London Buckingham Palace
William IV
Prince George of Cumberland
Princess Caroline of Wales and Princess
Charlotte
London Guildhall Art Gallery
George Dance the Younger
John Philip Kemble as Coriolanus (1798)
Richard Clark
Sir William Curtis Bt.
Sir William Curtis of Cullands Grove, 1st Bt.
(loan)
London National Army Museum
General Sir John Moore
General Sir Robert Brownrigg, 1st Bt.
William Craven, 7th Baron and 1st Earl of
Craven
London National Gallery
John Julius Angerstein
Queen Charlotte
London National Portrait Gallery
26 Paintings including:
George IV
Caroline Amelia Elizabeth of Brunswick
London Sir John Soane's Museum
Sir John Soane (1829)
London Tate Britain
13 works including:
Lady Georgiana Fane
Philadelphia Hannah, Viscountess Cremorne
London V&A
Head of a Lady (sketch)
Head of an Old Lady (sketch, unfinished)
Lady Lea (unfinished)
Paulina, wife of Sir Codrington Edmund
Carrington
Queen Caroline of Brunswick (1798)
Sir Codrington Edmund Carrington
London Wallace Collection
George IV
A Lady
Margaret, Countess of Blessington
Miss Sally Siddons
London (Dulwich) DPG
William Linley
London (Hampstead) Fenton House, NT
William IV
London (Hampstead) Kenwood
(Iveagh Bequest)
Miss Louisa Georgina Augusta Anne Murray
Longleat, Wiltshire
The 1st Marquess of Bath
Isabella Elizabeth, Marchioness of Bath and
her Children
Thomas Thynne, 1st Marquess of Bath
Manchester City Art Gallery
Sir Robert Peel, 1st Bt
James Curtis
Manchester Whitworth Art Gallery
Richard Payne-Knight
Montacute House, Somerset NT
Anthony Haldmand

Henry Raeburn: The Archers

Mount Stewart, County Down NT
Robert Stewart, 2nd Marquess of
Londonderry
Newcastle upon Tyne Laing Art Gallery
Group of Four Figures
Mrs Littleton
Normanby Hall, Lincolnshire
Mrs Alice Wood
Norwich St Andrew's Hall
Charles Harvey
Norwich Shire Hall
Thomas William Coke, 1st Earl of Leicester
Oxford All Souls
John Tracy, 7th Viscount Tracy of Rathcoote
Sir Charles Richard Vaughan
Oxford Christ Church
The Rt Hon. George Canning
William Bissett
William Eden, 1st Baron Auckland
Oxford Examination Schools
George IV
Oxford Jesus College
John Nash
Oxford Merton College
The Hon. Shute Barrington
Oxford Pembroke College
Sir Thomas Le Breton
Oxford University College
The Rt Hon. William Wyndham
Thomas Plumer
Penshurst Place, Kent
William IV when Duke of Clarence
Perth Art Gallery
John Murray, 4th Duke of Atholl
Thomas Graham, Baron Lynedoch
Plas Newydd, Isle of Anglesey NT
Henry William Paget, 1st Marquess of
Anglesey (1817)
The Hon. Berkeley Thomas Paget
Polesden Lacey, Surrey NT
•William Henry and Jacob Howell
Pattisson (The Pattisson Children) (1817)
Port Sunlight Lady Lever Art Gallery
Eleanor, Countess of Harborough
Thomas Gataker of Mildenhall
Ragley Hall, Warwickshire
George IV when Prince Regent
Sledmer House, Yorkshire
Elizabeth, Lady Sykes
Mrs John Robinson Foulis

Sir Mark and Lady Masterman-Sykes and
his brother, Tatton
Southampton City Art Gallery
Dr John Moore, Archbishop of Canterbury
Stratfield Saye, Hampshire
Henry Bathurst, 3rd Earl Bathurst
Marchioness Worcester, later Duchess of
Beaufort
Marianne, Marchioness Wellesley
Sudbury Hall, Derbyshire NT
Edward Vernon, Archbishop of Canterbury
Henry Venables Vernon, 3rd Baron
Swansea Glynn Vivian Art Gallery
Sir Robert Peel
Tabley House, Cheshire
Georgiana Maria Leicester as Hope
Tatton Park, Cheshire NT
Elisabeth Sykes, Mrs Wilbraham Egerton
(collaboration)
Upton House, Warwickshire NT
William IV when Duke of Clarence
Wallingford, Berkshire Council Chamber
Jacob Pleydell-Bouverie, 2nd Earl of Radnor
Wellington, Berkshire College
Arthur Wellesley, 1st Duke of Wellington
Wilton House, Wiltshire
Count Semion Vorontsov
Windsor Castle RC
47 works including:
Pope Pius VII
Sir Walter Scott
Windsor Guildhall
George IV
Woburn Abbey, Bedfordshire
John Russell 6th Duke of Bedford

HENRY RAEBURN
Stockridge, near Edinburgh 1756 –
Edinburgh 1823
Scottish portraitist who documented
the great age of Edinburgh (the Athens
of the North) and its thinkers and
philanthropists. His virtuoso handling of
paint demonstrates his confidence: he
painted directly onto the canvas without
prior drawing, giving a freshness and
exuberance to his sitters.
Abbotsford, Selkirkshire
Maxwell-Scott Collection
Sir Walter Scott

Aberdeen Art Gallery
10 paintings including:
Sir Robert and Lady Abercromby
Robert Adam, Architect
Bath Holburne Museum of Art
Lady Helen Boyle
Thomas Mare of Lauriston
Berwick-upon-Tweed Art Gallery
Mrs Janet Scott
Birkenhead Williamson Art Gallery
Andrew Buchanan of Arden Connel
Bowhill, Selkirkshire
Sir Walter Scott
Viscount Melville
Bradford Cartwright Hall
Mrs Anne Stewart of St Fort
Cambridge Fitzwilliam Museum
William Glendonwyn
Cardiff National Museum of Wales
Mrs Douglas of Brigton
Mrs Todd
Castle Fraser, Aberdeenshire NTS
Charles Mackenzie Fraser
Charlecote Park, Warwickshire NT
Katherine Ramsay
Sir Ewen Cameron Bt
Thomas Williamson Ramsay
Craigevar, Aberdeenshire NTS
The Hon. Sarah Semphill, Wife of Sir William
Forbes Bt
Sir William Forbes Bt
Dundee McManus Galleries
Mrs Bell of Goldilea
Mrs Moir of Leckie
Edinburgh NGS
38 paintings including:
Revd Dr Robert Walker skating on
Duddington Loch
Mrs Scott Moncrieff
Colonel Alastair Ronaldson Macdonell of
Glengarry
Edinburgh Royal Scottish Academy
John Pitcairn of Pitcairn, Provost of Dundee
Edinburgh Scottish National Portrait Gallery
19 paintings including:
Rear-Admiral Charles Inglis
Sir Walter Scot (1822)
Edinburgh Talbot Rice Gallery
Adam Ferguson
John Playfair

John Robinson
Thomas Elder
William Robertson
Floors Castle, Roxburghshire
Sir James Innesker, 5th Duke of Roxburghe
Forfar Museum and Art Gallery
Henry Dundas, Viscount Melville (1793)
Fyvie Castle, Aberdeenshire NTS
13 paintings including:
Isabella Macleod, Mrs James Gregory
Sir William Maxwell of Calderwood
Gawthorpe Hall, Lancashire NT
Robert Shuttleworth
Glasgow Art Gallery and Museum
18 paintings including:
Ann Pattison
Mr and Mrs Robert Campbell of Kailzie
Glasgow Burrell Collection
Colonel Bowes
Henry Mackenzie
Miss Macartney
Sir William Forbes of Pitsligo
Glasgow Hunterian Art Gallery
Master John Scott of Gala
Mrs Hay of Spot
Greenock McLean Museum and Art Gallery
Sir Francis Chantrey
Haddo House, Aberdeenshire NTS
The 4th Duke of Gordon
The Duchess of Gordon
Hill of Tarvit, Fife NTS
John Tait of Harviestoun
Mrs Tyndall Bruce of Falkland
Inverness Museum and Art Gallery
Grace Lockhart
Kilmarnock Dick Institute
James Anderson
Mrs George Anderson
Kirkcaldy Museum and Art Gallery
Sir James Stevenson Barnes
Leith, Midlothian Trinity House
Viscount Duncan of Camperdown
Liverpool Sudley House
A Girl sketching
Liverpool Walker Art Gallery
Ann Stirling
London Courtauld Institute
Mrs Malcolm
London National Gallery
•The Archers
London National Portrait Gallery
Francis Horner
Henry Mackenzie
Hugh William Williams
John Home
John Playfair
Sir John Sinclair Bt
London Tate Britain
The 1st Viscount Melville
Lady Dalrymple
Lieutenant-Colonel Bryce McMurdo
Mrs Cay
Mrs Charles Stuart (?)
Mrs Downey
Mrs H.W. Lauzun
Pringle Fraser
A Young Lady
London V&A
Mrs Hobson
William Hobson of Markfield
London (Hampstead) Kenwood
(Iveagh Bequest)
Sir John Sinclair as a Boy
Manchester City Art Gallery
Alexander Campbell of Hillyards
Alexander Gordon, 4th Duke of Gordon
Mrs Ahaftoe Clark and her Daughters
Montacute House, Somerset NT
Mrs Boswell
Robert Stewart
Newcastle upon Tyne Laing Art Gallery
Robert Allan of Kirkliston
Oxford Ashmolean Museum
Jacobina Copland

Paisley Museum and Art Galleries
Mrs Forbes
Pencarrow House, Cornwall
Molesworth-St Aubyn Collection
Sir Arscott Molesworth
Perth Museum and Art Gallery
Lady Sefton Steuart of Touch
Samuel Anderson
Sir Alexander Mackenzie
Polesden Lacey, Surrey NT
George and Maria Stewart as Children
Mrs Simpson
The Paterson Children
Sir William Macleod Bannatyne
Port Sunlight Lady Lever Art Gallery
Thomas Telford
Stanway House, Gloucestershire
Francis Charteris, Lord Elcho
Upton House, Warwickshire NT
The 13th Earl of Eglinton as a Boy
on Horseback
The MacDonald Children
Wolverhampton Art Gallery and Museum
William Fairlie of Fairlie

ALLAN RAMSAY
Edinburgh 1713 – Dover 1784
Scottish portraitist who settled in London.
His 'Italian Grand Manner' portraits
anticipate Reynolds's by several years
and, in Horace Walpole's words, his style
was 'formed to paint women'. He enjoyed
good society, the art of conversation and
travelling, making four trips to Italy.
Aberdeen Art Gallery
Miss Janet Shairp
Audley End, Essex EH
John Manners, Marquess of Granby (1745)
Barnard Castle Bowes Museum
Man in a Red Coat
Bath Holburne Museum of Art
John Sargent
John Sargent
Rosamund Chambers
Beningbrough Hall, Yorkshire NT
Robert Wood (1755)
Berwick-upon-Tweed Art Gallery
Miss Christine Grant
Birmingham CMAG
Mrs Martin (1761)
Cambridge Emmanuel College
Anthony Askew (1750)
Capesthorne Hall, Cheshire
Bromley Davenport Collection
Jean-Jacques Rousseau
Chirk Castle, Denbighshire
Colonel Myddelton Collection
Lady Anne Rushout (1743)
Dover Town Hall
Lord Chancellor Hardwicke
Drumlanrig Castle, Dumfriesshire
Archibald, 3rd Duke of Argyll
Francis, 2nd Duke of Buccleuch
William, 4th Duke of Queensbury
Dundee McManus Galleries
Edward Harvey (1747)
Edinburgh NGS
13 works including:
•Portrait of the Artist's Wife, Margaret
Lindsay

A Dead Child (sketch)
Jean-Jacques Rousseau
Edinburgh Scottish National Portrait Gallery
11 portraits including:
David Hume
James Murray, 2nd Duke of Athol
Floors Castle, Roxburghshire
A Lady
Glasgow Art Gallery and Museum
Archibald, 3rd Duke of Argyll (1749)
Captain Sir John Lindsay
Colonel John Stewart of Stewartfield (1742)
Henrietta Diana, Dowager Countess
of Stafford (1759)
Janet Grant, Countess of Hyndford
Glasgow Burrell Collection
Lady in White
Glasgow Hunterian Art Gallery
Dr William Hunter
Francis Hutcheson
George Bristow
Lady Anne Campbell, Countess of Strafford
Mrs Tracy Travell
Gorambury, Hertfordshire
Anna Maria Cockburn
Greenock McLean Museum and Art Gallery
A Naval Officer
Hill of Tarvit, Fife NTS
Captain Thomas Waller
Lady in a Blue Dress
Mrs Muir of Caldwell
Mrs Young
Ickworth, Suffolk NT
The Duc de Nivernois
Mary Lepel, Lady Hervey
Kendal Abbot Hall Art Gallery
Portrait of Julia Musgrave
Leicester NWMAG
The Hon. William Finch (1744)
Leith Hall, Aberdeenshire NTS
Jean Nesbit
Lady Banff
Liverpool Walker Art Gallery
Elizabeth Cotman
Emily, Countess of Kildare
London Buckingham Palace RC
George III
Queen Charlotte
London Guildhall Art Gallery
George III
Queen Charlotte
A Woman
London Courtauld Institute
Captain Sir William Peer Williams Bt (175[?])
London Foundling Hospital
Dr Richard Meade (1747)
London National Portrait Gallery
Philip Dormer Stanhope, 4th Earl
of Chesterfield
Self Portrait
London Tate Britain
Alexander Boswell, Lord Auchinleck (1754)
Lady Hall of Dunglass (1752)
A Man (1743)
Miss Ramsay in a Red Dress
Thomas, 2nd Baron Mansel of Margam,
with this Half-Brothers and Sister (1742)

Allan Ramsay: Flora Macdonald

London V&A
Mrs Everard
A Young Man
London (Greenwich) NMM
The Hon. Charles Stewart (1740)
Newcastle upon Tyne Laing Art Gallery
James Adams
Newhailes House, East Lothian NTS
Four portraits of the Dalrymple Family (1739)
Oxford Ashmolean Museum
• Flora Macdonald (1749)
Oxford St John's College
George III
George III
Queen Charlotte
Paisley Museum and Art Galleries
A Lady
Perth Museum and Art Gallery
Lady in Blue
Penrhyn Castle, Gwynned NT
William Colyear, Viscount Milsington
Port Sunlight Lady Lever Art Gallery
The Dinwiddie Sisters
Ragley Hall, Warwickshire
George III
Queen Charlotte
Scone Palace, Perthshire
The 7th Viscount Stormont
George III
Queen Charlotte
Stourhead, Wiltshire NT
Sir Richard Hoare, 1st Bt (1746)
Stratfield Saye, Hampshire
George III
Warwick County Museum
John Ward
Wimpole Hall, Cambridgeshire NT
Catherine Freeman
Charles Yorke I
Jemima, Marchioness Grey (1741)
The Hon Philip Yorke, later 2nd Earl of
Hardwicke (1741)
Windsor Castle RC
Prince George Augustus of Mecklenburg-
Strelitz
Prince William, later Duke of Clarence

JOSHUA REYNOLDS

Plympton, Devon 1723 – London 1792
Cool, intellectual and urbane, son of a
clergyman and with a good classical
education Reynolds was the natural choice
for the sitter who wished to present a
learned attitude. He made a hundred
portraits a year, for which he had the help
of a number of studio assistants.
His classical learning made him the
obvious candidate for first president of the
Royal Academy.
Aberdeen Art Gallery
Robert Ramsden
Alnwick Castle, Northumberland
Lady Lovaine
Hugh, 1st Duke of Northumberland
Althorp, Northamptonshire
15 paintings including:
Georgiana, Countess Spencer
Self Portrait
Antony House, Cornwall
James Buller of Morval
Thomas, 8th Earl of Westmorland
John, 9th Earl of Westmorland
Reginald Pole
Pipng Shepherd Boy
Arniston House, Midlothian
Henry Dundas, Lord Melville
Arundel Castle, Sussex
Lord Thomas Howard of Worksop
George IV
Ascott, Buckinghamshire NT
Lady Elizabeth Keppel
Miss Meyer as Hebe
Audley End, Essex English Heritage
Rear Admiral Matthew Whitwell (1755)

Joshua Reynolds: Mrs Siddons as the Tragic Muse

Barlaston, Staffordshire
Wedgwood Museum
Josiah Wedgwood (1782)
Sarah Wedgwood (1782)
Barnard Castle Bowes Museum
Mrs Thrale
Bath Holburne Museum of Art
Lucy Sneyd
Belfast Ulster Museum
Miss Theodosia Magill, 1st Countess
Clanwilliam
Belton House, Lincolnshire NT
Amelia Egerton, Lady Hume
Sir Abraham Hume Bt
Sir John Cust Bt
Miss Hume
Belvoir Castle, Leicestershire
The 4th Duke of Rutland
Captain Lord Robert Manners
Lady Tyrconnel
Lord Granby and his Sister
The Marquess of Granby
Berkeley Castle, Gloucestershire
Elizabeth, Countess of Berkeley
Augustus Keppel
Birmingham Barber Institute
Archbishop Richard Robinson
The Revd William Beele
A Young Man
Birmingham CMAG
Gawler Brothers
Dr John Thomas
Mrs Luther
The Roffey Family
Blackburn Art Gallery
William Fouden
Blenheim Palace, Oxfordshire
The 4th Duke of Marlborough and his Family
Elizabeth, Countess of Pembroke
Francis, Marquess of Tavistock
Duchess of Marlborough and Daughter

Lord Charles Spencer
George, 4th Duke of Marlborough
George, 4th Duke of Marlborough
Lord Robert Spencer
Blickling Hall, Norfolk NT
Countess of Ancram
Bowhill, Selkirkshire
Caroline, Countess of Dalkeith
Duchess of Buccleuch and her Daughter
Duchess of Buccleuch and her Daughter
(sketch)
Henry 3rd Duke of Buccleuch
Ladies Elizabeth and Henrietta Montagu
Lady Caroline Scott as Winter
Lord Dalkeith
Bowood, Wiltshire
1st Marquess of Lansdowne
Countess of Ilchester and Daughters
Hope Nursing Love
Kitty Fisher
Lady Louisa Fitzpatrick
'Lady Sarah Bunbury'
Mrs Baldwin
Strawberry Girl
Thomas Fitzmaurice
Bradford Cartwright Hall
John, 2nd Earl of Egmont, and his Wife,
Catherine
Bridlington Sewerby Hall Art Gallery
Nathanial Cholmley
Brighton Art Gallery
Head of a Boy
Bristol City Art Gallery
Edgcumbe, Williams and Selwyn
Thomas, 4th Lord Middleton
Broadlands, Hampshire
Lady Melbourne
Bury St Edmunds Manor House Museum
Augustus, 3rd Earl of Bristol
Buscot Park, Berkshire NT
Barbara St John, Lady Coventry (1764)

A Beggar Boy and his Sister
Mercury as Cut-Purse
Cambridge Fitzwilliam Museum
The Braddyll Family
Henry Vansittart
Lord Rockingham and Edmund Burke
Mrs Angelo
Cambridge Pembroke College
The Revd William Mason (1774)
Cambridge Trinity College
Prince William Frederick, later 2nd Duke of
Gloucester (1780)
Cardiff National Museum of Wales
The 2nd Baron Ducie
Charlotte Grenville with her Three Children
Colonel George Catchmaid Morgan
Sir William Watkins Wynn and his Wife
Castle Howard, Yorkshire
Margaret, Countess of Carlisle
Frederick, 5th Earl of Carlisle
Frederick, 5th Earl of Carlisle with George
Selwyn
Frederick, 5th Earl of Carlisle as Lord
Morpeth
Cawdor Castle, Nairn
John 1st Lord Cawdor
Charles Greville
Chatsworth, Derbyshire
The Devonshire Collection
Countess Spencer and Her Daughter
Duchess of Devonshire and Her Daughter
Georgiana, Duchess of Devonshire
Lady Elizabeth Foster
Lord Richard Cavendish
William Augustus, Duke of Cumberland
William, 3rd Duke of Devonshire
Dalmeny House, nr. Edinburgh
Contessa della Rena
Edward Gibbon
George Selwyn
Lady Almeira Carpenter
Lady in a Black Lace Mantle
Lord Rockingham
William Petty, Lord Shelburne
Doddington Hall Leeds City Art Gallery
Lord and Lady Pollington and their Son
Drumlanrig Castle, Dumfriesshire
Lady Elizabeth Montagu
Dunham Massey, Cheshire
The 5th Earl of Stamford
Dunrobin Castle, Sutherland
Countess of Sutherland
Dunster Castle, Somerset NT
Miss Luttrell
Eastnor Castle, Herefordshire NT
Miss Elizabeth Eliot
Edinburgh NGS
Alexander, later 10th Duke of Hamilton
Captain (later Admiral) Duncan
James Coutts
• The Ladies Waldegrave
A Little Girl
Sir David Lindsay, Bt of Evelick
Edinburgh Scottish National Portrait Gallery
Edmund Burke
John Murray, 4th Earl of Dunmore (1765)
Professor Adam Ferguson
The Revd William Robertson
Robert Hay Drummond, Archbishop of York
Sir William Forbes of Pitsligo, Bt
Elton Hall, Peterborough Proby Collection
Kitty Fisher
Archibald Bower
Charles Proby
John Joshua, 1st Earl Carysfort
John, 1st Lord Carysfort
Lady Carysfort
Master and Miss Proby
Thomas Proby
Erddig, Clwyd NT
Edward Kinaston
Euston Hall, Suffolk
Anne Duchess of Grafton
2nd Duke of Grafton

Joshua Reynolds: The Ladies Waldegrave

Maria Countess Waldegrave
Exeter Royal Albert Memorial Museum
Captain Charles Proby of Elton Hall
Thomas Dawson, 1st Viscount Cremorne
Firle Place, Sussex
Elizabeth Milbanke and Her Son
Marquess of Huntly
Sampson Gideon
The Lamb Children
Floors Castle, Roxburghshire
The Hon. Caroline Gawler
John Gawler
Sir John Thorold Bt
Fonmon Castle, South Glamorgan
Sir William Boothby
Robert Jones
Fyvie Castle, Aberdeenshire NT
Elizabeth Fortesque, Countess of Ancram
Glasgow Art Gallery and Museum
A Boy in van Dyck Dress
Isabella, Countess of Errol
Glasgow Hunterian Art Gallery
Lady Maynard
Mrs Brudenell
Nelly O'Brien
William Hunter
Goodwood, Sussex
The 3rd Duke of Richmond
Mary, 3rd Duchess of Richmond
Jane, Duchess of Gordon
Lady Charles Spencer
Gorhambury, Hertfordshire
The Four Children of James, 2nd Viscount Grimston
The Hon. Mrs Walter

Gosford House, East Lothian
Francis Charteris
Lord Delaval
Grimsthorpe Castle, Lincolnshire
Lord Brownlow Bertie
Peregrine, 2nd Duke of Ancaster
Peregrine 3rd Duke of Ancaster
Mary Duchess of Ancaster
Children of the 3rd Duke of Ancaster
Thomas Panton
Mrs Panton
Gunby Hall, Lincolnshire NT
Bennet Langton
Mary, Dowager Countess of Rothes
Hagley Hall, Stourbridge
Mr, later 1st Lord, Lyttelton
Hampton Court Palace RC
Saint Michael the Archangel slaying the Dragon (after Guido Reni)
Harewood House, Yorkshire
Anne, Countess of Harewood, with her Infant Daughter
Edward, 1st Earl of Harewood
Edwin, 1st Lord Harewood
Jane, Countess of Harrington
Lady Worsley
Mrs Hale as Euphrosyne
Mrs Hardinge
Hartland Abbey, Bideford
Paul Orchard
Mrs Orchard
Hatfield House, Hertfordshire
Chase Price (?)
Lady Salisbury
Highclere Castle, Berkshire

Sleeping Cupid
Holker Hall, Cumbria
Sir William Lowther
Sir William Lowther, Charles Turner, Lord Milltown and M. Huet
Holkham Hall, Norfolk
Charles James Fox
Houghton Hall, Norfolk
Cholmondeley Collection
The 1st Marquess of Cholmondeley
The Duchess of Ancaster
Ickworth, Suffolk NT
Sir Charles Davers, 6th Bt (1773)
Inveraray Castle, Argyll
Anne Lady Strafford
Lord Strafford
Ipswich Christchurch Mansion
Sir Hutchins Williams
Kedleston Hall, Derbyshire NT
Lady Caroline Curzon and Child
Nathanial, 2nd Lord Scarsdale
Killerton House, Devon NT
Sir Thomas Acland
Kingston Lacey, Dorset NT
Miss Payne and Mrs Woodley
Knole, Kent NT
Nine paintings including:
David Garrick
Dr Samuel Johnson
Wang-y-Tong
Leeds Temple Newsam House
Isabella, Lady Beauchamp
Frederick, Viscount Duncannon (?)
Lady Hertford
Leicester NWMAG

Charles Bothby Skrymshire
Liverpool Sudley Art Gallery
Mrs George Gostling
Mrs James Modyford Heywood
Liverpool Walker Art Gallery
Miss Elizabeth Ingram
London Guildhall Art Gallery
Lady Dorothea Harrison (1758)
Pope Paviarus
Sir Charles Pratt (1764)
Sir Thomas Harrison (1758)
Thomas Tomkins
London National Army Museum
Colonel John Barrington
Lord Ligonier
Marquess of Granby
London National Gallery
Anne, Countess of Albemarle
Captian Robert Orme (1756)
General Sir Banastre Tarleton (1782)
Lady Cockburn and her Sons
London National Portrait Gallery
26 paintings including:
Dr Samuel Johnson
Lawrence Sterne
Self Portrait
London Tate Britain
32 paintings including:
The Age of Innocence
George IV when Prince of Wales
Three Ladies adorning a Term of Hymen (1773)
London V&A
Entrance to Mr Thrale's Park, Streatham (sketch)

A Lady
A Lady (Miss Reynolds?) (sketch)
Mary Barnardiston
London Wallace Collection
12 paintings including:
Miss Jane Bowles
St John the Baptist in the Wilderness
London (Blackheath) Ranger's House EH
(on loan from the Wernher Collection)
Countess Bellemont
Lady Caroline Price
Richard Barwell
London (Brentford) Syon House
1st Duchess of Northumberland
Andrew Drummond
London (Dulwich) DPG
General on Horseback
Girl with a Baby (sketch)
The Infant Samuel
•Ms Siddons as the Tragic Muse
Recovery from Illness: An Allegory (sketch)
Robert Dodsley
Self Portrait
London (Greenwich) NMM
15 paintings including:
Viscount Augustus Keppel (1749)
London (Hampstead)
Kenwood (Iveagh bequest)
16 paintings including:
The Angerstein Children
Kitty Fisher as Cleopatra dissolving the Pearl
London (Richmond) Ham House NT
Charlotte Walpole, Countess of Dysart
London (Twickenham) Marble Hill House
A Man
Longleat, Wiltshire
Kitty Hunter
Lord Thurlow
Manchester City Art Gallery
Lord Cathcart
Lady Cathcart
Admiral Lord Hood
Lady Anstruther
Montacute House, Somerset NT
'Colonel Isaac Gale'
Elizabeth Hamilton (?)
Mount Edgcumbe House, Cornwall
Richard, 2nd Lord Edgcumbe
Muncaster Castle, Cumbria
Isabella, Lady Beauchamp
Frances Shepherd (Lady Irvine)
William Weddell
Mrs Weddell
Newcastle upon Tyne Laing Art Gallery
Mrs Elizabeth Riddelll
Newstead Abbey, Nottinghamshire
William Trevanion
Oxford Ashmolean
Captain Philemon Pownall (sketch)
Charity
Charles Fitzroy, 2nd Duke of Grafton
Dr Joseph Warton
James Paine, Architect, and his Son James
Miss Keppel, afterwards Mrs Thomas Meyrick
Oxford CCPG
General John Guise
Parham Park, Sussex
John Craufurd
Paxton House, Berwickshire
Patrick Home
Pencarrow House, Cornwall
Three portraits of Sir John Molesworth
William Molesworth
Mrs William Molesworth
Lady St Aubyn
Petworth House, Sussex
19 paintings including:
Death of Cardinal Beaufort
Kitty Fisher (1759)
Plymouth CMAG
The Age of Innocence
Charles Rogers (1777)
Miss Frances Reynolds

Mrs Joseph Harner
The Revd Samuel Reynolds
Self Portrait
Charles Cutliffe
Polesden Lacey, Surrey NT
Venus and the Piping Boy
Port Sunlight Lady Lever Art Gallery
Angelica Kauffmann
Elizabeth Gunning, Duchess of Hamilton and Argyll
The Hon. Mrs Peter Beckford (1782)
Lady Gertrude Fitzpatrick
Lady Ledell Phipps and her Son
The Misses Paine and Mrs Paine (1765)
Mrs Fortseque
Mrs Seaforth and her Child
Venus chiding Cupid
Powis Castle, Powys NT
Lady Henrietta Herbert
Raby Castle, Durham
Lady Catherine Powell
Captain Raby Vane
Ragley Hall, Warwickshire
The 1st Marquess of Hertford
Lord Waldegrave
Field Marshall Henry Seymour Conway
Horace Walpole, 3rd Earl of orford
Viscount Beauchamp
Mr Conway
Duke of Grafton
Rockingham Castle, Northamptonshire
Miss Goddard
Mrs Watson
Rousham Park, Oxfordshire
Cottrell-Dormer Collection
Lady Charles Cottrell-Dormer
Saltram Park, Devon NT
13 paintings including:
Francesco Bartolozzi
The Parker Children
Scone Place, Perthshire
William Murray, 1st Earl of Mansfield
Sherborne Castle, Dorset
Colonel Stephen Digby
Shugborough, Staffordshire NT
Admiral Lord Anson
Mary Vernon, Mrs Anson (1764)
Southampton City Art Gallery
Nehemiah Winter
Stirling Smith Art Gallery
Mrs Callander
Stourhead, Wiltshire NT
Thomas Veale Lane
Upton House, Warwickshire NT
The Earl and Countess of Ely (1775)
Waddesdon Manor, Buckinghamshire NT
11 paintings including:
Emily Pott as Thais
Mrs Sheridan as Saint Cecilia
A Fortune Teller
Wallington, Northumberland NT
Sir Walter Calverley Blackett
Watford Museum
Frances, Lady Essex
Weston Park, Shropshire
George Bridgman
Sir William Lowther
Wilton House Wiltshire
Augustus Hervey, 3rd Earl of Bristol
Charles, 3rd Duke of Marlborough
Elizabeth Countess of Pembroke
Elizabeth, Countess of Pembroke and her Son George, Lord Herbert
Elizabeth, Countess of Pembroke and her Son George, Lord Herbert
George, 4th Duke of Marlborough
Henry, 10th Earl of Pembroke
Henry, 10th Earl of Pembroke and his Son George, Lord Herbert
Lord Charles Spencer
Wimpole Hall, Cambridgeshire NT
The Duchess of Manchester and her Son
Windsor Castle RC
David Garrick

Edward, Duke of York
George III when Prince of Wales
Henry, Duke of Cumberland
Princess Sophia Matilda of Gloucester
Self Portrait
Thomas, Lord Erskine
William, Duke of Cumberland
Woburn Abbey, Bedfordshire
13 paintings including:
Francis, Marquess of Tavistock
Lady Elizabeth Keppel
York City Art Gallery
Captain John foote
Sir Conyers d'Arcy

GEORGE ROMNEY
Dalton in Furness 1734 – Kendal 1802
Romney established himself in London as a painter of historical subjects and portraits. He is best remembered today as the society portraitist who challenged Reynolds and Gainsborough by undercutting their prices. He typified many late eighteenth century English artists who produced portraits but whose preferred subject matter was imaginative history painting.
Anthony House, Cornwall NT
Jemima Pole Carew
Arbury Hall, Warwickshire
Sir Roger Newdigate
Ascott, Buckinghamshire NT
The Hon. Mrs Tickell
Barlaston, Staffordshire
Wedgwood Museum
Elizabeth Allen (1793)
Bath Holburne Museum
John Sargent
Major-General Sir John Burgoyne Bt.
Belton House, Lincolnshire NT
The 1st Baron Brownlow
Frances, Lady Brownlow
Peregrine Cust (1779)
Birkenhead Williamson Art Gallery
A horse (study)
Birmingham Barber Institute
John Smith
Birmingham CMAG
Lady Holte

George Romney: Self Portrait

Mrs Abraham Bracebridge and her Daughter
Blackburn Art Gallery
The Revil Dr Richard Scales
Mr Barton
Bolton Art Gallery
The tempest (four fragments)
Bradford, Cartwright Hall
James Ainstie
Brighton Art Gallery
Tom Hayley as Puck
Cambridge Fitzwilliam Museum
William Thomas Meyer (?)
Cambridge Trinity College
Prince William Frederick, 2nd Duke of Gloucester (1791)
Cardiff National Museum of Wales
Mrs Newbery
Castle Howard, Yorkshire
The 1st Marquess of Stafford
Castle Ward, County Down NT
Hon Edward Ward
Corsham Court, Wiltshire
Christine Methuen, Lady Boston
Frederick Irby, 2nd Lord Boston
Dunham Massey, Cheshire NT
George Henry Gret, 6th Earl of Stamford
The 5th Earl of Stamford
The Hon. Anchitel Grey
Lady Henrietta Cavendish Bentinck, Countess of Stamford
Eastnor Castle, Hertfordshire
The 1st Earl of Somers
Edinburgh National Gallery
Mrs William Bootle
Edinburgh Scottish National Portrait Gallery
Jane Maxwell, Duchess of Gordon
John McArthur
Major-General James Stuart
Forfar, Angus Art Gallery
David Scott MP of Dunninald
Fyvie Castle, Aberdeenshire NTS
Captain Arthur Forbes of Culloden
John West, 4th Earl of De La Warr
Mr William Marwood
Mrs Stratford Canning
Glasgow Art Gallery
Lieutenant-Colonel Sir Charles Stuart (1779)
Glasgow Burrell Collection

Richard Brinsley Sheridan
Glasgow Pollok House
Richard Cumberland
Glasgow University
Emma, Lady Hamilton
A Man (David Garrick?)
Miss Harriet Milles
Mrs Ralph Willett
Sir Thomas Rumbold
Harewood House, Yorkshire
John Thomas, 13th Earl of Clanricarde
Harrogate Art Gallery
The Rev J Hadfield
Hatfield House, Hertfordshire
James Cecil, 7th Earl and 1st Marquess of Salisbury
Ickworth, Suffolk NT
Lady Louisa Hervey, Countess of Liverpool
Kendal Abbot Hall Art Gallery
The Artist's Brother James, holding a Candle (1761)
Captain Robert Banks
John Postlethwaite
The Death of Wolfe (1759) (sketch)
The Four Friends: William Hayley with his Son, Thomas William Meyer, and the Artist (1796)
The Gower Family
Master Richard Meyler
Kingston Lacy, Dorset NT
Frances Woodley, Mrs Bankes
Knole, Kent NT
Samuel Foote
Lancaster CMAG
Dr Oliver Marton (1794)
Liverpool Sudley Art Gallery
Mrs Sargent
Liverpool Walker Art Gallery
A Child
Master Collingwood
Miss Collingwood
Mrs Collingwood
London Courtauld Institute
Georgiana, Lady Greville
Study of Hands (fragment)
London Guildhall Art Gallery
Captain Arthur Forbes of Culloden
Thomas Barrow
London National Portrait Gallery
14 paintings including:
• Self Portrait
Adam Walter and His Family
London Tate Britain
20 paintings including:
Jacob Morland of Capplethwaite
Mrs Johnstone and her Son
London V&A
Female Head
Serena
Young Man of the Maynard Family
London Wallace Collection
Mrs Robinson (Perdita)
London (Dulwich) DPG
Joseph Allen
William Hayley
London (Greenwich) NMM
The Hon. John Forbes (1778)
Lady Hamilton as Ariadne
Sir Charles Hardy
Sir Francis Geary
Sir Hyde Parker
Sir Joshua Rowley
Vice-Admiral George Darby
William Bentinck
London (Hampstead)
Kenwood (Iveagh Bequest)
Anne, Countess of Albermarle and her Son
Lady Hamilton at Prayer
Lady Hamilton at the Spinning Wheel
Miss Martindale
Mrs Crouch
Mrs John Chaworth Musters
Manchester City Art Gallery
Captain William Peere Williams

Melford Hall, Suffolk NT
Admiral Sir Hyde Parker Bt.
Captain Sir Hyde Parker
Merthyr Tydfill Cyfarthfa Castle
Mrs Thompson of Kendal
Oxford Ashmolean Museum
Sarah Siddons
Oxford Christ Church
Charles Agar, Earl of Normanton (1782)
David Murray, Viscount Stormont (1783)
The Duke of Portland
Edward Smallwell
Euseby Cleaver
The Revd John Wesley
Shute Barrington
Sir Archibald Macdonald
Oxford Exeter College
George Parker, Earl of Macclesfield
Oxford New College
John Oglander (1778)
Penrhyn Castle, Gwynned NT
Richard Pennant, Lord Penrhyn
Petworth House, Sussex NT
The Egremont Family
Mirth and Melancholy
Plas Newydd, Isle of Anglesey, NT
The Earl of Uxbridge
Port Sunlight Lady Lever Art Gallery
Miss Sarah Rodbard, later Lady Coot (1784)
Mrs Mary Oliver
Powis Castle, Montgomeryshire NT
Charlotte Clive
Rebecca Clive, Mrs Robinson
Preston Harris Museum and Art Gallery
John Flaxman
Mrs Threlfall and Mrs Anne Threlfall
Ragley Hall, Warwickshire
Admiral Lord Hugh Seymour (sketch)
Rotherham, Clifton Park Museum
Anne Verelst
Sizergh Castle, Cumbria NT
Cecilia Towneley
Charles Strickland
Charles Strickland
The Revd William Strickland
Sledmere House, Yorkshire
Sir Christopher and Lady Sykes (1786)
Sir William Tatton Egerton (1796)
Southampton City Art Gallery
Lord Ducie
Mrs Barton and her son Oliver
Stanway House, Gloucestershire
Susan Tracy and Two of her Children
Three Tracy Children
Stratford-upon-Avon RSCC
The Infant Shakespeare attended by Nature and the Passions
Titania reposing with her Indian votaries
Upton House, Warwickshire NT
William Beckford
Waddesdon Manor, Buckinghamshire NT
Emma, Lady Hamilton
The Hon. Lady Stuart (1779)
Mrs Jordan as Peggy in The Country Girl (1786)
Wakefield City Art Gallery
The Revd Daniel Wilson
Wallington, Northumberland NT
Sir John Trevelyan, 4th Bt.
Sir John Trevelyan, 5th Bt.
Wimpole Hall, Cambridgeshire NT
The 3rd Earl Hardwicke
Elizabeth, Countess of Hardwicke
The Hon. Charles Yorke
Wolverhampton Art Gallery
Thomas Gainsborough
Worcester City Art Gallery
Thomas Elwine of Coventry

GEORGE STUBBS
Liverpool 1724 - London 1806
Originally supported himself as a portraitist while studying anatomy in York. His dissections of horses and tireless sketches of their anatomy led to his publication of The Anatomy of the Horse in 1766, and to the creation of some of the most magnificent images of animals. His knowledge of anatomy was matched by a genius for design.

Althorp, Northamptonshire NT
Scape Flood
Ascott, Buckinghamshire NT
Five Mares
Pumpkin (1773)
Two Horses in a Paddock (1788)
Barlaston, Staffordshire
Wedgwood Museum
Portrait of Erasmus Darwin (1783)
Family Portrait (1780)
Portrait of Josiah Wedgwood I (1780)
Portrait of Richard Wedgwood (1780)
Portrait of Sarah Wedgwood (1780)
Bath Holburne Museum of Art
The Revd Carter Thelwell with his Wife and Daughter (1776)
Berkeley Castle, Gloucestershire
Groom and Horses
Cambridge Fitzwilliam Museum
Isabella Saltonstall as Una in Spenser's Faerie Queene (1782)
Joseph Smyth, Lieutenant of Whittlebury Forest on a Dapple Grey Horse
Euston Hall, Suffolk
Mares and Foals
Glasgow Hunterian Art Gallery
The Moose
The Nylghau
A Pygmy Antelope
Goodwood, Sussex
Hunting Scene
Hunting Scene
Racehorses in Training
Hull Ferens Art Gallery
Portrait of George Fothergill
Leeds Temple Newsam House
Phillis, a Pointer of Lord Clermonts
Lincoln Usher Gallery
A Cocker Spaniel
Liverpool Walker Art Gallery
Horse frightened by a Lion
Portrait of James Stanley (1755)

The Lincolnshire Ox
Molly Longlegs held by her Jockey
Three Brood Mares at Grass
A Lion and a Tiger (1772)
A Monkey
London National Gallery
Lady and Gentleman in a Carriage (1787)
The Millbanke and Melbourne Families
• Whistlejacket
London National Portrait Gallery
Self Portrait
London Tate Britain
14 paintings including:
Lion devouring a Horse (1769)
Mares and Foals in a Landscape
Reapers
London V&A
Goose with Outspread Wings
Lions and Lioness (1776)
Manchester City Art Gallery
Cheetah and Stag and Two Indians
Mount Stewart House, County Down, NT
Hambletonian
Parham Park, Sussex
A Kangaroo
Port Sunlight Lady Lever Art Gallery
Equestrian Self Portrait (1782)
The Farmer's Wife and the Raven
Hay Carting (1795)
Haymakers (1794)
Saltram Park, Devon NT
The Fall of Phaeton (1777)
Upton House, Warwickshire NT
Haymakers (1783)
Labourers (1779)
Reapers (1783)
Windsor Castle RC
16 paintings including:
The Prince of Wales's Phaeton (1793)

GIAN BATTISTA TIEPOLO
Venice 1696 - Madrid 1770
One of the greatest painters of the century and finest exponent of the Italian rococo, he was the last of the great Venetian artists. He travelled widely, painting frescos and altarpieces in palaces and churches in Italy and beyond, including decorative schemes in the Residenz at Würzburg, and the Royal Palace in Madrid.

Ascott, Buckinghamshire NT
Assumption of the Virgin
Barnard Castle Bowes Museum
The Harnessing of the Horses in the Sun (sketch)
Burghley House, Stamford
Christ on the Mount of Olives
Edinburgh NGS
• The Finding of Moses
The Meeting of Anthony and Cleopatra
London Courtauld Institute
12 paintings including:
Allegory of the Power of Eloquence (modello)
Saint Charles Borromeo meditating on the Crucifixion (modello) (1767)
London National Gallery

Elisabeth-Louise Vigée Lebrun: Countess Golovine

10 works including:
Allegory with Venus and Time
The Banquet of Cleopatra
London (Dulwich) DPG
Apollo and a Goddess
Diana
Fortitude and Wisdom
Joseph receiving Pharoah's Ring (attributed)
Oxford Ashmolean Museum
Young Woman with a Macaw

ELISABETH-LOUISE VIGÉE LEBRUN
Paris 1755 - Paris 1842
Daughter of an artist, wife of a picture dealer, and one of the most successful women painters of all time, she was an accomplished portraitist. Friend to Marie-Antoinette and Painter to the Queen, at the outbreak of the Revolution she travelled widely, working in Italy, Vienna, Prague, Dresden, Russia, England and Switzerland.

Birmingham Barber Institute
• Countess Golovine
Brighton Art Gallery
Self Portrait (attributed)
Fyvie Castle, Aberdeenshire NTS
Self Portrait
Ickworth, Suffolk NT
The 4th Earl of Bristol (1790)
Self Portrait (1791)
Knole, Kent NT
The Duchess of Dorset (1803)
London National Gallery
Mlle Brongniart
Self Portrait in a Straw Hat
London Wallace Collection
The Comte d'Espagnac (1786)
Mme de Perregaux (1789)
Polesden Lacey, Surrey NT
Etienne Vigée, the Artist's Brother (attributed)
Port Sunlight Lady Lever Art Gallery
Lady Hamilton as a Bacchante
Waddesdon Manor, Buckinghamshire NT
The Duchesse de Polignac (1783)

JEAN-ANTOINE WATTEAU
Valenciennes 1684 - Nogent-sur-Marne, near Paris 1721
Watteau invented an imaginary world of parks and gardens peopled by elegant figures dressed in theatrical silks and satins, playing music, dancing and relaxing. Known as fêtes galantes, this type of painting continued until the French Revolution, which effectively finished it off. Watteau himself died young, of tuberculosis.

Birmingham Barber Institute
Man playing a Hurdy-Gurdy (attributed)
Brodick Castle, Isle of Arran NTS
The Adventuress
• The Enchanter
Edinburgh NGS
'Fêtes Venitiennes'

'Le Dénicheur de Moineaux'
London National Gallery
The Scale of Love ('La Gamme d'Amour')
London Sir John Soane's Museum
'L'Accordée du Village'
London Wallace Collection
The Elysian Fields
Fête in a Park
Gilles and his Family
The Halt
Harlequin and Colombine
The Music Lesson
The Music Party
The Toilette
London (Dulwich) DPG
'Le Bal Champêtre'
Oxford Ashmolean Museum
'Le Repos Gracieux' (attributed)
Waddesdon Manor, Buckinghamshire NT
Harlequin, Pierrot and Scapin
York City Art Gallery
Le Défile

RICHARD WILSON
Pengoes, Powys, 1714 - Colomendy, Clywd 1782
The Welsh-born son of a clergyman, Wilson was given a classical education. The influence of his six years in Italy is seen on his return to Britain in the transposition of the golden light of the Roman Campagna onto scenes of British landscape. The largest collection of his work is in Cardiff.

Aberdeen Art Gallery
Ruin in a Clearing
Accrington Haworth Art Gallery
Castle near a Lake
Anglesey Abbey, Cambridgeshire NT
Gypsies at the Entrance to a Wood
Landscape with a Castle and a Lake
Landscape with a Tower
Windsor Forest
Barnard Castle Bowes Museum
River Scene with a Farmhouse
Belfast Ulster Museum
Farm with a Pond
Landscape with Bandits
Beningbrough Hall, Yorkshire NT
Francis Ayscough with the Prince of Wales
Birkenhead Williamson Art Gallery
Landscape
Landscape, Mountain and Cows
Old Welsh Bridge
Birmingham Barber Institute
River Dee near Eaton Hall
Birmingham CMAG
Okehampton Castle, Devon
Ruins of the Villa of Maecenas, Tivoli (1767)
Bournemouth
Russell-Cotes Art Gallery and Museum
On the Strada Nomentana

Gian Battista Tiepolo: The Finding of Moses

Richard Wilson: Niagara Falls

Brighton Art Gallery
Figures by a Lake
River View with Figures on a Bank
Bristol City Art Gallery
Diana and Callisto
Ruined Tower with Figures
Burnley Towneley Hall
Italian Landscape with Figures
Buscot Park, Berkshire
Faringdon Trustees
The Villa Chigi, Ariccia
Cambridge Fitzwilliam Museum
Apollo and the Seasons
Italian River Landscape with a Broken Bridge
Cardiff National Museum of Wales
21 paintings including:
Caernarvon Castle
Edinburgh National Gallery
Italian Landscape
River Scene with Castle and Figures
Edinburgh Scottish NPG
Flora MacDonald
Exeter Royal Albert Memorial Museum
Llyn Peris and Dolbadarn Castle, North Wales
Gloucester Art Gallery
Ariccia
The Convent on the Rock
Kew Gardens, Ruined Arch
Lake with Pavilion and Statue, Italy
The Tomb of the Horatii and the Curatii
Torre del Fiscale
The Villa of Hadrian
The Villa of Maecenas
Hull Ferens Art Gallery
Crow Castle, Llangollen
Italian Landscape with a Stone Pine
Kendal Abbot Hall Art Gallery
Crummockwater from near Loweswater
Chapel (attributed)
Leamington Spa Art Gallery
Faustulus discovering Romulus and Remus
near Rome
Leeds Temple Newsam House
Classical Landscape
Leicester Museum and Art Gallery
Head of a Capuchin (1752)
Landscape with Bathers
Liverpool Walker Art Gallery
Cader Idris and the Valley of the Mawddach
View of Snowdon
London Foundling Hospital
The Foundling Hospital
St George's Hospital
London National Gallery
Holt Bridge on the River Dee
The Valley of the Dee
London Royal Academy
Portrait of John Hamilton Mortimer
Self Portrait
London Tate Gallery
25 paintings including:
Rome: St Peter's and the Vatican from the
Janiculum
Westminster Bridge under Construction
(1744)
London V&A
Italian Lake Scene
Italian River Scene with Figures
Landscape, Evening, River Scene with Castle
Landscape, River Mouth with Peasants
dancing
London (Dulwich) DPG
Tivoli, the Cascades and the Villa of
Maecenas
London (Greenwich) NMM
Portrait of Thomas Smith
London (Hampstead)
Kenwood (Iveagh Bequest)
View of London from Highgate
London (Twickenham) Marble Hill House
The Thames near Marble Hill
Manchester City Art Gallery
Landscape with a Ruined Castle
overlooking a River

View on the River Arno, III (1764)
The Valley of the Mawddach
The Villa of Cicero
The Villa of Hadrian
Newcastle upon Tyne Laing Art Gallery
The Alban Hills
Newport, Gwent Art Gallery
A Backwater on the Severn
Nostell Priory, Yorkshire NT
Landscape
Nottingham Castle Museum
View of Snowdon
Oxford Ashmolean Museum
Aquae Albulae, near Tivoli
The Bathers
Pastoral Scene in the Campagna
The Ponte d'Augusto, Rimini
View from the Villa Madama, Rome
View of the Lago d'Agnano with the Bay of
Naples and Vesuvius in the Distance
A Weir on the River Po near Ferrara
Petworth House, Sussex NT
The Hermitage (1760)
View on the Arno
View on the Dee near Eaton Hall (1760)
Plymouth City Art Gallery
The Broken Bridge at Narni
Port Sunlight Lady Lever Art Gallery
Landscape with Diana and Callisto
Lake Albano, Castlegandolo
The Unransomed
The Villa of Maecenas, Tivoli
Southampton City Art Gallery
Classical Landscape, View on the Arno
Swansea Glynn Vivian Art Gallery
Lake Avernus
Landscape with a Castle
River Scene in Italy
Solitude
Upton House, Warwickshire NT
A Convent on a Rock
Wilton House, Wiltshire
Ariccia, a Fallen Tree
Ariccia, a Fallen Tree
The Tomb of the Horatii and the Curatii
Six views of Wilton House
Wolverhampton Art Gallery
•Niagara Falls
York City Art Gallery
Lake Avernus (attributed)

JOSEPH WRIGHT OF DERBY

Derby 1734 - Derby 1797
A provincial artist who has rightly
acquired an international reputation,
Wright was a specialist painter of dramatic
lighting effects: candlelit scenes in
darkened rooms, volcanic eruptions and
fireworks at night. A friend of pioneer
industrialists, inventors and scientists, he
painted portraits and scenes of scientific
experiments and industry to staggeringly
life-like effect. The best collection of his
works is still in his native Derby

Aberystwyth
School of Art Gallery and Museum
Vesuvius in Eruption
Belfast Ulster Museum
Virgil's Tomb (1785)
Birmingham CMAG
The Girandola
Broadlands, Hampshire
Knatchbull Collectioin
An Iron Forge (1772)
Cambridge Fitzwilliam Museum
Matlock Tor, Derbyshire
Portrait of Mrs John Ashton (1769)
Portrait of Viscount Fitzwilliam at the Age
of 19 (1764)
Cardiff National Museum of Wales
Lake Albano
Derby Art Gallery
35 paintings including:
•The Alchemist in search of the

Joseph Wright of Derby: The Alchemist in search of the Philosopher's Stone discovers Phosphorus

Philosopher's Stone discovers Phosphorus
A Philosopher lecturing upon the Orrery
Doncaster Art Gallery
William Brooke (1760)
Dunham Massey, Cheshire NT
Portrait of the Hon. John Gray
Eastbourne Towner Art Gallery
River Landscape with Cliffs and Houses in
the Distance
Exeter Royal Albert Memorial Museum
Landscape with Lake Nemi and a view of
Castelgandolfo (1792)
Gawthorpe Hall, Lancashire NT
Portrait of James Shuttleworth with
his Wife and Daughter
Grasmere Dove Cottage and the
Wordsworth Museum
Ullswater, The Lake District
Hatchlands, Surrey NT
Helen Goodwin (1782)
Lucy Stafford
Rev Henry Case Morewood (1782)
Kedleston Hall, Derbyshire NT
The Convent of San Cosimato
Nathanial Curzon, 2nd Lord Scarsdale
Self Portrait
View in Dovedale
Leeds Temple Newsam House
A Girl
Portrait of Samuel Oldknow
Leicester NWMAG
High Tor, Matlock, Derbyshire

Portrait of Mrs Catherine Swindell
Liverpool
University of Liverpool Art Gallery
Snowdon by Moonlight
Liverpool Walker Art Gallery
The Girandola
Fleetwood Hesketh
Mrs Fleetwood Hesketh
The Lady in Milton's Comus (1784)
Moonlit Scene (1792)
London Leighton House
Italian Landscape
London National Gallery
An Experiment with an Air Pump
Portrait of Mr and Mrs Thomas Coltman
London National Portrait Gallery
Portrait of Erasmus Darwin
Self Portrait
Portrait of Sir Richard Arkwright
Portrait of Thomas Day
London Tate Britain
An Iron Forge (1772)
A Moonlit Scene with a Lighthouse, Coast
of Tuscany
Sir Brooke Boothby reclining in a
Landscape (1781)
Portrait of Thomas Staniforth of Darnall,
Yorkshire (1796)
Vesuvius in Eruption with a View of the
Islands in the Bay of Naples
View of Catania with Mount Etna in the
Distance

London Wellcome Institute
Portrait of Richard Wright, Surgeon, of Derby
London (Hampstead) Kenwood
(Iveagh Bequest)
Two Girls dressing a Kitten by Candlelight
Macclesfield Christ Church
Portrait of Charles Roe
Manchester City Art Gallery
Portrait of the Hon. Thomas Bligh (?)
Portrait of Thomas Day (1770)
Newcastle upon Tyne Laing Art Gallery
Portrait of Lawrence Monck of Caenby,
Lincoln
A Member of the Monck Family
Portrait of Mrs Lawrence Monck
Nottingham
Castle Museum and Art Gallery
Portrait of Sir Richard Arkwright
Oxford Ashmolean
Italianate Lake Scene with a Waterfall
Preston Museum of Lancashire
Mrs James Hardman of Rochdale and
Allerton Hall
Sheffield Sheffield Galleries (Graves)
View of Dale Abbey, Derbyshire
Southampton City Art Gallery
Derbyshire Landscape
Wolverhampton Art Gallery and Museum
Portrait of Erasmus Darwin

1801-1900

Nineteenth-century paintings in British collections are, unsurprisingly, predominantly by British artists. The greatest collection of works by a single artist in the country must be the 300 or so paintings and many more drawings left to the nation by Turner and housed for the most part in the Clore galleries of Tate Britain. A huge body of Constable's work, including an unrivalled collection of oil studies, is owned by the Victoria and Albert Museum, some of which are on loan to Tate Britain. The nineteenth century also saw the founding of many of our great municipal galleries, which bought contemporary art ambitiously – hence the outstanding pre-Raphaelite collections in Birmingham (particularly rich in the works of the Brummie Burne-Jones), Liverpool and Manchester. Manchester council also employed Ford Maddox Brown to paint a series of pictures for their Town Hall. In contrast, public galleries in Britain were slow to respond to and collect works by avant-garde artists on the Continent. The Impressionist and Post-Impressionist paintings in this country were almost all bought not by institutions but by a small number of enlightened collectors early in the twentieth century, who bequeathed their picturesto the public. Most important among these were Samuel Courtauld, whose astonishing collection is housed in the Courtauld Institute Galleries in Somerset House, London, and the Davies sisters, Gwendoline and Margaret, who left over 260 works, dominated by Impressionists and Post Impressionists to the National Museum of Wales in Cardiff.

Sir Edward Burne-Jones: The Briar Rose series: The Prince enters the Briar Wood

ARNOLD BÖCKLIN
Basle 1827 - San Domenico near Fiesole 1901
Hailed as the most influential Swiss painter of the nineteenth century, Böcklin's highly emotionally charged works and other-worldly settings were hugely influential on the German-speaking world but never popular in Britain - there is only one to be seen in the country. Spending much of his life in Italy, he was inspired by classical mythology, the spirit of which infused his early naturalistic landscapes with poetic symbolism and heightened romantic style.
London (Walthamstow)
William Morris Gallery
• Silenus

FORD MADOX BROWN
Calais 1821 - London 1893
Born and raised on the Continent, Brown was profoundly influenced by the Nazarenes, the quasi-religious group of German painters working in Rome. Their religious and medieval subject matter, and use of clear colour, was adopted by Brown. His work had a tremendous impact on the young Rossetti and his circle of Pre-Raphaelites. His most important work was the decoration of the great chamber of Manchester Town Hall.
Aberdeen Art Gallery
The Romans building the Fort at Manchester (1879-80)
Birmingham CMAG
Ten works including:
• The Last of England (1855)
The Pretty Baa-Lambs (1851-9)
Work (1863)
Bodelwyddon Castle Denbighshire
Henry Fawcett and Dame Millicent Fawcett
Bradford Cartwright Hall
Wycliffe reading his Translation of the Bible

Ford Madox Brown: The Last of England (1855)

Buscot Park, Berkshire NT
Entombment (1868)
Cambridge Fitzwilliam Museum
Cordelia's Portion
The Last of England (1860)
Cardiff National Museum of Wales
King René's Honeymoon (1864)
View on the Medway
Carlisle
Tulie House Museum and Art Gallery
The Baptism of Saint Edwin AD 627
Glasgow Art Gallery and Museum
Wycliffe on Trial (1885)
Liverpool Walker Art Gallery
The Coat of Many Colours (1866)
Portrait of Millie Smith (1846)
Waiting: An English Fireside (1855)
London Tate Britain
The Brent at Hendon (1854)
Carrying Corn (1854)
Chaucer at the Court of Edward III (1856-68)
Portrait of Dykes Barry as a Child (1853)
The Hayfield (1855-6)

Jesus washing Peter's Feet (1852-6)
Lear and Cordelia (1849-54)
Platt Lane (1844)
'Take your Son Sir' (unfinished)
Manchester City Art Gallery
29 works including:
The English Boy
Work (1852-65)
Manchester Whitworth Art Gallery
The Execution of Mary Queen of Scots
Manchester Town Hall
12 paintings depicting the history of Manchester over 19 centuries
Nottingham
Castle Museum and Art Gallery
Cromwell and the Vaudois
Manfred in the Chamois Hunter's Hut
Oxford Ashmolean Museum
The Execution of Mary Queen of Scots (study)
Portrait of Mrs Madox
The Pretty Baa-Lambs (1852)
The Seed and Fruits of English Poetry (1853)

Lady Rivers and her Children
Port Sunlight Lady Lever Art Gallery
Cromwell on his Farm in Saint Ives, 1630 (1874)
Windemere (1855)
Southampton City Art Gallery
Cordelia's Portion
Wightwick Manor, Staffordshire NT
Portrait of William Michael Rossetti by Gaslight (1856)
The Young Mother
The Artist's Daughter Lucy
The Artist's Mother
The Artist's Sister-in-law
Mary Rossetti

SIR EDWARD BURNE-JONES
Birmingham 1833 - London 1898
Heavily influenced by the medieval subject matter of the Pre-Raphaelites and the teachings of his friend William Morris, Burne-Jones retreated from the realities of industrialising England to a dream-world of chivalric deeds, knights errant and dreaming damsels. His Briar Rose series in Buscot Park, depicting the questing prince among the sleeping ladies, exemplifies this genre of painting.
Birmingham CMAG
21 works including 12 paintings of the Story of Cupid and Psyche
Pygmalion and the Image
Brighton St Paul's
Altarpiece: the Annunciation and the Adoration of the Magi
Bristol City Art Gallery
The Garden Court
Saint George and the Dragon, VII: The Return
Burnley Towneley Hall
Wood Nymphs
Buscot Park, Berkshire NT
• 14 paintings of the Legend of the Briar Rose
Cardiff National Museum of Wales
Study of a Head
Venus Discordia
The Wheel of Fortune
Carlisle
Tulie House Museum and Art Gallery
Helen, a Mermaid
Compton, Surrey Watts Gallery
The Triumph of Love (4 panels)
Glasgow Art Gallery and Museum
The Angel (1881)
Danaë (the Tower of Brass)
Leicester NWMAG
Christ and the Twelve Apostles
Liverpool Walker Art Gallery
The Sleeping Knights
London Leighton House
The Sower (sketch)
Study of a Head
London Tate Britain
10 works including:
King Cophetua and the Beggar Maid (1884)
Love and the Pilgrim (1896-7)
The Morning of the Resurrection (1886)
London V&A

The Car of Love (unfinished)
Cupid's Hunting-Fields
The Feast of Peleus
Mill Girls dancing to Music by a River (1870)
A Peacock
Scene from La Roman de la Rose
Manchester City Art Gallery
Sibylla Delphica
Newcastle upon Tyne Laing Art Gallery
Laus Veneris
Norwich Castle Museum
Annunciation
Oxford Ashmolean Museum
The Building of the Brazen Tower
Plymouth CMAG
Venus Concordia
Port Sunlight Lady Lever Art Gallery
Ananias in the Fiery Furnace
Annunciation (1879)
Azarias in the Fiery Furnace
The Beguiling of Merlin (1874)
The Tree of Forgiveness (1882)
Sheffield Sheffield Galleries (Graves)
Cupid delivering Psyche
The Hours (1882)
Southampton City Art Gallery
10 paintings of the story of Perseus
Lancelot at the Chapel of the Holy Grail
Stalybridge Astley Cheetham Art Gallery
Saint Nicholas
Wightwick Manor, Staffordshire NT
Love Among the Ruins (1894)

MARY CASSATT
Allegheny City, now in Pittsburgh 1844 - Le Mesnil-Théribus, France 1926
Daughter of a Pittsburgh banker, Cassatt travelled widely in Europe before settling in Paris to study painting. Interested in the work of Courbet, Manet and the Impressionists, her introduction to Degas in 1877 led to his invitation to exhibit with the Impressionists. She was also an early patron of Impressionist works and encouraged her friends and family to do likewise.
Birmingham CMAG
A Woman
Glasgow Art Gallery and Museum
• The Little Sisters

PAUL CÉZANNE
Aix-en-Provence 1839 - Aix-en-Provence 1906
Cézanne's stated aim was 'to make museum art of Impressionism' - that is, to make something grave and permanent from the fleeting effects of nature aimed at by the Impressionists. His geometric

rigour and the way he applied paint with deliberate strokes, one next to the other, had a profound influence on Cubism in the early years of the twentieth century.
Cambridge Fitzwilliam Museum
The Edge of the Wood
Cardiff National Museum of Wales
Mountains at L'Estaque
Provençal Landscape: the Copse
Still Life with a Teapot
Edinburgh NGS
Landscape
Mont Sainte-Victoire
Glasgow Burrell Collection
The Château de Médan
Liverpool Walker Art Gallery
The Murder
London Courtauld Institute
The Lake at Annecy (1896)
Large Trees at the Jas de Bouffan
Man with a Pipe
Mont Sainte-Victoire
The Pond at Osny (1877)
Pot of Flowers and Pears
The Road with Bends
• Still Life with a Plaster Bust of Cupid
Two Card-Players
London National Gallery
11 paintings including:
Self Portrait
Bathers
London Tate Modern
The Gardener
Sheffield Sheffield Galleries (Graves)
The Jas de Bouffan

JOHN CONSTABLE

East Bergholt, Suffolk 1776 – Hampstead, London 1837
Together with Turner, one of the greatest English landscapists of nineteenth-century England and certainly the best loved. Constable was a painter of place, maintaining that 'I should paint my own places best', and in particular painted his native Suffolk, Hampstead where he later lived with his wife and family, Salisbury, Weymouth and Brighton, and West Sussex, which he discovered towards the end of his life.

John Constable: Golding Constable's Flower Garden

Aberystwyth
School of Art Gallery and Museum
Landscape with Trees
Anglesey Abbey, Cambridgeshire NT
The Opening of Waterloo Bridge
Barnsley Cannon Hall
Portrait of Mrs Tuder
Birmingham CMAG
Study of Clouds
Harwich Lighthouse
Bristol City Art Gallery
Near Keswick, Evening (1806)
Malvern Hall from the South West
Burnley Towneley Hall
The Gathering Storm (1819)
Bury, Lancashire Art Gallery
Hampstead Heath (attributed)
Cambridge Fitzwilliam Museum
12 works including:
East Bergholt (1808)
Sky Study with a Shaft of Sunlight
Cardiff National Museum of Wales
Cottage in a Cornfield
Coventry Herbert Art Gallery

Cloud Study
Edinburgh NGS
Dedham Vale
Noon, Hampstead Heath
On the Stour
Elton Hall, Peterborough
Proby Collection
Dedham Vale
Glasgow Art Gallery and Museum
Hampstead Heath
House by the Road
On the Wye, Herefordshire
Hull Ferens Art Gallery
Cloud Study
Ipswich Christchurch Mansion
Portrait of Abram Constable
Farm Carthorses in Harness
Portrait of Golding Constable
• Golding Constable's Flower Garden (1815)
Golding Constable's Vegetable Garden
The Mill Stream, Willy Lott's House (1816)
Portrait of Thomas Gosnall (attributed)
Willy Lott's House (1816)
Knightshayes Court, Devon NT
Field of Flowers and Berries in a Brown Pot
Poppies
Leeds City Art Gallery
Corner of Hampstead Ponds
The Field by the Wood
A Herald Angel
View of Dedham (sketch) (1814)
Leicester NWMAG
Unfinished Portrait of a Gentleman
Liverpool Walker Art Gallery
Seashore with Fishermen near a Boat
London Courtauld Institute
Cloud Study
London Guildhall Art Gallery
Salisbury Cathedral from the Meadow
London National Gallery
Weymouth Bay
Stratford Mill
The Hay Wain (1821)
Salisbury Cathedral from the River Avon
The Cornfield (1826)
Salisbury Cathedral from the Meadows (on loan)
The Cenotaph, Coleorton
London Tate Britain
41 paintings including:
Flatford Mill (1817)
The Opening of Waterloo Bridge
Sketch for 'Hadleigh Castle'
London V&A
103 works including:
The Hay Wain (full-scale study)
Old Sarum (1829)

Salisbury Cathedral from the Bishop's Grounds
Willy Lott's House, near Flatford Mill
London (Hampstead) Fenton House NT
View of Hampstead Heath under a Stormy Sky
London (Richmond) Ham House NT
Portrait of Louisa Manners (after Hoppner)
Portrait of Maria Lewes (after Reynolds)
Manchester City Art Gallery
Cottage in a Cornfield
Hampstead (1821)
Manchester Whitworth Art Gallery
Study of Clouds
Nayland, Suffolk Saint James
Christ Blessing the Sacrament
Newcastle upon Tyne Laing Art Gallery
Salisbury Cathedral (attributed)
Oxford Ashmolean Museum
Coast Scene
Dedham Vale from Langham (1812)
Golding Constable's house at East Bergholt
Study of Clouds
Summer Sunset
View at Hampstead looking Towards Harrow
Water Meadows near Salisbury
Port Sunlight Lady Lever Art Gallery
Cottage at East Bergholt (sketch)
East Bergholt Mill, The Glebe Farm
Rochdale Art Gallery
Stream with Trees on a Bank
Study of Cumulus Clouds
Sheffield Sheffield Galleries (Graves)
Landscape (1829)
Salisbury Cathedral
Swansea Glynn Vivian Art Gallery
Foxgloves
Upton House, Warwickshire NT

Suffolk Landscape (sketch)
Walsall New Art Gallery
Landscape with Clouds
Westcliff-on-Sea Beecroft Art Gallery
The River Stour looking towards Manningtree

JEAN-BAPTISTE-CAMILLE COROT

Paris 1796 – Paris 1875
Corot was one of the most successful, and remains one of the most popular, nineteenth-century landscape painters. His early works, including vibrant oil-sketches painted in Italy, were revolutionary in their crystalline treatment of light. His later landscapes are softer almost dreamlike views with characteristic wispy, almost monochrome, trees.
Barnard Castle Bowes Museum
Landscape with Cattle
Barnsley Cooper Art Gallery
Landscape with Two Peasant Women fishing
Birmingham Barber Institute
Mountains in the Limousin
Bournemouth Russell-Cotes Art Gallery and Museum
Landscape with a Bridge
Bristol City Art Gallery
Fontainebleau, the Forest
Cambridge Fitzwilliam Museum
Chestnut Grove
Daubigny's Pond, Auvers
Dutch Landscape (1854)
The Dyke (1866)
Landscape in the Roman Campagna
Cardiff National Museum of Wales
Castel Gandolfo
Distant View of Corbeil, Morning
Fisherman moored to the Bank
The Pond
Edinburgh NGS
10 paintings including:
The Artist's Mother
The Watering Place
Glasgow Art Gallery and Museum
The Crayfisher
Portrait of Mlle de Foudras (1872)
Pastoral, Souvenir of Italy (1873)
The Riverbank
The Woodcutter
Glasgow Burrell Collection
Peasant House near Fontainebleau
Sailing-boats in a Harbour
A Woman
Greenock McLean Museum and Art Gallery
Evening
Kilmarnock Dick Institute
Harvesting
Leeds City Art Gallery
'Les Châteaux'
Mont Valérian
Woodland
Liverpool Sudley House
The Cow at the Well

Paul Cézanne: Still Life with a Plaster Bust of Cupid

Jean-Baptiste-Camille Corot: Sunset, Figures under Trees

London National Gallery
24 works including:
The Roman Campagna, with the Claudian Aqueduct
The Four Times of Day
London V&A
Morning
Twilight
London Wallace Collection
Macbeth and the Witches
Manchester City Art Gallery
Rider in the Water
•Sunset, Figures under Trees
Manchester Whitworth Art Gallery
Saint-Brévain, near Saint-Nazaire
Oxford Ashmolean Museum
Lago di Piediluco, Umbria (1826)
Landscape near Ville d'Avray
Portraits of M. and Mme Bison (1852)
View of Olevano
Paisley Museum and Art Galleries
Foggy Morning, Ville d'Avray
The Mill Stream
Sheffield Sheffield Galleries (Graves)
'Au Petit Chaville'
Southampton City Art Gallery
Landscape
Normandy Breakwater
Ville d'Avray
Walsall New Art Gallery
Woman Reading

GUSTAVE COURBET
Ornans, Franche-Comté 1819 -
La Tour-de-Peilz, near Vevey 1877
An extravagantly bohemian character, fiercely republican and anti-clerical, he was arrested and sentenced for his part in the destruction of the Vendôme column in 1871, and fled to Switzerland, where he established a picture factory producing Swiss landscapes. His work is naturalistic and depicts scenes of everyday life in the form of portraits, self-portraits, nudes, still lifes and landscapes.
Barnard Castle Bowes Museum
View from Ornans
Birmingham Barber Institute
The Rock Arch, Étretat
Birnmingham CMAG
Venus and Psyche (study)
Bristol City Art Gallery
L'Eternité
Landscape, Ornans, the Valley of the Loue
Cambridge Fitzwilliam Museum
The Charente at Port Bertaud
'Dinant, la Roiche à Bayard'
The Glade
Cardiff National Museum of Wales
Portrait of Béatrice Bouvet, Aged Three
Edinburgh NGS
River in a Gorge
Trees in the Snow
The Wave
Glasgow Art Gallery and Museum
Flowers in a Basket
Still Life with Apple Pear and Orange
A Woman (attributed)
Glasgow Burrell Collection

Edgar Degas: Jockeys before the Race

•Alms for a Beggar at Ornans
Irises and Carnations
The Lady with the Parasol, Mlle Aubé
Pomegranates
Still Life of Fruit
The Washerwoman
Leeds City Art Gallery
The Women of the Village
Liverpool Walker Art Gallery
Low Tide at Trouville
London National Gallery
Young Ladies on the Banks of the Seine
Still Life with Apples and Pomegranates
Beach Scene
Landscape
London V&A
L'Immensité
Landscape with the Châtel St-Denis,
Scey- en-Varais, Doubs (1873)
London (Walthamstow)
William Morris Gallery
Still Life of Pears
Manchester City Art Gallery
The Brook of the Puits Noir
Oxford Ashmolean Museum
The Banks of the Stream (1873)
Winter Scene
Paisley Museum and Art Galleries
Snowy Landscape
Perth Museum and Art Gallery
Still Life, Peaches
Southampton City Art Gallery
Sea Piece at Honfleur (attributed)
York City Art Gallery
Swiss Landscape (1869)

EDGAR DEGAS
Paris 1834 - Paris 1917
Exhibited with the Impressionists but was not concerned like them with natural outdoor effects, declaring that 'no art was less spontaneous than mine'. Like the Impressionist circle, his subjects were of contemporary life - in particular, the ballet, circus, cabaret, café-concert and

the racecourse - and he was interested in the effects of artificial light.
Birmingham Barber Institute
•Jockeys before the Race
Portrait of Mlle Malo (pastel)
Birmingham CMAG
Roman Beggar Woman (1857)
Cambridge Fitzwilliam Museum
Two Women at the Café
Edinburgh NGS

Before the Performance
Portrait of Diego Martelli
Group of Dancers
Study of a Girl's Head
Woman Drying Herself
Glasgow Art Gallery and Museum
Dancers on a Bench (pastel)
Glasgow Burrell Collection
19 works including 13 pastels
and
Girl Looking through Opera Glasses
Portrait of M. Duranty
Leicester NWMAG
Sheep Returning to the Fold
Liverpool Walker Art Gallery
Woman Ironing
London Courtauld Institute
A Dancer
Lady with a Parasol
Two Ballerinas
Woman at the Window
London National Gallery
14 works (three on loan from Tate)
including:
Miss La La at the Cirque Fernando
Hélène Rouart in her Father's Study
Combing the Hair
London V&A
At the Ballet: Robert le Diable (1876)
Walsall New Art Gallery
Marguerite Degas, the Artist's Sister

EUGÈNE DELACROIX
Charenton-Saint-Maurice, near Paris
1798 - Paris 1863
Prime exponent of Romantic painting, admirer of Géricault, and interested in English art, especially in animal sporting paintings. His use of brilliant colour,

dramatic action and exotic subject matter is often compared to the cool classicism of Ingres, in order to demonstrate two diverse but contemporaneous strands of painting in the first half of the nineteenth century.
Birmingham Barber Institute
Carrying the Body of Saint Stephen (1862)
Birmingham CMAG
Portrait of Mme F. Simon (attributed)
Bristol City Art Gallery
Woman in a Red Turban (1831)
Cambridge Fitzwilliam Museum
Cers (study)
The Muse of Orpheus (study)
Odalisque (sketch)
Prudence, Force, Genius (sketch)
Edinburgh NGS
Arabs playing Chess
Glasgow Art Gallery and Museum
The Expulsion of Adam and Eve from the Garden of Eden (attributed)
Glasgow Burrell Collection
A White Horse
London National Gallery
Abel Widmer
Louis-Auguste Schwiter
Christ on the Cross (1853)
Ovid Among the Scythians (1859)
London V&A
The Good Samaritan (1852)
The Shipwreck of Don Juan (sketch)
London Wallace Collection
The Execution of Doge Marino Faliero
Faust and Mephistopholes
Nottingham
Castle Museum and Art Gallery
•Tam O'Shanter

CASPAR DAVID FRIEDRICH
Greifswald 1774 - Dresden 1840

Paul Gauguin: The Breton Shepherdess (1886)

A major figure in the Romantic movement, Freidrich's paintings contain powerful realism combined with intense emotional symbolism. In common with many German artists his work was viewed with suspicion in Britain until very recently, a fact which explains - but hardly excuses - his feeble representation in collections here.

London National Gallery
•Winter Landscape

PAUL GAUGUIN
Paris 1848 - Atuona, Marquesas Islands 1903
His early Impressionist work was succeeded by an increasingly abstracted style in which colour became all-important. His powerful personality and belief in the use of colour to express emotion exerted a great influence on his younger contemporaries, especially Van Gogh. Attracted by non-European art and life, he left France for the South Sea islands, where he remained until his death.

Birmingham Barber Institute
Bathers at Tahiti (1897)
Landscape at Pont Aven (attributed) (1888)
Cambridge Fitzwilliam Museum
Landscape (1873)
Edinburgh NGS
Jacob wrestling with the Angel (1888)
Martinique Landscape (1887)
Three Tahitian Women (1898)
Glasgow Art Gallery and Museum
Østervold Park, Copenhagen (1885)
London Courtauld Institute
Harvest at Brittany (1889)
Nevermore (1897)
'Te rerioa' (the Dream) (1897)
London National Gallery
Vase of Flowers (1896)
'Faa Iheihe' (on loan from Tate) (1898)
The Harvest: Le Pouldu (on loan from Tate) (1890)
Manchester City Art Gallery
Harbour Scene Dieppe
Newcastle upon Tyne Laing Art Gallery
•The Breton Shepherdess (1886)

THÉODORE GÉRICAULT
Rouen 1791 - Paris 1824
Dead at the age of 32, Géricault was the bright star of the Romantic movement. Painter of horses and of scenes of contemporary subjects, he spent two years in England, where his Raft of the Medusa was shown as a travelling exhibit and where he continued to study the horse. Despite the limited exposure of his work he exerted a tremendous influence on painters of the Romantic movement.

Cambridge Fitzwilliam Museum
Cart of Wounded Soldiers
Glasgow Burrell Collection
Grey Charger harnessed with Blue Trappings
'Le Haras'
A Piebald Stallion
•Prancing Grey Horse
The Stallion
Télémaque
Trumpeter of the Polish Lancers

Two Brown Horses
London National Gallery
A Horse Frightened by Lightning
London Wallace Collection
Cavalry Skirmish
Walsall New Art Gallery
Study of a Male Nude

VINCENT VAN GOGH
Groot-Zundwert 1853 - Auvers-sur-Oise 1890
Paradigm of the twentieth century's conception of the misunderstood genius, scorned in his own lifetime and recognised only after his death, Van Gogh is today one of the world's best-loved painters. His paintings possess a vibrancy characterised by his distinctive swirling brushwork and bright use of colour, often applied directly from the tube.

Birmingham Barber Institute
Peasant Woman digging (1885)
Cardiff National Museum of Wales
Landscape with Rain at Auvers (1890)
Edinburgh NGS
Bust of a Peasant (1886)
Fruit Trees in Blossom (1888)
Olive Trees (1889)
Glasgow Art Gallery and Museum
Portrait of Alexander Reid (1887)
'Le Moulin de Blute-Fin' Montmartre (1886)
London Courtauld Institute
Peach Blossom in the Crau (1889)
Self Portrait with Bandaged Ear (1889)
London National Gallery
•The Artist's Chair (1888-9)
A Field
Sunflowers
Wheatfield with Cypresses (1889)
Farms near Auvers (on loan from Tate) (1890)
Oxford Ashmolean Museum
The Restaurant 'La Sirène' Asnières (1887)

WILLIAM HOLMAN HUNT
London 1827 - London 1910

With Rossetti and Millais, co-founder of the Pre-Raphaelite movement initiated in 1848 in reaction to academic teaching. In love with the world of the Middle Ages and early Italian art, Hunt travelled to Egypt and the Holy Land to paint Biblical scenes with accurate settings. He also painted moralising scenes of contemporary life, dense with symbolism.

Aberdeen Art Gallery
Past and Present
Birmingham CMAG
Portrait of Dante Gabriel Rossetti (1853)
The Finding of the Saviour in the Temple (1854-60)
The Lantern-Maker's Courtship
May Morning on Magdalen Tower, Oxford (1888-91)
Self Portrait (1845)
Two Gentlemen of Verona (1851)
Bodelwyddon Castle Denbighshire
Portrait of Stephen Lushington
Cambridge Fitzwilliam Museum
Portrait of Cyril Benoni Holman Hunt (1880)
The Thames at Chelsea, Evening (1853)
Coventry Herbert Art Gallery
Copy of Rembrandt's Christ and the Woman Taken in Adultery
Leeds City Art Gallery
The Shadow of Death (1870-3)
Liverpool Sudley House
The Finding of the Saviour in the Temple
Liverpool Walker Art Gallery
The Eve of Saint Agnes (1847-57)
Portrait of Harold Rathbone (1893)
The Triumph of the Innocents (1876-87)
London Guildhall Art Gallery
The Eve of Saint Agnes (1848)
London Natural History Museum
Portrait of Professor Richard Owen
London St Paul's Cathedral
The Light of the World (1900)
London Tate Britain
The Awakening Conscience (1853)
Claudio and Isabella (1850)
Portrait of F.G. Stephens (1847)
The Haunted Manor (1849)
Portrait of John Hunt
Portrait of John Key
Our English Coasts, or 'Strayed Sheep' (1852)
The Ship (1875)
The Triumph of the Innocents (1883-4)
Manchester City Art Gallery
The Hireling Shepherd (1851)
The Lady of Shalott
The Lantern-Maker's Courtship
The Light of the World (1851-6)
The Scapegoat (1854-5)
The Shadow of Death (1870-3)
Study of Edith Holman Hunt (1884)
Newcastle upon Tyne Laing Art Gallery
Isabella and the Pot of Basil (1867)
Oxford Ashmolean Museum
The Afterglow in Egypt
A Converted British Family Sheltering a Christian Priest from the Persecution of the Druids (1850)
The Festival of Saint Swithin (1866-75)
London Bridge at Night (1863-6)
The Plain of Esdraelon
The Schoolgirl (Miriam Wilkinson) (1859)
Self Portrait at the Age of 14
Oxford Jesus College
John David Jenkins (1852)
Oxford Keble College
•The Light of the World
Port Sunlight Lady Lever Art Gallery
May Morning on Magdalen Tower, Oxford (1890)
The Scapegoat (1854-5)
Preston Harris Museum and Art Gallery
The Back of the Sphinx, Gizeh

Gustav Klimt: Portrait of Hermine Gallia (1904)

Sheffield Sheffield Galleries (Graves)
Little Nell and her Grandfather (1845)
Southampton City Art Gallery
Afterglow in Egypt (1854-63)
Torbay Torre Abbey
Family Group: The Children's Party
Wightwick Manor Staffordshire NT
The Artist's Daughter Gladys
Worthing Museum and Art Gallery
Bianca

JEAN-AUGUSTE-DOMINIQUE INGRES
Montauban 1780 - Paris 1867
The arch-exponent of Classicism, Ingres's paintings possess a cool, glassy finish. A superb draughtsman and great admirer of Raphael, he lived in Italy for 18 years, earning an income as a portraitist to French tourists. Although his portraits are now seen as among his finest achievements, he saw himself as

a painter of 'histories', scenes from the Bible and the Classics painted in the grand manner.

Birmingham Barber Institute
Paolo and Francesca
Hull Ferens Art Gallery
Portrait of a Lady (attributed)
London National Gallery
Monsieur de Norvins
Angelica saved by Ruggiero
Oedipus and the Sphinx
Pindar and Ictinus
•Madame Moitessier
London V&A
Henri IV of France Surprised by the Spanish Ambassador
Sleeping Nude

GUSTAV KLIMT
Vienna 1862 - Vienna 1918
Klimt's highly distinctive works betray the fact that he achieved far greater success as a decorator, particularly in the medium of mosaic, than as an actual painter. A founding member of the Vienna 'Sezession', he was highly influenced by the work of Japanese artists and by British painters such as Burne-Jones.

London National Gallery
•Portrait of Hermine Gallia (1904)

Edouard Manet: Still Life with a Ham

EDOUARD MANET
Paris 1832 - Paris 1883
One of the greatest painters of his century, Manet reacted against academic painting in favour of contemporary subjects, which he sought to invest with gravitas. He particularly admired the sombre tonalities of the Spanish masters, especially of Velázquez. He was of immense influence on the Impressionist movement and was in turn influenced by them.
Birmingham Barber Institute
Portrait of Carolus Duran (unfinished) (1876)
Cardiff National Museum of Wales
Barge at Argenteuil
Church at Petit Montrouge (1870)
Dead Rabbit at a Window
Glasgow Burrell Collection
'Aux Folies Bergère'
A Café in the Place du Théâtre Français, Paris (pastel)
Portrait of Marie Colombier (pastel)
Still Life of Fruit
•Still Life with a Ham
Vase with a Pink Rose and a Yellow Rose
A Woman (pastel)
London Courtauld Institute
The Bar at the Folies Bergère (1882)
'Dejeuner sur l'Herbe'
'Marguerite de Conflans en toilette de bal'
London National Gallery
Music in the Tuileries Gardens (1862)
The Execution of Maximilian
Eva Gonzales (1870)
Corner of a Café Concert
Woman with a Cat (on loan from Tate)
Oxford Ashmolean Museum
Landscape with a Village Church

JOHN EVERETT MILLAIS
Southampton 1829 - London 1896
The precociously brilliant Millais was a co-founding member of the Pre-Raphaelite Brotherhood. A technical genius, and perhaps the most celebrated of all his contemporaries, he abandoned the principals of the Pre-Raphaelites and the avant-garde to become a very wealthy and highly fashionable society painter.
Aberdeen Art Gallery
Bright Eyes (1877)
The Convalescent (1875)
Portrait of George de Maurier (1882)
Self Portrait (1883)
Birmingham CMAG
The Blind Girl (1856)
The Enemy Sowing Tares
My Second Sermon (1864)
The Poacher's Wife (unfinished) (1860)
Three Sword Hilts (1838)
Waiting (1854)
The Widow's Mite (1870)
Blackpool Grundy Art Gallery
The Letter Box
Bodelwyddon Castle Denbighshire
Portrait of Thomas Carlyle
Bolton Art Gallery
The Somnambulist (1871)
Brighouse Smith Art Gallery
Reflection (1873)
Bristol City Art Gallery
The Bridge at Lammermoor (1878)
Cambridge Fitzwilliam Museum
The Bridesmaid (1851)

Portrait of Mrs Coventry Patmore (1851)
Cardiff National Museum of Wales
Jephthah (1867)
Dundee McManus Galleries
On the Balcony
Puss-in-boots (1877)
Edinburgh NGS
Sweetest Eyes that were ever seen
Elton Hall, Peterborough
Proby Collection
The Minuet
Egham, Surrey Royal Holloway College
The Princes in the Tower (1878)
Princess Elizabeth in Prison at Saint James's (1879)
Fyvie Castle, Aberdeenshire NTS
The Sound of Many Waters (1876)
Glasgow Art Gallery and Museum
The Forerunner (1896)
Portrait of Mrs Elder (1886)
The Ornithologist (1885)
Portrait of Revd John Caird
Portrait of William Ewart Gladstone
Hove Museum and Art Gallery
'Non Angli sed angeli'
Kilmarnock Dick Institute
Daydreams
Leeds City Art Gallery
Infancy
Youth
Manhood
Old Age
Music
Poetry
Liverpool Sudley House
Ferdinand lured by Ariel (sketch)
Landscape, Hampstead
Vanessa (1868)
Liverpool Walker Art Gallery
The Good Resolve (1877)
Lorenzo and Isabella (1849)
The Martyr of the Solway
Rosalind in the Forest
Self Portrait (1847)
Study of a Girl's Head
London Foundling Hospital
Portrait of Luther Holden
London Guildhall Art Gallery
My First Sermon (1863)
My Second Sermon (1864)
The Woodman's Daughter (1851)
London Leighton House

Portrait of Robert Rankin (1889)
London National Portrait Gallery
Portrait of the 3rd Marquess of Salisbury
Portrait of Benjamin Disraeli
Portrait of Sir Arthur Sullivan
Portrait of William Ewart Gladstone
Portrait of William Wilkie Collins
London Tate Britain
25 paintings including:
The Boyhood of Raleigh
Ophelia
London V&A
Portrait of Edward Robert Bulwer Lytton (1876)
Pizarro seizing the Inca of Peru
London (Camberwell)
South London Gallery
Portrait of the Marquis of Granby
Manchester City Art Gallery
11 works including:
•Autumn Leaves (1856)
Wandering Thoughts
Oldham Art Gallery
Boys Rabbiting
Departure of the Crusaders
Portrait of Thomas Oldham Barlow
Oxford Christ Church
Portrait of William Ewart Gladstone (1885)
Perth Museum and Art Gallery
Portrait of Effie Gray (1873)
Just Awake (1865)
Portrait of Sir Robert Pullar (1896)
Port Sunlight Lady Lever Art Gallery
Portrait of Alfred, Lord Tennyson (1881)
The Black Brunswicker (1860)
An Idyll of 1745 (1884)
Lingering Autumn (1890)
Little Speedwell's Darling Blue (1892)
The Nest (1887)
Sir Isumbras at the Ford (1857)
Spring, Apple Blossoms (1859)
St Helier Jersey Museum
A Jersey Lily

Picture of Health (Alice the Artist's Daughter)
Sheffield Sheffield Galleries (Mappin)
The Proposal
Southampton City Art Gallery
Flowing to the Sea (1871)
Stratford-upon-Avon RSCC
Portrait of Lord Ronald Sutherland Gower
Wednesbury Art Gallery and Museum
Boy playing a Hurdy-Gurdy (1843)
Wightwick Manor, Staffordshire NT
Effie Gray: The Foxglove (1853)
Othello and Desdemona

CLAUDE MONET
Paris 1840 - Giverny 1926
It was Monet's painting Impression Sunrise that gave rise to the term Impressionism. Monet sought to capture the fleeting effects of nature, frequently painting the same motif - such as a haystack, poplar trees or the façade of Rouen cathedral - seen at different times of day, in different seasons and weather conditions, to observe the variance of light on a single subject.
Aberdeen Art Gallery
'Falaise à Fecamp' (1881)
Birmingham Barber Institute
The Church at Varangeville (1882)
Cambridge Fitzwilliam Museum
'Le Printemps'
Rocks at Port-Coton with the Lion Rock (1886)
Cardiff National Museum of Wales
Ten works including:
Poplars on the Epte
•Rouen Cathedral, Sunset (1894)
Water-lilies (1906)
Edinburgh NGS
Haystacks, Snow Effect
Poplars on the Epte
Glasgow Art Gallery and Museum
Vétheuil

Claude Monet: Rouen Cathedral, Sunset

View at Ventimiglia (1884)
Liverpool Walker Art Gallery
The Thaw on the Seine near Bennecourt
London Courtauld Institute
Antibes (1888)
Autumn effect, Argenteuil (1873)
Vase of Flowers
London National Gallery
15 works including:
Bathers at La Grenouillère (1869)
The Thames below Westminster
The Gare St-Lazare (1877)
The Water-Lily Pond (1899)
London Tate Modern
Water-Lilies (on loan from the National
Gallery)
Southampton City Art Gallery
The Church at Vétheuil (1880)
Swansea Glynn Vivian Art Gallery
Boats in Holland near Zaandam
Walsall New Art Gallery
The Narrow Path on the Cliff at
Varangeville

SAMUEL PALMER
London 1805 - Redhill, Surrey 1881
The most important member of 'The
Ancients', as the followers of William Blake
called themselves, Palmer produced
mainly pastoral landscapes, rich with
Christian symbolism but balanced with an
outward wealth of detail. His greatest
works are usually regarded as those he
made during his stay in the Kent village of
Shoreham in 1826-34.
Cardiff National Museum of Wales
● The Rising of the Skylark
London Tate Britain
Coming from evening Church (1830)
The Gleaning Field
A Hilly Scene
The Waterfalls, Pistil Mawddach, North
Wales
Manchester City Art Gallery
The Bright Cloud
Oxford Ashmolean Museum
Cornfield Bordered by Trees
Pastoral Scene
Rest on the Flight into Egypt

CAMILLE PISSARRO
St Thomas, West Indies 1830 –
Paris 1903
Pissarro's subtle, sensitive depictions of
the townscapes of Paris, Rouen and Le
Havre secured his position as a leading
exponent of the Impressionist movement.
Born in the West Indies, he arrived in Paris
in 1855 where he was taught by Corot
before meeting Monet in 1859. He
remained true to Impressionist principals
all his life and was the only artist to exhibit
in all their exhibitions.
Birmingham Barber Institute
The Pond at Montfoucault (1875)
Birmingham CMAG
'Le Pont de Boïeldieu à Rouen, Soleil
Couchant' (1896)
Cambridge Fitzwilliam Museum
Garden at Pontoise (1882)
'La Route de Pont-Marly'
Cardiff National Museum of Wales
The Pont-Neuf, Paris (1902)
Sunset at Rouen (1898)
Edinburgh NGS

Samuel Palmer: The Rising of the Skylark

The Marne at Chennevières
Glasgow Art Gallery and Museum
The Towpath (1864)
The Tuileries Gardens (1900)
Glasgow Barber Institute
'Le Marché' (pastel)
Ipswich Christchurch Mansion
The House of Père Gallien at Pontoise
(1866)
Leicester NWMAG
The Road, Snow Effect
London Courtauld Institute
Festival at the Hermitage, Pontoise
Lordship Lane Station, Dulwich (1871)
The Quays at Rouen (1883)
London National Gallery
View from Louveciennes
Fox Hill, Upper Norwood (1870)
The Avenue, Sydenham (1871)
Portrait of Cézanne (1874)
The Côte des Boeufs at L'Hermitage (1877)
The Little Country Maid (on loan from Tate)
(1882)
The Pork Butcher (on loan from Tate)
(1883)
A Wool Carder (on loan from Tate)
(1880)
Portrait of Felix Pissarro (on loan from
Tate) (1881)
London Tate Modern
The Pilot's Jetty, Le Havre (1903)
Self Portrait (1903)
Manchester City Art Gallery
The Old Bridge at Bruges (1903)

Village Street, Louveciennes (1871)
Manchester Whitworth Art Gallery
Quay at Pontoise, after Rain
Oxford Ashmolean Museum
14 paintings including:
The Artist's Wife sewing near a Window
(1885)
Autumn, Morning Mist, Eragny (1902)
● Vue de ma Fenêtre, Eragny
Southampton City Art Gallery
Louveciennes (1870)

PIERRE-AUGUSTE RENOIR
Limoges 1841 - Cagnes 1919
Renoir initially worked in Paris as a painter
of porcelain. He met his fellow
Impressionists, Monet and Sisley, in the
1860s and, like them, painted landscapes
and scenes of contemporary life.

From the 1880s he moved away from
Impressionism, concentrating on images
of the human figure and the nude.
Aberdeen Art Gallery
La Roche-Guyon
Birmingham Barber Institute
A Woman
Birmingham CMAG
Saint-Tropez
Cambridge Fitzwilliam Museum
'Le Coup de Vent'
Study of a Girl
Cardiff National Museum of Wales
Head of a Girl
'La Parisienne' (1874)

Seated Couple
Edinburgh NGS
Mother and Child
Glasgow Art Gallery and Museum
Portrait of Mme Charles Fray (1901)
The Painter's Garden, Cagnes-sur-Mer
Still Life (1908)
Glasgow Burrell Collection
Lady with Auburn Hair (pastel)
Leeds City Art Gallery
After the Bath (pastel)
London Courtauld Institute
Portrait of Ambroise Vollard (1908)
● 'La Loge' (1874)
The Outskirts of Pont-Aven
Woman Tying her Shoe
London National Gallery
A Nymph by a Stream
At the Theatre
Boating on the Seine
The Umbrellas
Moulin Huet Bay, Guernsey (1883)
Lakeside Landscape
A Bather
Head of a Girl (on loan from Tate)
London Tate Modern
Misia Sert (on loan from the National
Gallery) (1904)
Dancing Girl with Tambourine (on loan
from the National Gallery) (1909)
Dancing Girl with Castanets (on loan from
the National Gallery) (1909)
Nude on a Couch (1914-15)
Peaches and Almonds (1901)
Manchester City Art Gallery
Seated Nude
Seated Woman
Oxford Ashmolean Museum
'Le Jardin de Montmartre'
Nude Figure of a Girl
Still Life, Sculpture and Porcelain (1919)
Southampton City Art Gallery
Portrait of Herr Wilhelm Mühlfeld (1910)
Walsall New Art Gallery
The Olive Trees at Cagnes-sur-Mer

DANTE GABRIEL ROSSETTI
London 1828 - Birchington on Sea,
Kent 1882
Poet and painter, son of an Italian political
exile, brother of poet Christina, Rossetti
was a co-founder of the Pre-Raphaelite
Brotherhood, inspired by the literature
and art of the Middle Ages. Dante and
Arthurian legend were his principal
sources of inspiration. His later painting
is overtly sensual, depicting idealised
women as goddesses and femmes fatales.
Aberdeen Art Gallery
Mariana (1870)
Birmingham Barber Institute
The Blue Bower (1865)
Birmingham CMAG
'Beata Beatrix'
The Boat of Love

Dante Gabriel Rossetti: Dante's Dream on the Day of the Death of Beatrice (1880, replica)

Henri (Douanier) Rousseau: Tropical Storm with a Tiger

'La Donna della Finestra'
A Persian Youth
Proserpine (1882)
Bournemouth
Russell-Cotes Art Gallery and Museum
Venus Verticordia
Cambridge Fitzwilliam Museum
Girl at a Lattice (1862)
Joan of Arc (1882)
Cardiff National Museum of Wales
Fair Rosamund
Carlisle
Tulie House Museum and Art Gallery
Found (sketch)
Dundee McManus Galleries
•Dante's Dream on the Day of the Death
of Beatrice (1880, replica)
Edinburgh NGS
'Beata Beatrix' (replica)
Glasgow Art Gallery and Museum
'Regina cordium' Alice Wilding (1866)
Liverpool Sudley House
The Two Mothers (fragment)
Liverpool Walker Art Gallery
Dante's Dream (1870-1)
Llandaff, Glamorgan Cathedral
Triptych: the Seed of David (1858-64)
London Guildhall Art Gallery
'La Ghirlandata'
London Tate Britain
11 paintings including:
'Beata Beatrix' (1864)
'Ecce Ancilla Domini' (1850)
London V&A
The Day-Dream
Manchester City Art Gallery
Astarte Syriaca (1877)
The Bower Meadow
'Joli Coeur' (1867)
Nottingham

Castle Museum and Art Gallery
Marigolds
Port Sunlight Lady Lever Art Gallery
The Blessed Damozel (1879)
Pandora (pastel) (1878)
'Sibylla Palmifera' or 'Venus Palmera'
(1866-70)
Sheffield Sheffield Galleries (Graves)
A Musician
Wightwick Manor, Staffordshire NT
Jane Morris

HENRI (DOUANIER) ROUSSEAU
Laval 1844 – Paris 1910
Frequently referred to by his nickname
Le Douanier, which describes his job on
the Paris tollgates, Rousseau is regarded
as the prime exponent of the untutored
artist, and the greatest practitioner of

Naive Art. His works are characterised by
their vibrant colour, exotic subjects and
often dreamlike atmospheric quality.
London Courtauld Institute
The Toll-house
London National Gallery
•Tropical Storm with a Tiger (1891)
London Tate Gallery
Bouquet of Flowers

JOHN SINGER SARGENT
Florence 1856 - London 1925
Born and raised in Italy by expatriate
Americans, Sargent trained in Paris and
was inspired by the loose brushwork and
palette of the Impressionists, particularly
his friend Monet. In 1885 he established
himself in London, where he became a
highly popular and extraordinarily prolific

John Singer Sargent: The Vickers Sisters

portrait painter of late Victorian and
Edwardian society.
Aberdeen Art Gallery
Dr Robert Farquharson of Finzean
John Fyffe (1902)
Miss Popney Graeme
Mrs J.W. Crombie (1878)
Self Portrait (1876)
Shoeing the Ox
Birmingham CMAG
Katherine Lewis
Study of a Man's Head (1896)
Blenheim Palace, Oxfordshire
The 9th Duke of Marlborough and his
Family
Bodelwyddon Castle, Denbighshire
Joseph Chamberlain
Bradford Cartwright Hall
Mrs Ernest Hills
Cambridge Fitzwilliam Museum
Dorothy Barnard (1889)
Near the Mount of Olives, Jerusalem
Olives in Corfu
A Sicilian Peasant (study) (1907)
Venice, S. Maria della Salute
Cambridge University Library
Francis Jenkinson (1915)
Cardiff National Museum of Wales
The Painter Hercules Brabazon
Chatsworth, Derbyshire
The Acheson Sisters
Evelyn, Duchess of Devonshire (1902)
Doddington Hall, Lincolnshire
Jarvis Collection
Ena Mathias
Dundee McManus Galleries
William Brownlee, Provost of Dundee (1902)
Edinburgh NGS
Lady Agnew of Lochnaw
Mrs Ernest Hills of Redleaf

Edinburgh
Scottish National Portrait Gallery
Earl Haig
General Sir George F. Milne
Lord Horne
Sir Ian Hamilton
Farnham, Surrey Museum
Mrs Cecil Wade (1888)
Glasgow Art Gallery and Museum
Mrs George Batten singing (1895)
Sir David Richmond
Houghton Hall, Norfolk
Cholmondeley Collection
The Countess of Rocksavage
Leeds University Gallery
Sir Edmund Gosse
Leicester NWMAG
Field Marshall Viscount Allenby (sketch)
Liverpool Walker Art Gallery
Vespers
London Imperial War Museum
Gassed (1918)
London National Gallery
Lord Ribblesdale (1902)
London National Portrait Gallery
14 portraits including:
Dame Alice Ellen Terry (1889)
General Officers of the First World War
(1922)
London Tate Britain/Tate Modern
31 works including 11 Portraits of the
Wertheimer Family and
Carnation, Lily, Lily, Rose
London (Blackheath) Ranger's House EH
(on loan from the Wernher Collection)
Portrait of Lady Wernher
Lyme Park, Cheshire NT
Ethel Pottinger, Lady Knaresborough
Manchester City Art Gallery
Albanian Olive-Gatherers (1909)
An Italian Sailor
Mrs Duxbury and her Daughter
Newcastle upon Tyne Laing Art Gallery
Mrs Henry Richardson
Oxford Ashmolean Museum
The Steps of the Church of SS. Domenico e
Sisto, Rome (1906)
Paisley Museum and Art Galleries
Lady Williamson
Port Sunlight Lady Lever Art Gallery
On his Holidays, Norway (1901)
Sheffield Sheffield Galleries (Graves)
•The Vickers Sisters (1884)
Smallhythe, Kent
Ellen Terry Memorial Museum
Ellen Terry as Lady Macbeth (sketch)
Southampton City Art Gallery
Major E.C. Harrison as a Boy
Truro Royal Cornwall Museum
The Archers

GEORGES SEURAT
Paris 1859 - Paris 1891
Despite his tragic death at the age of 32,
Seurat revolutionised art through his
technique of 'pointillism'. Influenced
especially by scientific writings on optics
and vision, Seurat systematically
experimented with light and shadow, the
emotional impact of colour and line, in an
attempt to produce a more scientific,
theoretical approach to painting.
Bristol City Art Gallery
Sunset
Cambridge Fitzwilliam Museum

The rue St-Vincent, Montmartre (1884)
Edinburgh NGS
The Barracks, Saint Denis
Study for the Bathers
Glasgow Art Gallery and Museum
House Among Trees
•Seated Man
The Seine (Study for the Bathers)
Liverpool Walker Art Gallery
White House, Ville d'Avray
London Courtauld Institute
Beach at Gravelines
The Bridge at Courbevoie (1886)
Le Chahut (study) (1889)
Man painting his Boat
Young Woman powdering Herself
London National Gallery
11 paintings including:
Bathers at Asnières and four sketches for it
Le Bec du Hoc Grandcamp (on loan from Tate)
The Channel of Gravelines, Grand Fort-Philippe

ALFRED SISLEY

Paris 1839 - Moret-sur-Loing, nr Paris 1899
A leading member of the Impressionists, if perhaps the least adventurous of them, Sisley painted almost only landscapes, greatly influenced by the work of Monet whom he had met while studying at the studio of Gleyre, in Paris. His parents were English and he stayed in this country for a short time, painting a series of views of the Thames.
Aberdeen Art Gallery
The Banks of the Loing (1897)
The Little Square (1874)
A Yard at Sablons (1885)
Bedford Cecil Higgins Art Gallery
The Quatorze Juillet in Marly-le-Roi
Birmingham CMAG
The Transept of the Old Church of Moret-sur-Loing, Rainy Weather
Bristol City Art Gallery
The Entrance to the Village
Cambridge Fitzwilliam Museum
The Flood, Pont-Marly (1876)
Street at Moret-sur-Loing
Cardiff National Museum of Wales
La Falaise a Penarth (1897)
Street in Moret-sur-Loing (1892)
Edinburgh NGS
Molesey Weir, Hampton Court
Snow Effect (pastel)
Glasgow Art Gallery and Museum
Boatyard at Saint-Mammès
Street in Moret-sur-Loing
Glasgow Burrell Collection
The Bell-Tower of Noisy-le-Roi
Leeds City Art Gallery
The Fields (1874)
Setting Sun (1875)
Leicester NWMAG
In Winter, Moret-sur-Loing (1889)
London Courtauld Institute
Boats on the Seine
Snow at Louveciennes
London National Gallery
The Watering Place at Marly-le-Roi
The Bridge at Sèvres (1877) (on loan from Tate)
The Path to the Old Ferry at By (1880) (on

loan from Tate)
The Small Meadows in Spring (1880) (on loan from Tate)
Manchester City Art Gallery
•A Normandy Farm (1874)
Norwich Castle Museum
'Une Rue à Sèvres' (1877)
Oxford Ashmolean Museum
A Bend in the Loing
Southampton City Art Gallery
Avenue of Chestnut Trees at La Celle, Saint-Cloud (1867)
Swansea Glynn Vivian Art Gallery
Banks of the Loing at Moret-sur-Loing

HENRI DE TOULOUSE-LAUTREC

Albi 1864 - Château de Malromé, nr Laugon, Gironde 1901
Severely injured and crippled in a childhood accident, Toulouse-Lautrec felt excluded from the aristocratic society into which he was born. He trained as an artist in Paris, settling in Montmartre where he drew and painted the seedy Parisian underworld of dance-halls, cabarets and brothels. An exceptional draughtsman, he remains most celebrated as a designer of posters.
Aberdeen Art Gallery
•Portrait of Charles Conder (sketch)
Birmingham Barber Institute
Woman Seated in a Garden (1890)
London Courtauld Institute
Jane Avril at the Entrance to the Moulin Rouge
The Tête-à-tête Supper
London National Gallery
Woman Seated in a Garden (1891)
Emile Bernard (1885) (on loan from Tate)
A Horsewoman (1899) (on loan from Tate)
The Two Friends (1894) (on loan from Tate)
Oxford Ashmolean Museum
'La Toilette' (1891)

JOSEPH WILLIAM MALLORD TURNER

London 1775 - London 1851
Immensely gifted, Turner was both a watercolourist and oil painter, concerned with capturing the raw emotional power of the elements with a spontaneity that placed him far beyond his contemporaries. His extraordinary talent was fuelled by a number of trips to the Continent. His bequest to the nation of almost 300 canvases and nearly 20,000 watercolours is housed, for the most part, in the Clore Gallery at Tate Britain.
Aberystwyth National Library of Wales
Dolbadarn Castle
Ascott, Buckinghamshire NT
Cicero at his Villa at Tusculum
Belfast Ulster Museum
The Dawn of Christianity (1841)
Birmingham Barber Institute
The Sun Rising through Vapour
Birmingham CMAG
The Pass of Saint Gotthard
Bury, Lancashire Art Gallery

Joseph William Mallord Turner: Snow Storm: Hannibal and his Army Crossing the Alps

Calais Sands at Low Water, Poissards gathering Bait
Cambridge Fitzwilliam Museum
Welsh Mountain Landscape
Edinburgh NGS
Somer Hill, Tonbridge
Glasgow Art Gallery and Museum
Italian Scene
Modern Italy: The Pifferari
Harewood House, Yorkshire
Plompton Rocks
Leicester NWMAG
Kilgerran Castle (1804)
Liverpool Sudley House
Emigrants embarking at Margate
Margate Harbour
Schloss Rosenau
The Wreck Buoy
Liverpool
University of Liverpool Art Gallery
The Eruption of Souffrier on 30 April 1812
Liverpool Walker Art Gallery
Landscape
Linlithgow Palace, Scotland
London National Gallery
Dutch Boats in a Gale (on loan)
Calais Pier
Sun rising through Vapour
Dido Building Carthage (1815)
Ulysses deriding Polyphemus
The Evening Star
The Fighting 'Temeraire' (1838)
Rain, Steam and Speed
London Sir John Soane's Museum
Admiral Tromp's Barge at the Entrance of the Texel
The Val d'Aosta
London Tate Britain
282 paintings including:
Self Portrait
•Snow Storm: Hannibal and his Army Crossing the Alps
Snow Storm: Steam Boat off a Harbour's Mouth
London V&A
East Cowes, Isle of Wight
Lifeboat and Manby Apparatus going off to a Stranded Vessel
Line fishing off Hastings
Saint Michael's Mount, Cornwall
Venice
London (Greenwich) NMM
The Battle of Trafalgar
London (Hampstead) Kenwood
(Iveagh Bequest)
Fishermen upon a Lee Shore in Squally Weather
Manchester City Art Gallery
Now for the Painter: Passengers going on

Board (1827)
Thomson's Aeolian Harp
Petworth House, Sussex NT
20 paintings including:
The Lake: Sunset Fighting Bucks
The Lake: Sunset a Stag Drinking
Chichester Canal
Brighton from the Sea
Port Sunlight Lady Lever Art Gallery
The Falls of the Clyde
Sheffield Sheffield Galleries (Graves)
The Festival of the Opening of the Vintage, Mâcon
Southampton City Art Gallery
The Wave
Sudeley Castle, Gloucestershire
Ashcombe Collection
Alexander Pope's Villa on the Thames
Tabley House, Cheshire
University of Manchester
Tabley, the seat of Sir J.F.Leicester Bt: Windy Day

JAMES ABBOTT MCNEILL WHISTLER

Lowell, Mass, US 1834 - London 1903
Cosmopolitan, a wit, dandy, and close friend of Oscar Wilde, Whistler introduced to Victorian England the doctrine of 'art for art's sake', the creation of aesthetic works, often given musical titles such as 'symphony' or 'harmony', free from the narrative or moralising subject matter and attitudes that were currently popular.
Birmingham Barber Institute
•Symphony in White, No 3
Cambridge Fitzwilliam Museum
William Stott of Oldham (?)
Cardiff National Museum of Wales

Nocturne
Nocturne: Snowstorm
Nocturne: Saint Mark's Venice
Edinburgh NGS
Arrangement in Grey and Green: J.J. Cowan
Glasgow Art Gallery and Museum
Arrangement in Grey and Black, No 2: Thomas Carlyle (1872-1874)
Glasgow Burrell Collection
Nocturne
Rough Seas
Glasgow Hunterian Art Gallery
74 paintings including:
Brown and Gold: Self Portrait
Green and Silver: The Great Sea (1899)
Red and Black: The Fan
Leeds City Art Gallery
Harmony in White and Blue (attributed)
London Tate Gallery
Nine paintings including:
Harmony in Gray and Green: Miss Cicely Alexander (1872)
Nocturne in Black and Gold: The Fire Wheel (1875)
Nocturne in Blue and Gold: Old Battersea Bridge
Nocturne in Blue and Silver: Cremorne Lights (1872)
Nocturne in Blue-Green (1871)
Symphony in White No 2: The Little White Girl (1864)
Three Figures in Pink and Grey (1868-1878)
Oxford Ashmolean Museum
The Shore, Pourville
Sheffield Sheffield Galleries (Graves)
The Dancing-Lesson
Portrait

James Abbott McNeill Whistler: Symphony in White, No 3

1901-2002

Compiling a representative list of twentieth-century paintings in British collections is more difficult than for any previous century and the following selection of artists attempts to strike a balance – uneasy at times – between international figures, who have few works in the country, and others represented by many works in many galleries. In doing so, there have inevitably been omissions, while the concentration on paintings – as opposed to sculpture or installations – has also affected the artists chosen. Britain's collection of twentieth-century works combines surprising strengths – for example the many paintings by Vuillard throughout the country – with sometimes shocking weaknesses – only a single painting by Munch, for example, and the very few works by the American abstract painters of the mid-century, confined to London and Edinburgh. Both strengths and weaknesses reflect the country's slow response to international modernism and the limited resources of many regional collections, particularly in the post-war period. Where impressive twentieth-century collections exist (Aberdeen, Leeds, Manchester and Southampton, to name only a few) they are usually the result of the imaginative and far-sighted purchase of predominantly British works. Bodies such as the National Art Collection Fund and the Contemporary Art Society have been essential aids to the strengthening of the nation's collections – as have private benefactors, as always. Notable among recent bequests have been the Estorick Collection of Italian Futurist art (1998), now housed in Islington in north London, and the collection of Dadaist and Surrealist works donated to the Scottish National Gallery of Modern Art by Gabrielle Keiller in 1995.

FRANCIS BACON
Dublin 1909 - Madrid 1992
One of the leading painters of the second half of the twentieth century, Bacon's characteristic images of screaming figures, desolate nudes and portraits are harrowing and bleakly individual. His pessimistic vision is summed up in his own words: 'Man now realises that he is an accident, that he is a completely futile being, that he has to play the game without a reason.'
Aberdeen Art Gallery
●Pope (study after Velázquez) (1951)
Belfast Ulster Museum
Head II (1949)
Birmingham CMAG
Figures in a Landscape (1956)
Cardiff National Museum of Wales
Study for a Self Portrait (1963)
Edinburgh SNGMA
Figure Study I
Study for a Portrait (1991)
Huddersfield Art Gallery
Figure Study II (The Magdalen)
Leeds City Art Gallery
Painting, 1950 (1950)
Leicester NWMAG
Lying Figure I (1959)
London Tate Britain/Modern
52 works including sketches and
Three Figures and Portrait (1975)
Three studies for Figures at the Base of a
Crucifixion (1944)
Triptych: August 1972 (1972)

Manchester City Art Gallery
Portrait of Henrietta Moraes (1965)
Manchester Whitworth Art Gallery
Portrait of Lucien Freud (qv)
Newcastle upon Tyne Hatton Gallery
Study for Figure VI (1956-1957)
Norwich Sainsbury Centre for Visual Arts
Head of a Man (1960)
Head of a Man I (1960)
Head of a Woman (1960)
Imaginary Portrait of Pope Pius XII (1955)
Study for a Portrait of P.L. II (1957)
Study for a Portrait of Van Gogh I (1956)
Study of a Nude (1952-1953)
Three Studies for a Portrait of Isabel
Rawsthorne (1965)
Two Figures in a Room (1959)

GIACOMO BALLA
Turin 1871 - Rome 1958
Largely self-taught, Balla became one of the leading Italian Futurist painters, interested in the depiction of the speed and motion of the machine age. His early paintings were conventional landscapes and portraits but he developed into one of the most adventurous and inventive of the Futurists, using photography and abstraction to convey the effects of movement.
London Estorick Collection
The Hand of the Violinist
London Tate Modern
● Abstract Speed - the Car has passed
(1913)

PETER BLAKE
Dartford, Kent 1932
Blake's interest in American popular imagery led directly to his involvement with the British Pop Art movement during the 1960s. During the next decade he developed a more naturalistic style and, in 1975, co-founded the Brotherhood of Ruralists, whose intention of working together in the

MAX BECKMAN
Leipzig 1884 - New York 1950
Leading German Expressionist, painter, writer and professor of art, who was dismissed as 'decadent' in 1933 when the Nazis came to power. He later settled in the United States. He drew on mythological subjects as well as painting the contemporary world and self portraits.
Brighton Art Gallery
'Paysage Montagneux' (1929)
London Tate Modern
● Carnival
The Funeral Procession of Alexander the
Great (1940)
Greek Dance in a Landscape (1937)
Southampton City Art Gallery
Lucretia

countryside was in emulation of nineteenth-century groups such as the Pre-Raphaelites.
Hull Ferens Art Gallery
The Letterman (1962)
Leicester NWMAG
I tasted this in Mexico when I was attending
a Bull Fight with Tony (1973)
London Tate Britain/Modern
The First Real Target (1961)
'The Meeting' or 'Have a Nice Day Mr
Hockney' (1981-1983)
On the Balcony (1955-1957)
Self Portrait with Badges (1961)
Manchester Whitworth Art Gallery
●Got a Girl

UMBERTO BOCCIONI
Reggio, Calabria 1882 - Sorte,
Verona 1916
Leading Italian Futurist painter and sculptor, who sought to reflect the speed and dynamism of the modern world in their works. A pupil of Balla, he took part in all the Futurist assemblies from 1910 to 1915 but was killed in action on the north Italian front in 1916.
London Estorick Collection
●Modern Idol (1911)
Study for 'The City Rises' (1910)

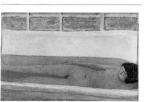

PIERRE BONNARD
Fontenay-aux-Roses, near Paris 1867 -
Le Cannet, France 1947
Termed an 'intimiste' for his paintings of simple, intimate moments: the feeding of the cat, the corner of the breakfast table, the play of light on the bathroom tiles. Bonnard married his companion, Marthe, in 1925 after 30 years of living together. She was his principal model, whom he repeatedly painted reclining in the bath.
Aberdeen Art Gallery
Vernonnet (1924)
Birmingham Barber Institute
The Doll's Dinner Party
Burton Agnes, Yorkshire Boynton Collection
Woman in a Red Dress

Cambridge Fitzwilliam Museum
House amidst Trees (1918)
Landscape (1902)
The Oil Lamp
Still Life (1922)
Le Repas
Cardiff National Museum of Wales
Sunlight at Vernon
Edinburgh SNGMA
View of the River Vernon
Lane at Vernonnet
Floors Castle, Roxburghshire
River Scene with a Yacht and a Barge
Glasgow Art Gallery and Museum
Edge of the Forest
Leeds City Art Gallery
Mother and Child (1894)
London Courtauld Institute
The Blue Balcony (Garden in Spring)
Landscape with Olive Trees and
a Chapel (1924)
Young Lady in an Interior
London Tate Modern
●The Bath (1925)
Bathing Woman seen from the Back
The Bowl of Milk
Coffee (1915)
Nude bending down (1923)
The Pont de la Concorde
Table laid for a Meal (1925)
Window at Le Cannet (1925)
Oxford Ashmolean Museum
Interior with a Nude Figure
A Path under the Trees
Southampton City Art Gallery
Two Poodles (1891)
Walsall New Art Gallery
The Seine at Vernon (1919) (Garman-Ryan
Collection)

GEORGES BRAQUE
Argenteuil-sur-Seine 1882 - Paris 1963
Profoundly influenced by the work of Cézanne, Braque was, with Picasso, the co-founder of Cubism, experimenting with faceted shapes and visual perception, maintaining that 'All my life my great preoccupation has been the painting of space.'
Edinburgh SNGMA
The Candlestick (1911)
Glasgow Art Gallery and Museum
●Still Life (1926)
London Tate Modern
Clarinet and a Bottle of Rum on a
Mantelpiece (1911)
Glass and Plate of Apples (1925)

Peter Blake: Got a Girl

Salvador Dalì: Autumn Cannibalism

Guitar and Jug (1927)
Mandola
Nude Bather (1925)
Still Life with Fish
Still Life (1924)
Oxford Ashmolean Museum
Still Life

MARC CHAGALL
Vitebsk (now Viciebsk) Belarus 1889 -
St-Paul-se-Vence, Alpes Maritimes 1985
Russian-born painter who worked in Paris
from 1923 and developed a highly
recognisable style of magic realism: lovers
fly with bouquets of flowers over dark
cities, green cows and blue sheep roam
the fields and the postman traces an arc in
the sky. His work was particularly
influential on the Surrealists.
London Tate Modern
The Blue Circus (1950)
Bouquet with Flying Lovers
The Dance and the Circus (1950)
•The Poet Reclining (1915)

GIORGIO DE CHIRICO
Vólos, Greece 1888 - Rome 1978
Born in Greece of Italian parents, de Chirico
trained in Athens and Munich before working
in Paris and Italy. In 1917 he co-founded the

Metaphysical Painting movement and his
reworking of the classical tradition, his
melancholic landscapes of empty squares
crossed by long shadows, had a deep
influence on almost all the Surrealists.
London Estorick Collection
Melancolia (1912)
The Revolt of the Sage (1916)
London Tate Modern
The Melancholy Departure (1916)
The Painter's Family (1926)
Manchester Whitworth Art Gallery
•The Philosopher (triptych)

SALVADOR DALÌ
Figueres 1904 - Figueres 1989
Spanish Surrealist who spent much of his
working life in Paris and the USA.
Profoundly influenced by the writings of
Freud and, in particular, the importance of
the dream: his paintings frequently contain
his characteristic soft watches, crutches
and ants. His post-war Christ of St John of
the Cross, now in Glasgow, is the most
powerful of his late religious work.
Edinburgh SNGMA
Bird (or Dove) (1928)
The Signal of Anguish (1936)
Glasgow St Mungo Museum

Christ of Saint John of the Cross (1951)
London Tate Modern
•Autumn Cannibalism (1936)
Forgotten Horizon (1936)
Metamorphoses of Narcissus (1934)
Mountain Lake - Beach Scene with
Telephone (1938)

ROBERT DELAUNAY
Paris 1885 - Montpellier 1941
With his Russian-born wife, Sonia, Delaunay
was the inventor of Orphic Cubism, in which
pure colour is applied to the faceted forms
of the Cubist style. His series of fragmented
images of Paris featuring the Eiffel Tower
are some of his most distinctive works, and
his coloured discs of 1912 are among the
earliest abstract works.
Edinburgh SNGMA
The Cardiff Team (1922-1923)
London Tate Modern
The City (study)
Endless Rhythm (1934)
Windows open simultaneously (1912)
Walsall New Art Gallery
•Portrait of Igor Stravinsky (1918)

ANDRÉ DERAIN
Chatou, near Paris 1880 - Garches 1954
A member of the so-called Fauve group of
painters. The term means 'savage' and was
coined by the critic Vauxcelles to describe
their wild application of paint and its bright
non-naturalistic usage. The exuberant
colours and free style, inspired by Van
Gogh and Matisse, was later abandoned by
Derain for a more restrained use of greys,
browns and olive greens.
Birmingham CMAG
Landscape near Cagnes
Birmingham Barber Institute
Bartolomeo Savona (1906)

André Derain: Barges on the Thames

Burton Agnes, Yorkshire Boynton Collection
Landscape near Chatou
Portrait of M. Georges Gabory (1921)
Portrait of Rita van Leer
Still Life of Fruit
Cambridge Fitzwilliam Museum
Portrait of Rita van Leer
Cardiff National Museum of Wales
The Church at Vers (1912)
Portrait of Mme Zborowska
Edinburgh SNGMA
Collioure (1905)
Glasgow Art Gallery and Museum
Blackfriars Bridge, London
Leeds City Art Gallery
•Barges on the Thames
Liverpool Walker Art Gallery
'L'Italienne'
London Courtauld Institute
Trees by a Lake, the Parc de Carrières,
Saint-Denis (1909)
London Tate Modern
Portrait of Henri Matisse (qv) (1905)
Landscape near Barbizon
Mme Derain in a White Shawl
The Painter and his Family
The Pool of London (1906)
Manchester City Art Gallery
Head of a Girl
Oxford Ashmolean Museum
Still Life of Plums

OTTO DIX
Untermhaus, near Gera 1891 -

Otto Dix: Nude Girl on a Fur (1932)

Singen 1969
Dix was a polemical painter, who emulated
the meticulous realism of Northern
Renaissance painters. His depictions of the
horrors of the First World War and
the corruptions of the post-war world
led to his work's being condemned by the
Nazis, as 'likely to adversely affect the
military will of the German people.'
Edinburgh SNGMA
•Nude Girl on a Fur (1932)

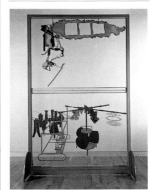

MARCEL DUCHAMP
Blainville, Normandy 1887 - Neuilly-sur-
Seine 1968
One of the seminal figures of twentieth-
century art, Duchamp challenged traditional
notions of what art is. His display of 'ready-
mades', such as the bicycle wheel or the
bottle rack, established a new hierarchy of
values: the concept is more important than
the execution of the work.
London Tate Modern
•The Bride stripped Bare by
her Bachelors Even (replica)
(1965-1966)
The Coffee Mill (1911)

MAX ERNST
Brühl, nr Cologne 1891 - Paris 1976
German Dadaist and later part of the
Surrealist group in Paris, he made a

number of frottage experiments by rubbing paper or canvas on tree bark to assemble a random work. Ernst also created 'collage-novels', and painted clear images of disturbing and puzzling scenes, frequently featuring birds and forests.

Edinburgh SNGMA
The Forest
The Great Lover
Hat in Hand, Hat on Head
The Joy of Life (1936)
Katharina Ondulata (collage)
Max Ernst showing a Girl the Head of his Father
Sea and Sun (1925)
She keeps her Secret
Towers (1914)
Woman with Umbrella
London Tate Modern
• Celebes (The Elephant Celebes) (1921)
The Entire City (1934)
Forest and Dove (1927)
Men shall know nothing of this (1923)
Moon in a Bottle (1955)
Pietà (Revolution by Night) (1923)
Manchester City Art Gallery
'La Ville Petrifiée' (1933)

LUCIAN FREUD
Berlin 1922
Grandson of Sigmund, the great Viennese father of psychoanalysis, Freud is a figurative, often hard-edged painter, preoccupied with the depiction of human flesh, its flaws boldly displayed. His works contain a physical intimacy, a sense of the artist's having exposed the body and soul of his sitter.
Cardiff National Museum of Wales
The Painter's Brother, Stephen
Edinburgh SNGMA
Two Men (1987-1988)
Hartlepool Gray Art Gallery
Head of a Woman (1970)
Liverpool University of Liverpool Art Gallery
Paddington Interior, Henry Diamond
Liverpool Walker Art Gallery
• Interior at Paddington
London National Portrait Gallery
Self Portrait (1962)
London Tate Britain/Modern
Portrait of Francis Bacon (stolen in Berlin 1988, and not recovered) (1952)
Girl with a White Dog (1950-1951)
Leigh Bowery (1991)
Naked Portrait (1972-1973)
Self Portrait (1946)
Standing among the Rags
Two Plants (1979-1980)
Manchester City Art Gallery
Girl with a Beret (1951)
Manchester Whitworth Art Gallery
A Man's Head, Self Portrait (1963)
Oxford Ashmolean Museum
Small Naked Portrait
Preston Harris Museum and Art Gallery
Still Life and a Sea Urchin

David Hockney: 'Le Plongeur'

Rochdale Art Gallery
Woman's Head with a Yellow Background (1963)
Southampton City Art Gallery
Bananas
Walsall New Art Gallery
Annabel (1967)
Kingcups, souvenir of Glen Artney (1967)
Portrait of Kitty (1948-1949)

ALBERTO GIACOMETTI
Stampa 1901 - Zurich 1966
The Swiss sculptor spent most of his working life in Paris where, in the 1930s, he joined the Surrealist movement and took part in the group's exhibitions and activities. Later, he was powerfully affected by existentialism, and his characteristically elongated figures have been seen as encapsulating the alienation and fragility of human existence.
London Tate Modern
Caroline (1965)
Caroline (1965)
Diego (1959)
Interior (1949)
Seated Man (1949)
Two Figures (1947)
Manchester City Art Gallery
Seated Woman (1949)
Norwich Sainsbury Centre for Visual Arts
• Diego (1950)
'Diego Assis' (1948)
'L'Arbre' (1950)

GEORGE GROSZ
Berlin 1893 - West Berlin 1959
Lacerating satirist of German society in the years following the First World War. His depictions of a corrupt military, black-

market profiteers and prostitutes led to his being fined for insulting the German army, and for immorality and blasphemy. Attracted by the Wild West, he left Germany in 1933 for the United States, where he remained until 1951.
London Tate Modern
• Suicide (1916)

DAVID HOCKNEY
Bradford 1937
Painter, etcher, film-maker and set designer, Hockney was a major participant in Britain's Pop Art movement during the 1960s. In the early 1970s he settled in California, where he painted the blue skies, swimming pools and lawns around Beverly Hills. His use of strong colour and flat paint surface can evoke a surrealist sense of the unreal.
Bradford Cartwright Hall
Bolton Junction, Eccleshill (1956)
• 'Le Plongeur'
Moorside Road, Fagley
Nude (1957)
Cardiff National Museum of Wales
The Actor (1964)
Edinburgh SNGMA
Rocky Mountains and Tired Indians (1965)
Hull Ferens Art Gallery
Life Painting for Myself (1962)
Liverpool Walker Art Gallery
Peter getting out of Nick's Pool
London Tate Britain/Modern
A Bigger Splash (1967)
The First Marriage (1962)
Man in Shower in Beverly Hills (1964)
Mr and Mrs Clark and Percy (1970-1972)
My Parents (1977)

Tea Painting in an Illusionistic Style (1961)
The Third Love Painting (1960)
Saltaire, Yorkshire Salt's Mill
About 200 paintings including:
Montcalm Interior (1997)
The Other Side
Salt's Mill, Saltaire (1997)
The Road across the Wolds (1997)
York City Art Gallery
Egyptian Head Disappearing into Descending Clouds (1961)

HOWARD HODGKIN
London 1932
Hodgkin's interest in Indian art is evident in the brightness of his almost wet-looking abstracts, which are painted on wood in preference to canvas, extending on to the frame itself. He maintains that although his work is non-representational it stems from an actual encounter with a particular person or event, or from a memory of a place.
Birmingham CMAG
Gardening (1963)
Bristol Museum and Art Gallery
Robyn Denny and Katherine Reid (1975)
Edinburgh SNGMA
Portrait of Mrs Rhoda Cohen (1962)
Kettering Art Gallery
Staff Meeting, Corsham (1959)
London Tate Britain/Modern
Clean Sheets (1979-1984)
Dinner at Smith Square (1975-1979)
Dinner at West Hill (1964-1966)
In a Hotel Garden (1974)
Interior of a Museum (1956-1959)
Mr and Mrs E.J.P. (1969-1973)
Mr and Mrs Stephen Buckley (1974-1976)
Mrs Nicholas Monro (1966-1969)
R.B.K. (1969-1970)
Rain (1984-1989)
Manchester City Art Gallery
The Hopes at Home
Manchester Whitworth Art Gallery
Interior at Oakwood Court (1978-1983)
Oldham Art Gallery
Husband and Wife (1963)
Southampton City Art Gallery
Simon Digby Talking (1972-1975)
Swindon Public Library
• Gramophone (1964-1967)

GWEN JOHN
Haverfordwest 1876 - Dieppe 1939
Largely neglected during her lifetime and living almost as a recluse, Gwen John was sister of the more famous Augustus, who predicted that in the future her work would be more highly regarded than his. She studied under Whistler in Paris and modelled for the sculptor Rodin. Her portraits and still lifes possess a subtle use of colour, delicacy of style and simplicity of composition.
Aberdeen Art Gallery
Seated Girl holding a Piece of Sewing
Birmingham Barber Institute
• Mère Poussepin
Birmingham CMAG
A Woman holding a Flower
Cambridge Fitzwilliam Museum
The Convalescent
Cardiff National Museum of Wales
A Birdcage
The Brown Teapot (study)
Girl in a Green Dress
Girl in Blue
Girl in Profile
Mère Poussepin
Sketch of a House under Trees in Winter
Study of a Seated Nude Girl
Study of a Young Woman in a Mulberry Dress
Edinburgh SNGMA
The Young Nun
Hull Ferens Art Gallery
The Seated Woman
Leeds City Art Gallery
Chloe Boughton-Leigh

Howard Hodgkin: Gramophone (1964-1967)

London National Portrait Gallery
Self Portrait
London Tate Britain/Modern
Chloe Boughton-Leigh
Convalescent
Dorelia in a Black Dress (1903)
A Lady Reading (1907-1908)
Nude Girl (1909-1910)
The Nun
Self Portrait
Manchester City Art Gallery
Flowers
Interior (1924)
The Letter (1924)
The Student (1903)
Sheffield Sheffield Galleries (Graves)
A Corner of the Artist's Room in Paris
Southampton City Art Gallery
Girl in a Mulberry Dress
Mère Poussepin
Swansea Glynn Vivian Art Gallery
The Nun
Tenby Museum and Art Gallery
Winifred John
York City Art Gallery
Young Woman in a Red Shawl

WASSILY KANDINSKY
Moscow 1866 - Neuilly-sur-Seine 1944
Russian-born artist who originally trained as a lawyer and became a central figure in the development of abstract art. In the 1920s he settled in Germany, where his influence was immense, through his publications (especially Concerning the Spiritual in Art) as well as his teaching at the radical Bauhaus art school. He believed that painting, like music, should aim for the emotional centre, and that this was effected through colour and form.
Oxford Ashmolean Museum
Murnau Staffelsee I
London Tate Modern
●Cossacks (1910-1911)
Swinging (1925)

ERNST-LUDWIG KIRCHNER
Abschaffenburg 1880 - Frauenkirch 1939
A member of Die Brücke ('The Bridge'), a group of German Expressionist painters who sought to link themselves with developments occurring in Paris, and whose works combined boldness of composition, style and colour. His work was declared 'degenerate' by the Nazis in 1938, a year before his suicide.
Edinburgh SNGMA
Japanese Theatre
London Tate Modern
●Bathers at Moritzburg

PAUL KLEE
Münchenbuchsee, nr Berne 1879 -
Muralto, nr Lucarno 1940
Swiss painter and etcher famous for 'taking a line for a walk'. The term expresses his free fantasy and the poetic, often childlike, results. As a teacher at the Bauhaus art school in Weimar and Dessau, and as a producer of theoretical writing, he was an influential figure. His work was proscribed by the Nazis in the 1930s, on grounds of its 'degeneracy'.
Edinburgh SNGMA
●Ghost of a Genius (1922)
London Tate Modern

The Castle Mountain of S (on paper) (1930)
Comedy (on paper) (1921)
They're biting (on paper) (1920)
Walpurgis Night (on paper) (1935)
A Young Lady's Adventure (on paper) (1922)

WILLEM DE KOONING
Rotterdam 1904 - 1989
Profoundly influenced by Kandinsky, de Kooning initially experimented with abstraction before leaving his native Holland for the USA, where he became a leading figure 'action painter'. He later worked in a harsh semi-realist mood, frequently depicting images of women in a deliberately crude and primitive style.
London Tate Modern
●The Visit (1966-1967)

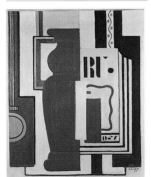

FERNAND LÉGER
Argetan, Orne 1881 - Gif-sur-Yvette,
Seine-et-Oise 1955
Léger worked in the Cubist idiom with Picasso and Braque, and later developed a form of round-edged Cubism. His subjects are always 'of the people': acrobats and card players, sailors and builders are shown as robot-like, monumental figures, often resembling machine parts, and outlined in heavy black contours.
Aberdeen Art Gallery
●Still Life with a Vase (1925)
Cambridge Fitzwilliam Museum
A Girl holding a Flower

Paul Klee: Ghost of a Genius (1922)

Chichester Pallant House
'Rouge et Bleu' (1939)
Edinburgh SNGMA
Study for the 'Constructors'
Tree Trunk on a Yellow Ground
Woman and Still Life (1921)
London Tate Modern
An Acrobat and his Partner (1948)
Keys, Composition (1928)
Leaves and Shell (1927)
Playing-card and Pipe (1928)
Still Life with a Beer Mug (1921-1922)
Two Women holding Flowers (1954)
Manchester City Art Gallery
Painting (1926)

ROY LICHTENSTEIN
New York 1923
Purest exponent of American Pop Art, best known for his comic-strip paintings in which a single frame is enlarged. The black contour lines, primary colours painted in flat unmodelled areas or as dots, the starburst and the thought bubble were all used by Lichtenstein to replicate the popular comic-strip and bestow on it a kind of monumentality.
Edinburgh SNGMA
●In the Car (1963)
London Tate Modern
Interior with Waterlilies (1991)
Whaam! (1963)

L.S. LOWRY
Stretford, nr Manchester 1887 -
Glossop, Derbyshire 1976

Manchester-born painter of the urban and industrial scenes of nearby Salford. He chose to work outside the mainstream tradition, painting factory chimneys, slag heaps, schools and terraced streets in a deliberately naive style, and peopled by 'matchstick men'.
Aberdeen Art Gallery
Barges on a Canal (1941)
Derelict Building (1941)
Belfast Ulster Museum
Street Scene (1947)
Birmingham CMAG
An Industrial Town (1944)
Bradford Cartwright Hall
Industrial Landscape, Ashton-under-Lyne (1952)
Bury, Lancashire Art Gallery
A Riverbank (1947)
Capesthorne Hall, Cheshire
Bromley Davenport Collection
View of Capesthorne Hall (1954)
Coventry Herbert Art Gallery
Ebbw Vale (1960)
Derby Art Gallery
Houses near a Mill (1941)
Doncaster Art Gallery
Seascape
Eccles Monks Hall Museum
The Bandstand, Peel Park (1928)
Edinburgh SNGMA
Canal and Factories (1955)
Glasgow Art Gallery and Museum
River Scene (1942)
VE Day (1945)
Village Square (1943)
Huddersfield Art Gallery
Huddersfield (1965)
Level Crossing (1961)
Kirkcaldy Museum and Art Gallery
An Old Street (1937)
Leamington Spa Art Gallery and Museum
The Mission Room (1937)
Leeds City Art Gallery
Industrial Landscape: The Canal (1945)
A Lancashire Cotton Worker (1944)
Leicester NWMAG
Industrial Landscape (1950)
Lincoln Usher Gallery
View of a Town (1936)
Liverpool Walker Art Gallery
The Fever Van (1935)
London Imperial War Museum
Going to Work (1943)
London Science Museum
A Manufacturing Town (1922)
London Tate Britain
Coming out of School (1927)
Dwelling, Ordsall Lane, Salford (1927)
Hillside in Wales (1962)
Industrial Landscape (1955)
The Old House, Grove Street (1948)
The pond (1950)
A Young Man (1955)
London (Greenwich) NMM
Greenwich Reach towards Deptford Power Station (1959)
Manchester City Art Gallery
An Accident (1926)
Coming Home from the Mill (1928)
An Island (1942)
Laying a Foundation Stone (1936)
An Organ-Grinder, Holgate Street, Hulme, Manchester (1934)
Piccadilly Gardens, Manchester (1954)
St Augustine's Church, Manchester (1945)
Waiting for the Shop to open (1943)
Manchester Whitworth Art Gallery
Ancoats Hospital Outpatients' Hall (1952)
In a Park (1963)
Industrial Scene (1965)
Lake Landscape (1950)
Middlesbrough Art Gallery
The Old Town Hall and St Hilda's Church,

Ernst-Ludwig Kirchner: Bathers at Moritzburg

Middlesbrough (1959)
Newcastle upon Tyne Laing Art Gallery
Old Chapel, Newcastle upon Tyne (1965)
River Scene (1935)
Newport, Gwent Museum and Art Gallery
Francis Street, Salford (1957)
Norwich Castle Museum
Landscape with Farm Buildings (1954)
Nottingham Castle Museum and Art Gallery
The Arrest (1927)
Industrial Panorama (1953)
Oldham Art Gallery
The Procession (1927)
Preston Harris Museum and Art Gallery
Mill Workers (1948)
Rochdale Art Gallery
Our Town (1947)
Rugby Art Gallery and Museum
Monday Morning (1946)
Salford The Lowry
47 paintings including:
Coming from the Mill (1930)
Market Scene, Northern Town (1939)
•Street Scene, Saint Simon's Church (1928)
Sheffield Sheffield Galleries (Graves)
Street Scene
Southampton City Art Gallery
The Canal Bridge (1949)
The Floating Bridge, Southampton (1956)
Southport Atkinson Art Gallery
Street Scene (1935)
Stockport Art Gallery
Crowther Street, Stockport (1930)
Old Steps, Stockport
Stoke-on-Trent
Potteries Museum and Art Gallery
The Empty House (1934)
Sunderland Museum and Art Gallery
The River Wear at Sunderland (1961)
Swindon Museum and Art Gallery
A Procession
Winter in Pendlebury (1943)
Wakefield Art Gallery
The Tollbooth, Glasgow (1947)
York City Art Gallery
The Bandstand, Peel Park, Salford (1931)
Clifford's Tower, York (1953)

RENÉ MAGRITTE
Lessines, Hainault 1898 - Brussels 1967
The Belgian Surrealist René Magritte was interested in the power of the dream. His familiar motifs include the picture within a picture, bowler-hatted men and veiled women - the latter perhaps a reference to his mother's suicide. His imagery often instils a feeling of unease, anxiety or menace.
Birmingham Barber Institute
The Taste of Sorrow (1948)
Cardiff National Museum of Wales
•Le Masque Vide (1928)
Edinburgh SNGMA

René Magritte: Le Masque Vide (1928)

The Black Flag (1937)
The Magic Mirror (1929)
Representation
Threatening Weather (1929)
London Tate Modern
Man with a Newspaper (1928)
The Reckless Sleeper (1927)

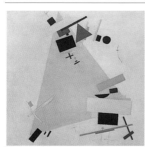

KASIMIR MALEVICH
Kiev 1878 - Leningrad, now St Petersburg, 1935
Russian pioneer of the avant-garde during the second decade of the twentieth century, Malevich was the founder of Suprematism, which held that form and colour were the most important elements in a painting. The logical development of his 'non-objective sensation' led to works such as White on White, but he later returned to figurative art.
London Tate Modern
•Dynamic Suprematism (1915)

FRANZ MARC
Munich 1880 - nr Verdun 1916
Marc was a founder member of the German Expressionist movement Der Blaue Reiter ('The Blue Rider'), so called after Marc's and Kandinsky's love of mounted riders and the colour blue. His most memorable images are powerful compositions of horses, painted with non-naturalistic use of colour and form. He was killed in action at Verdun in 1916.
Leicester NWMAG
•Red Woman

HENRI MATISSE
Le Cateau-Cambésis, Picardy 1869 - Nice 1954
One of the great colourists of the twentieth century and producer of some of the century's most dazzling paintings. He declared that he wanted his work to replicate the comfort of the easy chair to the tired viewer. In old age, in order to overcome the handicaps of arthritis, he developed the use of cut-out gouache shapes mounted on paper.
Burton Agnes, Yorkshire Boynton Collection
Green Nets, Etretat
Cambridge Fitzwilliam Museum
The Bulgarian Blouse
Etretat
The Studio under the Roof
Edinburgh SNGMA
•The Painting-Lesson (1919)
Floors Castle, Roxburghshire
Bowl of Flowers
Landscape
Glasgow Art Gallery and Museum
Head of a Young Girl

The Pink Tablecloth (1925)
Liverpool Walker Art Gallery
The Bridge
London National Gallery
Portrait of Greta Moll (1908)
London Tate Modern
10 works including:
Portrait of André Derain (qv) (1905)
The Snail (papier-collé) (1953)
Oxford Ashmolean Museum
Nude Female seated on a Sofa
Sheffield Sheffield Galleries (Graves)
Seated Woman ('La Femme au Peignoir') (1942)

JOAN MIRÓ
Barcelona 1893 - Mallorca 1983
Like Dalí and Picasso, Miró was from Spain, but he spent his working life in Paris. Described by Breton as 'the most surrealist of us all', he developed an individual style which was deliberately primitive and highly detailed. Miró claimed that hunger combined with staring at cracks in the wall made him hallucinate and helped him to visualise unusual and strange forms.
Edinburgh SNGMA
•Composition (1925)
Head of a Catalan Peasant (with Tate)
Maternity (1924)
Painting (1927)
London Tate Modern
Head of a Catalan Peasant (with Scottish National Gallery of Modern Art)
Message from a Friend (1964)
Painting (1927)
A Star caresses the Breast of a Negress (1938)
Woman and Bird by Moonlight (1949)

AMEDEO MODIGLIANI
Livorno 1884 - Paris 1920
An Italian-born artist working in Paris, he was principally a painter of portraits and elegantly distinctive and elongated figures, which combine a modernity typified by simplification with elements of a more traditional style. The sensual curves of his female nudes are particularly erotic.
Cambridge Fitzwilliam Museum
Portrait of a Young Woman Seated
London Courtauld Institute
•Seated Nude
London Estorick Collection
Doctor François Brabander (1918)
London Tate Modern
A Girl
Portrait of Hanka Zborowska (1918)
The Little Peasant (1919)
Norwich Sainsbury Centre
Head of Hanka Zborowska (1918)

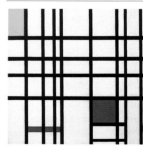

PIET MONDRIAN
Amersfoort 1872 - New York 1944
Developed a particularly rigorous form of abstraction based on his interest in theosophy and eastern mysticism. In what he termed his Neo-Platonic Plastic Mathematics, he reduced his paintings to their purest form - horizontal and vertical, black and white, and the three primary colours. He left Europe for New York in 1940.
Edinburgh
Scottish National Gallery of Modern Art
Composition (1932)
London Tate Modern
Church at Zoutelande (1910)
Composition B with Red (1935)
Composition with Grey, Red, Yellow and Blue
Composition with Red and Blue
•Composition with Red, Yellow and Blue
Tree

GIORGIO MORANDI
Bologna 1890 - Grizzana 1964
Briefly influenced by de Chirico's metaphysical work, Morandi remained in his native Bologna, painting independently from any school or movement. He is best known for his meditative still lifes, which feature simple arrangements of ordinary objects painted in light greys, creams and pinks.
Birmingham CMAG

Henri Matisse: The Painting-Lesson (1919)

•Still Life
Edinburgh SNGMA
Still Life (1962)
London Tate Modern
Still Life (1946)

EDVARD MUNCH
Løten 1863 - Ekely 1944
Norwegian painter, friend of Strindberg, and forerunner of Expressionism, Munch produced iconic images of isolated and anguished figures. His themes of alienation and despair were particularly influential on the German Expressionists, and the neurotic and often hysterical quality of his work reflects a particularly twentieth-century sensibility.
London Tate Modern
•The Sick Child (1907)

PAUL NASH
London 1889 - Boscombe, Hants 1946
Official war artist in both world wars, exhibitor of powerful images of shattered landscapes, and influenced by the Surrealists during the 1930s.
His best-known works are probably those made during the Second World War, which possess a visionary quality that places him in the tradition of Blake and Palmer.
Aberdeen Art Gallery
Northern Adventure
Wood on the Downs (1929)
Belfast Ulster Museum
St Pancras, Lilies (1927)
Birmingham City Museum and Art Gallery
Landscape of the Moon's First Quarter (1943)
Oxenbridge Pond (1928)
Blackpool Grundy Art Gallery
•Sanctuary Wood
Bradford Cartwright Hall
Views: Mediterranean
Cambridge Fitzwilliam Museum
Coronilla (1929)
November Moon (1942)
Cheltenham Art Gallery
St Pancras
Chichester Pallant House
Dead Spring (1929)
Coventry Herbert Art Gallery
The Stockyard
Dudley Art Gallery
Dymchurch
Edinburgh SNGMA
Berkshire Downs (1922)
Landscape of the Brown Fungus (1943)
Landscape of the Vernal Equinox (1944)
Token
Glasgow Art Gallery and Museum
Through a Window, Riviera
Harrogate Art Gallery
Cactus
Hull Ferens Art Gallery

Giorgio Morandi: Still Life

Michaelmas Landscape (1943)
The Rye Marshes (1932)
Leeds City Art Gallery
Circle of Monoliths
The Shore (1923)
Still Life with Bog Cotton
Leicester NWMAG
Nostalgic Landscape (1923-1938)
Liverpool Walker Art Gallery
Landscape of the Moon's Last Phase
London Imperial War Museum
The Battle of Britain (1940)
The Battle of Germany
The Defence of Albion
A Howitzer Firing
The Menin Road (1919)
The Mule Track
Spring in the Trenches, Ridge Wood (1917)
We are making a New World
The Ypres Salient at Night (1918)
London Tate Britain/Modern
14 paintings including:
Equivalents for the Megaliths
Flight of the Magnolia (1944)
Harbour and Room (1932-1936)
Landscape at Iden (1929)
Landscape from a Dream (1936-1938)
Pillar and Moon (1932-1942)
Totes Meer (Dead Sea)
Voyages of the Moon (1934-1937)
London (Camberwell)
South London Art Gallery
Buckinghamshire Landscape
Manchester City Art Gallery
Nocturnal Landscape (1938)
Sandling Park, Kent (1924)
Wounded, Passchendaele
Sheffield Sheffield Galleries (Graves)
Iver Heath, Snow (1927-1928)
Southampton City Art Gallery
The Archer
Landscape of the Malvern Distance
Swansea Glynn Vivian Art Gallery
Landscape of the Bagley Woods
York City Art Gallery
Winter Sea (1925-1937)

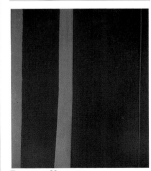

BARNETT NEWMAN
New York 1905 - New York 1970
American Minimalist and Abstract

Expressionist, Newman's abstractions aimed to provide the viewer with a mystical experience of pure colour achieved through the enveloping size of the canvas. His trademark style made use of thin vertical strips of colour, that he called zips, which 'opened up' large areas of colour. He was a great influence on painters of the 1960s.
London Tate Modern
•Adam (1951-1952)
Eve (1950)

BEN NICHOLSON
Denham, Bucks 1894 - London 1982
English pioneer of abstraction, Nicholson's paintings, in which objects are seen from a multiplicity of viewpoints, reflect his early interest in Cubism. His three-dimensional monochrome works show his response to the purity of the minimalism of the Dutch artist Piet Mondrian.
Aberdeen Art Gallery
Still Life on Table, March
Belfast Ulster Museum
Painting (1935)
Birmingham City Museum and Art Gallery
Still Life: Dolomites (1950)
Bristol City Art Gallery
Oval and Steeple
Porthmoer Beach (1930)
Cardiff National Museum of Wales
Two Forms
Chichester Pallant House
•Still Life (Cerulean) (1946)
Coventry Herbert Art Gallery
Two Forms (1946-1947)
Dudmaston, Shropshire NT
Four Squares, Two Circles (1963)
Edinburgh SNGMA
June 1961: Green Goblet and Blue Square (1961)
Painter's Relief: Plover's Egg Blue (1940)
Painting (1937)
Walton Wood Cottage, No 1 (1928)
White Relief (1935)
White Relief: Paros (1961-1962)
Glasgow City Art Gallery
Still Life (1946-1950)
Hull University Art Collection
Head and Mug in a Greek Landscape (1932)
Kendal Abbot Hall Art Gallery
Cold Fell (1922)

Crowned Head, The Queen (1932)
Still-Life Composition (1936)
Leeds City Art Gallery
Still Life with a Guitar
Leicester NWMAG
Still Life
Liverpool Walker Art Gallery
Prince and Princess (1932)
London Courtauld Institute
Painting 1937 (1937)
London Tate Britain/Modern
20 paintings including:
Guitar (1933)
'Le Quotidien' (1932)
Manchester City Art Gallery
'Au Chat Botté' (1932)
Composition, Still Life (1946)
St Ives' Bay, Sea with Boats (1931)
Still Life (1950)
Newcastle upon Tyne Laing Art Gallery
Design
Nottingham Castle Museum and Art Gallery
Bistre II
Oxford Ashmolean Museum
Still Life with Flag (1945)
Sheffield Sheffield Galleries (Graves)
Profile in Brown
Southampton City Art Gallery
Two Forms (1940-1942)
Stromness, Orkney Pier Arts Centre
Painted Relief (1939)
Still Life
Swindon Museum and Art Gallery
Composition in Black and White (1933)
Wakefield Art Gallery
Piquet (1933)

Jackson Pollock: Yellow Islands

EMILE NOLDE
Nolde, Schleswig-Holstein 1867 - Seebüll, Schleswig-Holstein 1956
Foremost German Expressionist. Profoundly influenced by Munch and Van Gogh, he caused a great stir with his religious pictures. Later, in Berlin, he painted scenes of city life, but is best known for his landscapes: dramatic and simplified scenes, in which colour is used for great emotional impact and intensity.
Edinburgh SNGMA
Head (1913)
London Tate Modern
•The Sea B (1930)

PABLO PICASSO
Malaga 1881 - Mougins 1973
Prodigiously talented Spanish painter, giant of the twentieth century, he spent his working life in France. Together with Braque developed Cubism, fragmenting the visible world into faceted planes. But while others developed Cubism into pure abstraction, Picasso returned to the human figure and human condition that remained his subjects throughout his life.
Cambridge Fitzwilliam Museum
•Head of a Woman
Edinburgh SNGMA
Guitar Gas-jet and Bottle
Portrait of Dora Maar
Mother and Child (1903)
The Soler Family (1940)
Glasgow City Art Gallery
The Flower-Seller (1901)
London National Gallery
Child with a Dove (on loan)
London Tate Modern
16 paintings including:
Nude Woman in a Red Armchair (1932)
Reclining Nude with a Necklace (1968)
Seated Nude (1909-1910)
The Three Dancers (1925)
Weeping Woman (1937)
Oxford Ashmolean Museum
Blue Roofs (1901)

JACKSON POLLOCK
Cody, Wy, US 1912 - East Hampton 1956
Abstract Expressionist who claimed that he wanted 'to express my feelings rather than illuminate them'. His so-called 'action paintings' trace the action of the painter on the surface of the canvas. Pollock saw his work as a reflection of the modern age – the fragmentary nature of post-atomic fraction and the inchoate strains of jazz.
Edinburgh SNGMA
Untitled Composition
London Tate Modern
No 23 (1948)
Summertime 9A
Untitled (Naked Man with Knife) (1938-1941)
•Yellow Islands (1952)

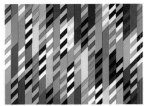

BRIDGET RILEY
London 1931
Riley is best known for the style she developed in the 1960s known as Op-art, a term used to describe the unsettling optical effects caused by her disturbing, and often eye-hurting, arrangement of black lines on white canvas. Now using colour, she continues to develop and explore the effects of line and the impact of colour.
Cambridge Fitzwilliam Museum
Shadowplay (1990)
Glasgow Art Gallery and Museum
Punjab (1971)
Kendal Abbot Hall Art Gallery
•Conversation (1992)
Leeds City Art Gallery
Winter Palace (1981)
London Tate Britain/Modern
Achaian (1981)
Cantus Firmus (1972-1973)
Deny II (1967)
Fall (1963)
Hesitate (1964)
Late Morning (1967-1968)
Nataraja (1993)
To a Summer's Day (1980)
Manchester City Art Gallery
Zephyr
Manchester Whitworth Art Gallery
Search (1966)

MARK ROTHKO
Dvinsk, Russia, now Daugavpils, Latvia
1930 - New York 1970
Russian-born American painter influenced by the European Surrealists, Rothko developed as a painter of entirely abstract works for which he made huge spiritual claims. His 'colour field' paintings, typified by the series he bequeathed to the Tate, are rectangles of colour bleeding into background colour.
London Tate Gallery
13 works including the 9 paintings • Black and Red on Maroon (1958-1959), presented by the artist and often hung together.

GINO SEVERINI
Cortona 1883 - Paris 1966
Having studied in Paris and associated with artists in the Picasso and Braque circle, Severini imbibed the tenets of Cubism, putting them into practice when he became a co-founder of the Italian Futurist movement in 1910. His works celebrate and attempt to capture movement as in his many paintings of dancing figures.
Chichester Pallant House
•'Danseuse', No. 5
London Estorick Collection

Mark Rothko: Black and Red on Maroon (1958-1959)

The Boulevard (1910-1911)
Dancer (Ballerina and Sea) (1913)
Quaker Oats - Cubist Still Life (1917)
London Tate Modern
Suburban Train arriving in Paris (1915)

WALTER SICKERT
Munich 1860 - Bathampton, Somerset
1942
Influenced by Degas's depiction of contemporary subject matter and his investigations into the effect of artificial light, Sickert painted the theatre, music hall, street and café. In 1911 he co-founded the Camden Town Group, and painted scenes of the grubby and unfashionable Mornington Crescent. Particularly memorable is the series of 'Camden Town Murders'.
Aberdeen Art Gallery
Gaité Rochechouard
Hampstead
'Il Canareggio'
Pimlico
The Beshet Shop
Aberdeen University
The Milkman
Attingham Park, Shropshire NT
Lady in Blue
Bath Victoria Art Gallery
Portrait of Lady Noble
The Serpentine
View of Bath from Belvedere
Violets
Belfast Ulster Museum
Easter
Suspense
Birmingham Barber Institute
The El Dorado, Paris
Birmingham CMAG
Dieppe Races
The Gallery of the Old Mogul
The Horses of St Mark's, Venice

The Miner
The Quai Duquesne and the Arcades de la Poissonnerie, Dieppe
The Rue Pecquet, Dieppe (1900)
Bolton Art Gallery
Portrait of Mme Pauline de Talleyrand de Périgord, Marquise de Castellané
Bradford Cartwright Hall
Leslie Banks as Petruchio and Edith Evans as Katherina in The Taming of the Shrew
Brighton Art Gallery
Portrait of the Hon. Lady Fry
Bristol City Art Gallery
Army and Navy
The Horses of St Mark's, Venice (1901)
Othello
Mrs Robert Campbell
Burton Agnes, Yorkshire Boynton Collection
Mr Sheepshanks's House, Bath
Canterbury Royal Museum and Art Gallery
Romeo and Juliet at Reculver, Kent
Cambridge Fitzwilliam Museum
12 works including:
Girl and Looking-Glass (Little Rachel)
The Old Bedford (1894-1895)
Cardiff National Museum of Wales
Camden Town
The Palazzo Eleanora Duse, Venice
Chichester Pallant House
Hubby and Wilson Steer (1905)
Les Arcades de la Prisonniers, Quai Duqcrosse, Dieppe
Dundee McManus Galleries
'La Soierie de Torqueville' (1912)
Eastbourne Tower Art Gallery
The Painter and his Muse
Edinburgh SNGMA
Corner of St Mark's, Venice
Dieppe (1900)
Envermeu
High-Steppers
Portrait of Israel Zangwill (1904)
The Rue Pecquet, Dieppe
The Rural Dean
Seascape
Exeter Royal Albert Memorial Museum
Reclining Nude
Glasgow Art Gallery and Museum
Barnsbury
Dieppe Harbour
Lansdown Crescent, Bath
Portrait of Sir Hugh Walpole (1929)
La Darse
Glasgow Hunterian Art Gallery
Clodgy Point, Cornwall

A Shop in Dieppe
Gloucester CMAG
Glencors (after Gilbert)
Harrogate Art Gallery
The New Bedford
Hastings Museum and Art Gallery
Portrait of Signor de Rossi (1901)
Hove Museum of Art
The Laundry Shop
Huddersfield Art Gallery
View of Ramsgate Harbour (1930)
Hull Ferens Art Gallery
The Hôtel Royal, Dieppe
Idyll
Hull University Art Collection
L'Eglise du Pollet, Dieppe
Mornington Crescent Nude
Ipswich Christchurch Mansion
Street Scene
Kirkcaldy Museum and Art Gallery

Evening
Lobster on a Tray
The Marché aux Loques, Dieppe
Resting
Wellington House, Academy
'What shall we do for the rent?'
Leeds City Art Gallery
13 works including:
The Open Window
Self Portrait
Leicester NWMAG
The Bart and the Bums
Dover
The Yellow Sleeve
• Mornington Crescent (1905)
Lincoln Usher Gallery
Reclining Nude Figure
London Courtauld Institute
Portrait of Mrs Barrett (1906)
Queen's Road Station, Bayswater
Plage Dieppe, the Bathing Huts
San Trovaso, Venice
Sweet Violets, White and Blue Violets in a Patterned Bowl
View of Dieppe with the Eglise du Pollet
London National Portrait Gallery
Portrait of George Jacob Holyoak
Portrait of Philip Wilson Steer
Self Portrait
Portrait of Sir Winston Churchill
Portrait of William Maxwell
Aitken, 1st Baron Beaverbrook
London Tate Britain/Modern
36 paintings including:
'Ennui'
'La Hollandaise'
Miss Earhart's Arrival
The New Bedford (1915-1916)
London Theatre Museum
Winnifred Emery as Rosamund in Sowing the Wind
W.S. Penley as Lord Fancourt Babberley in Charley's Aunt
London (Camberwell)
South London Art Gallery
The Sick Doctor
Manchester City Art Gallery
13 works including:
Jack the Ripper's Bedroom

Stanley Spencer: Resurrection of the Dead Soldiers

Portrait of Victor Lecour (1924)
Manchester Whitworth Art Gallery
The Church of St Jacques, Dieppe
Newcastle upon Tyne Laing Art Gallery
Venice, St Mark's Square
Northampton Central Museum
Mrs Vera Beuren and Child
Norwich Castle Museum
The Red Shop, Auberville
Nottingham Castle Museum and Art Gallery
'Noctes Ambrosianae'
Oldham Art Gallery
Barnet Fair
Oxford Ashmolean Museum
'Ennui'
Her Majesty's
The Lady in the Gondola (1895)
The Rue Aguado, Dieppe
Venice, St Mark's, the West Front (1895)
Paisley Museum and Art Galleries
The Porte Saint-Denis, Paris
Peterborough Museum and Art Gallery
The Third Republic: View of the Porte
Saint-Denis (1932)
Plymouth CMAG
Little Rachel
Street Scene in Dieppe
Portsmouth CMAG
The Belgian Cocottes (1906)
Preston Harris Museum and Art Gallery
Two Women
Rochdale Art Gallery
The Fair, Dieppe
Salford Museum and Art Gallery
Reflected Ornaments
Sheffield Sheffield Galleries (Graves)
Chagford, Devon
A Dead Hare
Portrait of Fred Winter
Soldiers of King Albert the Ready (1914)
A Woman
Southampton City Art Gallery
The Juvenile Lead (Self Portrait)
The Mantelpiece
Red Sky at Night, St Mark's
The Tichborne Claimant
The Sinn Feiners
Southport Atkinson Art Gallery
The Little Theatre (1890)
Stoke-on-Trent
Potteries Museum and Art Gallery
Idyll (after Gilbert)
Portrait of Maurice Asselin
The Waves
Stratford-upon-Avon RSCC
Fabia Drake as Lady Macbeth, Stratford, 1933
Swansea Glynn Vivian Art Gallery
'La Nera'
Wakefield Art Gallery
Ethel Sands descending the Staircase at
Newington
Worthing Museum and Art Gallery
Home, Sweet Home
York City Art Gallery
The Butcher's Shop
Old Heffel of Rowton House
The Rue de la Boucherie with the Church of
St Jacques, Dieppe (1903)
Venice, the Piazzetta
The Visitor

STANLEY SPENCER

Cookham, Berks 1891 - Cliveden 1959
Like a twentieth-century William Blake, Spencer was an eccentric and idiosyncratic artist. Most memorably he painted his Thames-side Berkshire village of Cookham repeatedly, often as background to biblical narratives. His style derives much from the German primitives, and offers unusual viewpoints and dramatic imagery.

Aberdeen Art Gallery
Clipped Yews
Crucifixion (1922-1924)

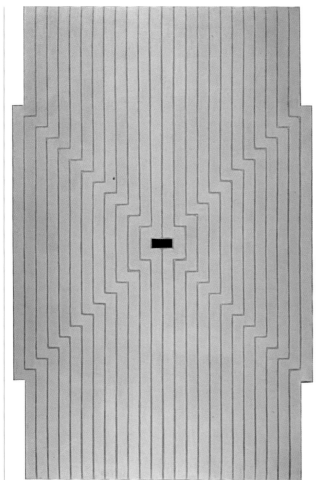

Frank Stella: Six Mile Bottom

Reunion (1945)
Southwold
Belfast Ulster Museum
The Betrayal
Portrait of Daphne Spencer (1951)
Scene from the Marriage at Cana in Galilee
(1935)
Birmingham City Museum and Art Gallery
Old Tannery Mills (1939)
The Psychiatrist (1945)
Resurrection, tidying (1945)
Rock Gardens, Cookham Dean
Bradford Cartwright Hall
Cookham from Cookham Dean
Near Southwold, Suffolk
Burghclere, Berkshire
Sandham Memorial Chapel
Decoration of the chapel comprising
19 paintings including:
•Resurrection of the Dead Soldiers
Cambridge Fitzwilliam Museum
Cottages at Burghclere
Landscape in North Wales (1938)
Love among the Nations
Love on the Moor
Sarajevo, Bosnia (1922)
Self Portrait (1939)
Self Portrait with Patricia Preece
Cambridge Girton College
Portrait of Mary Lucy Cartwright (1958)
Cardiff National Museum of Wales
Snowdon from Llanfrothen
Souvenir of Switzerland (1934)
Cheltenham Art Gallery
Village Gossips, Gloucestershire
Cookham-on-Thames
Stanley Spencer Gallery
12 paintings including:
The Betrayal (1914)
Christ overturning the Money-changer's
Table (1921)

Sunbathers at Orkney (1935)
Coventry Herbert Art Gallery
Miss Ashwanden in Cookham
Dundee McManus Galleries
The Ferry Hotel Lawn, Cookham (1936)
Edinburgh SNGMA
Christ delivered to the People (1950)
Fire Alight (1936)
Glasgow Art Gallery and Museum
The Glen, Port Glasgow (1952)
The Vale of Health, Hampstead
Hull Ferens Art Gallery
Greenhouse and Garden (1937)
Nude Portrait of Patricia Preece (1935)
The Red House
Hull University Art Collection
Villagers and Saints (1933)
Kettering Alfred East Gallery
Violinist
Leamington Spa Art Gallery and Museum
Cookham Rise
Leeds City Art Gallery
Christ's Entry into Jerusalem
Family Group: Hilda, Unity and Dolls
Gardening
Gardens in the Pound, Cookham
Madonna Lilies, Cookham
Separating fighting Swans
The Sisters
Leicester NWMAG
Adoration of Old Men (1937)
Liverpool Walker Art Gallery
Saturday Afternoon
Villas at Cookham
London Imperial War Museum
Convoys arriving with Wounded at a
Dressing-Station at Smol, Macedonia,
September 1916
Shipbuilding on the Clyde series (eight
paintings)
London Tate Britain/Modern

23 paintings including:
Double Nude Portrait: The Artist and his
Second Wife (1936)
Mending Cowls, Cookham (1914)
The Resurrection, Cookham (1923-1927)
Saint Francis and the Birds (1935)
Swan-Upping at Cookham (1914-1919)
Manchester City Art Gallery
The Boatbuilder's Yard, Cookham (1936)
Cookham Moor (1937)
A Village in Heaven (1937)
Manchester Whitworth Art Gallery
Soldiers Washing
Newcastle upon Tyne Laing Art Gallery
The Lovers (The Dustman)
Newport, Gwent Museum and Art Gallery
Sausage Shop
Nottingham Castle Museum and Art Gallery
Landscape, Cookham Dean
Peonies
Oxford Ashmolean Museum
Crows at Cookham (1936)
Plymouth CMAG
The Blue Garden Nursery (1955)
Preston Harris Museum and Art Gallery
Hill Zion (Resurrection series)
Wisteria
Reading, Berkshire Museum of Reading
Self Portrait
Rochdale Art Gallery
Bellrope Meadow, Cookham (1936)
Rugby Art Gallery and Museum
Portrait of Richard Carline (1923)
Sheffield Sheffield Galleries (Graves)
Helter-Skelter (1937)
Zacharias and Elizabeth (with Tate)
Southampton City Art Gallery
Portrait of Patricia Preece
Pound Field, Cookham
The Resurrection with the Raising of
Jairus's Daughter
Swansea Glynn Vivian Art Gallery
Garden at Whitehouse, Northern Ireland
The Marriage at Cana, Bride and Groom
York City Art Gallery
Deposition and the Rolling Away of the Stone

FRANK STELLA

Malden, Mass, US 1936
American artist, interested in minimalism and Abstract Expressionism, Stella has experimented by making works in series, working through a particular investigation into colour, space and structure. His declared wish was to 'force illusionistic space out of the painting at a constant rate by using regulated pattern.' His more recent paintings and sculptures were inspired by the patterns of cigar smoke.

London Tate Modern
Salta nel mio Sacco (1984)
•Six Mile Bottom

EDOUARD VUILLARD

Cuiseaux, Saône-et-Loire 1868 -
La Baule 1940
Like Bonnard, Vuillard painted scenes of domestic life, intimate records of family work and meals, which also led to their description as 'intimist'. His paintings of the family home often include his mother and maternal grandmother, who both lived with him. The deliberate flat patterning of his early work gave way to a more traditional approach.

Aberdeen Art Gallery
•Interior: The Card Party
Birmingham Barber Institute
Woman arranging her Hair
Birmingham CMAG
The Meal
Bristol City Art Gallery
Interior with Mme Hessel and her Dog (1910)
Burton Agnes, Yorkshire Boynton Collection
Missia at the Piano
Cambridge Fitzwilliam Museum
Interior with a Lady and a Dog (1910)
'Pot de Grès et de Fleurs' (1909)
Edinburgh SNGMA
The Candlestick
'Deux Oeuvrières dans l'atelier de couture'
'La Causette'
The Open Window
The Pink Room
Pot of Flowers
Glasgow Art Gallery and Museum
Interior of the Drawing Room
The Lady in Green
Lunch in the Country (pastel)
Mother and Child
The Table
Glasgow Burrell Collection
'La Salle à Manger' (pastel)
Leeds City Art Gallery
Mlle Nathanson in the Artist's Studio
Liverpool Walker Art Gallery
Mme Hessel on the Sofa
London Courtauld Institute
Woman at her Toilette
London National Gallery
Portrait of Mme André Wormser and her
Children
London Tate Modern
The Chimney Piece (1905)
(on loan from National Gallery)
Lunch at Villeneuve-sur-Yonne
(on loan from National Gallery)
Girl in an Interior
Landscape (1900)
Southampton City Art Gallery
The Manicure
Two People

ANDY WARHOL

Pittsburgh 1930 - New York 1987
American Pop artist noted for his silkscreen prints of the 1960s depicting consumer goods such as Campbell's soup cans as well as famous figures such as Elvis Presley, Marilyn Monroe and Jackie Kennedy/Onassis. The cult of celebrity was a theme he played on, famously stating that 'In the future everyone will be famous for 15 minutes.'

Edinburgh SNGMA
Jacqueline Kennedy II
Portrait of Maurice (1976)
London National Portrait Gallery
Four Portraits of Queen Elizabeth II
London Tate Gallery
Electric Chair (1964)
Marilyn Diptych (1962)
Self Portrait (1967)
Self Portrait (1986)
Wolverhampton Art Gallery and Museum
•Jacqueline (1964)

GALLERIES

Where to see paintings in galleries and houses across Britain: a selective guide.

The appearance of a particular artist in this list does not mean that their work always be on view. Temporary exhibitions and necessary conservation mean that works are occasionally removed from their permanent homes. Items from the Royal Palaces may sometimes be included in exhibitions at the Queen's Gallery, Buckingham Palace and items from the Tate collections may be on display at St Ives, Liverpool, Modern or Britain. In addition many stately homes only allow visitors by appointment. Readers are therefore advised to telephone institutions before visiting to confirm that the items they wish to see are available or arrange a viewing.

LONDON
Central and Greater

CENTRAL LONDON

APSLEY HOUSE
THE WELLINGTON MUSEUM
149 Piccadilly, London, WIJ 7NT
Tel: 020 7499 5676
Fax: 020 7493 6576
Website: www.apsleyhouse.org.uk
Collection includes work by: Jan Brueghel; Correggio; van Dyck; Elsheimer; Goya; Guercino; de Hooch; Murillo; Reynolds; Ribera; Rosa; Rubens; Steen; Velázquez; Wilkie.

BANQUETING HOUSE
Whitehall, London, SW1A 2ER
Tel: 020 7930 4179
Fax: 020 7930 8268
Website: www.hrp.org.uk
Collection includes work by: Rubens.

BARBER-SURGEON'S HALL
Monkwell Square, London, EC2Y 5BL
Tel: 020 7606 0741
Collection includes work by: Holbein the Younger.

BRITISH MUSEUM
Great Russell Street
London WC1B 3DG
Tel: 020 7636 1555
Fax: 020 7623 8616
Website: www.thebritishmuseum.ac.uk
The British Museum Prints and Drawings Department holds approximately 50,000 drawings and over two million prints dating from the beginning of the 15th century up to the present day. They cover the history of drawing and printmaking as fine arts, with large holdings of the works of such important artists as Dürer, Michelangelo, Raphael, Rembrandt and Goya.

BUCKINGHAM PALACE
London SW1A 1AA
Tel: 020 7321 2233
Fax: 020 7930 9625
Website: www.royal.gov.uk
Collection includes work by: Canaletto; Claude; Duccio; van Dyck; Freud; Hals, Hilliard; Nash; Vermeer; da Vinci.

COURTAULD INSTITUTE GALLERY
Somerset House, Strand, London, WC2R 0RN
Tel: 020 7848 2526
Website: www.courtauld.ac.uk
Collection includes work by: Angelico; Bellini; Bonnard; Bordone; Botticelli; Bruegel the Elder; Campin; Cézanne; Claude; Constable; Correggio; Cranach the Elder; Daddi; Dégas; Derain; van Dyck; Gaddi; Gainsborough; Gauguin; van Gogh; Gossaert; Goya; van Leyden; Lotto; Lippi (Fillipo); Manet; Massys;

Master of the St Bartholomew Altarpiece; Modigliani; Monet; Nicholson; Parmigianino; Pissarro; Raeburn; Ramsay; Renoir; Ercole de'Roberti; Rubens; Seurat; Sickert; Sisley; Tiepolo; Tintoretto; Toulouse-Lautrec; Palma Vecchio; Veronese; Vuillard; van der Weyden.

ESTORICK COLLECTION OF MODERN ITALIAN ART
39A Canonbury Square, London, N1 2AN
Tel: 020 7704 9522
Fax: 020 7704 9531
Website: www.estorickcollection.com
Collection includes work by: Balla; Boccioni; de Chirico; Guttuso; Modigliani.

GUILDHALL ART GALLERY
Guildhall Yard, London, EC2P 2EJ
Tel: 020 7606 3030
Fax: 020 7332 3342
Website: www.guildhall-art-gallery.org.uk
and collage.cityoflondon.gov.uk
Collection includes work by: Constable; Copley; Hunt; Millais; Rossetti.

KENSINGTON PALACE STATE APARTMENTS
London, W8 4PX
Tel: 0870 7515170
Website: www.hrp.org.uk
Collection includes work by: Carracci; Tintoretto; van Dyck.

IMPERIAL WAR MUSEUM
Lambeth Road, London, SE1 6HZ
Tel: 020 7416 5320
Website: www.iwm.org.uk
Collection includes work by: Lowry; Nash; Sargent; Spencer.

LAMBETH PALACE
Lambeth Road, London, SE1 7JU
Tel: 020 7898 1200
(telephone appointments only)
Collection includes work by: Holbein the Younger.

LEIGHTON HOUSE
12 Holland Park Road, London, W14 8LZ
Tel: 020 7602 3316
Fax: 020 7371 2467
Website: www.rbkc.gov.uk/
leightonhousemuseum/general
Collection includes work by: Burne Jones; Leighton; Millais; Wright of Derby.

MANSION HOUSE
London, EC4N 8BH
Tel: 020 7626 2500
(Telephone appointments only)
Collection includes work by: Avercamp; Jan Brueghel I; van de Capelle; Cuyp; Dou; Hals, Hobbema; de Hooch; Kalf; van Mieris; Ruisdael; Steen; van de Velde the Younger.

MUSEUM OF LONDON
London Wall, London, EC2Y 5HN
Tel: 020 7600 3699

Fax: 020 7600 1058
Website: www.museumoflondon.org.uk
Collection includes work by: Canaletto; Lawrence; Weight.

NATIONAL ARMY MUSEUM
Royal Hospital Road, Chelsea
London, SW3 4HT
Tel: 020 7730 0717
Website: www.national-army-museum.ac.uk
Collection includes work by: Reynolds.

NATIONAL GALLERY
Trafalgar Square, London, WC2N 5DN
Tel: 020 7747 2885
Fax: 020 7747 2423
Website: www.nationalgallery.org.uk
The National Collection of western European painting. Over two thousand paintings from the thirteenth century to 1900 containing works by most major artists of the intervening centuries.

NATIONAL PORTRAIT GALLERY
St Martin's Place, London, WC2H 0HE
Tel: 020 7306 0055
Website: www.npg.org.uk
Collection includes work by: Brown; van Dyck; Freud; Gainsborough; Hockney; Hogarth; Holbein the Younger; Holman Hunt; van Honthorst; John; Lawrence; Millais; Raeburn; Ramsay; Reynolds; Sargent; Sickert; Stubbs; Wright of Derby.

NATURAL HISTORY MUSEUM
Cromwell Road, London, SW7 5BD
Tel: 020 7942 5000
Website: www.nhm.ac.uk
Collection includes work by: Holman Hunt.

QUEEN'S GALLERY
Buckingham Palace, London, SW1A 1AA
Tel: 020 7321 2233
Fax: 020 7930 9625
Website: www.royal.gov.uk
Houses temporary exhibitions of items from the Royal Collection.

ST PAUL'S CATHEDRAL
London, EC4M 8AD
Tel: 020 7236 4128
Fax: 020 7248 3104
Website: www.stpauls.co.uk
Collection includes work by: Holman Hunt.

SCIENCE MUSEUM
Exhibition Road, London, SW7 2DD
Tel: 0870 870 4771
Fax: 020 7942 4302
Website: www.sciencemuseum.org.uk
Collection includes work by: Lowry.

SIR JOHN SOANE'S MUSEUM
13 Lincoln's Inn Fields
London, WC2A 3BP
Tel: 020 7440 4263
Fax: 020 7831 3957

Website: www.soane.org
Collection includes work by: Canaletto; Fuseli; Hogarth; Reynolds; Turner; Watteau.

TATE BRITAIN
Millbank, London, SW1P 4RG
Tel: 020 7887 8008
Website: www.tate.org.uk/britain

TATE MODERN
Bankside, London, SE1 9TG
Tel: 020 7887 8008
Website: www.tate.org.uk/modern
The Tate collection combines the National Collection of British Art with the National Collection of Modern Art from 1900 to the present day. Tate Britain displays the British Collection, but works by major twentieth-century and contemporary British artists can be shown in either venue. Works from the Tate collection are also shown in their satellites in Liverpool and St Ives.

THOMAS CORAM FOUNDATION FOR CHILDREN (FOUNDLING HOSPITAL ART TREASURES)
40 Brunswick Square, London, WC1N 1AZ
Tel: 020 7278 2424
Collection includes work by: Gainsborough; Hogarth; Millais; Ramsay; Reynolds.

VICTORIA AND ALBERT MUSEUM
Cromwell Road, London, SW7 2RL
Tel: 020 7942 2000
Website: www.vam.ac.uk
Collection includes work by: William Blake; Botticelli; Boucher; Jan Brueghel I; Burne Jones; Canaletto; Constable; Corot; Courbet; Dégas; Delacroix; Fuseli; Gainsborough; Hilliard; Holbein the Younger; Ingres; Millais; Perugino; Raeburn; Ramsay; Raphael; Rembrandt; Reynolds; Rossetti; Rubens; Stubbs; Terborch; Tintoretto; Turner; van de Velde the Younger.

WALLACE COLLECTION
Hertford House. Manchester Square
London, W1U 3BN
Tel: 020 7563 9500
Fax: 020 7224 2155
Website: www.the-wallace-collection.org.uk
Collection includes work by: Boucher; Canaletto; Claude; Corot; Cuyp; Daddi; Delacroix; Dou; van Dyck; Foppa; Fragonard; Gainsborough; Géricault; Hals; Hobbema; de Hooch; Memlinc; van Mieris; Murillo; Netscher; Poussin; Rembrandt; Reynolds; Rosa; Rubens; Ruisdael; del Sarto; Steen; Terborch; Titian; van de Velde the Younger; Velázquez; Vigée Lebrun; Watteau.

WELLCOME LIBRARY
183 Euston Road, London, NW1 2BE
Tel: 020 7611 8582
Fax: 020 7611 8703
Website:
http://library.wellcome.ac.uk/collections/

visual_ico.shtml
Collection includes work by: Elsheimer; West; Wright of Derby.

WESTMINSTER ABBEY
London, SW1P 3PA
Tel: 020 7222 5152
Fax: 020 7233 2072
Website: www.westminster-abbey.org
Collection includes the Westminster Retable and works by Canaletto.

GREATER LONDON

DULWICH PICTURE GALLERY
Gallery Road, London, SE21 7AD
Tel: 020 8693 5254
Website: www.dulwichpicturegallery.org.uk
Collection includes work by: Canaletto; Claude; Piero di Cosimo; Cuyp; Dou; van Dyck; Gainsborough; de Gelder; Hobbema; Hogarth; van Honthorst; Murillo; Poussin; Raphael; Rembrandt; Reynolds; Rosa; Rubens; Ruisdael; Tiepolo; van de Velde the Younger; Veronese; Watteau.

FENTON HOUSE
Windmill Hill, London, NW3 6RT
Tel: 020 7435 3471
Fax: 020 7435 3471
Website: www.nationaltrust.org.uk
Collection includes work by: Lawrence.

HAM HOUSE
Richmond, TW10 7RS
Tel: 020 8940 1950
Fax: 020 8332 6903
Website: www.nationaltrust.org.uk
Collection includes work by: Reynolds; van de Velde the Younger.

KENWOOD HOUSE
Hampstead Lane, London,
NW3 7JR
Tel: 020 8348 1286
Collection includes work by: Boucher; van de Cappelle; Cuyp; van Dyck; Gainsborough; Hals; Raeburn; Rembrandt; Reynolds; van de Velde the Younger; Vermeer; Wright of Derby.

MARBLE HILL HOUSE
Richmond Road, Twickenham
Middlesex, TW1 2NL
Tel: 020 8892 5115
Collection includes work by: Hogarth; Reynolds.

NATIONAL MARITIME MUSEUM
London, SE10 9NF
Tel: 020 8858 4422
Website: www.nmm.ac.uk
Collection includes work by: Canaletto; van de Cappelle; Gainsborough; Hogarth; Lowry; Ramsay; Reynolds; Ruisdael; Turner; van de Velde the Younger.

RANGER'S HOUSE
Chesterfield Walk, Blackheath
London SE10
Tel: 020 8853 0035
Collection includes work by: de Hooch, Lippi,
Reynolds, Sargent.

SOUTH LONDON GALLERY
65 Peckham Road, London, SE5 8UH
Tel: 020 7703 6120
Fax: 020 7252 4730
Website: www.southlondonart.com
Collection includes work by: Hogarth; Millais;
Nash; Sickert.

SYON HOUSE
Syon Park, Brentford
Middlesex, TW8 8JF
Tel: 020 8560 0881
Website: www.syonpark.co.uk
Collection includes work by: van Dyck;
Gainsborough; van Honthorst; Reynolds.

WILLIAM MORRIS GALLERY
Lloyd Park, Forest Road
London, E17 4PP
Tel: 020 8527 3782
Fax: 020 8527 7070
Website: www.lbwf.gov.uk/wmg
Collection includes work by: Böcklin.

EAST ANGLIA

Cambridgeshire, Essex, Norfolk, Suffolk

ANGLESEY ABBEY
Lode, Cambridgeshire, CB5 9EJ
Tel: 01223 811200
Fax: 01223 811200
Website: www.nationaltrust.org.uk
Collection includes work by: Canaletto;
Claude; Constable; Cuyp; Gainsborough.

AUDLEY END
Saffron Walden, Essex, CB11 4JF
Tel: 01799 522842
Fax: 01799 521276
Website: www.uttlesford.gov.uk/saffire/
places/audend.html
Collection includes work by: Canaletto;
Claesz; van Dyck; Holbein the Younger; van
Honthorst; Lawrence; Ramsay; Reynolds;
West.

**BURY ST EDMUNDS,
MANOR HOUSE MUSEUM**
Honey Hill, Bury St Edmunds,
Suffolk, IP33 1 HF
Tel: 01284 762081
Collection includes work by: Reynolds.

BLICKLING HALL
Blickling, Norwich,
Norfolk, NR11 6NF
Tel: 01263 738030
Fax: 01263 731660
Website: www.nationaltrust.org.uk
Collection includes work by: Canaletto;
Gainsborough; Reynolds.

CAMBRIDGE, EMMANUEL COLLEGE
Cambridge, CB2 3AP
Tel: 01223 334200
Fax: 01223 334426
Website: www.emma.cam.ac.uk
Collection includes work by: Ramsay.

CAMBRIDGE, FITZWILLIAM MUSEUM
Trumpington Street,
Cambridge, CB2 1RB
Tel: 01223 332900
Fax: 01223 332933
Website: www.fitzmuseum.cam.ac.uk

Collection includes work by: Bassano; William
Blake; Bonnard; Brown; Jan Brueghel;
Canaletto; Carracci; Cézanne; Claude;
Constable; Corot; Courbet; Cuyp; Dégas;
Delacroix; Dou; van Dyck; Elsheimer;
Gainsborough; Gauguin; Géricault;
Ghirlandaio; Guercino; Hals; van Heemskerck;
Hobbema; Hogarth; Holman Hunt; van
Honthorst; John; Jones; Léger; Lippi; Martini;
Matisse; Millais; Modigliani; Monet; Murillo;
Nash; Giovanni di Paolo; Picasso; Sebastiano
del Piombo; Pissarro; Poussin; Raeburn;
Rembrandt; Renoir; Reynolds; Rosa; Rossetti;
Rubens; Ruisdael; Sargent; Seurat; Sickert;
Sisley; Spencer; Steen; Stubbs; Tintoretto;
Titian; Turner; Palma Vecchio; Domenico
Veneziano; Veronese; Vuillard; Whistler;
Wright of Derby.

CAMBRIDGE, GIRTON COLLEGE
Cambridge, CB3 0JG
Tel: 01223 338999
Fax: 01223 338896
Website: www.girton.cam.ac.uk
Collection includes work by: Spencer.

CAMBRIDGE, KING'S COLLEGE
Cambridge, CB2 1ST
Tel: 01223 331100
Website: www.kings.cam.ac.uk
Collection includes work by: Rubens.

**CAMBRIDGE, MAGDALENE COLLEGE
(PEPYS LIBRARY)**
Cambridge, CB3 0AG
Tel: 01223 332100
Fax: 01223 462589
Website: www.magd.cam.ac.uk
Collection includes work by: van de Velde
the Younger.

CAMBRIDGE, PEMBROKE COLLEGE
Cambridge, CB2 1RF
Tel: 01223 338100
Fax: 01223 338163
Website: www.pem.cam.ac.uk
Collection includes work by: Reynolds.

CAMBRIDGE, ST JOHN'S COLLEGE
Cambridge, CB2 1TP
Tel: 01223 338600
Website: www.joh.cam.ac.uk
Collection includes work by: Holbein the
Younger.

CAMBRIDGE, TRINITY COLLEGE
Cambridge, CB2 1TQ
Tel: 01223 338400
Fax: 01223 338564
Website: www.trin.cam.ac.uk
Collection includes work by: Lawrence;
Reynolds.

CAMBRIDGE, UNIVERSITY LIBRARY
West Road
Cambridge, CB3 9DR
Tel: 01223 333000
Fax: 01223 333160
Website: www.lib.cam.ac.uk
Collection includes work by: Sargent.

ELTON HALL
Elton, Near Peterborough,
Cambridgeshire, PE8 6SH
Tel: 01832 280468
Fax: 01832 280584
Collection includes work by: Constable;
Gainsborough; Millais; Reynolds.

EUSTON HALL
Thetford, Norfolk, IP24 2QP
Tel: 01842 766366
Collection includes work by: Reynolds;
Stubbs.

FELLBRIGG HALL
Felbrigg, Norwich,
Norfolk, NR11 8PR
Tel: 01263 837444
Fax: 01263 837032
Website: www.nationaltrust.org.uk
Collection includes work by: Reynolds; van
de Velde the Younger.

HOLKHAM HALL
Wells-next-the-Sea,
Norfolk, NR23 1AB
Tel: 01328 710227
Website: www.holkham.co.uk
Collection includes work by: Canaletto;
Claude; van Dyck; Gainsborough; Reynolds;
Rubens.

HOUGHTON HALL
Houghton, Kings Lynn,
Norfolk, PE31 6UE
Tel: 01485 528569
Fax: 01485 528167
Website: www.houghtonhall.com
Collection includes work by: Reynolds;
Sargent.

ICKWORTH HOUSE
The Rotunda, Horringer,
Bury St Edmunds,
Suffolk, IP29 5QE
Tel: 01284 735270
Fax: 01284 735175
Website: www.stedmunds.co.uk/lifestyle/
ickworth-house.html
Collection includes work by: Gainsborough;
Hogarth; Lawrence; Ramsay; Reynolds;
Titian; Velázquez; Vigée Lebrun.

IPSWICH, CHRISTCHURCH MANSION
Christchurch Park, Ipswich,
Suffolk, IP4 2BE
Tel: 01473 433554
Website: www.ipswich.gov.uk/tourism/guide/
mansion.htm
Collection includes work by: Constable;
Gainsborough; Pissarro; Reynolds; Sickert.

NAYLAND, ST JAMES CHURCH
Nayland, Suffolk
Tel: 01206 262316
Collection includes work by: Constable.

**NORWICH CASTLE MUSEUM
AND ART GALLERY**
Castle Meadow, Norwich,
Norfolk, NR1 4JU
Tel: 01603 493625
Fax: 01603 493623
Website: www.norfolk.gov.uk/tourism/
museums/castle.htm
Collection includes work by: Burne Jones;
Gainsborough; Hobbema; Lowry; Sisley.

**NORWICH, SAINSBURY CENTRE FOR
VISUAL ARTS**
University of East Anglia,
Norwich, Norfolk, NR4 7TJ
Tel: 01603 593199
Fax: 01603 259401
Website: www.uea.ac.uk/scva
Collection includes work by: Bacon;
Giacometti; Modigliani; Moore.

**PETERBOROUGH MUSEUM
AND ART GALLERY**
Priestgate, Peterborough,
Cambridgeshire, PE1 1LF
Tel: 01733 343329
Fax: 01733 341928
Website: www.peterboroughheritage.org.uk
Collection includes work by: Sickert; Turner.

**WESTCLIFF-ON-SEA,
BEECROFT ART GALLERY**
Station Road, Westcliff-on-Sea,
Essex, SS0 7RA
Tel: 01702 347418
Website: www.beecroft-art-gallery.co.uk
Collection includes work by: Constable.

WIMPOLE HALL
Arrington, Royston,
Cambridgeshire, SG8 0BW
Tel: 01223 207257
Fax: 01223 207838
Website: www.wimpole.org
Collection includes work by: Ramsay;
Reynolds.

SOUTH EAST

East Sussex, West Sussex, Kent, Surrey

ARUNDEL CASTLE
West Sussex, BN18 9AB
Tel: 01903 883136
Fax: 01903 884581
Website: www.arundelcastle.org
Collection includes work by: van Dyck;
Gainsborough; Lawrence; Reynolds.

BRIGHTON MUSEUM AND ART GALLERY
4/5 Pavilion Buildings, Brighton
East Sussex BN1 1EE
Tel: 01273 290900
Fax: 01273 292851
Website: www.brighton-hove.gov.uk
/bhc/museums/brighton
Collection includes work by: Alma-Tadema;
William Blake; Cranach the Elder;
Gainsborough; Hogarth; Lawrence; Lievens;
Millais Reynolds; Sickert; Vigée Lebrun.

**CANTERBURY, ROYAL MUSEUM
AND ART GALLERY**
18 High Street, Canterbury,
Kent, CT1 2RA
Tel: 01227 452747
Fax: 01227 455047
Website: www.canterbury-artgallery.co.uk
Collection includes work by: Gainsborough;
Sickert.

CHICHESTER, PALLANT HOUSE GALLERY
9 North Pallant, Chichester
West Sussex, PO19 1TJ
Tel: 01243 774557
Fax: 01243 536038
Website: www.pallanthousegallery.com
Collection includes work by: Léger; Nash;
Nicholson; Severini; Sickert.

CLANDON PARK
West Clandon, Guildford
Surrey, GU4 7RQ
Tel: 01483 223479
Fax: 01483 223479
Website: www.nationaltrust.org.uk
Collection includes work by: Hogarth.

COMPTON, WATTS GALLERY
Down Lane, Compton, Guildford
Surrey, GU3 1DQ
Tel: 01483 810235
Website: www.wattsgallery.org.uk
Collection includes work by: Burne Jones;
Watts.

DOVER TOWN HALL
Biggin Street, Dover
Kent, CT16 1DQ
Tel: 01304 201200
Fax: 01304 201200
Website:

www.dover.gov.uk/townhall/home.htm
Collection includes work by: Ramsay.

EASTBOURNE, TOWNER ART GALLERY
High Street, Old Town,
Eastbourne, East Sussex, BN20 8BB
Tel: 01323 411688/417961
Fax: 01323 648182
Website: www.eastbourne.org/
entertainment/towner-art-gallery.htm
Collection includes work by: Sickert; Wright
of Derby.

EGHAM, ROYAL HOLLOWAY COLLEGE
Egham Hill, Egham
Surrey, TW20 0EX
Tel: 01784 434455
Website: www.egham.co.uk/info/rhbnc.html
Collection includes work by: Landseer;
Millais.

FARNHAM MUSEUM
Wilmer House, 38 West Street,
Farnham, Surrey, GU9 7DX
Tel: 01252 715094
Fax: 01252 715094
Website: www.waverley.gov.uk/
museumoffarnham/index.asp
Collection includes work by: Sargent.

FIRLE PLACE
Firle, Near Lewes
East Sussex, BN8 6LP
Tel: 01273 858335
Fax: 01273 858188
Website: www.firlestreet.freeserve.co.uk/
firle_place.html
Collection includes work by: van Dyck;
Gainsborough; Lawrence; Reynolds;
Tintoretto.

GOODWOOD HOUSE
Goodwood, Chichester,
Sussex, PO18 0PX
Tel: 01243 755 048
Fax: 01243 755 005
Website: www.goodwood.co.uk
Collection includes work by: Canaletto; van
Dyck; Reynolds; Stubbs.

HAMPTON COURT PALACE
Surrey, KT8 9AU
Tel: 020 8781 9500
Website: www.hrp.org.uk/webcode/
hampton_house.asp
Collection includes work by: Angelico;
Bassano; Bellini; Bordone; Bronzino; Jan
Brueghel, Pieter Bruegel the Elder; ter
Brugghen; Carracci; Correggio; Daddi; van
Dyck; Artemesia Gentileschi; Orazio
Gentileschi; Gossaert; Guercino; van
Heemskerck; Holbein the Younger; van
Honthorst; Lotto; Mantegna; Massys;
Parmigianino; Perugino; Pontormo; Raphael;
Reynolds; del Sarto; de la Tour; Tintoretto;
Titian; Palma Vecchio; van de Velde the
Younger; Veronese.

HASTINGS MUSEUM AND ART GALLERY
Johns Place, Bohemia Road,
Hastings, East Sussex TN34 1ET
Tel: 01424 781155
Fax: 01424 781165
Website: www.hastings.gov.uk/museum/
short_guide_bohemia.asp
Collection includes work by: Sickert.

HATCHLANDS PARK
East Clandon, Guildford, GU4 7RT
Tel: 01483 222482
Website: www.nationaltrust.org.uk
Collection includes Collection includes work
by: Wright of Derby.

KNOLE
Sevenoaks, Kent, TN15 0RP
Tel: 01732 462100
Fax: 01732 465528
Website: www.nationaltrust.org.uk
Collection includes work by: van Dyck; Gainsborough; Lawrence; Reynolds.

MAIDSTONE MUSEUM AND ART GALLERY
St Faith's Street, Maidstone,
Kent, ME14 1LH
Tel: 01622 754497
Fax: 01622 685022
Website: www.museum.maidstone.gov.uk
Collection includes work by: van de Velde the Younger.

PARHAM HOUSE
Parham Park, Near Pulborough,
West Sussex, RH20 4HS
Tel: 01903 742021
Fax: 01903 746557
Website: www.parhaminsussex.co.uk
Collection includes work by: Gainsborough; Reynolds; Stubbs.

PETWORTH HOUSE
Petworth, West Sussex, GU28 0AE
Tel: 01798 342207
Fax: 01798 342963
Website: www.nationaltrust.org.uk
Collection includes work by: William Blake; Bosch; Claude; Cuyp; van Dyck; Elsheimer; Fuseli; Gainsborough; Hobbema; Reynolds; Ruisdael; Titian; Turner; van der Weyden.

POLESDEN LACEY
Great Bookham, Dorking,
Surrey, RH5 6BD
Tel: 01372 452048
Fax: 01372 452023
Website: www.nationaltrust.org.uk
Collection includes work by: Cuyp; de Hooch; Lawrence; Master of the St Bartholomew Altarpiece; van Mieris; Perugino; Raeburn; Reynolds; Ruisdael; Terborch; van de Velde the Younger; Vigée Lebrun.

PRESTON MANOR
Preston Park, Brighton, BN1 6SD
Tel: 01273 292770
Website: www.brighton-hove.gov.uk/bhc/ museums/prestonmanor/index.html
Collection includes work by: Poussin.

SMALLHYTHE, ELLEN TERRY MEMORIAL MUSEUM
Smallhythe Place, Smallhythe,
Tenterden, Kent, TN30 7NG
Tel: 01580 762334
Fax: 01580 762334
Collection includes work by: Sargent.

TUNBRIDGE WELLS MUSEUM AND ART GALLERY
Civic Centre, Mount Pleasant,
Royal Tunbridge Wells, Kent, TN1 1JN
Tel: 01892 554171
Website:
www.tunbridgewells.gov.uk/museum/
Collection includes work by: Solomon.

WATFORD MUSEUM
194 Watford High Street, Watford,
Hertfordshire, WD17 2DT
Website: www.hertsmuseums.org.uk
Collection includes Collection includes work by: Reynolds.

WORTHING MUSEUM AND ART GALLERY
Chapel Road, Worthing,
West Sussex, BN11 1HP
Tel: 01903 221150
Fax: 01903 263646

Website:
www.worthing.com/living/local/museum.htm
Collection includes work by: Holman Hunt; Sickert.

SOUTH
Bedfordshire, Berkshire, Buckinghamshire, Hampshire, Hertfordshire, Oxfordshire.

ASCOTT
Wing, Near Leighton Buzzard,
Buckinghamshire, LU7 0PS
Tel: 01296 688242
Fax: 01296 681904
Website: www.nationaltrust.org.uk
Collection includes work by: Boucher; Cuyp; Gainsborough; Hobbema; Hogarth; Lotto; van Mieris; Reynolds; del Sarto; Steen; Stubbs; Rubens; Tiepolo; Turner.

ASHDOWN HOUSE
Lambourn, Newbury,
Berkshire, RG16 7RE
Tel: 01488 72584
Fax: 01793 861110
Website: www.nationaltrust.org.uk
Collection includes work by: van Honthorst.

BEDFORD, CECIL HIGGINS ART GALLERY
Castle Lane, Bedford,
Bedfordshire, MK40 3RP
Tel: 01234 211222
Fax: 01234 327149
Website: www.cecilhigginsartgallery.org
Collection includes work by: Sisley.

BLENHEIM PALACE
Woodstock,
Oxfordshire, OX20 1PX
Tel: 01993 811325
Fax: 01993 813527
Website: www.bleinheimpalace.com
Collection includes work by: Sargent; Reynolds.

BROADLANDS
Romsey,
Hampshire, SO51 9ZD
Tel: 01794 505010
Fax: 01794 505040
Website: www.broadlands.net
Collection includes work by: van Dyck; Lawrence; Reynolds.

BURGHCLERE, SANDHAM MEMORIAL CHAPEL
Harts Lane,
Burghclere, Newbury,
Berkshire, RG20 9JT
Tel: 01635 278394
Fax: 01635 278394
Website: www.nationaltrust.org.uk
Collection includes work by: Spencer.

BUSCOT PARK
Faringdon,
Oxfordshire, SN7 8BU
Tel: 01367 240786
Fax: 01367 241794
Website: www.buscot-park.com; www.faringdon-coll.com
Collection includes work by: Botticelli; Brown; Burne Jones; Gainsborough; Lawrence; Murillo; Sebastiano del Piombo; Rembrandt; Reynolds; Ribera; Rosa; Rubens; Palma Vecchio.

COOKHAM, STANLEY SPENCER GALLERY
The Kings Hall,
High Street, Cookham,
Berkshire, SL6 9SJ
Tel: 01628 471885

Website: www.stanleyspencer.org
Collection includes work by: Spencer.

GORHAMBURY HOUSE
Gorhambury,
St Albans, Hertfordshire, AL3 6AH
Tel: 01727 854051
Fax: 01727 843675
Collection includes work by: Ramsay; Reynolds.

HATFIELD HOUSE
Hatfield,
Hertfordshire, AL9 5NQ
Tel: 01707 287010
Fax: 01707 287033
Website: www.hatfield-house.co.uk
Collection includes work by: Hilliard; Lawrence; Reynolds.

HIGHCLERE CASTLE
Newbury, Berkshire,
RG20 9RN
Tel: 01635 253210
Website: www.highclerecastle.co.uk
Collection includes work by: Reynolds.

HINTON AMPNER HOUSE
Bramdean, Near Arlesford
Hampshire, SO24 0LA
Tel: 01962 771305
Fax: 01962 793101
Website: www.nationaltrust.org.uk
Collection includes work by: Fuseli.

LUTON, ST MARY'S PARISH CHURCH
Church Street, Luton,
Bedfordshire, LU1 3JF
Tel: 01582 721867
Collection includes work by: Fuseli.

OXFORD, ASHMOLEAN MUSEUM
Beaumont Street,
Oxford, OX1 2PH
Tel: 01865 278000
Fax: 01865 278018
Website: www.ashmol.ox.ac.uk
Collection includes work by: Angelico; Bellini; Bonnard; Braque; Bronzino; Brown; Jan Brueghel I; ter Brugghen; Burne Jones; Canaletto; Chardin; Claude; Constable; Corot; Piero di Cosimo; Courbet; Cuyp; Derain; van Dyck; Freud; Gainsborough; Giorgione; Giotto van Gogh; Gossaert; Hogarth; Holman Hunt; Kandinsky; Lippi; Matisse; Michelangelo; Monet; Nicholson; Palmer; Giovanni di Paolo; Pissarro; Poussin; Raeburn; Ramsay; Renoir; Reynolds; Rubens; Ruisdael; Sargent; Sickert; Spencer; Tiepolo; Tintoretto; Titian; Toulouse-Lautrec; Uccello; Vecchio; Veronese; Watteau; Whistler; Wright of Derby.

OXFORD, CHRIST CHURCH PICTURE GALLERY
Oxford, OX1 1DP
Tel: 01865 276150
Website: www.chch.ox.ac.uk/gallery
Collection includes work by: Angelico; Bassano; Botticelli; Duccio; Carracci; van Dyck; Gainsborough; van der Goes; Guercino; Hals; Lippi (Filippino); Lotto; Millais; Giovanni di Paolo; Pontormo; Reynolds; Rosa; Spranger; Tintoretto; Titian; Veronese.

OXFORD, JESUS COLLEGE
Oxford, OX1 3DW
Tel: 01865 279700
Fax: 01865 279687
Website: www.jesus.ox.ac.uk
Collection includes work by: Holman Hunt; Lawrence.

OXFORD, KEBLE COLLEGE
Oxford, OX1 3PG

Tel: 01865 272727
Fax:
Website: www.keble.ox.ac.uk
Collection includes work by: Holman Hunt.

OXFORD, NEW COLLEGE
Oxford, OX1 3BN
Tel: 01865 279555
Fax: 01865 279590
Website: www.new.ox.ac.uk
Collection includes work by: El Greco.

OXFORD, ST JOHN'S COLLEGE
Oxford, OX1 3JP
Tel: 01865 277300
Fax: 01865 277435
Website: www.sjc.ox.ac.uk
Collection includes work by: Ramsay.

OXFORD, WORCESTER COLLEGE
Oxford, OX1 2HB
Tel: 01865 278300
Fax: 01865 278387
Website: www.worcester.ox.ac.uk
Collection includes work by: Ruisdael.

PORTSMOUTH, CITY MUSEUM
Museum Road,
Old Portsmouth,
Hampshire, PO1 2LJ
Tel: 023 9282 7261
Fax: 023 9287 5276
Website: www.portsmouthsmuseums.co.uk
Collection includes work by: Sickert.

READING MUSEUM
The Town Hall,
Blagrave Street, Reading,
Berkshire, RG1 1QH
Tel: 01189 318660
Fax: 01189 751264
Website: www.royalhistory.org
Collection includes work by: Spencer.

ROUSHAM HOUSE
Rousham, Near Steeple Aston,
Bicester,
Oxfordshire, OX6 3QX
Tel: 01869 347110
Fax: 01869 347110
Website: www.rousham.org
Collection includes work by: Jones; Reynolds.

SOUTHAMPTON CITY ART GALLERY
Commercial Road,
Southampton,
Hampshire, SO14 7LP
Tel: 023 80 832277
Website:
www.southampton.gov.uk/leisure/arts
Collection includes work by: Bellany; Bellini; Bonnard; Brown; Burne Jones; Corot; Courbet; van Dyck; Forain; Freud; Gainsborough; Hodgkin; Holman Hunt; John; Jordaens; Lawrence; Lowry; Millais; Monet; Nash; Nicholson; Pissarro; Renoir; Reynolds; Rosa; Ruisdael; Sargent; Sickert; Sisley; Spencer; Turner; Vuillard; Wright of Derby.

STRATFIELD SAYE HOUSE
Near Reading,
Berkshire, RG7 2BZ
Tel: 01256 882882/882694
Fax: 01256 882882
Website: www.stratfield-saye.co.uk
Collection includes work by: Lawrence; Ramsay; Tintoretto.

WADDESDON MANOR
Waddesdon, Aylesbury,
Buckinghamshire, HP18 0JH
Tel: 01296 653226
Fax: 01296 653208

Website: www.waddesdon.org.uk
Collection includes work by: Boucher; Cuyp; Dou; Gainsborough; de Hooch; Master of the St Bartholomew's Altarpiece; Ruisdael; Reynolds; Terborch; van de Velde the Younger; Vigée Lebrun; Watteau.

WEST WYCOMBE PARK
West Wycombe,
Buckinghamshire, HP14 3AJ
Tel: 01494 513569
Website: www.nationaltrust.org.uk
Collection includes work by: Jordaens; Ribera; Rosa.

WINDSOR CASTLE
Windsor,
Berkshire, SL4 1NJ
Tel: 020 7321 2233
Fax: 020 7930 9625
Website: www.royal.gov.uk
Collection includes work by: Canaletto; van Dyck; Gainsborough; Hogarth; Holbein the Younger; van Honthorst; de Hooch; Lawrence; Massys; Memlinc; Ramsay; Rembrandt; Reynolds; del Sarto; Stubbs; van de Velde the Younger; Vermeer; Wright of Derby.

WOBURN ABBEY
Woburn,
Bedfordshire, MK17 9WA
Tel: 01525 290666
Fax: 01525 290271
Website: www.woburnabbey.co.uk
Collection includes work by: Canaletto; van de Cappelle; Carracci; Claude; Cuyp; van Dyck; Gainsborough; Lawrence; Murillo; Poussin; Reynolds; Ruisdael; Steen; van de Velde the Younger.

SOUTH WEST
Cornwall, Devon, Dorset, Somerset, Wiltshire.

ANTHONY HOUSE
Torpoint, Cornwall, PL11 2QA
Tel: 01752 812191
Collection includes work by: Reynolds.

ARLINGTON COURT
Arlington, Near Barnstaple,
Devon, EX31 4LP
Tel: 01271 850296
Fax: 01271 851108
Website: www.nationaltrust.org.uk
Collection includes work by: William Blake.

BATH, ASSEMBLY ROOMS
Bennett Street,
Bath, BA1 2QH
Tel: 01225 477789
Website: www.museumofcostume.co.uk
Collection includes work by: Gainsborough.

BATH, HOLBURNE MUSEUM OF ART
Great Pulteney Street,
Bath, BA2 4DB
Tel: 01225 466669
Fax: 01225 333121
Website: www.bath.ac.uk/Holburne
Collection includes work by: Gainsborough; Raeburn; Ramsay; Reynolds; Stubbs.

BATH, VICTORIA ART GALLERY
Bridge Street,
Bath, BA2 4AT
Tel: 01225 477772
Fax: 01225 477231
Website: www.victoriagal.org.uk
Collection includes work by: Lawrence; Sickert.

BOURNEMOUTH, RUSSELL-COTES ART GALLERY AND MUSEUM
East Cliff, Bournemouth,
Dorset, BH1 3AA
Tel: 01202 451800
Fax: 01202 451851
Website:
www.russell-cotes.bournemouth.gov.uk
Collection includes work by: Corot; Rossetti.

BOWOOD HOUSE
Calne, Wiltshire, SN11 0LZ
Tel: 01249 812102
Fax: 01249 821757
Website: www.bowood.org
Collection includes work by: Gainsborough;
Lawrence; Reynolds; Terborch.

BRISTOL CITY ART GALLERY
Queen's Road
Bristol BS8 1RL
Tel: 0117 922 3571
Website: www.bristol-city.gov.uk
Collection includes work by: Bellini; Burne
Jones; Claesz; Constable; Corot; Courbet;
Cranach; Delacroix; Gaddi; Gainsborough;
Hogarth; Jordaens; Lawrence; Nicholson;
Reynolds; Ruisdael; Seurat; Sickert; Sisley;
Vuillard.

CORSHAM COURT
Corsham, Wiltshire, SN13 0BZ
Tel: 01249 701610
Fax: 01249 701610
Website: www.corsham-court.co.uk
Collection includes work by: Bassano;
Claude; van Dyck; Gainsborough; Guercino;
Lippi, Filippo; Reynolds; Ribera; Rosa.

DORCHESTER, DORSET COUNTY MUSEUM
High West Street
Dorchester, Dorset DT1 1XA
Tel: 01305 262735
Fax: 01305 257180
Collection includes work by: Gainsborough.

KILLERTON HOUSE
Broadclyst, Near Exeter,
Devon, EX5 881345
Collection includes work by: Reynolds.

KINGSTON LACY
Wimborne Minster,
Dorset, BH21 4EA
Tel: 01202 883402
Fax: 01202 882402
Website: www.nationaltrust.co.uk
Collection includes work by: van Dyck;
Lawrence; Murillo; Sebastiano del Piombo;
Reynolds; Ribalta; Rosa; Rubens; Tintoretto;
Titian; Velázquez; Zurbaran.

KNIGHTSHAYES COURT
Bolham, Tiverton,
Devon, EX16 7RQ
Tel: 01884 254665
Fax: 01884 243050
Website: www.nationaltrust.org.uk
Collection includes work by: Constable;
Cranach the Elder.

LACOCK ABBEY
Lacock, Near Chippenham,
Wiltshire, SN15 2LG
Tel: 01249 730227
Fax: 01249 730227
Website: www.nationaltrust.org.uk
Collection includes work by: Gainsborough.

LONGLEAT
Warminster,
Wiltshire, BA12 7NW
Tel: 01985 844400
Fax: 01985 844885

Website: www.longleat.co.uk
Collection includes work by: van Dyck;
Lawrence; Reynolds; Tintoretto.

MONTACUTE HOUSE
Montacute, Somerset, TA15 6XP
Tel: 01935 823289
Fax: 01935 823289
Website: www.nationaltrust.org.uk
Collection includes work by: Gainsborough;
Reynolds.

MOUNT EDGCOMBE HOUSE
Cremyll, Torpoint,
Cornwall, PL10 1HZ
Tel: 01752 822236
Collection includes work by: Reynolds.

PENCARROW HOUSE
Washaway, Bodmin,
Cornwall, PL30 3AG
Tel: 01208 841369
Website: www.pencarrow.co.uk
Collection includes work by: Raeburn;
Reynolds.

PLYMOUTH CITY MUSEUM AND ART GALLERY
Drake Circus, Plymouth,
Devon, PL4 8AJ
Tel: 01752 304774
Fax: 01752 304775
Website: www.plymouthmuseum.gov.uk
Collection includes work by: Burne Jones;
Reynolds; Spencer.

ST IVES, TATE
Porthmeor Beach, St Ives,
Cornwall, TR26 1TG
Tel: 01736 796226
Website: www.tate.org.uk/stives
Collection includes work by various artists
from the Tate Collections concentrating on
artists from the school of St Ives.

SALTRAM PARK
Plympton, Plymouth,
Devon, PL7 1UH
Tel: 01752 333500
Fax: 01752 336474
Website: www.nationaltrust.org.uk
Collection includes work by: de Hooch;
Reynolds; Rubens; Stubbs.

SHERBORNE CASTLE
Sherborne, Dorset,
England, DT9 3PY
Tel: 01935 813182
Website: www.sherbornecastle.com
Collection includes work by: Reynolds.

STOURHEAD
Stourton, Warminster,
Wiltshire, BA12 6QD
Tel: 01747 841152
Fax: 01747 842005
Website: www.nationaltrust.org.uk
Collection includes work by: Poussin;
Ramsay.

SWINDON MUSEUM AND ART GALLERY
Bath Road, Old Town,
Swindon, Wiltshire, SN1 4BA
Tel: 01793 466556
Website: www.swindon.gov.uk
Collection includes work by: Hamilton;
Hodgkin; Lowry; Nicholson.

TORQUAY, TORRE ABBEY HISTORIC HOUSE AND GALLERY
The King's Drive, Torquay,
Devon, TQ2 5JE
Tel: 01803 293593
Fax: 01803 215948

Website:
www.torbay.gov.uk/index3.asp?page=675
Collection includes work by: Holman Hunt.

TRURO, ROYAL CORNWALL MUSEUM AND GALLERIES
River Street, Truro,
Cornwall, TR1 2SJ
Tel: 01872 272205
Fax: 01872 240514
Website: www.royalcornwallmuseum.org.uk
Collection includes work by: Hogarth;
Sargent.

WILTON HOUSE
Wilton, Salisbury,
Wiltshire, SP2 0BJ
Tel: 01722 746720
Fax: 01722 744447
Website: www.wiltonhouse.com
Collection includes work by: Jan Brueghel I;
van Dyck; van der Goes; Gossaert; van
Honthorst; Lawrence; van Leyden; van
Mieris; Rembrandt; Reynolds; Ribera; Rosa;
Rubens; Terborch; Tintoretto; van de Velde
the Younger.

MIDLANDS

Derbyshire, Gloucestershire, Herefordshire,
Leicestershire, Lincolnshire,
Northamptonshire, Nottinghamshire;
Shropshire, Staffordshire, Warwickshire,
West Midlands, Worcestershire

ALTHORP
Northampton, NN7 4HQ
Tel: 0870 1679000
Website: www.althorp.com
Collection includes work by: Reynolds; Rosa;
Stubbs.

ATTINGHAM PARK
Shrewsbury, Shropshire, SY4 4TP
Tel: 01743 708162
Fax: 01743 708175
Website: www.nationaltrust.org.uk
Collection includes work by: Lawrence;
Ribera; Rosa; Sickert.

BARLASTON, STAFFORDSHIRE WEDGWOOD MUSEUM
Barlaston,
Stoke-on-Trent,
Staffordshire, ST12 9ES
Tel: 01782 282818
Fax: 01782 223315
Website: www.wedgwoodmuseum.org.uk
Collection includes work by: Reynolds;
Stubbs.

BELTON HOUSE
Near Grantham,
Lincolnshire, NG32 2LS
Tel: 01476 566116
Fax: 01476 579071
Website: www.nationaltrust.org.uk
Collection includes work by: Reynolds.

BELVOIR CASTLE
Near Grantham,
Leicestershire, NG32 1PD
Tel: 01476 871002
Fax: 01476 870443
Website: www.belvoircastle.com
Collection includes work by: van Dyck;
Gainsborough; Murillo; Poussin; Reynolds;
Steen; van de Velde the Younger.

BERKELEY CASTLE
Gloucestershire, GL13 9BQ
Tel: 01453 810332
Website: www.berkeley-castle.com

Collection includes work by: Reynolds;
Stubbs.

BIRMINGHAM, BARBER INSTITUTE OF FINE ARTS
The University of Birmingham,
Edgbaston,
Birmingham, B15 2TS
Tel: 0121 414 7333
Fax: 0121 414 3370
Website: www.barber.org.uk/welcome.html
Collection includes work by: Bassano; Bellini;
Bonnard; Bordone; Botticelli; Canaletto; van
de Cappelle; Claude; Corot; Courbet; Cuyp;
Dégas; Delacroix; Derain; van Dyck;
Gainsborough; Gauguin; van Gogh; Gossaert;
Hals; Ingres; John; Lawrence; Magritte;
Manet; Martini; Massys; Monet; Murillo;
Pissarro; Poussin; Renoir; Reynolds; Rossetti;
Rubens; Ruisdael; Sickert; Steen; Tintoretto;
Toulouse-Lautrec; Turner; Veronese; Vigée
Lebrun; Vuillard; Whistler.

BIRMINGHAM CITY MUSEUMS AND ART GALLERY
Chamberlain Square,
Birmingham, B3 3DH
Tel: 0121 303 2834
Website: www.bmag.org.uk
Collection includes work by: Ayres; Bacon;
Botticelli; Brown; Burne Jones; Canaletto;
Cassatt; Christus; Claude; Constable;
Courbet; Dégas; Delacroix; Derain; Fuseli;
Gainsborough; Gentileschi (Orazio); Guercino;
Hodgkin; Holman Hunt; John; Jones; Lowry;
Martini; Memlinc; Millais; Morandi; Murillo;
Nash; Nicholson; Pissarro; Ramsay; Renoir;
Reynolds; Rosa; Rossetti; Rubens; Sargent;
Sickert; Sisley; Spencer; Turner; Vuillard;
Wallis; Wright of Derby.

BOUGHTON HOUSE
Kettering,
Northamptonshire, NN14 1BJ
Tel: 01536 515731
Fax: 01536 417255
Website: www.boughtonhouse.org.uk
Collection includes work by: Carracci; van
Dyck; Gainsborough; El Greco; van Honthorst;
Murillo; van de Velde the Younger.

BURGHLEY HOUSE
Stamford,
Lincolnshire, PE9 3JY
Tel: 01780 752451
Website: www.burghley.co.uk
Collection includes work by: Jan Brueghel I;
Cranach the Elder; van Dyck; Gainsborough;
Guercino; Lawrence; Rosa; Ruisdael; Tiepolo;
Veronese.

BUXTON MUSEUM AND ART GALLERY
Terrace Road, Buxton,
Derbyshire, SK17 6DU
Tel: 01298 24658
Fax: 01298 79394
Website:
www.derbyshire.gov.uk/azserv/libh024.htm
Collection includes work by: Lowry.

CHARLECOTE PARK
Warwick,
Warwickshire, CV35 9ER
Tel: 01789 470277
Fax: 01789 470544
Website: www.nationaltrust.org.uk
Collection includes work by: Gainsborough;
Raeburn.

CHATSWORTH
Bakewell,
Derbyshire, DE45 1PP
Tel: 01246 565300
Fax: 01246 583536

Website: www.chatsworth-house.co.uk
Collection includes work by: Bordone; van
Dyck; Hals; Landseer; Lawrence; Murillo;
Poussin; Reynolds; Rembrandt; Rosa;
Sargent; Tintoretto.

CHELTENHAM ART GALLERY AND MUSEUM
Clarence Street,
Cheltenham,
Gloucestershire, GL50 3JT
Tel: 01242 237431
Fax: 01242 262334
Website: www.cheltenhammuseum.org.uk/
home/home.asp
Collection includes work by: Dou; van Mieris;
Nash; Spencer; Steen.

COVENTRY, HERBERT ART GALLERY
Jordan Well,
Coventry, CV1 5QP
Tel: 024 7683 2381
Fax: 024 7683 2410
Website: www.coventrymuseum.org.uk
Collection includes work by: Constable;
Holman Hunt; Lawrence; Lowry; Nash;
Nicholson; Spencer.

CROFT CASTLE
Near Leominster,
Herefordshire, HR6 9PW
Tel: 01568 780246
Fax: 01568 780462
Website: www.nationaltrust.org.uk
Collection includes work by: Gainsborough;
Lawrence.

DERBY MUSEUM AND ART GALLERY
The Strand,
Derby, DE1 1BS
Tel: 01332 716659
Website: www.derby.gov.uk/museums
Collection includes work by: Lowry; Wright of
Derby.

DODDINGTON HALL
Doddington,
Lincoln, LN6 4RU
Tel: 01522 694308
Fax: 01522 685259
Website:
www.doddingtonhall.free-online.co.uk
Collection includes work by: Sargent.

DUDLEY ART GALLERY
St James' Road,
Dudley, DY1 1HU
Tel: 01384 815575
Fax: 01384 815576
Website: www.dudley.gov.uk/tourism/
dudleymuseum/index.asp
Collection includes work by: Nash.

DUDMASTON HALL
Quatt,
Near Bridgnorth,
Shropshire, WV15 6QN
Tel: 01746 780866
Fax: 01746 780744
Website: www.nationaltrust.org.uk
Collection includes work by: Nicholson.

DYRHAM PARK
Near Chippenham,
Gloucestershire, SN14 8ER
Tel: 01179 372501
Fax: 01179 371353
Website: www.nationaltrust.org.uk
Collection includes work by: Gainsborough;
Murillo.

EASTNOR CASTLE
Ledbury,
Herefordshire, HR8 1RL
Tel: 01531 633160

Website: www.eastnorcastle.co.uk
Collection includes work by: Reynolds.

**GLOUCESTER CITY MUSEUM
AND ART GALLERY**
Brunswick Road,
Gloucester, GL1 1HP
Tel: 01452 524131
Fax: 01452 410898
Website: www.glos-city.gov.uk/libraries/
templates/page.asp?URN=464
Collection includes work by: Gainsborough;
Lawrence; Sickert.

GUNBY HALL
Gunby,
Near Spilsby,
Lincolnshire, PE23 5SS
Tel: 01909 486411
Fax: 01909 486377
Website: www.gunbyhall.ic24.net
Collection includes work by: Reynolds.

GRIMSTHORPE CASTLE
Bourne,
Lincolnshire, PE10 0NB
Tel: 01778 591205
Collection includes work by: Reynolds.

HAGLEY HALL
Hagley,
Worcestershire, DY9 9LG
Tel: 01562 882408
Collection includes work by: Reynolds.

KEDLESTON HALL
Derby, DE22 5JH
Tel: 01332 842191
Fax: 01332 841972
Website: www.nationaltrust.org.uk
Collection includes work by: Cuyp; Reynolds;
Wright of Derby.

KETTERING, ALFRED EAST GALLERY
Sheep Street,
Kettering,
Northamptonshire, NN16 0AN
Tel: 01536 534274
Website: www.kettering.gov.uk/leisure/
cultural/artgallery/index.htm
Collection includes work by: Hodgkin;
Spencer.

**LEAMINGTON SPA ART GALLERY
AND MUSEUM**
Royal Pump Rooms,
The Parade,
Royal Leamington Spa,
Warwickshire, CV31 3PP
Tel: 01926 426559
Website:
www.royal-pump-rooms.co.uk/gallery
Collection includes work by: Lowry; Spencer.

**LEICESTER, NEW WALK MUSEUM AND
ART GALLERY**
53 New Walk,
Leicester, LE1 7FA
Tel: 0116 255 4100
Website: www.leicestermuseums.ac.uk/
museums/newwalk.html
Collection includes work by: Bacon; Peter
Blake; Burne Jones; Carracci; Constable;
Dégas; Hogarth; Lowry; Marc; Nash;
Nicholson; Pissarro; Poussin; Ramsay;
Sargent; Sisley; Sickert; Spencer; de la Tour;
Wright of Derby.

LINCOLN, USHER GALLERY
Lindum Road,
Lincoln, LN2 1NN
Tel: 01522 527980
Fax: 01522 560165
Website: www.lincolnshire.gov.uk/lccconnect/

culturalservices/Heritage/Usher.htm
Collection includes work by: Lowry; Sickert;
Stubbs.

NEWSTEAD ABBEY
Ravenshead,
Nottinghamshire, NG15 8NA
Tel: 01623 455900
Collection includes work by: Reynolds.

NORMANBY HALL
Normanby,
Scunthorpe,
Lincolnshire, DN15 9HU
Tel: 01724 720588
Website: www.northlincs.gov.uk/normanby
Collection includes work by: Lawrence;
Rubens.

**NOTTINGHAM CASTLE MUSEUM
AND ART GALLERY**
The Castle,
Nottingham, NG1 6EL
Tel: 0115 915 3700
Website: www.nottinghamcity.gov.uk/
whatson/museums/castle.asp
Collection includes work by: Brown;
Delacroix; Lowry; Nicholson; Rossetti; Sickert;
Spencer; Wright of Derby.

RAGLEY HALL
Alcester,
Warwickshire, B49 5NJ
Tel: 01789 762090
Fax: 01789 764791
Website: www.ragleyhall.com
Collection includes work by: Lawrence;
Ramsay; Reynolds.

ROCKINGHAM CASTLE
Rockingham,
Market Harborough,
Leicestershire, LE16 87H
Website: www.rockinghamcastle.com
Collection includes work by: Reynolds.

RUGBY ART GALLERY AND MUSEUM
Little Elborow Street,
Rugby,
Warwickshire, CV21 3BZ
Tel: 01788 533201
Fax: 01788 533204
Website: www.rugbygalleryandmuseum.org.uk
Collection includes work by: Lowry; Nash;
Spencer.

SHUGBOROUGH
Milford,
Near Stafford,
Staffordshire, ST17 0XB
Tel: 01889 881388
Website: www.staffordshire.gov.uk/live/
welcome.asp?id=24
Collection includes work by: Reynolds.

STANWAY HOUSE
Near Broadway,
Gloucestershire, GL54 5PQ
Tel: 01386 584469
Website:
www.visitcotswoldsandseveranvale.gov.uk/
attractions/details.asp?place_id=37
Collection includes work by: Raeburn.

**STOKE-ON-TRENT, POTTERIES MUSEUM
AND ART GALLERY**
Bethesda Street,
Hanley,
Stoke on Trent, ST1 3DW
Tel: 01782 232323
Fax: 01782 232500
Website: www.stoke.gov.uk/museums/pmag
Collection includes work by: Lowry; Sickert.

**STRATFORD-UPON-AVON ROYAL
SHAKESPEARE COMPANY COLLECTION**
Waterside,
Stratford-upon-Avon,
Warwickshire, CV37 6BB
Tel: 01789 262870
Collection includes work by: Fuseli; Millais;
Sickert.

SUDELEY CASTLE
Winchcombe,
Cheltenham,
Gloucestershire, GL54 5JD
Tel: 01242 602308
Fax: 01242 602959
Website: www.sudeleycastle.co.uk
Collection includes work by: Constable;
Claude; Reynolds; Ruisdael; Turner.

UPTON HOUSE
Banbury,
Warwickshire, OX15 6HT
Tel: 01295 670266
Website: www.nationaltrust.org.uk
Collection includes work by: Bosch; Boucher;
Bruegel the Elder; Canaletto; van de
Cappelle; Constable; David; Gainsborough;
El Greco; Goya; Hogarth; Holbein the
Younger; Lawrence; Lotto; Memlinc;
Patenier; Raeburn; Reynolds; Ruisdael; van
Saenredam; Schalken; Steen; Stubbs;
Tintoretto; van der Weyden.

WALSALL, NEW ART GALLERY
Gallery Square,
Walsall,
West Midlands, WS2 8LG
Tel: 01922 654400
Fax: 01922 654401
Website: www.artatwalsall.org.uk
Collection includes work by: Bonnard;
Constable; Corot; Dégas; Delaunay; Freud;
Géricault; Monet; Renoir; Reynolds.

WARWICK, WARWICKSHIRE MUSEUM
Market Hall,
Market Place,
Warwick,
Warwickshire, CV34 4SA
Tel: 01926 412500
Website: www.warwick-uk.co.uk/places-of-
interest/warwickshire-museum.asp
Collection includes work by: Ramsay.

**WEDNESBURY MUSEUM
AND ART GALLERY**
Holyhead Road,
Wednesbury,
West Midlands, WS10 7DF
Tel: 0121 556 0683
Website: www.smbc.sandwell.gov.uk/
SandwellDirect/LeisureDirect/Museums.htm
Collection includes work by: Millais.

WESTON PARK
Weston-under-Lizard,
Near Shifnal,
Shropshire, TF11 8LE
Tel: 01952 852100
Website: www.weston-park.com
Collection includes work by: Holbein the
Younger; Reynolds.

WIGHTWICK MANOR
Wightwick Bank,
Wolverhampton,
Staffordshire, WV6 8EE
Tel: 01902 761108
Fax: 01902 764663
Website: www.nationaltrust.org.uk
Collection includes work by: Brown;
Burne Jones; Hunt; Millais.

**WOLVERHAMPTON ART GALLERY
AND MUSEUM**
Lichfield Street,
Wolverhampton,
Staffordshire, WV1 1DU
Tel: 01902 552055
Fax: 01902 552053
Website:
www.scit.wlv.ac.uk/university/sles/gallery
Collection includes work by: Fuseli;
Gainsborough; Raeburn; Warhol; Wright of
Derby.

YORKS AND
HUMBERSIDE

Humberside, North Yorkshire, South
Yorkshire, West Yorkshire

BARNSLEY CANNON HALL MUSEUM
Cawthorne,
Barnsley,
South Yorkshire, S75 4AT
Tel: 01226 790270
Fax: 01226 792117
Website: www.barnsley.gov.uk/tourism/
cannonhall/countryhouse.asp
Collection includes work by: Canaletto; van
de Cappelle; Constable; Hogarth; van Mieris;
van de Velde the Younger.

BENINGBROUGH HALL
Beningbrough,
York, YO30 1DD
Tel: 01904 470666
Fax: 01904 470002
Website: www.npg.org.uk/live/benmenu.asp
Collection includes work by: Gainsborough;
Ramsay.

BRIGHOUSE, SMITH ART GALLERY
Halifax Road,
Brighouse,
West Yorkshire, HD6 2AF
Tel: 01484 719222
Fax: 01484 719222
Website: www.calderdale.gov.uk/ft_tourism/
arts/smith-art.html
Collection includes work by: Millais.

BURTON AGNES HALL
Burton Agnes,
Driffield,
North Yorkshire, YO25 0ND
Tel: 01262 490324
Website: www.burton-agnes.com
Collection includes work by: Bonnard; Cézanne;
Corot; Courbet; Derain; Gainsborough; Gauguin;
Manet; Matisse; Pissarro; Renoir; Sickert;
Vuillard.

CARTWRIGHT HALL
Lister Park,
Bradford,
West Yorkshire, BD9 4NS
Tel: 01274 751212/431212
Fax: 01274 481045
Website: www.bradford.gov.uk
Collection includes work by: Brown; Corot;
Gainsborough; Hockney; Lowry; Nash;
Raeburn; Reynolds; Sargent; Sickert;
Spencer.

CASTLE HOWARD
York,
North Yorkshire, YO60 7DA
Tel: 01653 648444
Fax: 01653 648529
Website: www.castlehoward.co.uk Collection
includes work by: van Dyck; Gainsborough;
Holbein the Younger; Lawrence; Reynolds;
Rosa; Rubens.

DONCASTER ART GALLERY
Chequer Road,
Doncaster,
West Yorkshire, DN1 2AE
Tel: 01302 734293
Fax: 01302 735109
Collection includes work by: Wright of Derby.

HAREWOOD HOUSE
Moorhouse,
Harewood,
Leeds, LS17 9LQ
Tel: 0113 218 1010
Fax: 0113 218 1002
Website: www.harewood.org
Collection includes work by: Bellini; Bordone;
Carracci; Gainsborough; El Greco; Lawrence;
Lotto; Sebastiano del Piombo; Reynolds;
Ribera; Tintoretto; Turner; Veronese.

HARROGATE, MERCER ART GALLERY
Royal Pump Room Museum,
Crown Place,
Harrogate,
North Yorkshire, HR1 2RY
Tel: 01423 556188
Fax: 01423 556130
Website: www.harrogate.gov.uk/museums
Collection includes work by: Nash; Sickert.

HUDDERSFIELD ART GALLERY
Princess Alexandra Walk,
Huddersfield,
West Yorkshire, HD1 2SU
Tel: 01484 221962
Collection includes work by: Bacon; Lowry;
Sickert.

HULL, FERENS ART GALLERY
Queen Victoria Square,
Hull, HU1 3RA
Tel: 01482 613902
Website: www.hullcc.gov.uk/museums/
ferens/index.php
Collection includes work by: Peter Blake;
Canaletto; Constable; Draper; Gysbrechts;
Hals; Hockney; John; Nash; Ribera; Ruisdael;
Sickert; Spencer; Stubbs; van de Velde the
Younger.

HULL, UNIVERSITY ART COLLECTION
The University of Hull,
Cottingham Road,
Hull, HU6 7RX
Tel: 01482 465192
Fax: 01482 465192
Website: www.hull.ac.uk/artcoll
Collection includes work by: Nicholson;
Sickert; Spencer.

LEEDS, CITY ART GALLERY
The Headrow,
Leeds, LS1 3AA
Tel: 0113 247 8248
Fax: 0113 244 9689
Website: www.leeds.gov.uk/artgallery
Collection includes work by: Bacon; Bonnard;
Lady Butler; Constable; Corot; Courbet;
Derain; Frost; Holman Hunt; John; Kramer;
Lawrence; Lowry; Millais; Nash; Nicholson;
Rego; Renoir; Riley; Sickert; Sisley; Spencer;
Vuillard; Whistler.

LEEDS, UNIVERSITY GALLERY
Parkinson Building,
Woodhouse Lane,
Leeds, LS2 9JT
Tel: 0113 343 2777
Fax: 0113 343 5561
Website: www.leeds.ac.uk/gallery
Collection includes work by: Fuseli; Sargent.

NOSTELL PRIORY
Doncaster Road,

Nostell,
Wakefield,
West Yorkshire, WF4 1QE
Tel: 01924 863892
Fax: 01924 865282
Website: www.nationaltrust.org.uk
Collection includes work by: Breughel;
Claude; Hogarth; van Mieris; Ruisdael.

ROCHDALE ART GALLERY
Touchstones,
Esplanade, Rochdale,
West Yorkshire, OL16 1AQ
Tel: 01706 342154
Website: www.visitrochdale.com/Leisure
Collection includes work by: Constable;
Freud; Lowry; Giovanni di Paolo; Sickert;
Spencer.

SEWERBY HALL
Church Lane,
Sewerby,
Bridlington,
Yorkshire, YO15 1EA
Tel: 01262 673769
Collection includes work by: Reynolds.

SHEFFIELD CITY ART GALLERIES
Surrey Street,
Sheffield, S1 1XZ,
Tel: 0114 278 2600
Fax: 0114 273 4705
Website: www.sheffieldgalleries.org.uk/
coresite/html/graves.asp
Collection includes work by: Burne-Jones;
Cézanne; Corot; Courbet; Holman Hunt; John;
Lawrence; Lowry; Murillo; Nash; Nicholson;
Sargent; Sickert; Spencer; Turner; Wright of
Derby.

SHEFFIELD MAPPIN ART GALLERY
Weston Park,
Sheffield, S10 2TP
Tel: 0114 276 2600
Fax: 0114 275 0957
Website: www.sheffieldgalleries.org.uk/
coresite/html/mappingallery.asp
Collection includes work by: Millais.

TEMPLE NEWSAM HOUSE
Temple Newsam Road,
Off Selby Road,
Leeds, LS15 0AE
Tel: 0113 264 7321
Website: www.leeds.gov.uk/templenewsam
Collection includes work by: Canaletto;
Reynolds; Ruisdael; Stubbs; Wright of Derby.

WHITBY, CAPTAIN COOK MEMORIAL MUSEUM
John Walker's House,
Grape Lane,
Whitby,
North Yorkshire, YO22 4BA
Tel: 01947 601900
Fax: 01947 601900
Website: www.cookmuseumwhitby.co.uk
Collection includes work by: Gainsborough.

WAKEFIELD ART GALLERY
Wentworth Terrace,
Wakefield,
West Yorkshire, WF1 3QW
Tel: 01924 305796
Fax: 01924 305770
Website: www.wakefield.gov.uk/community/
museumsarts
Collection includes work by: Lowry;
Nicholson; Sickert.

YORK ART GALLERY
Exhibition Square,
York, YO1 7EW
Tel: 01904 551861

Fax: 01904 551866
Website:
www.york.gov.uk/heritage/museums/art
Collection includes work by: Burra; Courbet;
Fuseli; Hockney; Hogarth; John; Lowry; van
Mieris; Murillo; Nash; Parmigianino; Reynolds;
del Sarto; Sickert; Spencer; Tiepolo; Turner;
Palma Vecchio.

NORTH WEST

Cheshire, Cumbria, Lancashire, Greater
Manchester, Merseyside

BIRKENHEAD, WILLIAMSON ART GALLERY
Slatey Road,
Birkenhead,
Merseyside, CH43 4UE
Tel: 0151 652 4177
Website: www.wirral-libraries.net/
info/artgall.htm
Collection includes work by: Raeburn.

BLACKBURN MUSEUM AND ART GALLERY
Museum Street,
Blackburn,
Lancashire, BB1 7AJ
Tel: 01254 667130
Fax: 01254 695370
Website: http://council.blackburnworld.com/
services/museum/index.htm
Collection includes work by: Lawrence;
Reynolds

BLACKPOOL, GRUNDY ART GALLERY
Queen Street,
Blackpool,
Lancashire, FY1 1PX
Tel: 01253 478170
Fax: 01253 478172
Website: www.blackpool.gov.uk
Collection includes work by: Nash.

BOLTON MUSEUM AND ART GALLERY
Le Mans Crescent,
Bolton,
Lancashire, BL1 1SE
Tel: 01204 332211
Fax: 01204 332241
Website: www.boltonmuseums.org.uk
Collection includes work by: Millais; Moran;
Sickert.

BURY ART GALLERY
Moss Street,
Bury,
Lancashire, BL9 0DR
Tel: 0161 253 5878
Fax: 0161 253 5915
Website: www.bury.gov.uk/culture/gallery.html
Collection includes work by: Constable;
Lowry; Symons; Turner.

CAPESTHORNE HALL
Siddington,
Macclesfield,
Cheshire, SK11 9JY
Tel: 01625 861221
Fax: 01625 861619
Website: www.capesthorne.com
Collection includes work by: Lowry.

DUNHAM MASSEY
Altrincham,
Cheshire, WA14 4SJ
Tel: 0161 941 1025
Fax: 0161 929 7508
Website: www.nationaltrust.org.uk
Collection includes work by: Guercino;
Reynolds; Wright of Derby.

GAWTHORPE HALL
Padiham,
Near Burnley,
Lancashire, BB12 8UA
Tel: 01282 771004
Fax: 01282 770178
Website: www.nationaltrust.org.uk
Collection includes work by: Raeburn; Wright
of Derby.

GRASMERE, THE WORDSWORTH TRUST
Dove Cottage, Grasmere,
Cumbria, LA22 9SH
Tel: 01539 435544
Fax: 01539 435748
Website: www.wordsworth.org.uk
Collection includes work by: Wright of Derby.

HOLKER HALL
Cark in Gartmel,
Grange over Sands,
Cumbria, LA11 7PL
Tel: 01539 558328
Collection includes work by: Reynolds.

KENDAL, ABBOT HALL ART GALLERY
Kendal,
Cumbria, LA9 5AL
Tel: 01539 722464
Fax: 01539 722494
Website: www.abbothall.org.uk
Collection includes work by: Freud;
Lawrence; Nicholson; Riley; Romney.

LEVENS HALL
Kendal,
Cumbria, LA8 0PD
Tel: 01539 560321
Fax: 01539 560669
Website: www.levenshall.co.uk
Collection includes work by: Rubens.

LIVERPOOL, TATE
Albert Dock,
Liverpool, L3 4BB
Tel: 0151 702 7401
Fax: 0151 702 7401
Website: www.tate.org.uk/liverpool
Collection includes work by various artists
from the Tate Collections.

LIVERPOOL, UNIVERSITY ART GALLERY
6 Abercromby Square,
Liverpool, L69 7WY
Tel: 0151 794 2348
Fax: 0151 794 2343
Website: www.liv.ac.uk/artgall/gallery.htm
Collection includes work by: Freud; Turner;
Wright of Derby.

LIVERPOOL, WALKER
William Brown Street,
Liverpool, L3 8EL
Tel: 0151 478 4199
Website: www.nmgm.org.uk
Collection includes work by: Bassano; Brett;
Brown; Burne Jones; Cézanne; Constable;
Courbet; Cranach the Elder; Dégas;
Delaroche; Derain; van Dyck; Elsheimer;
Fabritius; Freud; Fuseli; Gainsborough;
Hilliard; Hockney; Hogarth; Holman Hunt;
Lowry; Martini; Matisse; Michelangelo; Millais;
Monet; Murillo; Nash; Nicholson; Poussin;
Raeburn; Ramsay; Raphael; Rembrandt;
Reynolds; de'Roberti; Rosa; Rossetti; Rubens;
Sargent; Seurat; Stubbs; Turner; Veronese;
Vuillard; Waterhouse; Watts; West; Wright of
Derby; Yeames.

LYME PARK
Disley,
Stockport,
Cheshire, SK12 2NX
Tel: 01663 762023

Fax: 01663 765035
Website: www.nationaltrust.org.uk
Collection includes work by: Sargent.

LYTHAM ST ANNE'S TOWN HALL
South Promenade,
Lytham St Anne's,
Lancashire, FY8 1LW
Tel: 01253 721222
Fax: 01253 713754
Website: www.fylde.gov.uk
Collection includes work by: Fuseli.

MANCHESTER CITY ART GALLERY
Mosley Street,
Manchester, M2 3JL
Tel: 0161 234 1456
Fax: 0161 235 8899
Website: www.manchestergalleries.org
Collection includes work by: Bacon; William
Blake; Boucher; Brown; Burne Jones; van de
Cappelle; Caulfield; Claude; Constable; Corot;
Courbet; Cuyp; De Hooch; Derain; Dou; Duccio;
van Dyck; Ernst; Fragonard; Freud;
Gainsborough; Gauguin; Giacometti; van
Heemskerck; Hobbema; Hodgkin; Hogarth;
Holman Hunt; John; Kalf; Léger; Lowry;
Millais; Nash; Nevinson; Nicholson; Palmer;
Pissarro; Raeburn;
Renoir; Reynolds; Riley; Rossetti Ruisdael;
Sargent; Seurat; Sickert; Spencer; Steen;
Stubbs; Terborch; Turner;
Wright of Derby.

MANCHESTER TOWN HALL
Albert Square,
Manchester, M60 2LA
Tel: 0161 234 5000
Website: www.manchester.gov.uk
Collection includes work by: Brown.

MANCHESTER, WHITWORTH ART GALLERY
University of Manchester,
Oxford Road,
Manchester, M15 6ER
Tel: 0161 275 7450
Fax: 0161 275 7451
Website: www.whitworth.man.ac.uk
Collection includes work by: Bacon; Peter
Blake; Brown; de Chirico; Constable; Corot;
Freud; Hobbema; Hodgkin; Lawrence; Lowry;
Pissarro; Riley; Sickert; Spencer; Watts.

MUNCASTER CASTLE
Ravenglass,
Cumbria, CA18 1RQ
Tel: 01229 717614
Website: www.muncastercastle.co.uk
Collection includes work by: Reynolds

OLDHAM GALLERY
Greaves Street,
Oldham,
Greater Manchester, OL1 1AL
Tel: 0161 911 4657
Fax: 0161 911 4669
Website: www.galleryoldham.org.uk/
Collection includes work by: Hodgkin; Lowry;
Millais; Sickert

PORT SUNLIGHT, LADY LEVER ART GALLERY
Port Sunlight Village,
Bebington,
Wirral,
Merseyside, L62 5EQ
Tel: 0151 478 4136
Fax: 0151 478 4140
Website: www.nmgm.org.uk
Collection includes work by: Alma-Tadema;
Brown; Burne Jones; Constable;
Gainsborough; Holman Hunt; Lawrence;
Millais; Ramsay; Reynolds; Rossetti; Sargent;
Stubbs; Turner; Vigée Lebrun

PRESTON, HARRIS MUSEUM AND ART GALLERY
Market Square,
Preston,
Lancashire, PR1 2PP
Tel: 01772 258248
Website: www.visitpreston.com/whats_on/
museums/harris.htm
Collection includes work by: Freud; Holman
Hunt; Lowry; Sickert; Spencer.

PRESTON, MUSEUM OF LANCASHIRE
Stanley Street,
Preston,
Lancashire, PR1 4YP
Tel: 01772 264075
Fax: 01722 264079
Website: www.lancashire.gov.uk/education/
lifelong/museums/mol.html
Collection includes work by: Wright of Derby.

SALFORD MUSEUM AND ART GALLERY
Peel Park,
Salford, M5 4WU
Tel: 0161 736 2649
Fax: 0161 745 9490
Collection includes work by: Sickert.

SALFORD, THE LOWRY
Pier 8,
Salford Quays, M50 3AZ
Tel: 0161 876 2020
Fax: 0161 876 2021
Website: www.thelowry.com
Collection includes work by: Lowry.

SOUTHPORT, ATKINSON ART GALLERY
Lord Street,
Southport,
Merseyside, PR8 1DH
Tel: 0151 934 2110
Fax: 0151 934 2109
Collection includes work by: Lowry; Sickert.

STALEYBRIDGE, ASTLEY CHEETHAM ART GALLERY
Trinity Street,
Stalybridge,
Cheshire, SK15 2BN
Tel: 0161 338 6767
Website: www.tameside.gov.uk/
museumsandgalleries/astleycheetham.html
Collection includes work by: Burne Jones.

STOCKTON-ON-TEES, PRESTON HALL MUSEUM
Yarm Road,
Stockton-on-Tees,
Cleveland, TS3 3RH
Tel: 01642 781184
Fax: 01642 788107
Collection includes work by: de la Tour.

STOCKPORT ART GALLERY
Wellington Road South,
Stockport,
Greater Manchester, SK3 8AB
Tel: 0161 474 4453/4454
Fax: 0161 480 4960
Website: www.stockport.gov.uk
Collection includes work by: Lowry.

SUDLEY HOUSE
Mossley Hill Road,
Liverpool, L18 8BX
Tel: 0151 724 3245
Website: www.nmgm.org.uk
Collection includes work by: Corot;
Gainsborough; Holman Hunt; Lawrence;
Millais; Raeburn; Reynolds; Rossetti; Turner.

TABLEY HOUSE
Knutsford,
Cheshire, WA16 0HB

Tel: 01565 750151
Fax: 01565 653230
Website: www.tableyhouse.co.uk
Collection includes work by: Fuseli;
Lawrence; Reynolds.

TATTON PARK
Knutsford,
Cheshire, WA16 6QN
Tel: 01625 534400
Fax: 01625 534403
Website: www.tattonpark.org.uk
Collection includes work by: Canaletto;
Carracci; Chardin; van Dyck; Guercino;
Lawrence; Poussin; Rosa; van de Velde the
Younger.

TOWNELEY HALL
Towneley Park,
Off Todmorden Road,
Burnley,
Lancashire, BB11 3RQ
Tel: 01282 424213
Fax: 01282 436138
Website: www.towneleyhall.org.uk
Collection includes work by: Burne Jones;
Constable; Zoffany.

NORTH

Durham, Northumberland, Teeside, Tyne and
Wear

ALNWICK CASTLE
Alnwick,
Northumberland, NE66 1NQ
Tel: 01665 510777
Fax: 01665 510876
Website: www.alnwickcastle.com
Collection includes work by: Canaletto; van
Dyck; Lotto; Sebastiano del Piombo;
Reynolds; del Sarto; Tintoretto; Titian; Palma
Vecchio.

AUCKLAND CASTLE
Bishop Auckland,
County Durham, DL14 7NR
Tel: 01388 601627
Fax: 01388609323
Website: www.auckland-castle.co.uk
Collection includes work by: Zurbaran.

**BERWICK-UPON-TWEED BOROUGH
MUSEUM AND ART GALLERY**
The Barracks, The Parade,
Berwick-upon-Tweed,
Northumberland, TD15 1DQ
Tel: 01289 301869
Collection includes work by: Dégas; Raeburn;
Ramsay.

BARNARD CASTLE BOWES MUSEUM
Barnard Castle,
County Durham, DL12 8NP
Tel: 01833 690606
Fax: 01833 637163
Website: www.bowesmuseum.org.uk
Collection includes work by: Boucher;
Canaletto; Corot; Courbet; Fragonard;
Gainsborough; Goya;
El Greco; van Heemskerck; Ramsay;
Reynolds; Sassetta; Tiepolo

**CARLISLE TULLIE HOUSE MUSEUM AND
ART GALLERY**
Castle Street,
Carlisle, Cumbria, CA3 8TP
Tel: 01228 534781
Fax: 01228 810249
Website: www.tulliehouse.co.uk
Collection includes work by: Brown; Burne
Jones; Rossetti.

GATESHEAD SHIPLEY ART GALLERY
Prince Consort Road,
Gateshead,
Tyne and Wear, NE8 4JB
Tel: 0191 477 1495
Fax: 0191 478 7917
Website: www.twmuseums.org.uk
Collection includes work by: ter Brugghen;
Tintoretto.

HARTLEPOOL, GRAY ART GALLERY
Sir William Gray House,
Clarence Road,
Hartlepool,
Cleveland, TS24 8BT
Tel: 01429 523438
Fax: 01429 523477
Website: www.destinationhartlepool.co.uk
Collection includes work by: Freud.

MIDDLESBROUGH ART GALLERY
320 Linthorpe Road,
Middlesbrough,
Cleveland, TS1 3QY
Tel: 01642 247445
Fax: 01642 358138
Collection includes work by: Lowry

NEWCASTLE, HATTON GALLERY
The Quadrangle,
University of Newcastle upon Tyne,
Newcastle upon Tyne, NE1 7RU
Tel: 0191 222 6059
Fax: 191 222 6059
Website: www.ncl.ac.uk/hatton
Collection includes work by: Bacon; Rosa.

NEWCASTLE, LAING ART GALLERY
New Bridge Street,
Newcastle upon Tyne, NE1 8AG
Tel: 0191 232 7734
Fax: 0191 222 0952
Website: www.twmuseums.org.uk
Collection includes work by: Burne Jones;
Constable; Gauguin; Holman Hunt; Lawrence;
Lowry; Martin; Nash; Nicholson; Raeburn;
Ramsay; Reynolds; Sargent; Sickert; Spencer;
Wright of Derby.

RABY CASTLE
Staindrop,
County Durham, DL2 3AH
Tel: 01833 660202
Website: www.rabycastle.co.uk
Collection includes work by: Reynolds.

**SUNDERLAND MUSEUM AND
WINTER GARDENS**
Burden Road,
Sunderland,
Tyne and Wear, SR1 1PP
Tel: 0191 553 2323
Fax: 0191 553 7828
Website: www.twmuseums.org.uk
Collection includes work by: Lowry.

WALLINGTON
Cambo,
Morpeth,
Northumberland, NE61 4AR
Tel: 01670 773600
Fax: 01670 774420
Website: www.nationaltrust.org.uk
Collection includes work by: Gainsborough;
Reynolds.

SCOTLAND

ABERDEEN ART GALLERY
Schoolhill,
Aberdeen, AB10 1FQ

Tel: 01224 523700
Fax: 01224 632133
Website: www.aberdeencity.gov.uk
Collection includes work by: Bacon; Bonnard;
Brown; Courbet; Hogarth; Holman Hunt; van
Honthorst; John; Léger; Lowry; Millais;
Monet; Nash; Nicholson; Raeburn; Ramsay;
Renoir; Reynolds; Rossetti; Sargent;
Segantini; Sickert; Sisley; Spencer; Toulouse-
Lautrec; Vuillard.

ABBOTSFORD
Melrose,
Roxburghshire, TD6 9BQ
Tel: 01896 752043
Fax: 01896 752916
Website: www.melrose.bordernet.co.uk
Collection includes work by: Raeburn.

ARNISTON HOUSE
Gorebridge,
Midlothian, EH23 4RY
Tel: 01875 830 515
Website: www.arniston-house.co.uk
Collection includes work by: Reynolds.

BLAIR CASTLE
Blair Athol,
Pitlochry,
Perthshire, PH18 5TI
Tel: 01796 481207
Website: www.blair-castle.co.uk
Collection includes work by: Lawrence; van
Honthorst.

BOWHILL
Selkirk,
Borders, TD7 5ET
Tel: 01750 22204
Fax: 01750 22204
Website: www.heritageontheweb.org and
www.bowhill.org
Collection includes work by: Claude;
Canaletto; Gainsborough; Raeburn; Reynolds.

BRODICK CASTLE
Brodick,
Isle of Arran, KA27 8HY
Tel: 01770 302202
Fax: 01770 302312
Website:
www.nts.org.uk/properties_frmset.htm
Collection includes work by: Dou; Fragonard;
Gainsborough; Watteau.

BRODIE CASTLE
Brodie, Forres,
Moray, IV36 2TE
Tel: 01309 641371
Fax: 01309 641600
Website:
www.nts.org.uk/properties_frmset.htm
Collection includes work by: Dou.

CASTLE FRASER
Sauchen, Inverurie,
Aberdeenshire, AB51 7LD
Tel: 01330 833463
Fax: 01330 833819
Website:
www.nts.org.uk/properties_frmset.htm
Collection includes work by: Raeburn.

CAWDOR CASTLE
Nairn, IV12 5RD
Tel: (01667) 404615
Fax: (01667) 404674
Website: www.cawdorcastle.com
Collection includes work by: Reynolds.

CRAIGIEVAR CASTLE
Alford,
Aberdeenshire, AB33 8JS
Tel: 01339 883635

Fax: 01339 883280
Website:
www.nts.org.uk/properties_frmset.htm
Collection includes work by: Raeburn.

CULZEAN CASTLE
Maybole,
Ayrshire, KA19 8LE
Tel: 01655 884455
Fax: 01655 884503
Website:
www.nts.org.uk/properties_frmset.htm
Collection includes work by: van Dyck; van
de Velde the Younger.

DALMENY HOUSE
South Queensferry,
EH30 9TQ
Tel: +44/ (0)131 331 1888
Fax: +44/ (0)131 331 1788
website: www.dalmeny.co.uk
Collection includes work by: Reynolds.

DRUMLANRIG CASTLE
Near Thornhill,
Dumfries & Galloway, DG3 4AQ
Tel: 01848 330248
Fax: 01848 331682
Website: www.drumlanrigcastle.org.uk
Collection includes work by: Cuyp; van Dyck;
Gainsborough; Holbein; Murillo; Ramsay;
Rembrandt; Reynolds; Ruisdael.

DUNROBIN CASTLE
Golspie,
Sutherland, KW10 6SF
Tel: 01408 633177
Fax: 01408 634081
Collection includes work by: Reynolds.

DUNDEE MCMANUS GALLERIES
Albert Square,
Dundee, DD1 1DA
Tel: 01382 432084
Fax: 01382 432052
Website: www.dundeecity.gov.uk/mcmanus
Collection includes work by: Millais; Raeburn;
Ramsay; Rossetti; Sargent; Sickert; Spencer.

**EDINBURGH, NATIONAL GALLERY OF
SCOTLAND (ROYAL SCOTTISH ACADEMY)**
The Mound,
Edinburgh, EH2 2EL
Tel: 0131 624 6509
Fax: 0131 220 0917
Website: www.nationalgalleries.org
Collection includes work by: Avercamp;
Bassano; Bordon; Botticelli; Boucher;
Cézanne; Chardin; Claude; Constable; Corot;
Correggio; Courbet; Cranach the Elder; Cuyp;
Daddi; David; Dégas; Delacroix; Dou; Dyce;
van Dyck; El Greco; Elsheimer; Gainsborough;
Gauguin; van Gogh; van der Goes; Goya;
Guercino; Hals; Hobbema; Lippi; Lotto;
Massys; Millais; Monet; Murillo; Perugino;
Pissarro; Poussin; Raeburn; Ramsay;
Raphael; Rembrandt; Renoir; Reynolds; Rosa;
Rossetti; Rubens; Ruisdael; Sargent; Seurat;
Sisley; Steen; Tiepolo; Tintoretto; Titian;
Turner; Velázquez; van de Velde the
Younger; Vermeer; Veronese; del Verrocchio;
Watteau; Whistler; Zurbaran.

**EDINBURGH, SCOTTISH NATIONAL
GALLERY OF MODERN ART**
75 Belford Road,
Edinburgh, EH4 3DR
Tel: 0131 624 6326
Fax: 0131 343 2802
Website: www.nationalgalleries.org
Collection includes work by: Bacon; Bonnard;
Bordone; Braque; Dalí; Delaunay; Derain; Dix;
Ernst; Freud; El Grecco; Hockney; Hodgkin;
Holbein; John; Kirchner; Klee; Léger;

Lichtenstein; Lowry; Magritte; Matisse; Miró;
Mondrian; Morandi; Nash; Nicholson; Nolde;
Picasso; Pollock; Sickert; Spencer; Vuillard;
Warhol.

**EDINBURGH, SCOTTISH NATIONAL
PORTRAIT GALLERY**
1 Queen Street,
Edinburgh, EH2 1JD
Tel: 0131 624 6401
Fax: 0131 558 3691
Website: www.nationalgalleries.org
Collection includes work by: van Dyck;
Gainsborough; Raeburn; Ramsay; Reynolds;
Sargent.

EDINBURGH, TALBOT RICE GALLERY
University of Edinburgh,
Old College,
South Bridge,
Edinburgh, EH8 9YL
Tel: 0131 650 2210
Fax: 0131 650 2213
Website: www.trg.ed.ac.uk
Collection includes work by: Hobbema;
Raeburn; Rosa; Ruisdael; Steen; Veronese.

FLOORS CASTLE
Kelso,
Roxburghshire, TD5 7SF
Tel: 01573 223333
Fax: 01573 226056
Website: www.floorscastle.com
Collection includes work by: Bonnard;
Gainsborough; Matisse; Raeburn; Ramsay;
Reynolds; Ruisdael; van de Velde the
Younger.

FORFAR MUSEUM AND ART GALLERY
Meffan Institute,
20 West High Street,
Forfar,
Angus, DD8 1BB
Tel: 01307 464123
Website: www.angus.gov.uk
Collection includes work by: Raeburn.

FYVIE CASTLE
Fyvie,
Aberdeenshire, AB53 8JS
Tel: 01651 891266
Fax: 01651 891107
Website:
www.nts.org.uk/properties_frmset.htm
Collection includes work by: Batoni;
Gainsborough; Lawrence; Millais; Raeburn;
Reynolds; Vigée Lebrun.

GLASGOW ART GALLERY AND MUSEUM
Kelvingrove,
Glasgow, G3 8AG
Tel: 0141 287 2699
Fax: 0141 287 2690
Collection includes work by: Bellini; Bonnard;
Bordone; Botticelli; Braque; Brown; Jan
Brueghel I; Burne Jones; Cassatt; Constable;
Corot; Courbet; Cuyp; Delacroix; Derain;
Gauguin; Giorgione; van Gogh; Hobbema;
Kalf; Lippi (Filippino); Lowry; Matisse; van
Mieris; Millais; Monet; Murillo; Nash;
Nicholson; Picasso; Pissarro; Raeburn;
Ramsay; Rembrandt; Renoir; Reynolds;
Ribera; Rosa; Rossetti; Rubens; Ruisdael;
Saenredam; Sargent; Seurat; Sickert; Sisley;
Spencer; Tintoretto; Turner; Vecchio;
Vuillard; Whistler.

GLASGOW, BURRELL COLLECTION
2060 Pollokshaws Road,
Glasgow, G43 1AT
Tel: 0141 6497151
Fax: 0141 287 2597
Website: www.glasgow.gov.uk
Collection includes work by: Bellini; Cézanne;

Chardin; Corot; Courbet; Cranach the Elder; Daumier; Dégas; Delacroix; Gainsborough; Géricault; Gossaert; Hals; Manet; Memlinc; Raeburn; Ramsay; Rembrandt; Renoir; Reynolds; Ribera; Sisley; Vuillard; Whistler.

GLASGOW GALLERY OF MODERN ART
Queen Street,
Glasgow, G1 3AZ
Tel: 0141 229 1996
Fax: 0141 204 5316
Collection includes work by: Howson; McFadyen; Riley.

GLASGOW, POLLOK HOUSE
2060 Pollokshaws Road,
Glasgow, G43 1AT
Tel: 0141 649 7151
Fax: 0141 616 6521
Website:
www.nts.org.uk/properties_frmset.htm
Collection includes work by: William Blake; Goya; El Greco; Sebastiano del Piombo; Murillo; Steen.

GLASGOW, ST MUNGO'S GALLERY
2 Castle Street,
Glasgow, G4 0RH
Tel: 0141 552 5523
Collection includes work by: Dalí.

GLASGOW, HUNTERIAN ART GALLERY
University of Glasgow,
Hillhead Street,
Glasgow, G12 8QQ
Tel: 0141 330 5431
Fax: 0141 330 3618
Website: www.hunterian.gla.ac.uk
Collection includes work by: Chardin; Murillo; Raeburn; Ramsay; Rembrandt; Reynolds; Rosa; Rubens; Sickert; Steen; Stubbs; Whistler.

GOSFORD HOUSE
Longniddry,
East Lothian,
EH23 0PX
Tel : 01875 870 201
Collection includes work by: Reynolds.

GREENOCK, McLEAN MUSEUM AND ART GALLERY
15 Kelly Street,
Greenock,
Strathclyde, PA16 8JX
Tel: 01475 715624
Fax: 01475 715626
Website:
www.inverclyde.gov.uk/museum/index.htm
Collection includes work by: Corot; Raeburn; Ramsay.

HADDO HOUSE
Ellon,
Aberdeenshire, AB41 7EQ
Tel: 01651 851440
Fax: 01651
Website:
www.nts.org.uk/properties_frmset.htm
Collection includes work by: Lawrence; Raeburn.

HILL OF TARVIT
Cupar,
Fife, KY15 5PB
Tel: 01334 653127
Fax: 01334 653127
Website:
www.nts.org.uk/properties_frmset.htm
Collection includes work by: Claesz; Cuyp; Raeburn; Ramsay.

INVERARAY CASTLE
Inveraray, Argyll,

PA32 8XE.
Tel: 01499 302203
Fax: 01499 30242
Website: www.inveraray-castle.com
Collection includes work by: Reynolds.

INVERNESS MUSEUM AND ART GALLERY
Castle Wynd,
Inverness, IV2 3EB
Tel: 01463 237114
Fax: 01463 225293
Website: www.highland.gov.uk
Collection includes work by: Turner.

KILMARNOCK, DICK INSTITUTE
Elmbank Avenue,
Kilmarnock,
Ayrshire, KA1 3BU
Tel: 01563 554300
Fax: 01563 554311
Website: www.east-ayrshire.gov.uk/internet/frames/community.htm
Collection includes work by: Corot; Millais; Raeburn.

KIRKCALDY MUSEUM AND ART GALLERY
War Memorial Gardens,
Kirkcaldy,
Fife, KY1 1YG
Tel: 01592 412860
Fax: 01592 412870
Website:
Collection includes work by: Lowry; Raeburn; Sickert.

LEITH HALL
Huntly,
Aberdeenshire, AB54 4NQ
Tel: 01464 831216
Website:
www.nts.org.uk/properties_frmset.htm
Collection includes work by: Ramsay; Ribera.

LEITH, TRINITY HOUSE MUSEUM
99 Kirkgate,
Leith, Edinburgh,
Midlothian, EH6 6BJ
Tel: 0131 554 3289
Collection includes work by: Reynolds.

NEWHAILES
Musselburgh,
East Lothian, EH21 6RY
Tel: 0131 665 1546
Fax: 0131 653 5597
Website:
www.nts.org.uk/properties_frmset.htm
Collection includes work by: Ramsay.

PAISLEY MUSEUM AND ART GALLERIES
High Street,
Paisley,
Renfrewshire, PA1 2BA
Tel: 0141 889 3151
Fax: 0141 889 9240
Website: www.renfrewshire.gov.uk
Collection includes work by: Corot; Courbet; Raeburn; Ramsay; Sickert

PAXTON HOUSE
Berwick upon Tweed,
TD15 1SZ
Tel: 01289 386291
Fax:01289 386660
website: www.paxtonhouse.com
Collection includes work by: Reynolds.

PERTH MUSEUM AND ART GALLERY
George Street,
Perth,
Perthshire, PH1 5LB
Tel: 01738 632488
Fax: 01738 443505
Website:

www.pkc.gov.uk/ah/perth_museum.htm
Collection includes work by: Courbet; Lawrence; Millais; Raeburn.

SCONE PALACE
Scone,
Perthshire, PH2 6BD
Tel: 01738 552300
Fax: 01738 552588
Website: www.scone-palace.co.uk
Collection includes work by: Ramsay; Reynolds.

STIRLING, SMITH ART GALLERY AND MUSEUM
40 Albert Place,
Dumbarton Road,
Stirling, FK8 2RQ
Tel: 01786 471917
Fax: 01786 449523
Collection includes work by: Reynolds.

STROMNESS, PIER ARTS CENTRE
28-30 Victoria Street,
Stromness,
Orkney, KW16 3AA
Tel: 01856 850209
Fax: 01856 851462
Website: www.stir.ac.uk/town/smith/
Collection includes work by: Nicholson.

WALES

ABERYSTWYTH, NATIONAL LIBRARY OF WALES
Aberystwyth,
Ceredigion, SY23 3BU
Tel: 01970 632800
Fax: 01970 615709
Website: www.llgc.org.uk
Collection includes work by: Turner.

ABERYSTWYTH SCHOOL OF ART GALLERY AND MUSEUM
The University of Wales, Buarth Mawr
Aberystwyth,
Ceredigion, SY23 1NE
Tel: 01970 622460
Fax: 01970 622461
Website: www.aber.ac.uk/art
Collection includes work by: Wright of Derby.

BODELWYDDON CASTLE
Bodelwyddan, Rhyl,
Denbighshire, LL18 5YA
Tel: 01745 584060
Fax: 01745 584563
Website: www.bodelwyddan-castle.co.uk
Collection includes work by: Ford Maddox Brown; Hunt; Millais; Sargent.

BRECON, BRECKNOCK MUSEUM
Captain's Walk,
Brecon,
Powys, LD3 7DW
Tel: 01874 624121
Fax: 01874 611281
Website: www.powys.gov.uk
Collection includes work by: Jones.

CARDIFF, NATIONAL MUSEUM OF WALES
Cathays Park,
Cardiff, CF1 3NP
Tel: 029 20 397951
Fax: 029 20 573351
Website: www.nmgw.ac.uk
Collection includes work by: Bacon; Bonnard; Botticelli; Brown; Burne Jones; Canaletto; van de Cappelle; Cézanne; Claude; Constable; Corot; Courbet; Cuyp; Daumier; Derain; van Dyck; El Greco; Ford Maddox Brown; Freud; Fuseli; Gainsborough; van Gogh; Guercino;

Hockney; Hogarth; John; Jones; Magritte; Manet; Millais; Monet; Nicholson; Palmer; Pissarro; Poussin; Raeburn; Renoir; Reynolds; Ribera; Richards; Rosa; Rossetti; Rubens; Sargent; Sickert; Sisley; Spencer; Watteau; Whistler; Wilson.

CHIRK CASTLE
Chirk,
Wrexham, LL14 5AF
Tel: 01691 777701
Fax: 01691 774706
Website: www.nationaltrust.org.uk
Collection includes work by: Ramsay.

ERDDIG
Wrexham, LL13 0YT
Tel: 01978 355314
Fax: 01978 313333
Website: www.nationaltrust.org.uk
Collection includes work by: Gainsborough.

FONMON CASTLE
Barry,
South Glamorgan, CF62 3ZN
Phone: 01446 710206
Fax: 01446 711687
Collection includes work by: Reynolds.

NEWPORT MUSEUM AND ART GALLERY
John Frost Square,
Newport,
Gwent, NP9 1PA
Tel: 01633 840064
Fax: 01633 222615
Website: www.newport.uk
Collection includes work by: Lowry; Spencer.

PENRHYN CASTLE
Bangor, LL57 4HN
Tel: 01248 353084
Fax: 01248 371281
Website: www.nationaltrust.org.uk
Collection includes work by: Bouts; Canaletto; Gainsborough; Rembrandt; Steen.

PLAS NEWYDD
Llanfairpwll,
Anglesey, LL61 6DQ
Tel: 01248 714795
Website: www.nationaltrust.org.uk
Collection includes work by: van Dyck; Lawrence.

POWIS CASTLE
Welshpool, SY21 8RF
Tel: 01938 554338
Website: www.nationaltrust.org.uk
Collection includes work by: Gainsborough; Reynolds.

SWANSEA, GLYNN VIVIAN ART GALLERY
Alexandra Road,
Swansea, SA2 5DZ
Tel: 01792 655006/651738
Fax: 01792 651713
Website: www.swansea.gov.uk
Collection includes work by: Constable; John; Jones; Lawrence; Monet; Nash; Sickert; Spencer.

TENBY MUSEUM AND ART GALLERY
Castle Hill,
Tenby,
Pembrokeshire, SA70 7BP
Tel: 01834 842809
Fax: 01834 842809
Website: www.tenbymuseum.free-online.co.uk
Collection includes work by: John.

NORTHERN IRELAND

BELFAST ULSTER MUSEUM
Botanic Gardens,
Belfast, BT9 5AB
Tel: 028 9038 3000
Fax: 028 9038 3003
Website: www.ulstermuseum.org.uk
Collection includes work by: Bacon; Gainsborough; Howard; Jordaens; Lawrence; Lowry; Nash; Nicholson; Reynolds; Sickert; Turner; Wright of Derby.

MOUNT STEWART HOUSE
Newtownards,
County Down, BT22 2AD
Tel. 028 4278 8387/8487
Fax: 028 4278 8569
Website: www.nationaltrust.org.uk
Collection includes work by: Lawrence; Stubbs.

JERSEY

JERSEY MUSEUM
The Weighbridge,
St Helier,
Jersey, JE2 3NF
Tel: 01534 633300
Fax: 01534 633301
Website: www.jerseyheritagetrust.org
Collection includes work by: Millais.

INDEX

Entries in *Italics* refer to titles of paintings

A

Alma-Tadema, Lawrence
In the Tepidarium 134
Altdorfer, Albrecht 147
Christ Taking Leave of His Mother 147
Andrea del Sarto 147
Domenico di Jacopo di Matteo Becuccio 147
Andrea del Verrocchio
Virgin Adoring the Child 147
Angelico, Fra 143
Christ Glorified in the Court of Heaven 143
Angerstein, Julius 10, 14
Antonello da Messina 143
Crucifixion 143
St Jerome in his Study 2
Apsley House 12
Avercamp, Hendrick 152
Winter Scene with Skaters near a Castle 152
Ayres, Gillian
A Midsummer Night 137

B

Bacon, Francis 178
Figure Study II (Study for the Magdalen) 131
Pope (Study after Velázquez) 178
Triptych - August 1972 31
Two Figures in a Room 88
Balla, Giacomo 177
Abstract Speed - the Car has Passed 178
The Hand of the Violinist 113
Barber, Dame Nellie 17
Barber Institute 17
Bassano, Jacopo 147
Adoration of the Shepherds (attrib) 147
Batoni, Pompeo 10
Colonel William Gordon of Fyvie, 1735-1816 38
Beaumont, Sir George 10, 14
Beckford, William 12
Beckman, Max 177
Carnival 178
Bellany, John
Bethel 52
Bellini, Giovanni 143
Descent into Limbo 73
Head of a boy 143
Bermejo, Bartolomé 143
Saint Michael Triumphant over the Devil 143
Birmingham City Art Gallery 15
Blake, Peter 177
Got a Girl 178

Blake, William 160
The Dance of Albion 83
Elohim creating Adam 70-71
Nebuchadnezzar 130
Sir Geoffrey Chaucer and the Nine and Twenty Pilgrims on their Journey to Canterbury 160
Boccioni, Umberto 177
Modern Idol 178
Böcklin, Arnold
Silenus 170
Bonnard, Pierre 177
The Bath 178
Two Dogs 105
Bordone, Paris 147
Rest on the Flight into Egypt 147
Bosch, Hieronymous 147
Christ Mocked 147
Botticelli, Sandro 143
Mars and Venus 24-5
The Virgin Adoring the Sleeping Christ Child 144
Boucher, François 160
Daphnis and Chloë (Shepherd watching a Sleeping Shepherdess) 49
The Rising of the Sun 160
Bouts, Dieric 144
The Entombment 144
Bowes Museum 15
Braque, Georges 177
Clarinet and Bottle of Rum on Mantelpiece 111
Still Life 178
Brett, John
The Stonebreaker 52-3
Bronzino, Agnolo 147
An Allegory with Venus and Cupid 33
Portrait of Piero de Medici 147
Brown, Ford Madox 170
The Last of England 170
Manfred on the Jungfrau 131
Work 48
Bruegel, Jan I, 12, 152
Vase of Flowers 152
Bruegel the Elder, Pieter 148
Christ and the Woman taken in Adultery 81
The Death of the Virgin 126
Landscape with the Flight into Egypt 148
The Massacre of the Innocents 26
Brugghen, Hendrick ter 152
Bagpipe Player 152
Burne-Jones, Edward 170
The Briar Rose Series: The Prince enters the Briar Wood 170
King Cophetua and the Beggar Maid 34
Laus Veneris (The Praising of Venus) 27
The Wheel of Fortune 72
Burra, Edward
Silver Dollar Bar 64
Burrell, Sir William 19
Burrell Collection 17, 19

C

Campin, Robert 144
The Entombment (triptych) 144
The Virgin and Child in an Interior 138
Canaletto, Antonio 10-11, 160
Venice: the Grand Canal with the Palazzo Balbi 160
Cappelle, Jan van de 152
A Calm 152
Caravaggio, Michelangelo Merisi da 152
Boy Bitten by a Lizard 112
Supper at Emmaus 152
Carr, Rev Holwell 14
Carracci, Annibale 15, 148
The Butcher's Shop 53
Man Drinking 148
Cassat, Mary 170
The Little Sisters 170
Caulfield, Patrick
Inside a Weekend Cabin 114
Cézanne, Paul 18, 170-71
Mont Saint Victoire 101
The Murder 124
Still Life with a Plaster Bust of Cupid 171
Chagall, Marc 179
The Poet Reclining 179
Chardin, Jean-Baptiste-Siméon
The Governess 160
The House of Cards 62
Charles I, as collector 8-10
Chatsworth House 12
Chirico, Giorgio de 179
The Philosopher 179
Christie, James 10
Christus, Petrus 144
Christ as the Man of Sorrows 82
Portrait of a young Man 144
Cimabue, Giovanni 142
Virgin and Child Enthroned with Two Angels 142
Claude Lorraine 10, 152
Coast View with Perseus and the Origins of Coral 100
Landscape with Ascanius shooting the Stag of Silva 152
Landscape with Erminia and the Shepherd 132
Coke, Thomas (of Holkham Hall) 10
Constable, John 171
Golding Constable's Flower Garden 171
Hampstead, looking towards Harrow 106
The Haywain 100
Corot, Jean-Baptiste-Camille
Sunset, Figures under Trees 171
Correggio (Antonio Allegri) 12, 148
The School of Love 148
Cosimo, Piero di
The Forest Fire 94-5
Courbet, Gustave 172
Alms for a Beggar at Omans 172
Young Ladies of the Village 49

Courtauld Institute 19
Courtauld, Samuel 19
Cranach the Elder, Lucas 148
Adam and Eve 30
The Nymph of the Fountain 34
The Stag Hunt 148
Cuyp, Aelbert 153
View of Dordrecht 153

D

Daddi, Bernardo 142
Crucifixion (triptych) 142
Daddi, Taddeo
Crucifixion and Lamentation over the dead Christ 142
Dalí, Salvador 179
Autumn Cannibalism 179
The Christ of Saint John of the Cross 82
Daumier, Honoré-Victorin
The Heavy Burden 53
Lunch in the Country 134
David, Gerard 144
The Legend of Saint Nicholas 144
Davies, Gwendoline and Margaret 19
Degas, Edgar 172
Edmond Duranty 85
Jockeys before the Race 172
Delacroix, Eugène 172
Tam O'Shanter 172
Delaroche, Paul
Napoleon Crossing the Alps 38
De la Tour, Georges 155
The Choirboy 155
The Dice Players 66
Delaunay, Robert 179
Portrait of Igor Stravinsky 179
Derain, André 179
Barges on the Thames 179
Dix, Otto 179
Nude Girl on a Fur 179
Domenico Veneziano 144
Annunciation 144
Dou, Gerrit 153
Interior with a Woman Playing a Clavicord 152
Draper, Herbert
Ulysses and the Sirens 121
Duccio di Buoninsegna 142
The Annunciation 142
Duchamp, Marcel 179
The Bride Stripped Bare by her Bachelors Even 179
Dulwich Picture Gallery 14
Dürer, Albrecht 148
Saint Jerome 148
Dyce, William
The Man of Sorrows 128

E

Egg, Augustus
The Travelling Companions 50
El Greco 148-9
Allegorical Night Scene 87
The Disrobing of Christ 79
The Tears of Saint Peter 149
Elsheimer, Adam 154
Judith and Holofernes 134
Epstein collection, Walsall 17
Epstein, Mrs Kathleen 17
Ernst, Max 179-80
Celebes (the Elephant Celebes) 179
Evelyn, John 10
Eyck, Jan van 144
Portrait of Giovanni Arnolfini and his Wife 85
Portrait of a Young Man 144

F

Fabritus, Carel 154
Self Portrait 154
Fitzwilliam Collection 14
Fonthill 12
Foppa, Vincenzo
The Young Cicero Reading 57
Forain, Jean-Louis
The Fisherman 65
Fragonard, Jean-Honoré 161
The Fountain of Love 161
The Swing 29
Francesca, Piero della
The Baptism of Christ 75
Freud, Lucian 180
Interior at Paddington 180
Small Naked Portrait 89
Friedrich, Caspar David 172-3
Water Landscape 172
Frith, William Powell
The Derby Day 50-51
The Fair Toxophilites 67
Frost, Terry
Brown Verticals 101
Fuseli, Johann Heinrich 161
The Three Witches from Macbeth 161

G

Gaddi, Taddeo 142
Crucifixion and Lamentation over the Dead Christ 142
Gainsborough, Thomas 11, 161
Mr and Mrs George Byam and their Eldest Daughter 161
Gauguin, Paul 173
The Breton Shepherdess 172
Nevermore 128-9
The Vision after the Sermon (Jacob and the Angel) 74
Gelder, Aert de
Jacob's Dream 74
Gentile da Fabriano 144
Virgin and Child with Angels 144
Gentileschi, Artemesia 154
Self Portrait asd Pittura 154
Gentileschi, Orazio 154
Joseph and Potiphar's Wife 154
The Rest on the Flight into Egypt 78
George III 11
Géricault, Théodore 173
Prancing Grey Horse 173
Ghirlandaio, Domenico, 144
The Virgin and Child 144
Giacometti, Alberto 180
Diego 180
Seated Woman 88
Giorgione 148
The Adoration of the Kings 148-9
Giotto di Bondone 142
Pentecost (attrib) 142
Giovanni de Paolo 145
Crucifixion 145
Goes, Hugo van der 145
Trinity Altarpiece 145
Gossaert, Jan 148
Hercules and Deianeira 28, 148
Goya, Francisco de
The Interior of a Prison 129
Boys Playing at Seesaw and Boys Playing at Soldiers 63
Scene at a Bullfight: Spanish Entertainment 162
Greville, Mrs Ronnie 12
Griffier, Jan
Noah's Ark 104
Grosz, George
Suicide 116, 131
Guercino (Giovanni Francesco Barbieri) 154
The Betrayal of Christ 154
Guttoso, Renato
A Hero of the Proletariat 39
Gysbrechts, Cornelius
Trompe l'Oeil Studio Wall with Vanitas Still Life 108

H

Hals, Frans 154-5
A Man (The Laughing Cavalier) 154
Portrait of an Unknown Man 138
Hamilton, Richard
Adonis in Y-Fronts 21
Interior Study (A) 59
Hawkins, Henry
Penrhyn Slate Quarry 54-5
Hazlitt, William 11
Heemskerck, Maerten van 149
Self Portrait 149
Hess, Hans 21

Hilliard, Nicholas 149
Queen Elizabeth (The Pelican Portrait) 149
A Young Man Leaning against a Tree among Roses 30
Hobbema, Meindert 155
The Avenue, Middelharnis 154
Hockney, David 180
'Le Plongeur' 180
Peter Getting out of Nick's Pool 135
We Two Boys Together Clinging 28
Hodgkin, Howard 180
Gramophone 180
Hogarth, William 10, 162
The Battle of the Pictures 10
Before and After 110
Heads of Six of Hogarth's Servants 59
The Rake's Progress III, The Rose Tavern 86
Self Portrait with his Pig 162
Holbein the Younger, Hans 149
Archbishop Warham 149
Jean de Dinteville and George de Selve: "The Ambassadors" 109
Holloway College 16
Holloway, Thomas 16
Honthorst, Gerrit van 155
Charles I 155
Hooch, Pieter de 155
Courtyard of a House in Delft 155
Howard, Ken
Ulster Crucifixion 74
Howson, Peter
Patriots 87
Hunt, William Holman
The Awakening Conscience 32

I

Ingres, Jean-Auguste-Dominique 173
Madame Moltessier 173

J

John, Gwen 180
Mère Poussepin 180
Jones, Thomas
Buildings in Naples 106
Radnorshire 163

K

Kalf, Willem 155
Still Life with a Drinking Horn 155
Kandinsky, Wassily 181
Cossacks 181
Kirchner, Ernst-Ludwig 181
Bathers at Moritzburg 181
Klee, Paul 181
Ghost of a Genius 181

Klimt, Gustav 173
Portrait of Hermine Gallia 173
Kooning, Willem de 181
The Visit 181
Kramer, Jacob
The Day of Atonement 122

L

Laing Art Gallery 15
Landseer, Edwin
Laying Down the Law 105
Man Proposes, God Disposes 76-7
Lawrence, Sir Thomas 11, 163
William Henry and Jacob Howell Pattison 163
Léger, Fernand 181
Still Life with a Vase 181
Leicester City Art Gallery 21
Leighton, Frederic Lord 15
Captive Andromache 16-17
Leonardo de Vinci 145
The Virgin of the Rocks 145
Lever, William Hesketh 16
Leyden, Lucas van 149
The Card Players 149
Lichtenstein, Roy 181
In the Car 181
Lievens, Jan
The Raising of Lazarus 81
Lippi, Fillipino 145
The Wounded Centaur 145
Lippi, Filippo 145
Virgin and Child with Angels and Saints 145
Lorenzetti, Pietro 142
Saint Sabinus before the Governor of Tuscany (attrib) 142
Lotto, Lorenzo 149
A Lady with a Drawing of Lucretia 149
Lowry, Laurence Stephen 181
Coming from the Mill 54
Street Scene, St Michael's Church 181

M

Magritte, René 182
Le Masque Vide 182
The Taste of Sorrow 127
Malevich, Kasimir 182
Dynamic Suprematism 182
Manchester 'Great Art Treasures Exhibition' 14-15
Manet, Édouard 174
A Bar at the Folies-Bergère 46-7
Still Life with a Ham 174
Mantegna, Andrea 8, 145
The Elephants 8-9
The Triumphs of Caesar 145
Marc, Franz 182
Red Woman 182

WITHDRAWN

Martin, John
The Bard 102
The Destruction of Sodom and Gomorrah 76
Martini, Simone 142
Christ discovered in the Temple 79
Saint John the Evangelist 142
Masaccio 145
The Virgin and Child 145
Massys, Quinten 149
A Grotesque Old Woman 87, 149
Master of the St Bartholomew Altarpiece 136
The Deposition 146
Matisse, Henri 182
The Painting Lesson 182
McFadyen, Jock
Depression 89
Memlinc, Hans 146
The Virgin of the Annunciation (attrib) 146
Messina, Antonello da
St Jerome in his Study 56
Michelangelo Buonarroti 150
The Entombment 150
Mieris, Frans van 156
A Sick Woman and her Doctor 156
Millais, John Everett 174
Autumn Leaves 174
The Black Brunswicker 27
Spring (Apple Blossoms) 98
Miró, Joan 182
Composition 182
Modigliani, Amedero 182
Seated Nude 182
Mondrian, Piet 182
Composition 115
Composition with Red Yellow and Blue 182
Monet, Claude 174
The Church at Varengeville 113
Rouen Cathedral, Sunset 174
Water Lilies 19
Moran, Thomas
Nearing Camp, Evening, Upper Colorado River 4-5, 102
Morandi, Giorgio 182
Still Life 183
Moore, Henry
Sleeping Shelterers (Two Women and a Child) 41
Munch, Edvard 183
The Sick Child 183
Murillo 156
The Marriage at Cana 156

N

Nash, Paul 183
Sanctuary Wood 183
Totes Mere (Dead Sea) 42
Winter Sea 99
National Gallery 12 -14

Impressionism 19
National Gallery of Scotland 11
National Museum of Wales 19
National Trust, picture collections 12
Netscher, Caspar
The Lace Maker 58
Nevinson, Christopher R.W.
Searchlights 36
Newman, Barnett 183
Adam 183
Nicholson, Ben 183
Still Life (Cerulean) 183
Nolde, Emile 183
The Sea 183

O

Os, Jan van
Fruit 98
(detail) 92

P

Palma Vecchio 150
Venus and Cupid in a Landscape 150
Palmer, Samuel 175
The Magic Apple Tree 133
The Rising of the Skylark 175
Paolo, Giovanni di
St John the Baptist Retiring to the Desert 110-11
Parliament, sale of pictures by 10
Parmigianino (Francesco Mazzola) 150
A Scholar 150
Patenier, Joachim 150
The Destruction of Sodom and Gomorrah 150
Pembroke, Earls of 11
Perugino 146
The Archangel Raphael with Tobias 146
Picasso, Pablo, 183
Head of a Woman 183
Nude Woman in a Red Armchair 28
The Three Dancers 120
Weeping Woman 43
(detail) 22
Piero della Francesca 146
The Nativity 146
Piero di Cosimo 146
A Satyr Mourning over a Nymph 146
Pissaro, Camille 175
Vue: de ma Fenêtre 175
Polesden Lacey 12
Pollock, Jackson 183
Summertime: Number 9A 138-9
Yellow Islands 183
Pontormo, Jacopo da 150
The Story of Joseph 150
Poussin, Nicolas 11, 156
Cephalus and Aurora 73
A Dance to the Music of Time 97

Landscape with the Ashes of Phocion 96-7
The Sacrament of Extreme Unction 90
The Shepherds in Arcadia 118
Tancred and Ermenia 27
The Triumph of David 156

R

Raeburn, Henry 11, 164
The Archers 164
Ramsay, Alan 164
Flora Macdonald 165
Portrait of the Artist's Wife 164
Raphael 11, 150
The Crucified Christ with the Virgin Mary, Saints and Angels 114
Holy Family with the Palm Tree 150
Rego, Paula
The Artist in her Studio 57
Rembrandt van Rijn 157
Belshazzar's Feast 118-19
Ecce Homo 124
Self Portrait 84
Young Girl leaning on a Windowsill 156
Young Woman in Bed 35
Renoir, Pierre Auguste 175
A Gust of Wind 94-5
La Loge 175
Reynolds, Joshua 11, 165
Georgiana, Duchess of Devonshire, Lady Georgiana Cavendish 136
The Ladies Waldegrave 166
Mrs Siddons as the Tragic Muse 165
Ribera 157
Hecate 157
Richards, Ceri
Cycle of Nature 97
Riley, Bridget 184
Conversation 184
Roberti, Ercole de' 144
Pietà 78, 144
Roberts, William
Les Routiers 44, 67
Rogier van den Weyden 147
The Magdalen Reading 147
Romney, George 11, 167
The Gower Family 60
Self Portrait 167
Rosa, Salvator 157
Rocky Landscape with a Hermit 157
L'Umana Fragilità 108
Rossetti, Dante Gabriel 175
Beata Beatrix 123
Dante's Dream on the Day of the Death of Beatrice 175
Rothko, Mark 184
Black and Red on Maroon 184
Black on Maroon 82
Rousseau, Henri (Douanier) 176
Tropical Storm with a Tiger 176
Royal Academy Summer Exhibition 15
Royal Holloway College 16

Rubens, Peter Paul 10, 12, 157
Cain Slaying Abel 125
The Judgement of Paris 25
Landscape in Flanders 107
Portrait of Susanna Lunden 157
Venus Mourning Adonis 127
Ruisdal, Jacob van 158
The Banks of a River 158

S

Sainsbury Centre for the Visual Arts, Norwich 17
Saenredam, Pieter 158
Interior of San Bravo, Haarlem 158
Sargent, John Singer 176
Gassed 43
The Vickers Sisters 176
Sassetta 146
Miracle of the Holy Sacrament 146
Schalken, Gottfried (attrib)
Boys Flying Kites 65
Sebastiano del Piombo 150
The Judgment of Solomon 150
The Raising of Lazarus 81
Segantini, Giovanni
An Idyll 133
Seguier, William 12
Seurat, Georges-Pierre 176
Bathers at Asnières 49
The Chahut 61
Seated Man 176
Sunset 107
Young Woman Powdering Herself 139
Severini, Gino
Danseuse No 5 184
Sickert, Walter Richard 184
Mornington Crescent 184
Noctes Ambrosianae 65
Sisley, Alfred 177
A Normandy Farm 177
Soane, Sir John 14
Solomon, Abraham
The Acquittal 111
Waiting for the Verdict 111
South German School (signed H. Letter)
The Battle of Lepanto, 7 August 1571 36
Spencer, Stanley 185
Map Reading and Bed Making 40
Resurrection of the Dead Soldiers 184
Shipbuilding on the Clyde 54-5
Southwold 64
A Village in Heaven 132-3
Spranger, Bartholomeus 151
The Adoration of the Kings 151
Steen, Jan 158
The Fat Kitchen 158
A School for Boys and Girls 51
Stella, Frank 185
Six Mile Bottom 185
Stubbs, George 168

Cheetah and Stag with Two Indians 104
Hambletonian 104-05
Whistlejacket 168
White Horse Frightened by a Lion 103
Symons, Mark
The Day after Christmas 63

T

Tate Modern 21
Terborch, Gerard 159
Interior with a Dancing Couple 159
Thompson, Elizabeth (Lady Butler)
Scotland Forever 37
Tiepolo, Gian Battista 168
The Finding of Moses 168
Tintoretto (Jacopo Robusti) 151
*Christ Washing the Feet of the
Apostles* 151
Titian 11, 151
Bacchus and Ariadne 35
The Death of Actaeon 77
Diana and Actaeon 151
The Rape of Lucretia 33
The Three Ages of Man 109
Thomas, Trevor 21
Toulouse-Lautrec, Henri de 177
Portrait of Charles Conder 177
Turner, Joseph Mallord
William 10, 11, 177
*Rain, Steam and Speed: The Great
Western Railway* 113
*Snow Storm: Hannibal and his Army
Crossing the Alps* 177
*Snow Storm, Steamboat off a Harbour's
Mouth* 102-03

U

Ucello, Paulo, 146
The Battle of San Romano 37
The Hunt 66-7
Saint George and the Dragon 146

V

Van Dyck, Anthony 153
Cupid and Psyche 80
*Johann, Count of Nassau, with his Wife
and Family* 153
*Philip Herbert 4th Earl of Pembroke and
his family* 85
The Stoning of Saint Stephen 122
*Venetia Stanley, Lady Digby, on her
Deathbed* 91
Van Gogh, Vincent 173
The Artist's Chair 173
Rain, Auvers 107
Self Portrait with Bandaged Ear 128
Sunflowers 137

Velázquez, Diego 12, 159
*The Infant Balthasar Carlos as a
Sportsman with Three Dogs* 158
Old Woman Cooking Eggs 58
Waterseller 13
Velde the Younger, Willem van de 159
*Calm: a Dutch Flagship Coming to
Anchor* 159
Vermeer, Jan 159
The Guitar Player 60
*Interior with a Young Woman standing at
the Virginals* 159
Young Woman Seated at a Virginal 135
Verocchio, Andrea del 147
Virgin Adoring the Child 147
Veronese (Paolo Caliari) 151
Hermes, Herse and Aglauros 151
Vigée Lebrun, Elisabeth-Louise 168
Countess Golovine 168
Vuillard, Edouard 185
Interior: the Card Party 185

W

Walker Gallery 15
Wallis, Henry
The Death of Chatterton 90-91
Warhol, Andy 185
Jacqueline 185
Marilyn Diptych 85
(detail) 69
Waterhouse, John William
Echo and Narcissus 31
Watteau, Jean-Antoine 168
The Enchanter 168
Watts, George Frederic
Love and Death 25
The Rider on the Pale Horse 77
Weight, Carel
Anger 125
Wellington, Duke of 11-12
West, Benjamin
The Death of Nelson 39
Westminster Retable 143
Whistler, James Abbott McNeill 177
Symphony in White, No 3 177
Wilkie, David
*Chelsea Pensioners Reading the Gazette of
the Battle of Waterloo* 40
Wilson, Richard 10, 168
Niagara Falls 168
Wilton Diptych 143
Wilton House 12
Woburn Abbey 'Venetian Room' 11
Wright of Derby, Joseph 169
*The Alchemist in search of the
Philosopher's Stone discovers
Phosphorous* 169
*The Annual Girandola at the Castel Sant'
Angelo, Rome* 136
*A Philosopher giving that Lecture on the
Orrery in which a Lamp is put in place of*

the Sun 56
*The Widow of an Indian Chief Watching
the Arms of her Deceased Husband* 126

Y

Yeames, William Frederick
And when did you last see your Father? 41

Z

Zoffany, Johan
*Charles Townley's Library at 7 Park
Street, Westminster* 135

PICTURE CREDITS

Cover: Jan Gossaert *Hercules and Deianeira (detail)*, The Barber Institute **Back cover:** David Hockney *Peter getting out of Nick's Pool (detail)*©David Hockney. Board of the Trustees of the National Galleries and Museums on Merseyside (Walker Art Gallery) **P2:** **Antonello da Messina** *St. Jerome in his Study* ©The National Gallery **P4-5:** **Thomas Moran** *Nearing Camp, Evening, Upper Colorado River* Bolton Museum and Art Gallery **P6-7:** **Pablo Picasso** *Weeping Woman (detail)*©Succession Picasso/DACS 2002. Tate London, **William Roberts** *Les Routiers (detail)*©Estate of John Roberts, care of Mischon de Reya Solicitors, London. Reproduced with the kind permission of the Trustees of the National Galleries and Museums of Northern Ireland, **Andy Warhol** *Marilyn Diptych (detail)*©The Andy Warhol Foundation for the Visual Arts, Inc./ARS, NY and DACS, London 2002/Tate London, **Jan van Os** *Flowers and Fruit (detail)*, Warrington Museum and Art Gallery/The Bridgeman Art Library, **George Grosz** *Suicide (detail)*©DACS 2002, Tate London **P8-9:** **Andrea Mantegna** *The Triumphs of Caesar: The Elephants*, The Royal Collection©HM Queen Elizabeth II **P10:** **William Hogarth** *The Battle of the Pictures* The British Museum **P11:** **The Venetian Dining Room at Woburn Abbey, Bedfordshire**©The Marquess of Tavistock and the Trustees of the Bedford Estates. By kind permission of the Marquess of Tavistock and the Trustees of the Bedford Estates **P12:** **The Red Drawing Room, Polesdon Lacey, Surrey**. The Bridgeman Art Library **P13:** **Diego Valasquez** *The Waterseller of Seville*, Apsley House, The Wellington Museum/The Bridgeman Art Library **P14:** **Interior, Dulwich Picture Gallery**. Andrew Crowley **P15:** **Exterior, Bowes Museum.** The Bowes Museum. Queen Victoria visits the Great Art Treasures Exhibition©Corbis **P16-17:** **Frederic Lord Leighton** *Captive Andromache* Manchester Art Gallery/The Bridgeman Art Library **P18-19:** **Exterior,New Art Gallery, Walsall**©Roderick Coyne **Claude Monet** *Water-Lilies* National Museums and Galleries of Wales, Cardiff **P20-21:** **Richard Hamilton** *Adonis in Y-Fronts*©Richard Hamilton 2002. All Rights Reserved, DACS. Wolverhampton Art Gallery/The Bridgeman Art Library **Part 1 P22:** **Pablo Picasso** *Weeping Woman (detail)*©Succession Picasso/DACS 2002. Tate London. **P24-25:** **Sandro Botticelli** *Venus and Mars*, Peter Paul Rubens *The Judgment of Paris*©The National Gallery, **GF Watts** *Love and Death*,The Whitworth Art Gallery **P26-27:** **Pieter Brueghel the Elder** *The Massacre of the Innocents*,The Royal Collection©HM Queen Elizabeth II, **Nicolas Poussin** *Tancred and Erminia*,The Barber Institute, **Sir John Everett Millais** *The Black Brunswicker*,The Lady Lever Gallery/The Bridgeman Art Library, Trustees of the National Museums and Galleries on Merseyside, **Edward Burne-Jones** *Laus Veneris*, The Laing Art Gallery **P28-29:** **Pablo Picasso** *Nude in a red armchair*©Succession Picasso/DACS 2002, Tate London, **David Hockney** *We Two Boys Together Clinging*©David Hockney, The Bridgeman Art Library, **Jan Gossaert** *Hercules and Deianeira*, The Barber Institute, **Jean-Honoré Fragonard** *The Swing*, The Wallace Collection **P30-31:** **Francis Bacon** *Triptych* 1972©Estate of Francis Bacon/ARS, NY and DACS, London 2002, Tate London, **Lucas Cranach the Elder** *Adam and Eve*,The Courtauld Institute Gallery, **Nicholas Hilliard** *Young Man Leaning Against a Rose Tree*, The Victoria and Albert Museum/The Bridgeman Art Library, **John William Waterhouse** *Echo and Narcissus*, Board of Trustees of the National Museums and Galleries Merseyside (The Walker Art Gallery) **P32-33:** **Titian** *The Rape of Lucretia*, Fitzwilliam Museum, **William Holman Hunt** *The Awakening Conscience*, Tate London, **Bronzino** *Allegory with Venus and Cupid*©The National Gallery **P34-35:** **Rembrandt** *YoungWoman in Bed*©The National Gallery of Scotland, **Edward Burne-Jones** *King Cophetua and the Beggar Maid*, Tate London, **Lucas Cranach the Elder** *The Nymph of the Fountain*, Board of Trustees of the National Museums and Galleries Merseyside (The Walker Art Gallery), **Titian** *Bacchus and Ariadne*©The National Gallery **P36-37:** **CRW Nevinson** *Searchlights*, Manchester City Art Galleries, ©Courtesy of the Artist's Estate/The Bridgeman Art Library, **Paulo Uccello** *The Battle of San Romano*©The National Gallery, **H Letter** *Battle of Lepanto*, The National Maritime Museum, **Elizabeth Butler(Lady Butler)** *Scotland Forever!* ©Courtesy of the Artists Estate/The Bridgeman Art Library **P38-39:** **Renato Guttoso** *Head of a Proletariat* ©DACS 2002, Estorick Collection **Pompeo Batoni** *Colonel William Gordon of Fyvie*©National Trust of Scotland/Fyvie Castle/The Bridgeman Art Library, **Samuel West** *Death of Nelson*, **Paul Delaroche** *Napolean crossing the Alps*, Board of Trustees of the National Museums and Galleries Merseyside (The Walker Art Gallery) **P40-41:** **WF Yeames** *And when did you last see your Father?* Board of the Trustees of the National Museums and Galleries (The Walker Art Gallery), **Stanley** *Spencer Map Reading Bedmaking*©Estate of Stanley Spencer 2002. All Rights Reserved, DACS/National Trust Photographic Library, **Henry Moore** *Sleeping Shelterers*, reproduced by permission of the Henry Moore Foundation/Robert & Lisa Sainsbury Collection, University of East Anglia, **David Wilkie** *Chelsea Pensioners*, The Wellington Museum/The Bridgeman Art Library **P42-43:** **Pablo Picasso** *Weeping Woman*©Succession Picasso/DACS2001, Tate London, **John Singer Sargent** *Gassed*©The Imperial War Museum, **Paul Nash** *Totes Meer (Dead Sea)*©Tate London **Part 2 P44:** **William Roberts** *Les Routiers (detail)*©Estate of John Roberts, care of Mischon de Reya Solicitors, London. Reproduced with the kind permission of the Trustees of the National Galleries and Museums of Northern Ireland **P46-47:** **Edouard Manet** *A Bar at the Folies-Bergere*, Courtauld Institute Gallery **P48-49:** **Ford Maddox-Brown** *Work*, Manchester City Art Galleries, **Georges Seurat** *Bathers at Asni res*©The National Gallery, **Gustave Courbet** *The Village Maidens*, Leeds Museums and Art Galleries (City Art Gallery)/The Bridgeman Art Library, **François Boucher** *Daphnis and Chloe(Shepherd watching a Shepherdess Sleep)*, The Wallace Collection **P50-51:** **Augustus Egg** *The Travelling Companions*, Birmingham Museums and Art Gallery, **Jan Steen** *A School for Boys and Girls*, National Gallery of Scotland, **William Powell Frith** *The Derby Day*, Tate London **P52-53:** **John Brett** *The Stonebreaker*, Board of Trustees of the National Galleries and Museums Merseyside (The Walker Art Gallery), **John Bellany** *Bethel*©Courtesy of the Artist's Estate/Bridgeman Art Library, **Honore Daumier** *The Heavy Burden*, Glasgow Museums: The Burrell Collection, **Annibale Carracci** *The Butcher's Shop*, Christ Church Gallery **P54-55:** **Stanley Spencer** *Shipbuilding on the Clyde: Riveters*©Estate of Stanley Spencer 2001. All Rights Reserved, DACS/The Imperial War Museum, **L S Lowry** *Coming from the Mill*©The Lowry Collection, **Henry Hawkins** *Penrhyn Quarry*, National Trust Photographic Library/Penrhyn/Douglas Pennant Collection **P56-57:** **Antonello da Messina** *St Jerome in his Study*©The National Gallery, **Vincenzo Foppa** *Young Cicero Reading*©The Trustees of the Wallace Collection, **Paula Rego** *The Artist in her Studio*©Paula Rego, Courtesy of Marlborough Fine Art/Leeds Museums and Galleries (City Art Gallery)/The Bridgeman Art Library, **Joseph Wright of Derby** *A Philosopher giving a Lecture on the Orrery*©Derby Museum and Art Gallery **P58-59:** **Caspar Nietscher** *The Lace Maker*©The Wallace Collection, **William Hogarth** *Heads of Six of Hogarth's Servants*©Tate London, **Diego Valazquez** *An Old Woman Cooking Eggs*©National Gallery of Scotland, **Edouard Vuillard** *The Manicure*©ADAGP, Paris and DACS, London 2002, Southampton City Art Gallery/The Bridgeman Art Library, **Richard Hamilton** *Interior Study (a)*©Richard Hamilton 2002. All Rights Reserved, DACS/Swindon Art Gallery **P60-61:** **Jan Vermeer** *Girl with a Guitar*, Kenwood House/The Bridgeman Art Library, **George Romney** *The Gower Family*, Abbot Hall Art Gallery/The Bridgeman Art Library, **Georges Seurat** *(Study for) Le Chahut*, Courtauld Institute Galleries **P62-63:** **Jean-Siméon Chardin** *The House of Cards*©The National Gallery, **Mark Symons** *The Day After Christmas*©Bury Art Gallery and Museum/The Bridgeman Art Library, **Francisco de Goya** *Boys playing at See-Saw*, **Francisco de Goya** *Boys playing at Soldiers*, Glasgow Museums: Stirling Maxwell Collection, **Godfried Schalken** *Boys flying Kites*, Upton House, National Trust Photographic Library **P64-65:** **Stanley Spencer** *Southwold*©Estate of Stanley Spencer 2002. All Rights Reserved, DACS. Aberdeen Art Gallery, **Jean Louis Forain** *The Fisherman*©ADAGP, Paris and DACS, London 2002. Southampton City Art Gallery/ The Bridgeman Art Library, **Walter Sickert** *Noctes Ambrosiane* ©Estate of Walter R. Sickert 2002. All Rights Reserved, DACS, Castle Museum and Art Gallery, Nottingham/The Bridgeman Art Library, **Edward Burra** *Silver Dollar Bar*©Estate of Edward Burra. Courtesy of Alex Reid & LeFevre Ltd. (The LeFevre Gallery) London, York City Art Gallery/The Bridgeman Art Library **P66-67:** **Paolo Uccello** *The Hunt*, Ashmolean Museum, **William Roberts** *Les Routiers*©Estate of John Roberts, care of Mischon de Reya Solicitors, London. Reproduced with the kind permission of the Trustees of the National Galleries and Museums of Northern Ireland, **Georges de la Tour** *The Dice Players*, Preston Hall Museum/The Bridgeman Art Library, **William Powell Frith** *Fair Toxophilites*, Royal Albert Memorial Museum/The Bridgeman Art Library **Part 3 P68:** **Andy Warhol** *Marilyn Diptych (detail)*©The Andy Warhol Foundation for the Visual Arts, Inc./ARS, NY and DACS, London 2002/Tate London **P70-71:** **William Blake** *Elohim Creating Adam*, Tate London **P72-73:** **Edward Burne-Jones** *Wheel of Fortune*, National Museum and Gallery, Wales; **Nicolas Poussin** *Cephalus and Aurora*©The National Gallery, **Giovanni Bellini** *Christ's Descent into Limbo*, Bristol Museum and Art Gallery/The Bridgeman Art Library **P74-75:** **Aert de Gelder** *Jacob's Dream*, Dulwich Picture Gallery; **Paul Gauguin** *The Vision after the Sermon*, National Gallery of Scotland; **Ken Howard** *Ulster Crucifixion Triptych*©Ken Howard: reproduced with kind permission of the Trustees of the National Museums and Galleries of Northern Ireland; **Piero della Francesca** *The Baptism of Christ*©National Gallery **P76-77:** **Edwin Landseer** *Man proposes, God disposes*, Royal Holloway and Bedford New College/Bridgeman Art Library; **George Frederick** *Watts Rider on the Pale Horse*, Board of the Trustees of the National Museums and Galleries on Merseyside (Walker Art Gallery); **Titian** *Death of Actaeon*©National Gallery; **John Martin** *The Destruction of Sodom and Gomorrah*, Laing Art Gallery, Newcastle **P78-79:** **El Greco** *The Disrobing of Christ* National Trust Photographic Library/Upton House (Bearsted Collection); **Ercole de' Roberti** *Pieta*, **Simone Martini** *Christ discovered in the Temple*, Board of Trustees of the National Museums and Galleries of Merseyside (Walker Art Gallery); **Orazio Gentileschi** *The Rest on the Flight into Egypt*, Birmingham Museums and Art Gallery **P80-81:** **Anthony Van Dyck** *Cupid and Psyche*, The Royal Collection©HM Queen Elizabeth II; **Jan Lievens** *The Raising of Lazarus*, Royal Pavilion, Libraries & Museums, Brighton & Hove/Bridgeman Art Library; **Pieter Brueghel the Elder** *Christ and the Woman taken in Adultery*, Courtauld Institute Gallery; **Sebastiano del Piombo** *The Raising of Lazarus*©National Gallery **P82-83:** **Salvador Dali** *Christ of St. John of the Cross*©Salvador Dali, Gala-Salvador Dali Foundation, DACS, London 2002: Glasgow Museums/the St Mungo Museum of Religious Life & Art; **Petrus Christus** *The Man of Sorrows*, Birmingham Museums and Art Gallery; **William Blake** *Dance of Albion*, British Museum/Bridgeman Art Library; **Mark Rothko** *Black on Maroon*©Kate Rothko Prizel and Christopher Rothko/DACS 1998, Tate London **P84-85:** **Edgar Degas** *Duranty*, Glasgow Museums: The Burrell Collection; **Anthony Van Dyck** *The 4th Earl of Pembroke and his Family*, Collection of the Earl of Pembroke, Wilton House/Bridgeman Art Library; **Jan Van Eyck** *The Arnolfini Marriage*©The National Gallery; **Andy Warhol** *Marilyn Diptych*©The Andy Warhol Foundation for the Visual Arts, Inc./ARS, NY and DACS, London 2002; **Rembrandt van Rijn** *Self-portrait*, Kenwood House/The Bridgeman Art Library **P86-87:** **El Greco** *Allegorical Night Scene*, Harewood House, **William Hogarth** *A Rake's Progress III: the Rake at the Rose Tavern*, Courtesy of the Trustees of Sir John Soane's Museum/The Bridgeman Art Library; **Quentin Massys** *Grotesque Old Woman*©The National Gallery; **Peter Howson** *Patriots*©Peter Howson/Courtesy of Angela Flowers Gallery, Glasgow Museums: Gallery of Modern Art **P88-89:** **Alberto Giacometti** *The Artist's Mother*©ADGP, Paris and DACS, London 2002, Manchester City Art Galleries; **Jock McFadyen** *Depression* ©Jock McFadyen, Glasgow Museums: Gallery of Modern Art; **Lucian Freud** *Small Naked Portrait*©Lucian Freud, Ashmolean Museum; **Francis Bacon** *Two Figures in a Room*©Estate of Francis Bacon/ARS, NY and DACS, London 2002, Sainsbury Centre for the Visual Arts, the Robert and Lisa Sainsbury Collection/James Austin **P90-91:** **Henry Wallis** *Death of Chatterton*, Birmingham Museum Art Gallery; **Nicolas Poussin** *Extreme Unction*, Belvoir Castle/The Bridgeman Art Library; **Anthony van Dyck** *Venetia Stanley, Lady Digby, on her Deathbed*, by permission of the Trustees of Dulwich Picture Gallery **Part 4 P92:** **Jan van Os** *Flowers and Fruit (detail)*, Warrington Museum and Art Gallery/The Bridgeman Art Library **P94-95:** **Pierre-Auguste Renoir** *The Gust of Wind*, The Fitzwilliam Museum, **Piero di Cosimo** *The Forest Fire*, The Ashmolean Museum **P96-97:** **Nicolas Poussin** *Landscape with the Ashes of Phocion*, Board of the Trustees of the National Galleries and Museums on Merseyside (The Walker Art Gallery), **Nicolas Poussin** *A Dance to the Music of Time*, The Wallace Collection, **Ceri Richards** *Cycle of Nature*©Estate of Ceri Richards 2002. All Rights Reserved, DACS. The National Museum and Gallery, Wales. **P98-99:** **John Everett Millais** *Apple Blossoms – Spring*, Lady Lever Art Gallery/The Bridgeman Art Library, **Jan van Os** *Flowers and Fruit*, Warrington Museum and Art Gallery/The Bridgeman Art Library, **Paul Nash** *Winter Sea*, York City Art Gallery ,Tate London, 2002 **P100-101:** **Terry Frost** *Brown Verticals*©Terry Frost 2002. Leeds Museums and Galleries (City Art Gallery)/The Bridgeman Art Library, **Claude Lorrain** *The Origin of Coral*, Holkham Hall/The Bridgeman Art Library, **Paul Cezanne** *Mont St. Victoire*, Courtauld Institute Gallery, **John Constable** *The Haywain*©The National Gallery **P102-103:** **Thomas Moran** *Nearing Camp, Evening on the Upper Colorado River*, Bolton Museum and Art Gallery, **JMW Turner** *Snow Storm-Steam Boat off a Harbour's Mouth*, Tate London, **John Martin** *The Bard*, Laing Art Gallery, **George Stubbs** *Horse Frightened by a Lion*, Board of the Trustees of the National Museums and Galleries Merseyside (Walker Art Gallery **P104-105:** **Pierre Bonnard** *Two Dogs*, ADAGP, Paris and DACS, London 2002, Southampton City Art Gallery/The Bridgeman Art Library, **George Stubbs** *Cheetah and Stag with Two Indians*, Manchester City Art Galleries, **George Stubbs** *Hambletonian*, Mount Stewart House and Garden/National Trust Photographic Library, **Edwin Landseer** *Laying Down the Law*, Devonshire Collection, Chatsworth. By permission of the Duke of Devonshire and the Chatsworth Settlement Trustees, **Jan Griffier** *Noah's Ark*, Bristol City Museum and Art Gallery/The Bridgeman Art Library **P106-107:** **John Constable** *Hampstead, looking towards Harrow* Manchester City Art Galleries, **Peter Paul Rubens** *Landscape in Flanders*, Barber Institute, **Vincent Van Gogh** *Rain at Auvers*, **Thomas Jones** *Buildings in Naples* The National Museum and Gallery, Wales, **George Pierre Seurat** *Sunset*, Bristol City Museum and Art Gallery/The Bridgeman Art Library **P108-109:** **Hans Holbein the Younger** *Jean de Dinteville and Georges de Selve (The Ambassadors)*©The National Gallery, **Cornelius Gysbrechts** *Vanitas (Still Life-Trompe L'Oeil)*, Ferens Art Gallery, Hull City Museums and Art Gallery/The Bridgeman Art Library, **Salvator Rosa** *L'Umana Fragilita*, The Fitzwilliam Museum, **Titian** *The Three Ages of Man*, Duke of Sutherland Collection, on loan to the National Gallery of Scotland, **P110-111:** **Abraham Solomon** *Waiting for the Verdict* and *The Aquittal (Not Guilty)*, Tunbridge Wells Museum and Art Gallery, **William Hogarth** *Before* and *After*, The Fitzwilliam Museum, **Georges Braque** *Clarinet and Bottle of Rum on a Mantlepiece*©ADAGP, Paris and DACS, London 2002. Tate London. **Giovanni di Paolo** *Saint John the Baptist retiring to the Desert*©The National Gallery **P112-113:** **Claude Monet** *The Church at Varengeville*, The Barber Institute, **Giacomo Balla** *The Hand of the Violinist*©DACS 2002. The Estorick Collection, **JMW Turner** *Rain, Steam and Speed-The Great Western Railway*, **Michaelangelo Mersi da Caravaggio** *Boy bitten by a Lizard*©The National Gallery **P114-115:** **Raphael** *The Crucified Christ with the Virgin Mary, Saints and Angels (The Mond Crucifixion)*©The National Gallery, **Patrick Caulfield** *Inside a Weekend Cabin*©Patrick Caulfield 2002. All Rights Reserved, DACS, **Piet Mondrian** *Composition 1932*©2002 Mondrian/Holtzman Trust c/o Beeldrecht, Amsterdam, Holland & DACS, London. **Part 5 P116:** **George Grosz** *Suicide (detail)*©DACS 2002, Tate London **P118-119:** **Rembrandt van Rijn** *Belshazzar's Feast*©National Gallery. **Nicolas Poussin** *Shepherds in Arcadia* By Permission of the Duke of Devonshire and the Chatsworth Settlement Trustees **P120-121:** **Herbert Draper** *Ulysses and the Sirens*, Ferens Art Gallery, Hull City Museums and Art Galleries/Bridgeman Art Library. **Pablo Picasso** *The Three Dancers*©Succession Picasso/DACS 2002, Tate London

P122-123: **Jacob Kramer** *The Day of Atonement*©Care of Mischon de Reya Solicitors, London, Leeds Museums and Galleries (City Art Gallery)/The Bridgeman Art Library. **Dante Gabriel Rossetti** *Beata Beatrix*, Tate London. **Anthony van Dyck** *The Stoning of St Stephen*, Tatton Park/National Trust Photographic Library **P124-125:** **Carel Weight** *Anger*©Estate of the Artist, Museum of London/The Bridgeman Art Library. **Rembrandt van Rijn** *Ecce Homo*©National Gallery. **Paul Cézanne** *The Murder,* Board of the Trustees of the National Museums and Galleries on Merseyside (Walker Art Gallery). **Peter Paul Rubens** *Cain Slaying Abel*, Courtauld Institute Gallery **P126-127:** **Rene Magritte** *The Taste of Sorrow*©ADAGP, Paris and DACS, London 2002, Barber Institute. **Joseph Wright of Derby** *The Widow of an Indian Chief Watching the Arms of her Deceased Husband*, Derby Museum and Art Gallery. **Pieter Brueghel** *The Death of the Virgin*, Upton House/National Trust Photographic Library. **Peter Paul Rubens** *Venus Mourning Adonis*, By Permission of the Trustees of Dulwich Picture Gallery **P128-129:** **Paul Gauguin** *Nevermore*, Courtauld Institute Galleries, **Vincent Van Gogh** *Self-Portrait with Bandaged Ear* Courtauld Institute Galleries. **William Dyce** *The Man of Sorrows*, National Gallery of Scotland. **Francisco Goya** *Interior of the Jail,* The Bowes Museum, Barnard Castle/The Bridgeman Art Library **P130-131:** **Francis Bacon** *Figure Study II (Study for the Magdalene)*©Estate of Francis Bacon 2002. All Rights Reserved, DACS, Huddersfield Art Gallery. **William Blake** *Nebuchadnezzar*, Tate London. **Ford Madox Brown** *Manfred on the Jungfrau,* Manchester City Art Galleries, City Art Gallery. **George Grosz** *Suicide*©DACS 2002, Tate London **P132-133:** **Claude** *Erminia and the Shepherds*, Collection of the Earl of Leicester, Holkham Hall/Bridgeman Art Library. **Giovanni Segantini** *An Idyll*, Aberdeen Art Gallery. **Stanley Spencer** *A Village in Heaven*©Estate of Stanley Spencer 2002, All Rights Reserved, DACS, Manchester City Art Galleries. **Samuel Palmer** *Magic Apple Tree,* Fitzwilliam Museum/Bridgeman Art Library **P134-135:** **David Hockney** *Peter Getting out of Nick's Pool*©David Hockney. Board of the Trustees of the National Galleries and Museums on Merseyside (Walker Art Gallery). **Johann Zoffany** *Charles Townleys' Library at 7 Park Street, Westminster*, Townley Hall Art Gallery and Museum/Bridgeman Art Library. **Lawrence Alma-Tadema** *The Tepidarium,* Lady Lever Art Gallery /Bridgeman Art Library, Trustees of the National Museums and Galleries on Merseyside. **Honore Daumier** *Lunch in the Country*, National Gallery and Museum Wales. **Jan Vermeer** *A Young Woman Seated at a Virginal*©National Gallery **P136-137:** **Vincent van Gogh** *Sunflowers*©National Gallery, **Joseph Wright of** *Derby The Annual Girandola at the Castel Sant'Angelo,* Board of the Trustees of the National Museums and Galleries Merseyside (Walker Art Gallery). **Joshua Reynolds** *Georgiana, Duchess of Devonshire, Lady Georgiana Cavendish*, Devonshire Collection, Chatsworth. By Permission of the Duke of Devonshire and the Chatsworth Settlement Trustees. **Gillian Ayres** *A Midsummer Night*©Gillian Ayres 2002, Gimpel Fils Gallery, London, Birmingham Museum and Art Gallery **P138-139:** **Frans Hals** *Portrait of an Unknown Man,* Fitzwilliam Museum. **Robert Campin** *The Virgin and Child in an Interior*©National Gallery. **Georges Seurat** *Young Woman Powdering Herself,* Courtauld Institute Galleries. **Jackson Pollock** *Summertime: Number 9a*©ARS, NY and DACS, London 2001, Tate London. **Chronology:** *The Westminster Retable*©Dean and Chapter of Westminster, **Giovanni di Paolo** *Crucifixion (Predella)*, Rochdale Art Gallery, **Giovanni Bellini** *Head of a Boy*, **Simone Martini** *St. John the Evangelist*, The Barber Insitutute, **Maerten van Heemskerck** *Self Portrait*, **Filippo Lippi** *Triptych: Madonna and Angels with figures of the Donor and Saints,* **Domenico Veneziano** *The Miracle of St. Zenobius*, The Fitzwilliam Museum, **Agnolo Bronzino** *Portrait of Piero De'Medici,* The Ashmolean Museum, **Annibale Carracci** *Man Drinking*, **Filippino Lippi** *The Wounded Centaur*, Christ Church, **Robert Campin** *Entombment Triptych*, **Paris Bordone** *Rest on the Flight into Egypt*, **Pieter Brueghel I** *Landscape with the Flight into Egypt*, The Courtauld Gallery, **Lucas Cranach the Elder** *The Stag Hunt*, **Hans Memlinc** *The Annunciation*, Glasgow Museums: The Burrell Collection,**Andreas Mantegna** *The Triumphs of Caesar: Trumpters, Bearers of Standards and Banners*, Royal Collection©HM Queen Elizabeth II, **Jacopo Bassano** *Adoration of the Shepherds*, **Andrea Del Sarto** *Beccucio Bicchieraio*, **Andrea del Verrocchio** *Madonna and Child*, National Gallery of Scotland, **Gerard David** *Three Legends of St. Nicholas Triptych*, **Sandro Botticelli** *Virgin adoring the sleeping Christ Child*, Duke of Sutherland Collection, on loan to the National Gallery of Scotland, **Gentile da Fabriano** *Madonna and Child,* **Hugo van der Goes** *Trinity Altarpiece (The Holy Trinity)* The Royal Collection ©HM Queen Elizabeth II (on loan to the National Gallery of Scotland), **Michaelangelo Buonarroti** *The Entombment*, **Lorenzo** *Lotto A Lady with a drawing of Lucretia*, **Albrecht Dürer** *Saint Jerome*, **Correggio** *Venus with Mercury and Cupid*, **Hieronymus Bosch** *Christ Mocked*, **Rogier van der Weyden** *The Magdalen Reading,* **Albrecht Altdorfer** *Christ taking leave of his Mother*, **Paolo** *Uccello Saint George and the Dragon*, **Piero di Cosimo** *A Satyr mourning over a Nymph,* **Perugino** *The Archangel Raphael with Tobias,* **Master of the Saint Bartholomew Altarpiece** *The Deposition,* **Masaccio** *The Virgin and Child,* **Leonardo da Vinci** *The Virgin of the Rocks,* **Domenico Ghirlandaio** *The Virgin and Child*, **Jan van Eyck** *A man in a turban*, **Petrus Christus** *Portrait of a young man*, **Dieric Bouts** *The Entombment,* **The Wilton Diptych**, **Fra Angelico** *Christ Glorified in the Court of Heaven,* **Antonello da Messina** *Christ Crucified*, **Bartolomé Bermejo** *Saint Michael triumphant over the Devil with the Donor Don Antonio Juan,* **Cimabue** *Virgin and Child*, **Duccio di Buoninsegna** *The Annunciation*, **Attributed to Giotto di Bondone** *Pentecost*, **Pietro Lorenzetti** *Saint Sabinus before the Governor of Tuscany*©The National Gallery, London **Anthony Van Dyck** *Count John of Nassau*, Firle Place **Murillo** *The Marriage Feast at Cana*, Barber Institute **Frans van Mieris** *A Sick Woman and her Doctor*, Glasgow Museums: Art Gallery & Museum, Kelvingrove **Salvator Rosa** *Rocky Landscape with Hermit*, Board of the Trustees of the National Museums and Galleries (Walker Art Gallery) **Jan van de Cappelle** *A Calm*, National Museum and Gallery, Wales II **Guercino** *The Betrayal*, **Palma Vecchio** *Venus and Cupid*, **Veronese** *Hermes, Herse and Aglauros*, Fitzwilliam Museum **Gerrit Dou** *Lady Playing a Clavichord*, **Nicolas Poussin** *The Triumph of David*, **Rembrandt van Rijn** *Girl leaning on a Windowsill*, Dulwich Picture Gallery **Adam Elsheimer** *Judith and Holofernes*, **Jusepe Ribera** *La Carcasse: A Witch being drawn to the Sabbath on the skeleton of a Monster*,The Victoria & Albert Museum **Jan Brueghel I** *A Vase of Flowers*, **Claude Lorrain** *Ascanlus shooting the stag of Sylvia*, **Hendrick Ter-Brugghen** *A Man Playing the Bagpipes*, **Joachim Patenir** *The Destruction of Sodom and Gommorah*, Ashmolean Museum **Albert Cuyp** *View of Dordrecht*, Ascott/National Trust Photographic Library **Sebastiano del Piombo** *Judgement of Solomon*, Kingston Lacey/National Trust Photographic Library **Frans Hals** *The Laughing Cavalier*,The Wallace **Collection Gerrit van Honthorst** *Charles I* ©National Portrait Gallery **Raphael** *Holy Family with a Palm Tree* **and Titian** *Diana and Actaeon*, Duke of Sutherland Collection, on loan to the National Gallery of Scotland **Artemesia Gentileschi** *Self-Portrait as Pittura*, **Orazio Gentileschi** *Joseph and Potiphar's Wife*, The Royal Collection©HM Queen Elizabeth II **Hendrick Avercamp** *A Winter Scene with Skaters near a Castle*, **Caravaggio** *The Supper at Emmaus*, **Carel Fabritius** *Self Portrait*, **Meindert Hobbema** *The Avenue at Middleharnis*, **Pieter de Hooch** *The Courtyard of a House in Delft*, **Willem Kalf** *Still life with the Drinking Horn of the Saint Sebastian Archers' Guild, Lobster and Glasses*, **Peter Paul Rubens** *Portrait of Susanna Lunden*, **Jacopo da Pontormo** *Joseph with Jacob in Egypt*, **Bartholomeus Spranger** *Adoration of the Kings*©The National Gallery, **Parmigianino** *Portrait of a Man with a Book*, York City Art Gallery **Tintoretto** *Christ washing the Disciples Feet*, Shipley Art Gallery **Thomas Jones** *A View of Radnorshire*, National Museum and Gallery, Wales **William Blake** *Sir Geoffrey Chaucer and the nine and twenty pilgrims on their journey to Canterbury*, Glasgow Museums: The Stirling Maxwell Collection, Pollok House **Willem Van de Velde the Younger** *Calm: A Dutch flagship coming to anchor before a light air*©National Maritime Museum **Jean-Baptiste-Siméon Chardin** *The Governess*, Tatton Park/National Trust Photographic Library **Gerard Ter Borch** *An Officer making his bow to a Lady*, Polesden Lacey/National Trust Photographic Library **Diego Velazquez** *Don Balthasar Carlos*, Ickworth/National Trust Photographic Library **Jacob Ruisdael** *The Banks of a River*, **Pieter Saenredam** *Interior of church, Haarlem*©National Gallery of Scotland **William Hogarth** *The Painter and his Pug*, Tate London **Jean Honoré Fragonard** *Fountain of Love*, **François Boucher** *The Rising of the Sun* by kind permission of the Trustees of The Wallace Collection **Jan Vermeer** *A young woman standing at a Virginal*, **Henry Raeburn** *The Archers*, **George Stubbs** *Whistlejacket*©The National Gallery, **Francisco de** *Goya Scene at a Bullfight: Spanish Entertainment*, Ashmolean Museum **Antonio Canaletto** *View on the Grand Canal*, Ferens Art Gallery, Hull City Museums and Galleries **Thomas Gainsborough** *Mr. and Mrs. George Byam and their eldest daughter, Selina*, Holburne Museum of Art **Jan Steen** *The Fat Kitchen*, Cheltenham Art Gallery & Museums **Joshua Reynolds** *Mrs Siddons as the Tragic Muse*, Dulwich Picture Gallery **Joshua Reynolds** *The Ladies Waldegrave*, National Gallery of Scotland **Allan Ramsay** *Portrait of Flora Macdonald*, Ashmolean Museum **Allan Ramsay** *The Painter's Wife, Margaret Lindsay*, National Gallery of Scotland, **George Romney** *George Romney* By Courtesy of the National Portrait Gallery, London, **Gian Battista Tiepolo** *The Finding of Moses*, National Gallery of Scotland, **Ford Maddox Brown** *The Last of England*, Birmingham Museum & Art Gallery, **Henri Toulouse-Lautrec** *Portrait of Charles Conder*, Aberdeen Art Gallery & Museums, **Gustav Klimt** *Portrait of Hermine Gaillia*, **JMW Turner** *Snowstorm: Hannibal and his Army Crossing the Alps*, Tate London, **Camille Pissarro** *Vue de ma Fenêtre, Eragny*, Ashmolean Museum, **Arnold Böcklin** *Silenus*, William Morris Gallery, **Dante Gabriel Rossetti** *Dante's Dream*, McManus Galleries, **Antoine Watteau** *The Enchanter*, Brodick Castle/The National Trust for Scotland **Paul Gauguin** *Breton Shepherdess*, Laing Art Gallery, **Eugene Delacroix** *Tam O'Shanter*, Nottingham Castle Museum and Art Gallery, **Joseph Wright of Derby** *The Alchemist in search of the Philosopher's Stone*, Derby Museum and Art Gallery, **Jean-Auguste-Dominique Ingres** *Madame Moitessier*, **Vincent Van Gogh** *The Artist's Chair*, **Caspar David-Friedrich** *Winter Landscape* ©The National Gallery, **Paul Cezanne** *Still Life with Plaster Cupid*, **Pierre-Auguste Renoir** *La Loge*, Courtauld Institute Gallery, **Edgar Degas** *Jockeys before a Race*, **E. Vigée-Lebrun** *Countess Golovine*, The Barber Institute, **John Everett Millais** *Autumn Leaves*, **Alfred Sisley** *A Normandy Farm*, Manchester City Art Galleries, City Art Gallery, **Claude Monet** *Rouen Cathedral*, **Samuel Palmer** *The Rising of the Skylark*, **National Museum of Wales**, **Mary Cassat** *The Sisters*, **Gustave Courbet** *Alms for a Beggar at Ornans*, **Edouard Manet** *Still Life with a Ham*, Glasgow Museums: The Burrell Collection, **Georges Seurat** *Seated Man*, Glasgow Museums: Art Gallery and Museum Kelvingrove, **Theodore Gericault** *Prancing Grey Horse*, Glasgow Museums: The Burrell Collection, **Stanley Spencer** *The Resurrection of the Soldiers*©Estate of Stanley Spencer 2002. All Rights Reserved, DACS. National Trust Photographic Library. **Giorgio de Chirico** *The Philosopher (central panel from triptych)*©DACS 2002. The Whitworth Art Gallery. **Rene Magritte** *The Empty Mask*©ADAGP, Paris and DACS, London 2002. National Museum and Gallery, Wales. **Alberto Giacometti** *Diego*©ADAGP, Paris and DACS, London 2002. The Sainsbury Centre for the Visual Arts/James Austin. **Giorgio Morandi** *Still Life*©DACS 2002. Birmingham Museums and Art Gallery. **Georges Braque** *Still Life*©ADAGP, Paris and DACS, London 2002. Glasgow Museums: Art Gallery&Museum, Kelvingrove. **Pablo Picasso** *Head of a Woman*©Succession Picasso/DACS2002. The Fitzwilliam Museum. **L S Lowry** *A Street Scene (St. Simon's Church)*©The Lowry Collection, Salford. **JM Whistler** *Symphony in White, N° III*, Barber Institute. **Amedeo Modigliani** *Female Nude*, The Courtauld Institute Gallery. **Robert Delaunay** *Portrait of Igor Stravinsky*©L&M Services B.V.Amsterdam 20010910/Walsall New Art Gallery. **Howard Hodgkin** *Gramophone*©Howard Hodgkin. Swindon Art Gallery. **Lucian Freud** *Interior at Paddington*©Lucian Freud. Board of the Trustees of the National Museums and Galleries on Merseyside (Walker Art Gallery). **Paul Nash** *Sanctuary Wood*, Grundy Art Gallery, Tate London, 2002. **Umberto Boccioni** *Modern Idol*, Estorick Collection. **Bridget Riley** *Conversation*©Bridget Riley, All Rights Reserved. Courtesy Karsten Schubert, London. **Ben Nicholson** *Still Life (Cerulean)*©Angela Verren-Taunt 2002, All Rights Reserved, DACS. **Gino Severini** *Danseuse N°5*©ADAGP, Paris and DACS, London 2002. Pallant House Gallery. **Francis Bacon** *Pope I - Study after Pope Innocent X by Velasquez*©Estate of Francis Bacon 2002. All Rights Reserved, DACS. **Fernand Léger** *Nature Mort avec Vase*©ADAGP, Paris and DACS, London 2002. **Edouard Vuillard** *The Card Party*©ADAGP, Paris and DACS, London 2002. Aberdeen Art Gallery and Museums. **Joan Miró** *Composition*©ADAGP, Paris and DACS, London 2002. **Otto** *Dix Nude Girl on a Fur*©DACS2002. **Paul Klee** *Ghost of a Genius*©DACS 2002. **Roy Lichtenstein** *In the Car*©The Estate of Roy Lichtenstein/DACS 2002. The Scottish National Gallery of Modern Art. **All of the following: Tate London.** **George Grosz** *Suicide*©DACS 2002. **Giacomo Balla** *Abstract Speed: The Car Has Passed*© DACS 2002, Tate London. **Mark Rothko** *Black on Maroon*©Kate Rothko Prizel and Christopher Rothko/DACS 2002. **Max Beckmann** *Carnival*©DACS 2002. **Pierre Bonnard** *The Bath*©ADAGP, Paris and DACS, London 2002. **Marc Chagall** *The Poet Reclining*©ADAGP, Paris and DACS, London 2002. **Salvador Dalì** *Autumnal Cannibalism*©Salvador Dalì, Gala-Salvador Dalì Foundation, DACS, London 2002. **Marcel Duchamp** *The Bride Stripped Bare by her Bachelors, Even (The Large Glass)*©Succession Marcel Duchamp/ADAGP, Paris and DACS, London 2002. **Max Ernst** *Celebes*©ADAGP, Paris and DACS, London 2002. **Wassily Kandinsky** *Cossacks*©ADAGP, Paris and DACS, London 2002. **Ernst Ludwig Kirchner** *Bathers at Moritzburg*©Dr. Wolfgang & Ingeborg Henze-Ketterer, Wichtrach/Bern. **Piet Mondrian** *Composition with Red, Yellow, and Blue*©2002 Mondrian/Holtzman Trust c/o Beeldrecht, Amsterdam, Holland & DACS, London. **Edvard Munch** *The Sick Child*©Munch Museum/Munch-Ellingsen Group, BONO, Oslo, DACS, London 2002. **Barnett Newman** *Adam*©ARS, NY and DACS, London 2002. **Jackson Pollock** *Yellow Islands*©ARS, NY and DACS, London 2002. **Willem de Kooning** *The Visit*©Willem de Kooning Revocable Trust/ARS, NY and DACS, London 2002. **Frank Stella** *Six Mile Bottom*©ARS, NY and DACS, London 2002. **Emil Nolde** *The Sea B*©Nolde-Stiftung Seebüll. **Kasimir Malevich** *Dynamic Suprematism* (no estate). **All of the following: The Bridgeman Art Library.** **El Greco** *Tears of St. Peter*, The Bowes Museum, **Hans Holbein the Younger** *William Warham*, Lambeth Palace, **Lucas van Leyden** *The Card Players*, collection of the Earl of Pembroke, Wilton House, **Taddeo Gaddi** *Crucifixion and Lamentation*, Bristol Museum and Art Gallery, **Sassetta** *The Miracle of the Holy Sacrament*, The Bowes Museum, **Georges de la Tour** *The Choirboy*, New Walk Museum, Leicester City Museum Service, **Francisco de Zurbaran** *Asher*, Auckland Castle **Richard Wilson** *The Falls of Niagara* Wolverhampton Art Gallery, **Sir Thomas Lawrence** *The Masters Patterson* Polesden Lacey,National Trust, **Henri Rousseau** *Tiger in a Tropical Storm (Surprised!)* The National Gallery, **John Constable** *Golding Constable's Flower Garden*, Ipswich Borough Council Museums and Galleries, **Edward Burne-Jones** *'The Briar Rose' series: the Prince enters the Briar Wood*, Faringdon Collection, Buscot, **William Holman** *Hunt The Light of the World*, Keble College, **John Singer Sargent The Vickers Sisters**, Sheffield City Art Galleries, **Jean Baptiste Camille Corot** *Sunset: Figures under Trees*, Manchester City Art Gallery, **Andre Derain** *Barges on the Thames*©ADAGP, Paris and DACS, London 2002. Leeds Museums and Art Galleries (City Art Gallery). **David Hockney** *Le Plonguer: board and diver*©David Hockney. Bradford Art Galleries and Museums. **Franz Marc** *The Red Woman*, New Walk Museum, Leicester City Museums. **Gwen John** *Mere Poussepin*©Estate of Gwen John 2002. All Rights Reserved, DACS. Southampton City Art Gallery. **Andy Warhol** *Jacqueline*©The Andy Warhol Foundation for the Visual Arts, Inc./ARS, NY and DACS, London 2002. Wolverhampton Art Gallery. **Peter Blake** *Got a Girl*©Peter Blake 2002, All Rights Reserved, DACS. Whitworth Art Gallery. **Henri Matisse** *Painting Lesson*©Succession H Matisse/DACS, London 2002. Scottish National Gallery of Modern Art. **Walter Sickert** *Mornington Crescent*©Estate of Walter R. Sickert 2002, All Rights Reserved, DACS. Leicester Museum Services.